0,1
ifc/title

Grant Morrison
Writer

Steve Yeowell
Jill Thompson
Dennis Cramer
Illustrators

Daniel Vozzo
Colorist

Clem Robins
Letterer

Sean Philips
Rian Hughes
Original covers

Rian Hughes
Cover and design

THE INVISIBLES
created by
Grant Morrison

THE INVISIBLES:

Say You Want a Revolution

THE INVISIBLES:
Say You Want a Revolution

THE INVISIBLES:
SAY YOU WANT A REVOLUTION
Published by DC Comics.
Cover, introduction and compilation
copyright © 1996 DC Comics.
All rights reserved.

Originally published in single magazine
form as THE INVISIBLES 1-8.
Copyright © 1994, 1995 Grant Morrison.
All Rights Reserved.
All characters, their distinctive
likenesses and related elements featured
in this publication are trademarks
of Grant Morrison. VERTIGO is a
trademark of DC Comics.
The stories, characters and incidents
featured in this publication are entirely
fictional. DC Comics does not read or
accept unsolicited submissions of ideas,
stories or artwork.

DC Comics
1700 Broadway, New York, NY 10019
A Warner Bros. Entertainment Company.
Printed in Canada. Seventh Printing.
ISBN: 1-56389-267-7.
ISBN 13: 978-1-56389-267-7

Cover and publication design
by Rian "Carpal Tunnel" Hughes.

2,3
indicia/masthead
introduction | 1

indicia &
masthead

SUSTAINABLE FORESTRY INITIATIVE
Certified Fiber Sourcing
www.sfiprogram.org
Fiber used in this product line meets the sourcing requirements
of the SFI program. www.sfiprogram.org PWC-SFICOC-260

Before I wrote this introduction I decided to speak to Grant Morrison about it so, being without the powers of telepathy, phoned him. The phone rang three times...and then I received the shrill rebuttal of a fax signal.

I was about to replace the phone when something stopped me. And I listened. I had never really listened to a fax signal before. I'd always considered it kind of neutral. A kind of blank. Kind of like a blank pin or page.

A tinnitus tone...followed by sucking emptiness...then the tone again...

And as I listened to that dislocated whistle, that static vibration, unchanging yet changing, indifferent, inchoate... I began to hear other sounds, I began to listen to — or rather create — a kind of inner-ear orchestration. I heard whispers. I heard laughter. With an absurd hop, skip and limp of the imagination, I even fancied I heard the distant stammer of the Godhead.

Then I sobered up a little and thought of THE INVISIBLES. How like the tone of a fax signal it is.

Like Grant's phone message, it is answerable to no one...and at first may seem impenetrable.

Like Grant's anti-phone message, we must bring our own meaning to it. We must, to extend and mutilate a metaphor, rip out the bleeding hearts of significance from the sacrificial victims of our own experiences, and hold them up before the cold and pitiless brilliance of Tonatiyu, as manifested in Grant himself.

For with patience and cunning we find that THE INVISIBLES, like so much of Grant's work and even like Grant himself, is eminently penetrable. It cries out for penetration, and when penetrated, yields its lush riches.

And the riches in this book, in this collection, are indeed riches. From the deft characterization of Dane McGowan and his strange fellow Invisibles, to the moving portraits of Byron and Bysshe and Mary Shelley, even to an amusing if contentious interpretation of that dull, farting semi-dwarf De Sade, this comic sparkles. The intricate interweaving of the Arcadia storyline in particular is worth the price of admission alone.

When Grant recently wrote an introduction to one of my own books, ENIGMA, he offered the reader some memories he had of times spent with me. I would now, in the spirit of damnation, and in an attempt to illustrate more clearly the caliber of the man whom I'm proud to call my friend, like to reciprocate, by sharing with you two memories of my own.

The time in Barcelona, on a chill yet sun-soaked Ramblas, when Grant and I were trying to decide upon a title for the collaboration we were, and hopefully still are, planning to execute.

Amid the scent of rude tobacco and flowers, we happened by pure chance to cast our eyes upon row upon row of homosexual pornographic literature. As one, our eyes alighted upon a singularly mischievous glossy cover, showing a naked young thing with brazen eyes. The title of that lewd publication was...

"BIZARRE BOYS!" we both breathed, staring with astonishment at each other before returning our grateful gaze to the magazine in question. We had a kind of mental intercourse, a porno epiphany when our two minds were, for a bizarre moment, united.

We had found our title.

More important, I think, we had found each other.

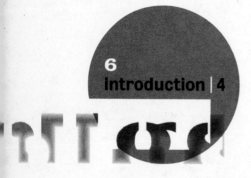

And later, in San Diego, in a crowded and smoke-filled hotel room shortly before dawn, I remember looking across from my position on the bed to see Grant, prostrate on the floor, his eyes redder than a sexually excited Orang Utan's arse, intoning a poignant salutation to water. Yes, to water! For here is a man who, at the very death-rattle of night, when most of us are drunkenly content to crawl into our own or others' beds, here is a man who still has time to pay homage to that clear running lifeblood of the planet!

Grant, I salute thee!

THE INVISIBLES, I salute thee!

I salute also the astonishing achievement of the various artists who have so obviously given themselves fully to this project, to bring Grant's beautiful creations to life.

Steve Yeowell, Jill Thompson, Dennis Cramer, and all the others who have worked on this book deserve our thanks and gratitude.

In parting, if you are reading this introduction, unsure whether to buy this book or not, I implore you. In the name of art, in the name of sex, in the name of liberty, buy it. Or steal it. No, on second thought don't steal it. Cajole someone else into buying it for you. Whatever you do, read it.

Listen to it.

Listen to this dislocated whistle...listen to this white noise.

Penetrate it.

Allow yourself to be penetrated.

For this is a great comic. And The Invisibles is a great movement.

And Grant Morrison, who as I write is a sick man in more ways than one, is a great mind. And a great writer.

Peter Milligan

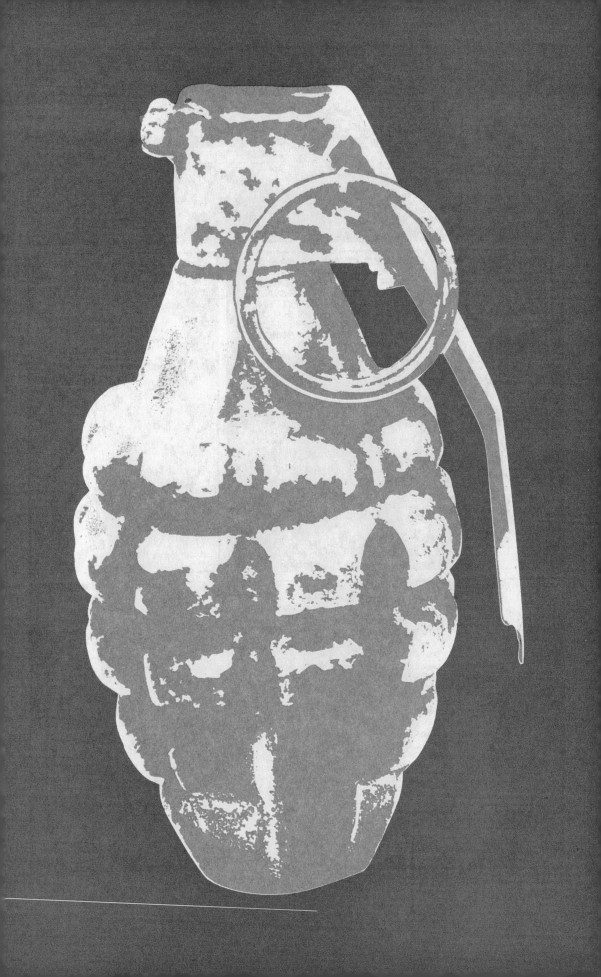

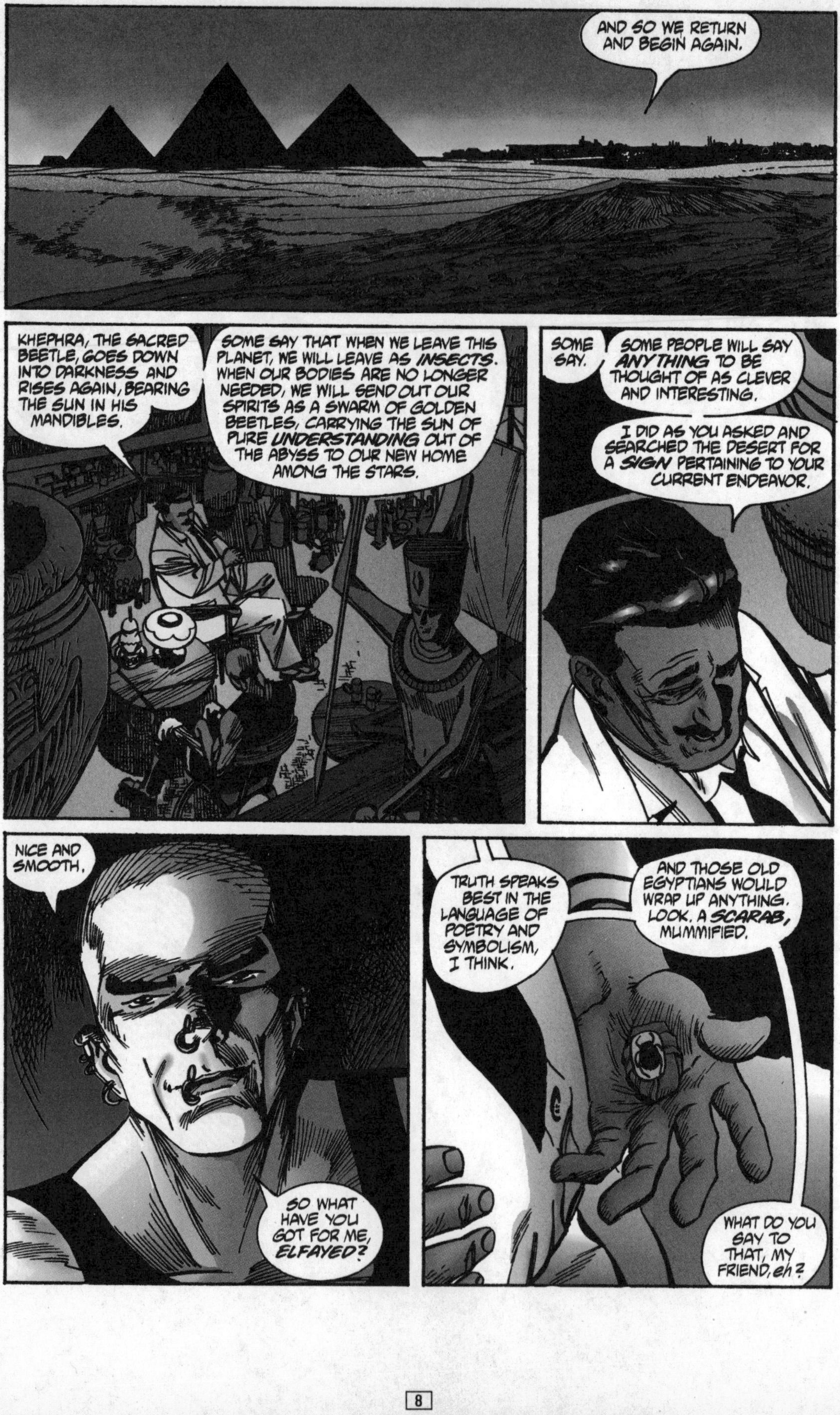
AND SO WE RETURN AND BEGIN AGAIN.
KHEPHRA, THE SACRED BEETLE, GOES DOWN INTO DARKNESS AND RISES AGAIN, BEARING THE SUN IN HIS MANDIBLES.
SOME SAY THAT WHEN WE LEAVE THIS PLANET, WE WILL LEAVE AS INSECTS. WHEN OUR BODIES ARE NO LONGER NEEDED, WE WILL SEND OUT OUR SPIRITS AS A SWARM OF GOLDEN BEETLES, CARRYING THE SUN OF PURE UNDERSTANDING OUT OF THE ABYSS TO OUR NEW HOME AMONG THE STARS.
SOME SAY.
SOME PEOPLE WILL SAY ANYTHING TO BE THOUGHT OF AS CLEVER AND INTERESTING.
I DID AS YOU ASKED AND SEARCHED THE DESERT FOR A SIGN PERTAINING TO YOUR CURRENT ENDEAVOR.
NICE AND SMOOTH.
SO WHAT HAVE YOU GOT FOR ME, ELFAYED?
TRUTH SPEAKS BEST IN THE LANGUAGE OF POETRY AND SYMBOLISM, I THINK.
AND THOSE OLD EGYPTIANS WOULD WRAP UP ANYTHING. LOOK. A SCARAB, MUMMIFIED.
WHAT DO YOU SAY TO THAT, MY FRIEND, eh?

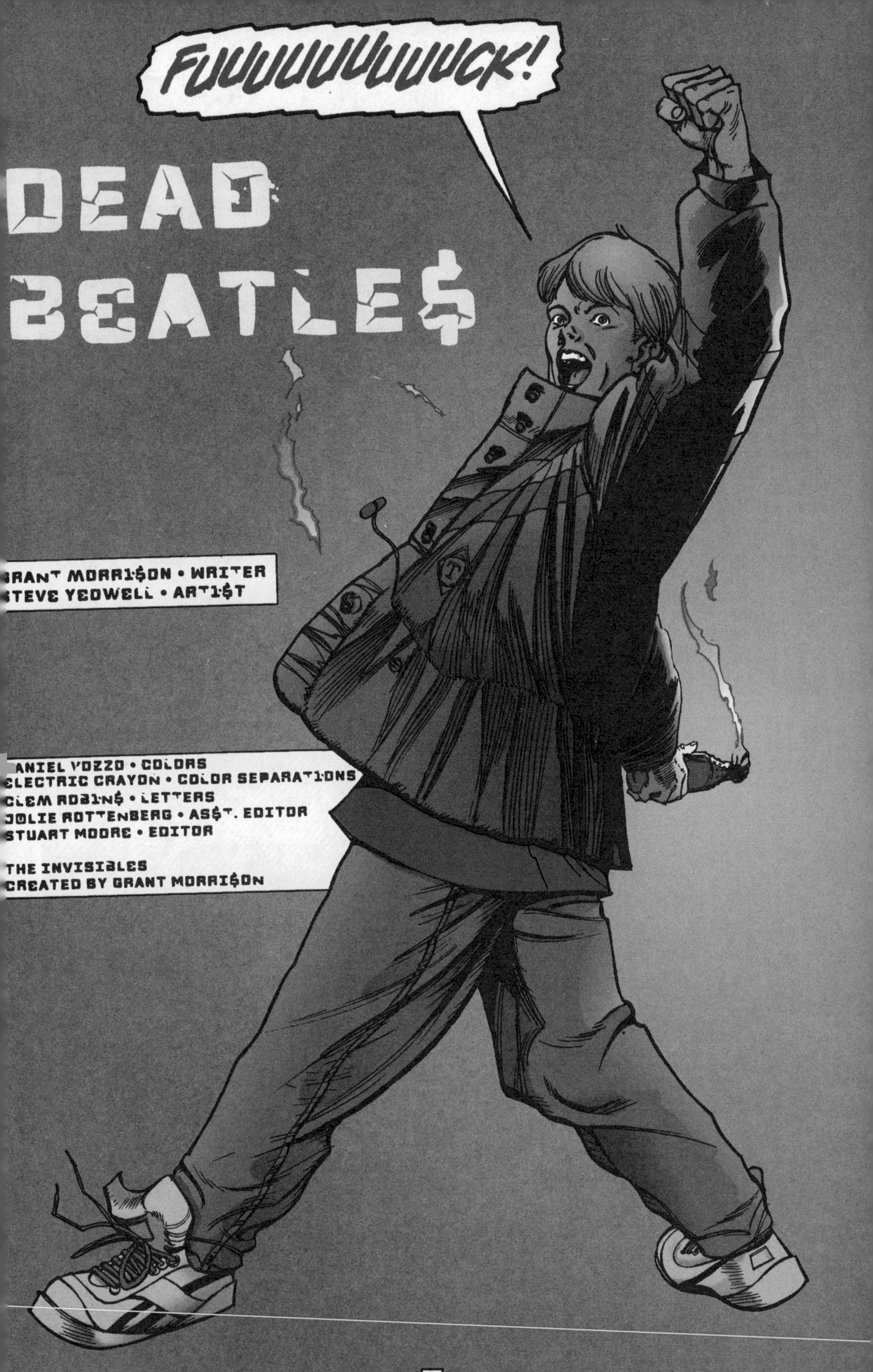
FUUUUUUUUUUCK!
DEAD BEATLE$
RANT MORRI$ON • WRITER
TEVE YEOWELL • ARTI$T
ANIEL VOZZO • COLORS
ELECTRIC CRAYON • COLOR SEPARATIONS
CLEM ROBIN$ • LETTERS
JULIE ROTTENBERG • AS$T. EDITOR
STUART MOORE • EDITOR
THE INVISIBLES
CREATED BY GRANT MORRI$ON

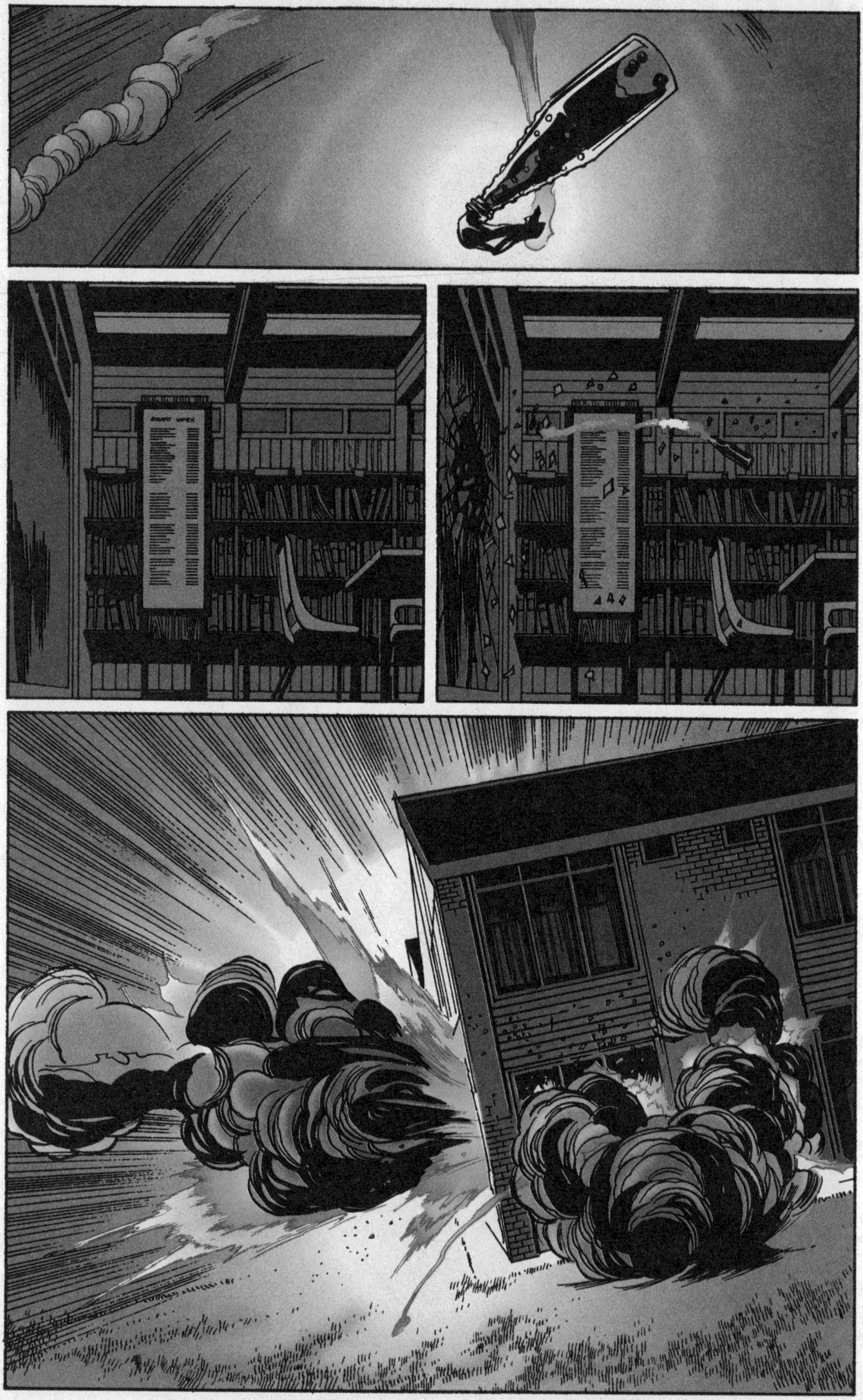

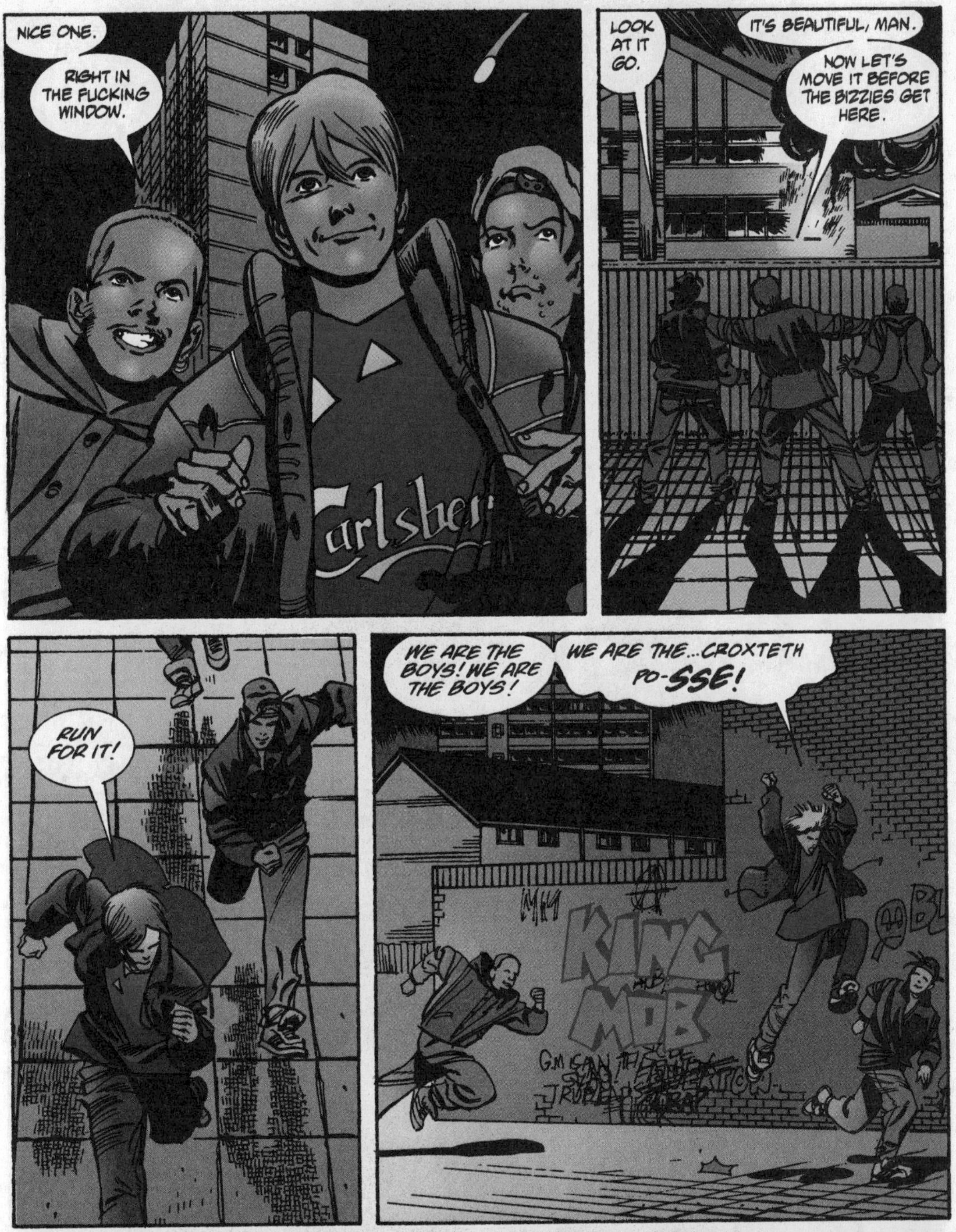
NICE ONE.
RIGHT IN THE FUCKING WINDOW.
LOOK AT IT GO.
IT'S BEAUTIFUL, MAN.
NOW LET'S MOVE IT BEFORE THE BIZZIES GET HERE.
RUN FOR IT!
WE ARE THE BOYS! WE ARE THE BOYS!
WE ARE THE...CROXTETH PO-SSE!
KING MOB
HAHAHAHAHAHA

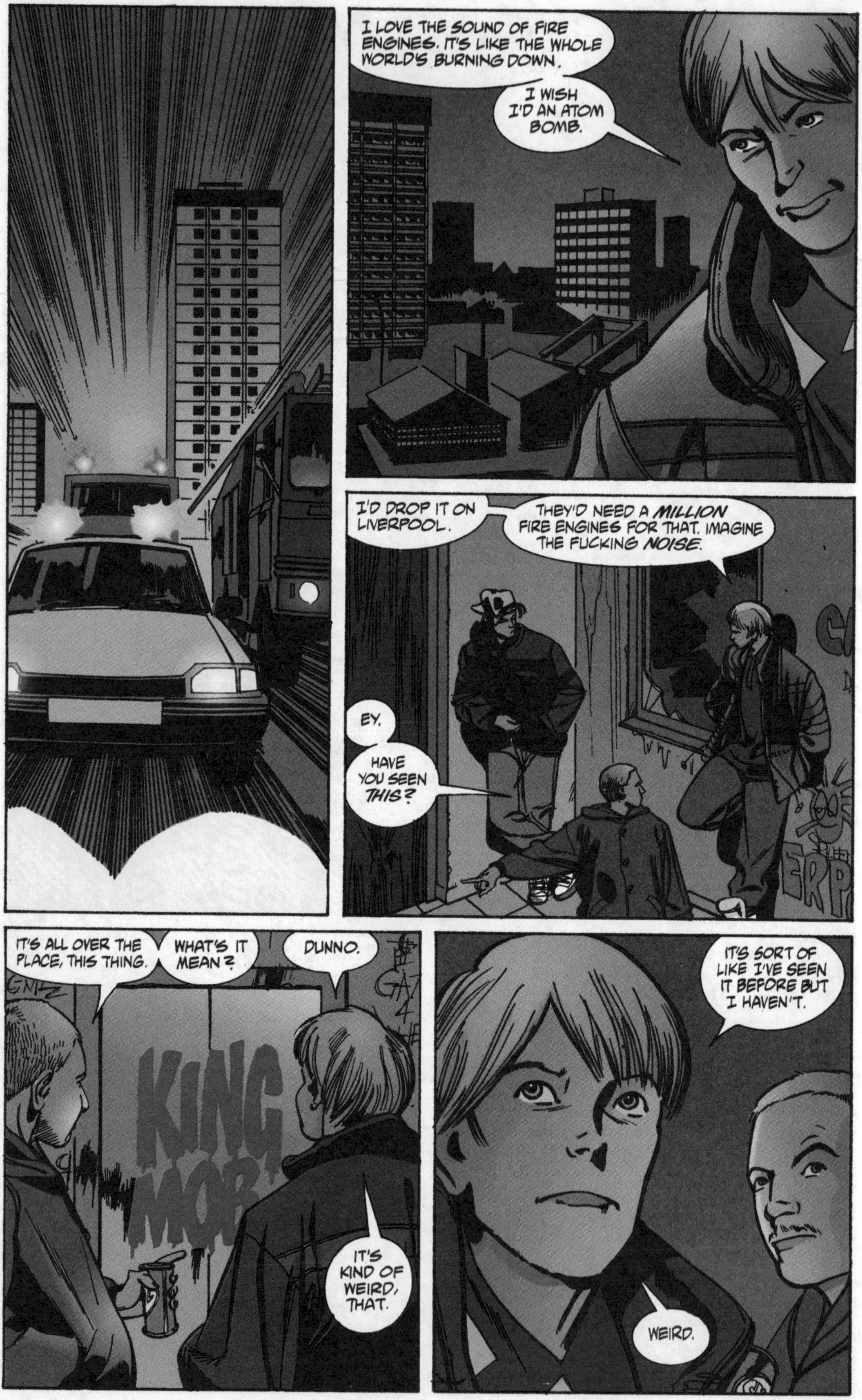
I LOVE THE SOUND OF FIRE ENGINES. IT'S LIKE THE WHOLE WORLD'S BURNING DOWN.
I WISH I'D AN ATOM BOMB.
I'D DROP IT ON LIVERPOOL.
THEY'D NEED A *MILLION* FIRE ENGINES FOR THAT. IMAGINE THE FUCKING *NOISE*.
EY.
HAVE YOU SEEN *THIS*?
IT'S ALL OVER THE PLACE, THIS THING.
WHAT'S IT MEAN?
DUNNO.
KING MOB
IT'S KIND OF WEIRD, THAT.
IT'S SORT OF LIKE I'VE SEEN IT BEFORE BUT I HAVEN'T.
WEIRD.

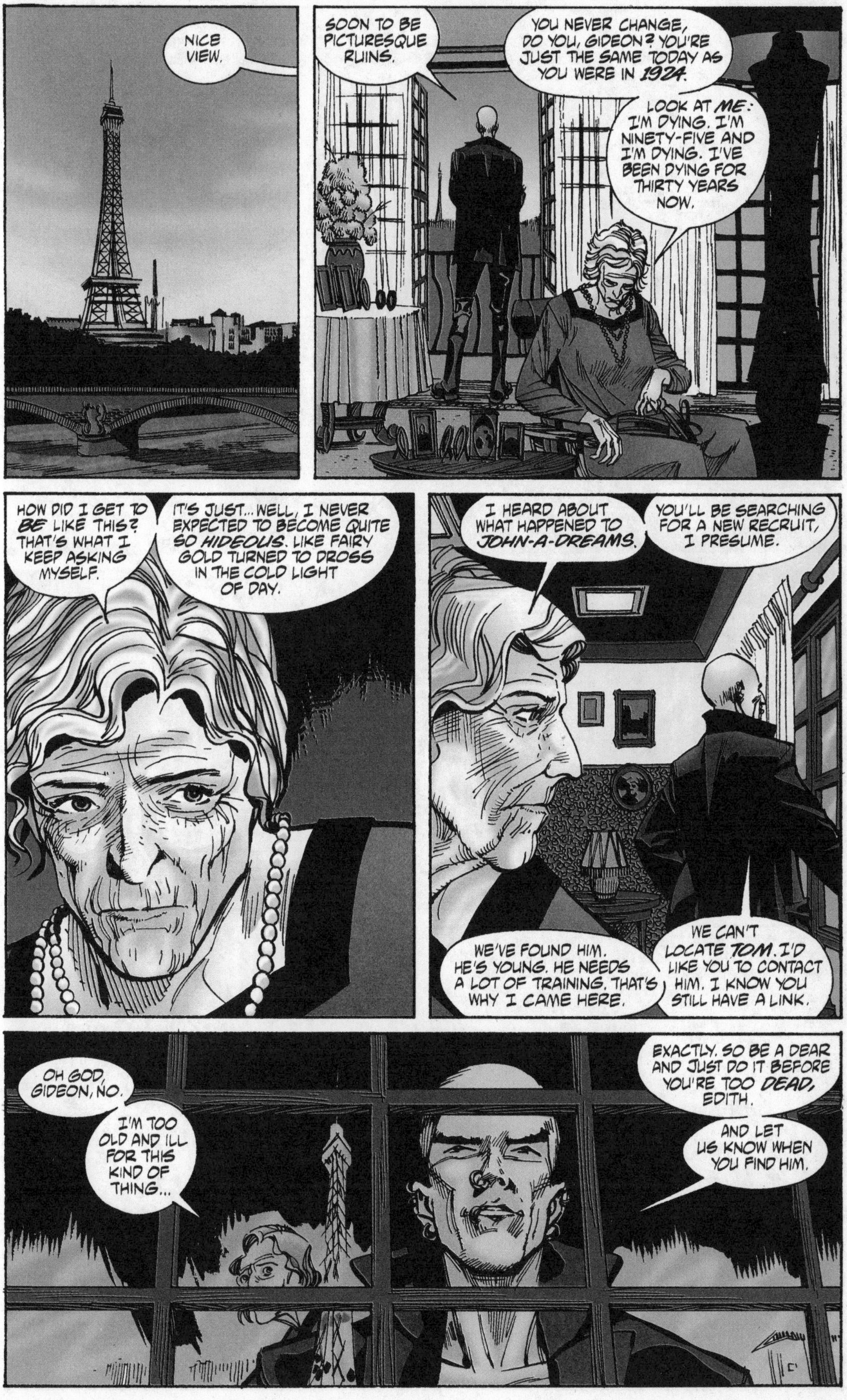
NICE VIEW.
SOON TO BE PICTURESQUE RUINS.
YOU NEVER CHANGE, DO YOU, GIDEON? YOU'RE JUST THE SAME TODAY AS YOU WERE IN 1924.
LOOK AT ME: I'M DYING. I'M NINETY-FIVE AND I'M DYING. I'VE BEEN DYING FOR THIRTY YEARS NOW.
HOW DID I GET TO BE LIKE THIS? THAT'S WHAT I KEEP ASKING MYSELF.
IT'S JUST... WELL, I NEVER EXPECTED TO BECOME QUITE SO HIDEOUS. LIKE FAIRY GOLD TURNED TO DROSS IN THE COLD LIGHT OF DAY.
I HEARD ABOUT WHAT HAPPENED TO JOHN-A-DREAMS.
YOU'LL BE SEARCHING FOR A NEW RECRUIT, I PRESUME.
WE'VE FOUND HIM. HE'S YOUNG. HE NEEDS A LOT OF TRAINING. THAT'S WHY I CAME HERE.
WE CAN'T LOCATE TOM. I'D LIKE YOU TO CONTACT HIM. I KNOW YOU STILL HAVE A LINK.
OH GOD, GIDEON, NO.
I'M TOO OLD AND ILL FOR THIS KIND OF THING...
EXACTLY. SO BE A DEAR AND JUST DO IT BEFORE YOU'RE TOO DEAD, EDITH.
AND LET US KNOW WHEN YOU FIND HIM.

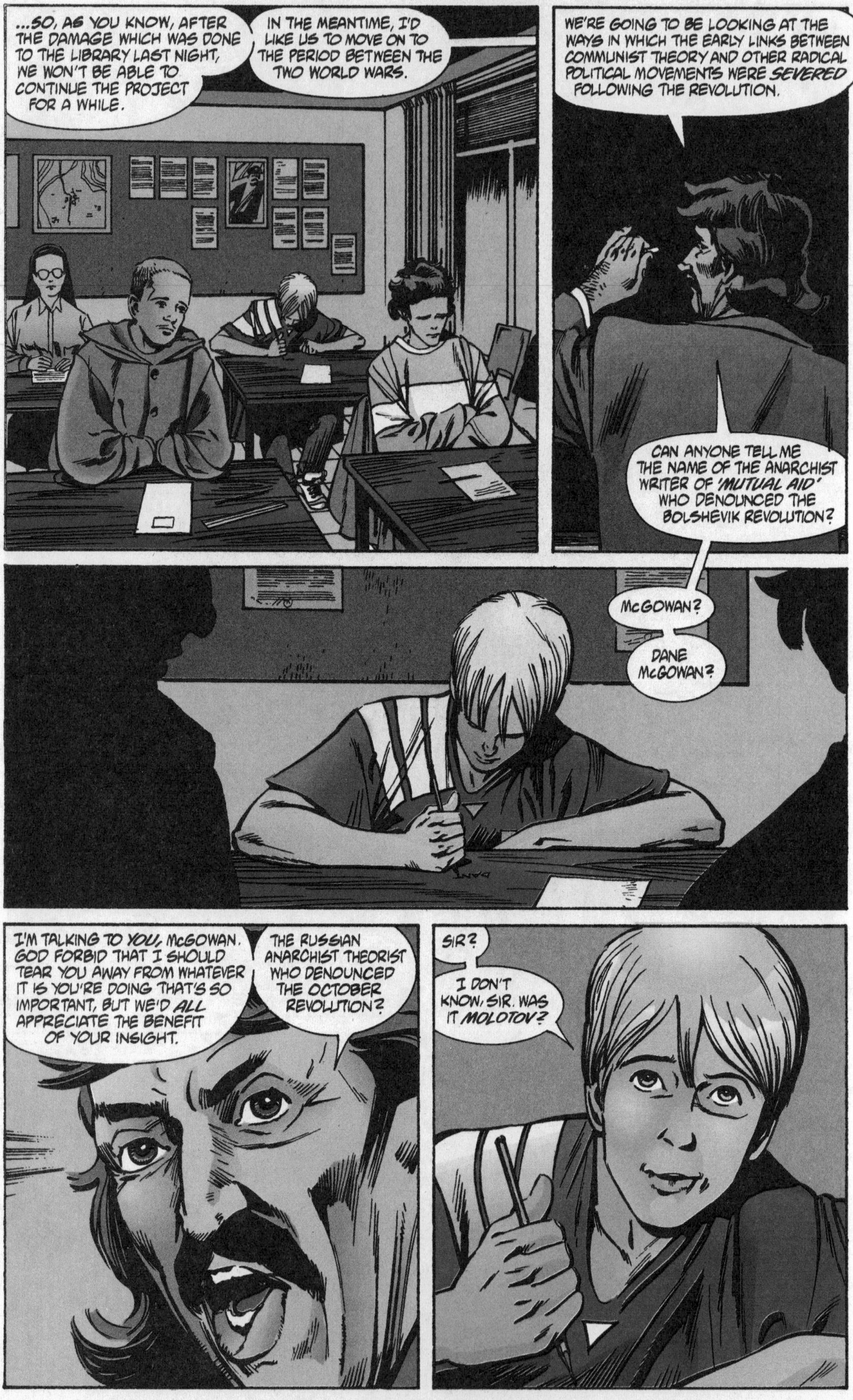

...SO, AS YOU KNOW, AFTER THE DAMAGE WHICH WAS DONE TO THE LIBRARY LAST NIGHT, WE WON'T BE ABLE TO CONTINUE THE PROJECT FOR A WHILE.
IN THE MEANTIME, I'D LIKE US TO MOVE ON TO THE PERIOD BETWEEN THE TWO WORLD WARS.
WE'RE GOING TO BE LOOKING AT THE WAYS IN WHICH THE EARLY LINKS BETWEEN COMMUNIST THEORY AND OTHER RADICAL POLITICAL MOVEMENTS WERE SEVERED FOLLOWING THE REVOLUTION.
CAN ANYONE TELL ME THE NAME OF THE ANARCHIST WRITER OF 'MUTUAL AID' WHO DENOUNCED THE BOLSHEVIK REVOLUTION?
McGOWAN?
DANE McGOWAN?
I'M TALKING TO YOU, McGOWAN. GOD FORBID THAT I SHOULD TEAR YOU AWAY FROM WHATEVER IT IS YOU'RE DOING THAT'S SO IMPORTANT, BUT WE'D ALL APPRECIATE THE BENEFIT OF YOUR INSIGHT.
THE RUSSIAN ANARCHIST THEORIST WHO DENOUNCED THE OCTOBER REVOLUTION?
SIR?
I DON'T KNOW, SIR. WAS IT MOLOTOV?

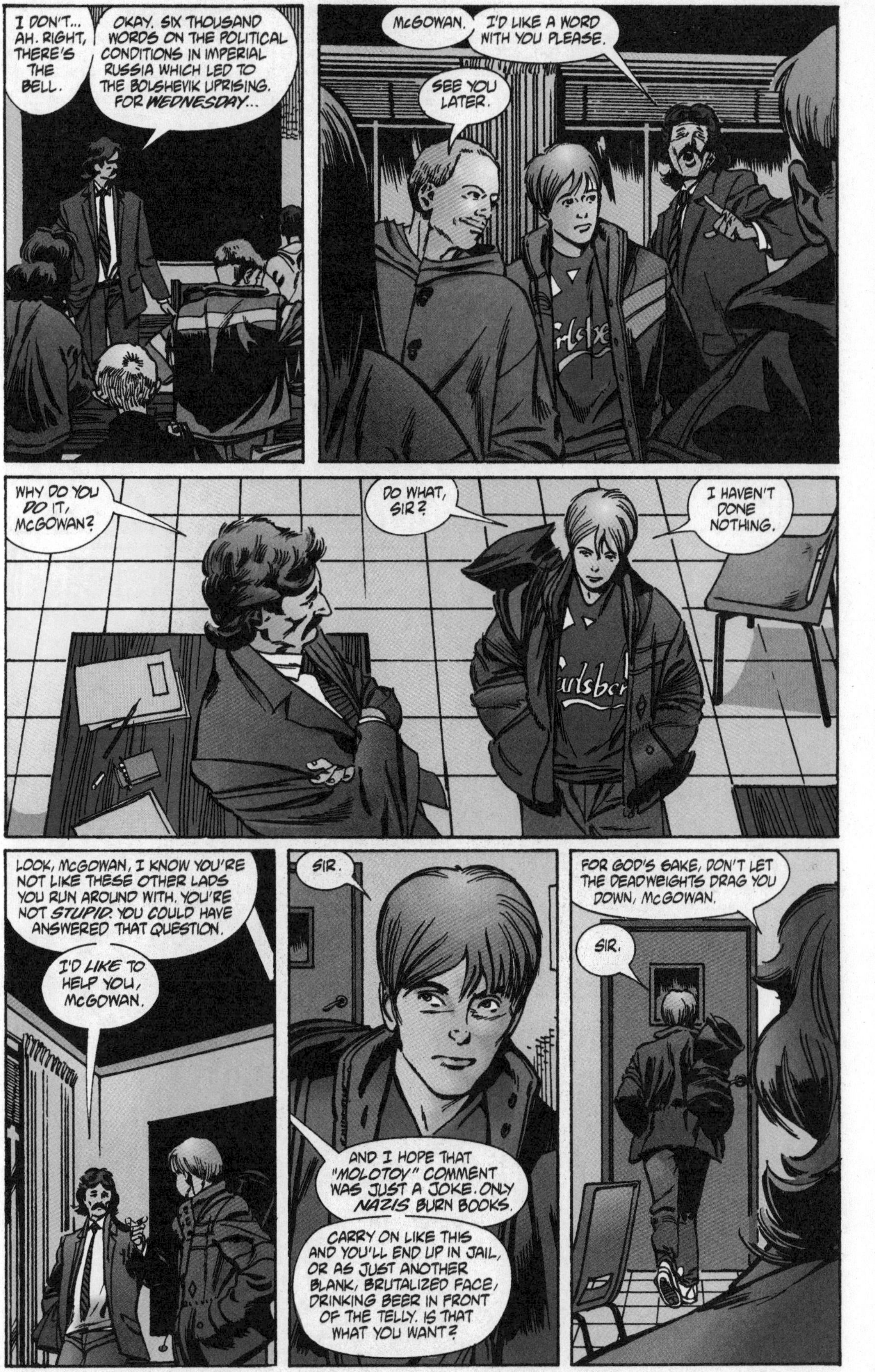
I DON'T... AH. RIGHT, THERE'S THE BELL.
OKAY. SIX THOUSAND WORDS ON THE POLITICAL CONDITIONS IN IMPERIAL RUSSIA WHICH LED TO THE BOLSHEVIK UPRISING. FOR *WEDNESDAY*...
McGOWAN.
I'D LIKE A WORD WITH YOU PLEASE.
SEE YOU LATER.
WHY DO YOU *DO* IT, McGOWAN?
DO WHAT, SIR?
I HAVEN'T DONE NOTHING.
LOOK, McGOWAN, I KNOW YOU'RE NOT LIKE THESE OTHER LADS YOU RUN AROUND WITH. YOU'RE NOT *STUPID*. YOU COULD HAVE ANSWERED THAT QUESTION.
I'D *LIKE* TO HELP YOU, McGOWAN.
SIR.
AND I HOPE THAT "MOLOTOV" COMMENT WAS JUST A JOKE. ONLY *NAZIS* BURN BOOKS.
CARRY ON LIKE THIS AND YOU'LL END UP IN JAIL, OR AS JUST ANOTHER BLANK, BRUTALIZED FACE, DRINKING BEER IN FRONT OF THE TELLY. IS THAT WHAT YOU WANT?
FOR GOD'S SAKE, DON'T LET THE DEADWEIGHTS DRAG YOU DOWN, McGOWAN.
SIR.

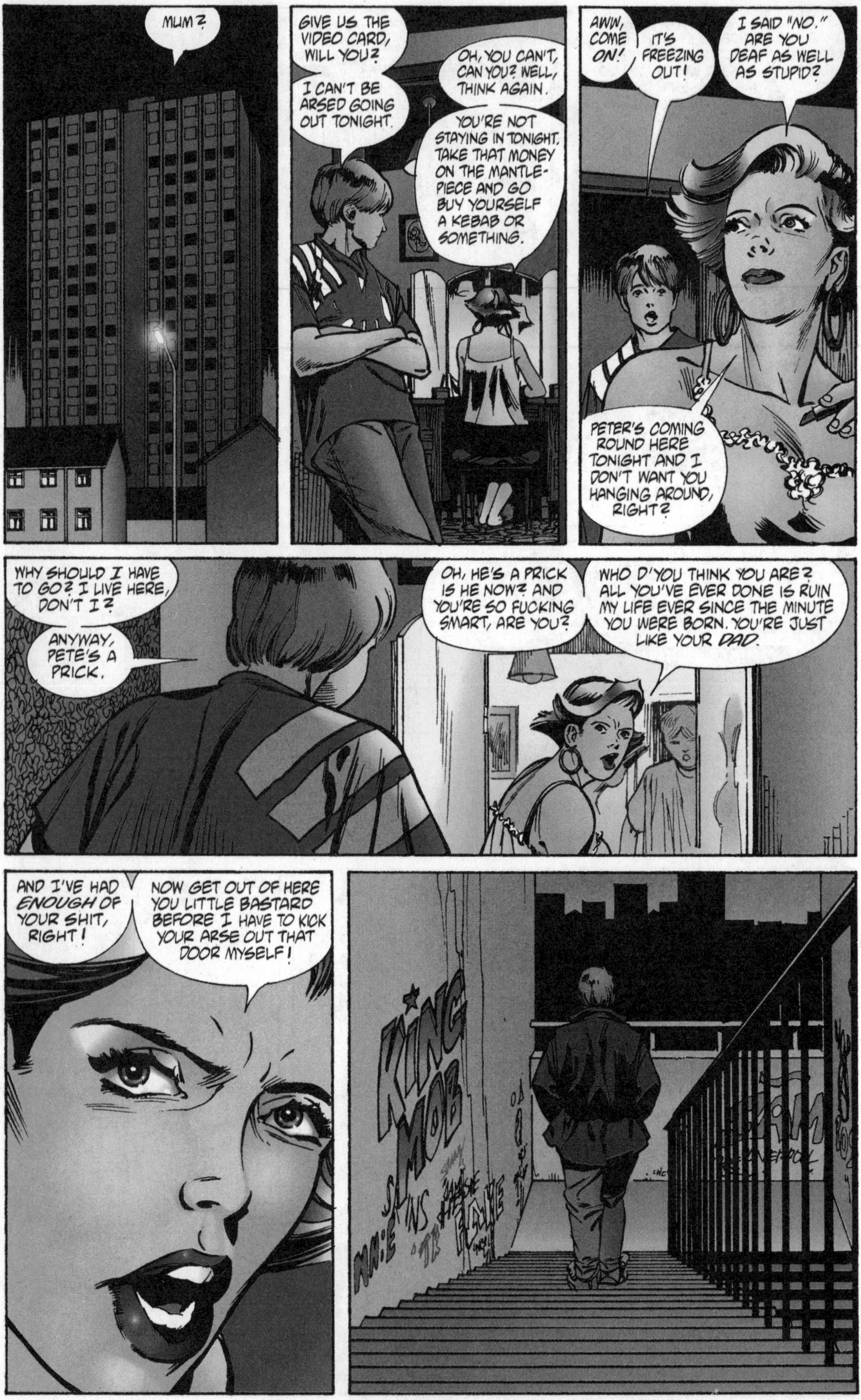
MUM?
GIVE US THE VIDEO CARD, WILL YOU?
I CAN'T BE ARSED GOING OUT TONIGHT.
OH, YOU CAN'T, CAN YOU? WELL, THINK AGAIN.
YOU'RE NOT STAYING IN TONIGHT. TAKE THAT MONEY ON THE MANTLE-PIECE AND GO BUY YOURSELF A KEBAB OR SOMETHING.
AWW, COME ON!
IT'S FREEZING OUT!
I SAID "NO." ARE YOU DEAF AS WELL AS STUPID?
PETER'S COMING ROUND HERE TONIGHT AND I DON'T WANT YOU HANGING AROUND, RIGHT?
WHY SHOULD I HAVE TO GO? I LIVE HERE, DON'T I?
ANYWAY, PETE'S A PRICK.
OH, HE'S A PRICK IS HE NOW? AND YOU'RE SO FUCKING SMART, ARE YOU?
WHO D'YOU THINK YOU ARE? ALL YOU'VE EVER DONE IS RUIN MY LIFE EVER SINCE THE MINUTE YOU WERE BORN. YOU'RE JUST LIKE YOUR DAD.
AND I'VE HAD ENOUGH OF YOUR SHIT, RIGHT!
NOW GET OUT OF HERE YOU LITTLE BASTARD BEFORE I HAVE TO KICK YOUR ARSE OUT THAT DOOR MYSELF!
KING MOB

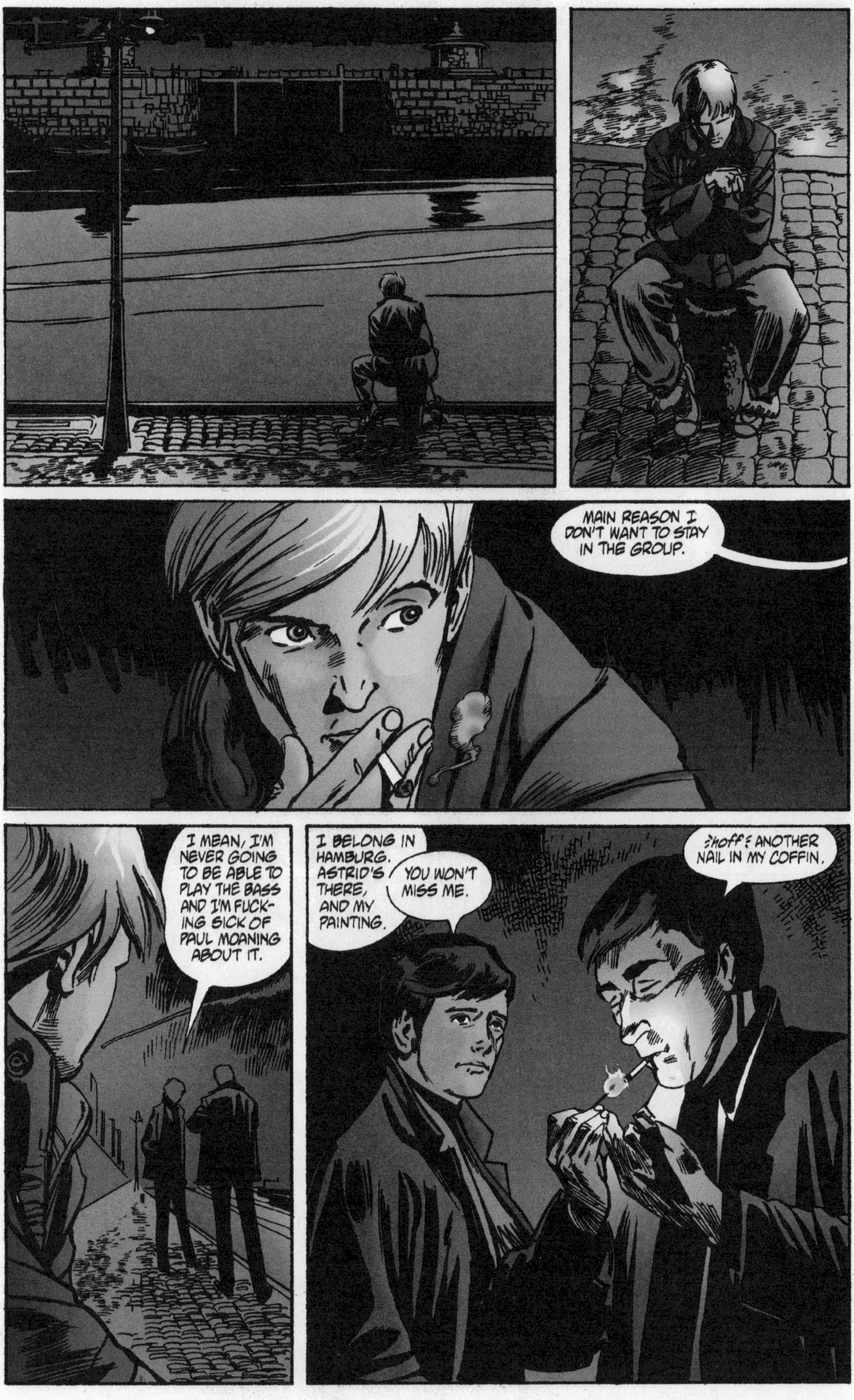
MAIN REASON I DON'T WANT TO STAY IN THE GROUP.
I MEAN, I'M NEVER GOING TO BE ABLE TO PLAY THE BASS AND I'M FUCKING SICK OF PAUL MOANING ABOUT IT.
I BELONG IN HAMBURG. ASTRID'S THERE, AND MY PAINTING.
YOU WON'T MISS ME.
hoff ANOTHER NAIL IN MY COFFIN.

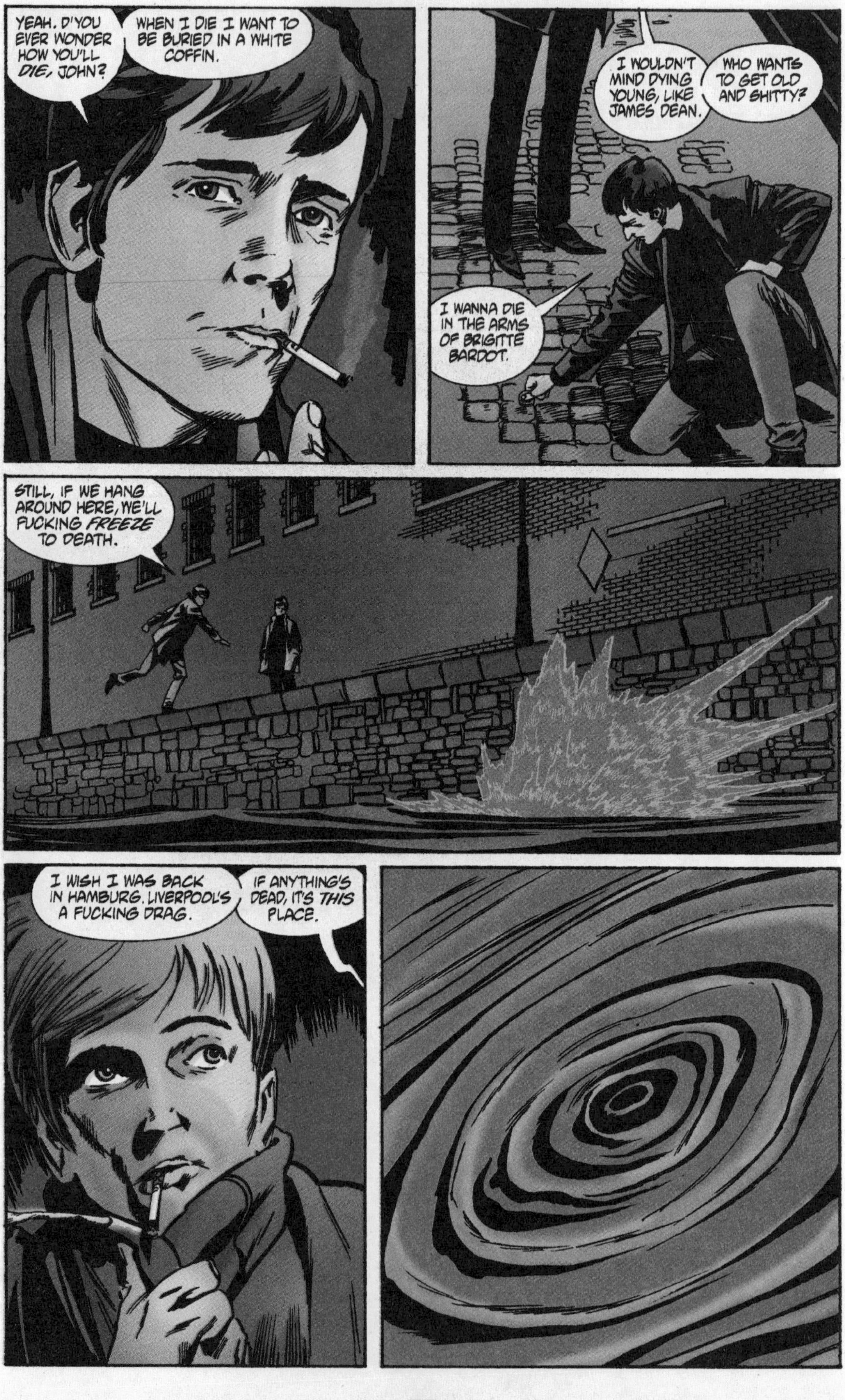
YEAH. D'YOU EVER WONDER HOW YOU'LL DIE, JOHN?
WHEN I DIE I WANT TO BE BURIED IN A WHITE COFFIN.
I WOULDN'T MIND DYING YOUNG, LIKE JAMES DEAN.
WHO WANTS TO GET OLD AND SHITTY?
I WANNA DIE IN THE ARMS OF BRIGITTE BARDOT.
STILL, IF WE HANG AROUND HERE, WE'LL FUCKING FREEZE TO DEATH.
I WISH I WAS BACK IN HAMBURG. LIVERPOOL'S A FUCKING DRAG.
IF ANYTHING'S DEAD, IT'S THIS PLACE.

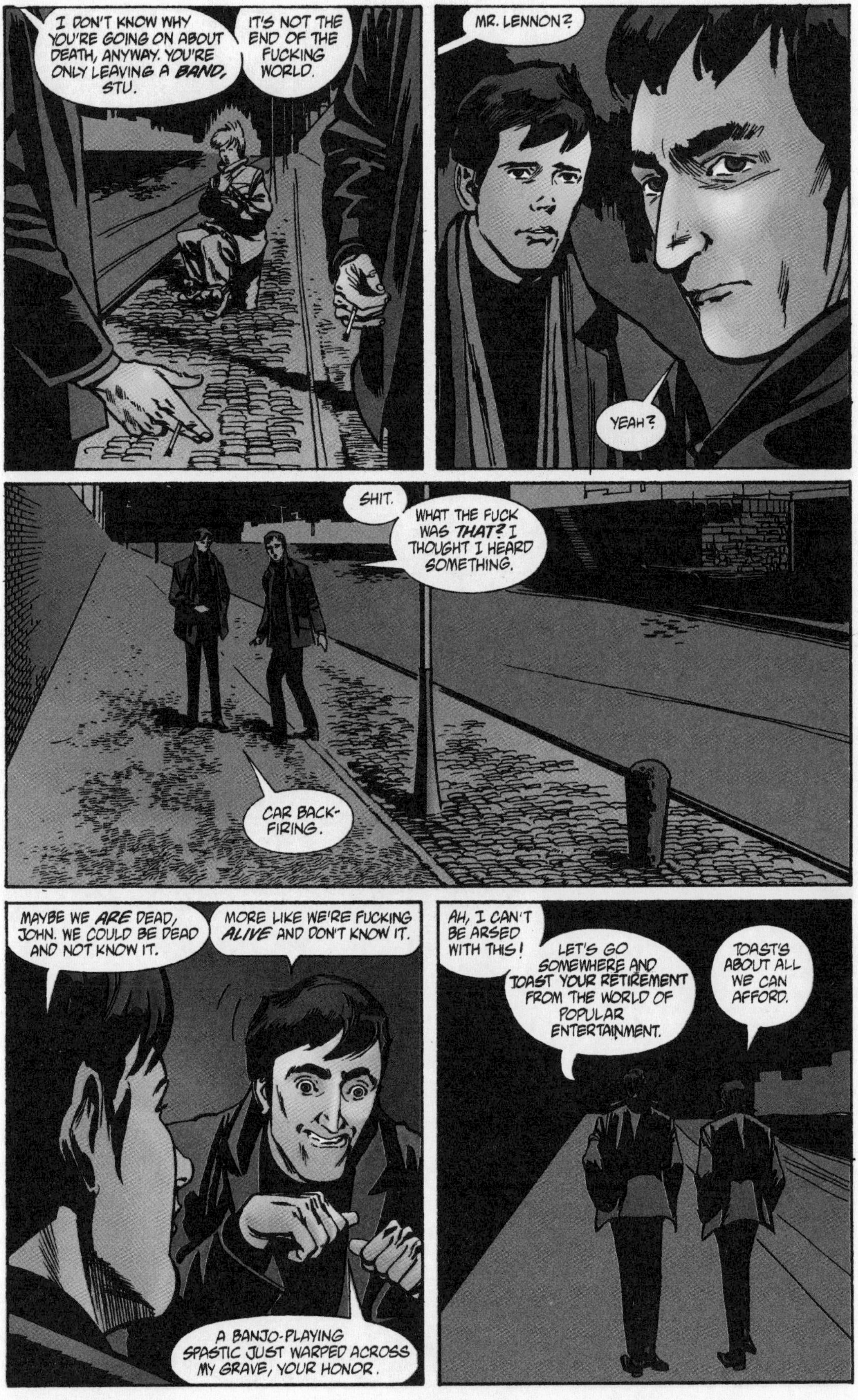
I DON'T KNOW WHY YOU'RE GOING ON ABOUT DEATH, ANYWAY. YOU'RE ONLY LEAVING A BAND, STU.
IT'S NOT THE END OF THE FUCKING WORLD.
MR. LENNON?
YEAH?
SHIT.
WHAT THE FUCK WAS THAT? I THOUGHT I HEARD SOMETHING.
CAR BACK-FIRING.
MAYBE WE ARE DEAD, JOHN. WE COULD BE DEAD AND NOT KNOW IT.
MORE LIKE WE'RE FUCKING ALIVE AND DON'T KNOW IT.
A BANJO-PLAYING SPASTIC JUST WARPED ACROSS MY GRAVE, YOUR HONOR.
AH, I CAN'T BE ARSED WITH THIS!
LET'S GO SOMEWHERE AND TOAST YOUR RETIREMENT FROM THE WORLD OF POPULAR ENTERTAINMENT.
TOAST'S ABOUT ALL WE CAN AFFORD.

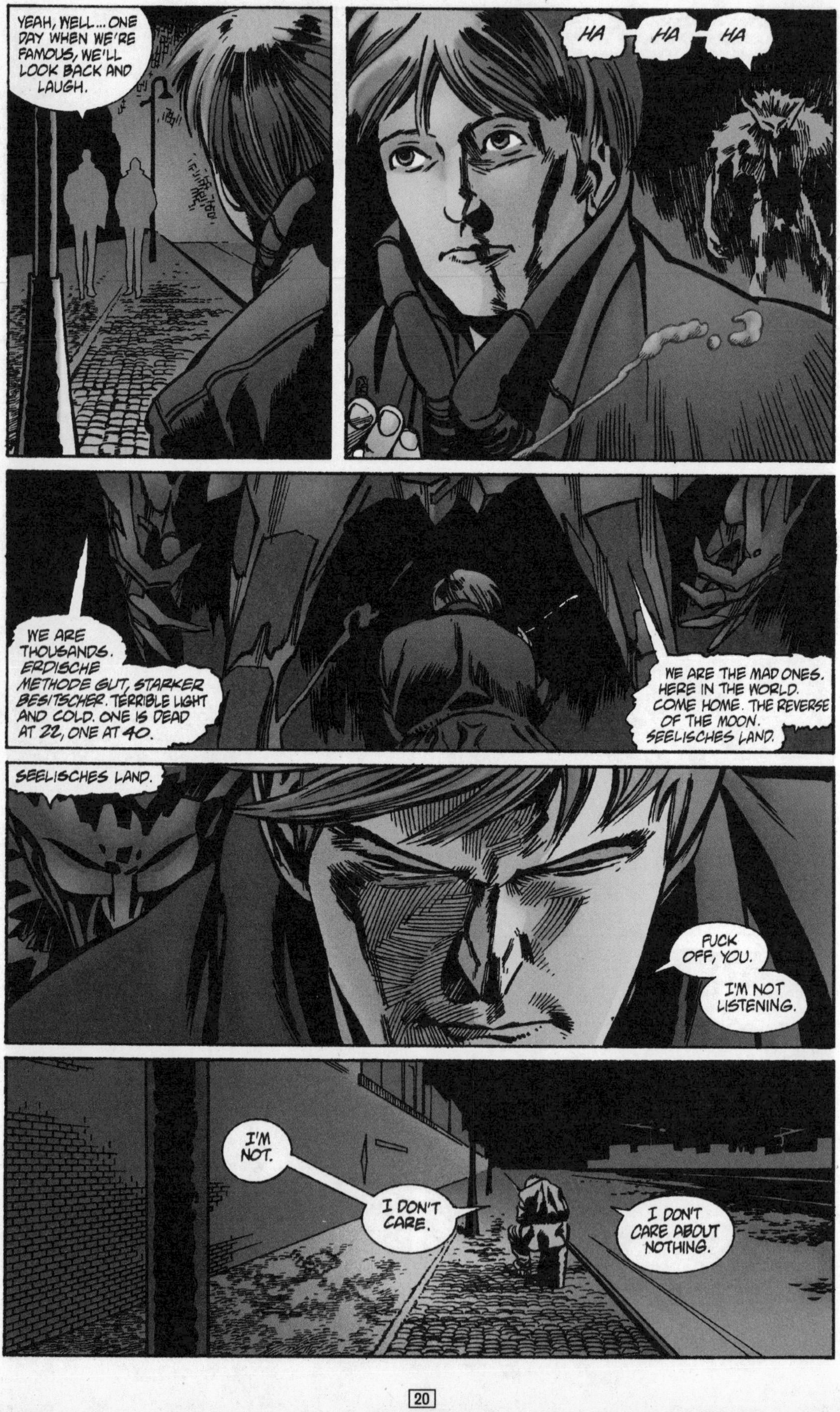

YEAH, WELL... ONE DAY WHEN WE'RE FAMOUS, WE'LL LOOK BACK AND LAUGH.
HA
HA
HA
WE ARE THOUSANDS. ERDISCHE METHODE GUT, STARKER BESITSCHER. TERRIBLE LIGHT AND COLD. ONE IS DEAD AT 22, ONE AT 40.
WE ARE THE MAD ONES. HERE IN THE WORLD. COME HOME. THE REVERSE OF THE MOON. SEELISCHES LAND.
SEELISCHES LAND.
FUCK OFF, YOU.
I'M NOT LISTENING.
I'M NOT.
I DON'T CARE.
I DON'T CARE ABOUT NOTHING.

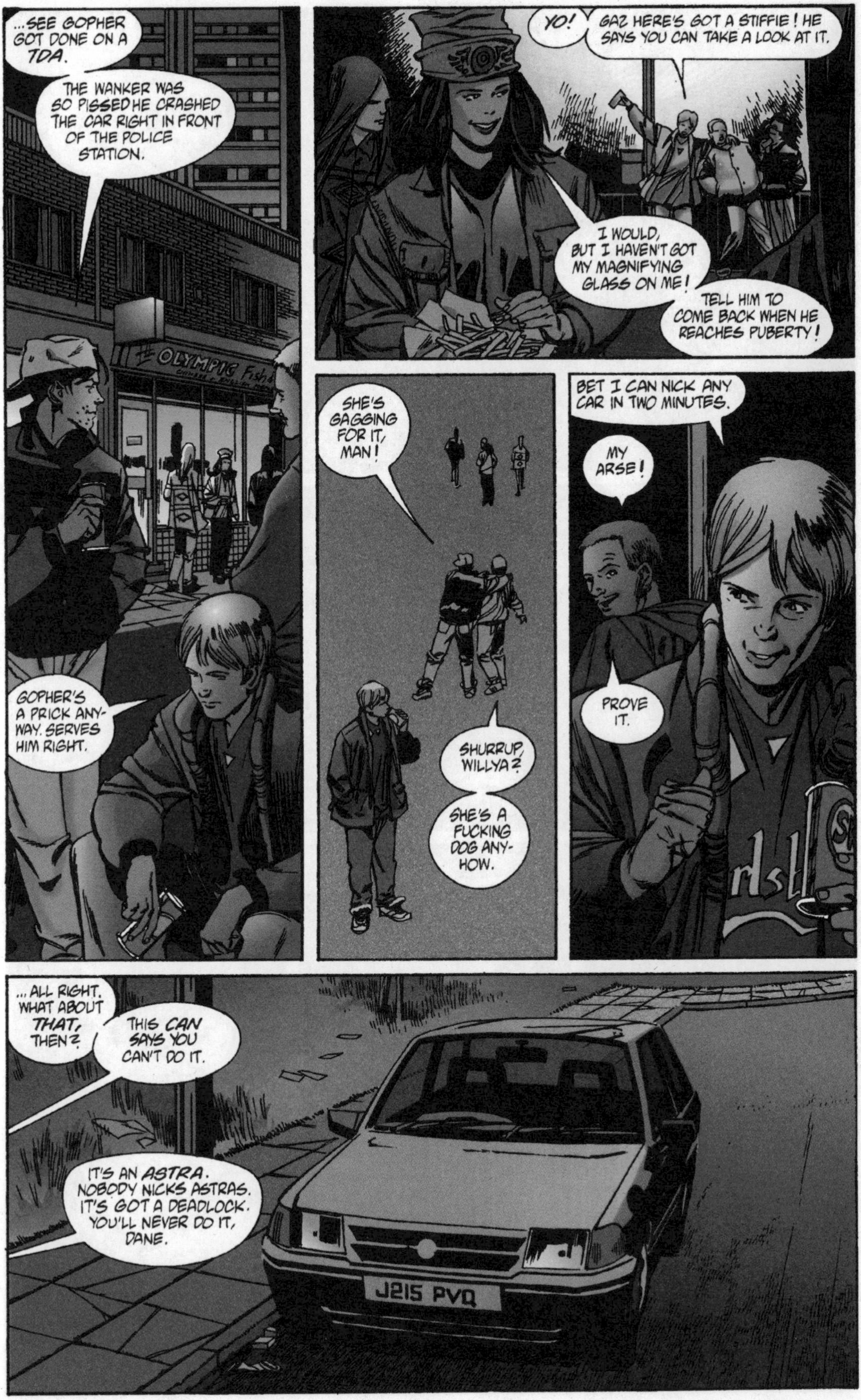
...SEE GOPHER GOT DONE ON A TDA.
THE WANKER WAS SO PISSED HE CRASHED THE CAR RIGHT IN FRONT OF THE POLICE STATION.
OLYMPIC Fish
GOPHER'S A PRICK ANY-WAY. SERVES HIM RIGHT.
YO!
GAZ HERE'S GOT A STIFFIE! HE SAYS YOU CAN TAKE A LOOK AT IT.
I WOULD, BUT I HAVEN'T GOT MY MAGNIFYING GLASS ON ME!
TELL HIM TO COME BACK WHEN HE REACHES PUBERTY!
SHE'S GAGGING FOR IT, MAN!
SHURRUP, WILLYA?
SHE'S A FUCKING DOG ANY-HOW.
BET I CAN NICK ANY CAR IN TWO MINUTES.
MY ARSE!
PROVE IT.
...ALL RIGHT. WHAT ABOUT THAT, THEN?
THIS CAN SAYS YOU CAN'T DO IT.
IT'S AN ASTRA. NOBODY NICKS ASTRAS. IT'S GOT A DEADLOCK. YOU'LL NEVER DO IT, DANE.
J215 PVQ

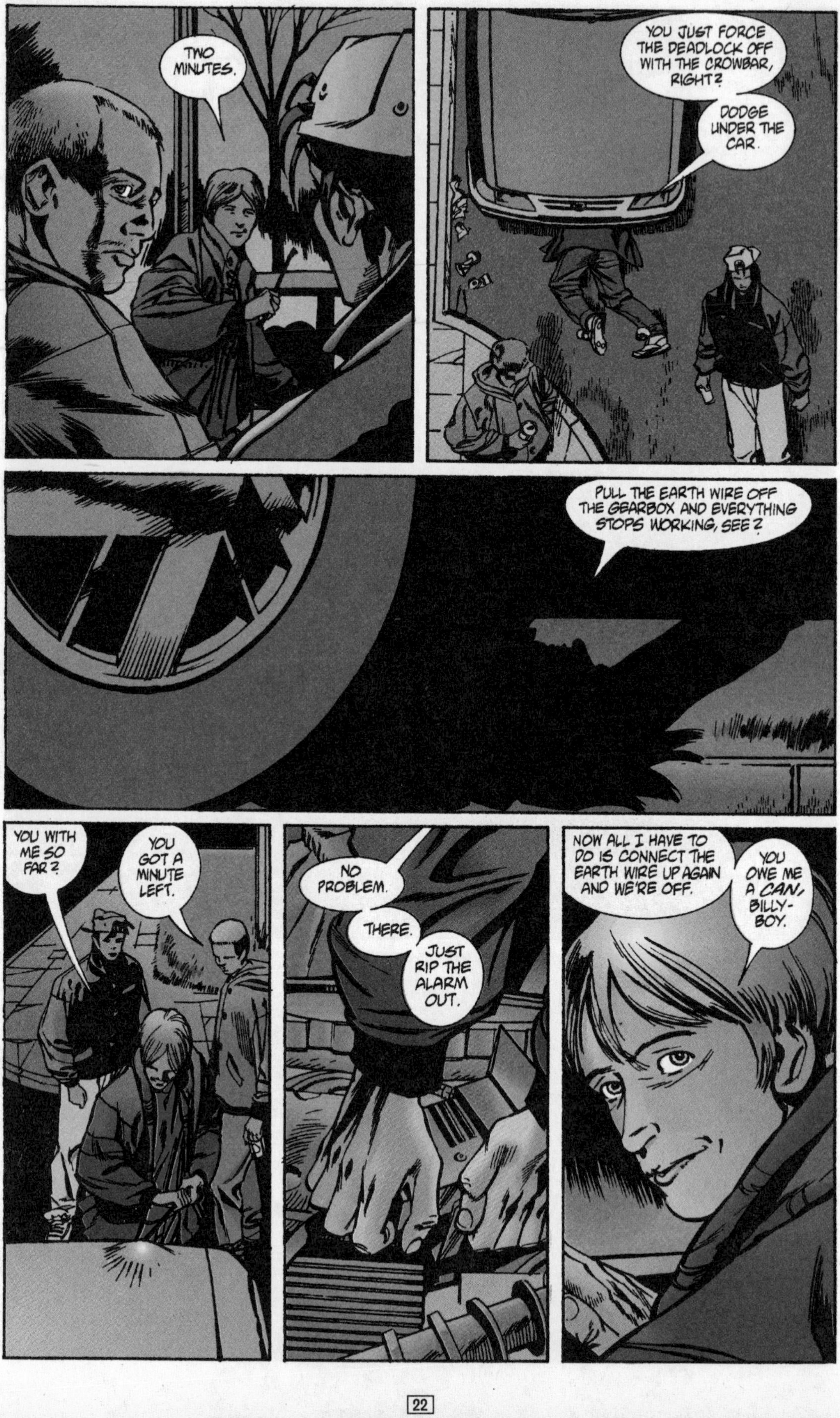
TWO MINUTES.
YOU JUST FORCE THE DEADLOCK OFF WITH THE CROWBAR, RIGHT?
DODGE UNDER THE CAR.
PULL THE EARTH WIRE OFF THE GEARBOX AND EVERYTHING STOPS WORKING, SEE?
YOU WITH ME SO FAR?
YOU GOT A MINUTE LEFT.
NO PROBLEM.
THERE.
JUST RIP THE ALARM OUT.
NOW ALL I HAVE TO DO IS CONNECT THE EARTH WIRE UP AGAIN AND WE'RE OFF.
YOU OWE ME A *CAN*, BILLY-BOY.

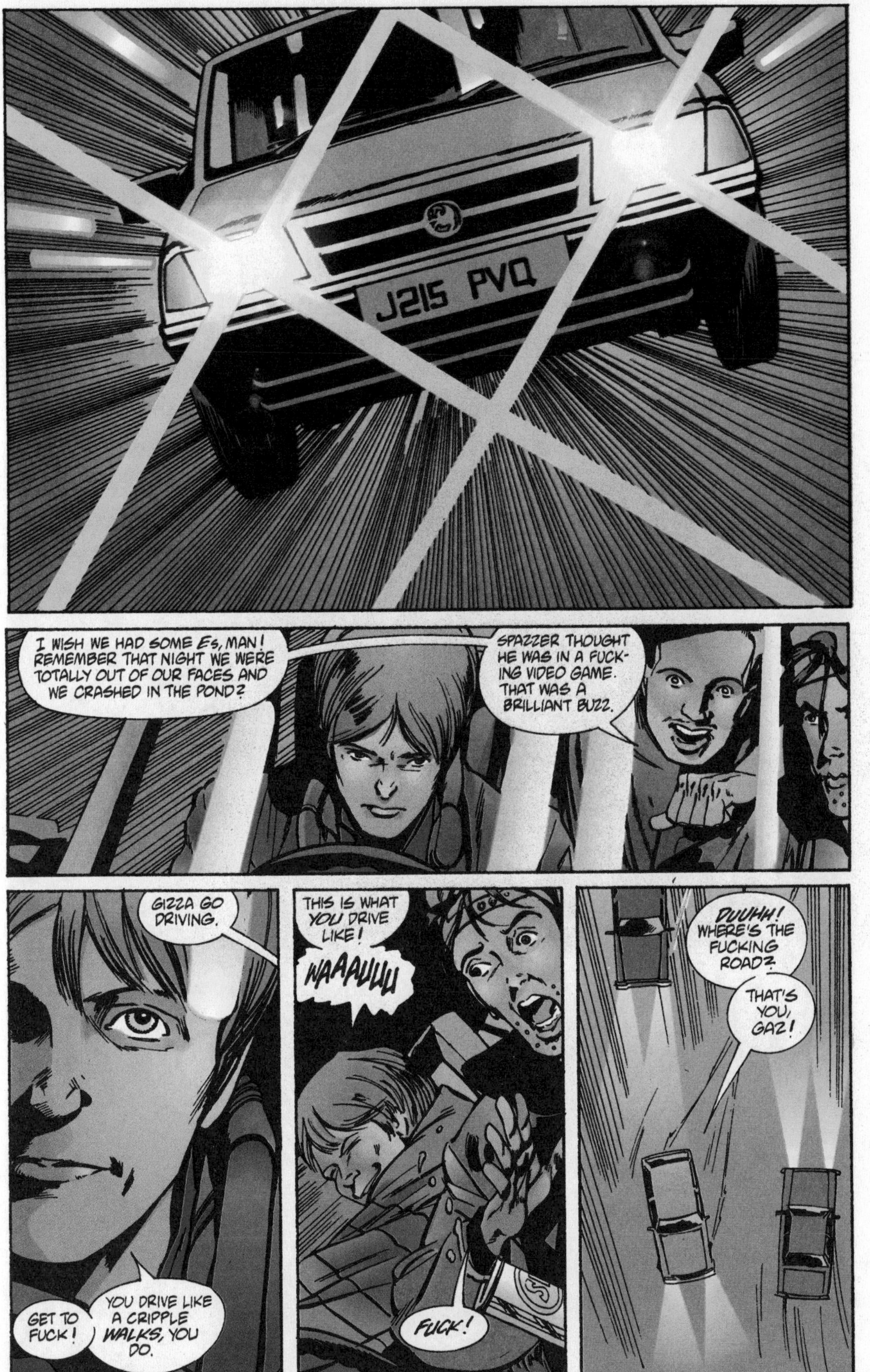

J215 PVQ
I WISH WE HAD SOME *Es*, MAN! REMEMBER THAT NIGHT WE WERE TOTALLY OUT OF OUR FACES AND WE CRASHED IN THE POND?
SPAZZER THOUGHT HE WAS IN A FUCKING VIDEO GAME. THAT WAS A BRILLIANT BUZZ.
GIZZA GO DRIVING.
YOU DRIVE LIKE A CRIPPLE *WALKS*, YOU DO.
GET TO FUCK!
THIS IS WHAT *YOU* DRIVE LIKE!
WAAAUUU
FUCK!
DUUHH! WHERE'S THE FUCKING ROAD?
THAT'S YOU, GAZ!

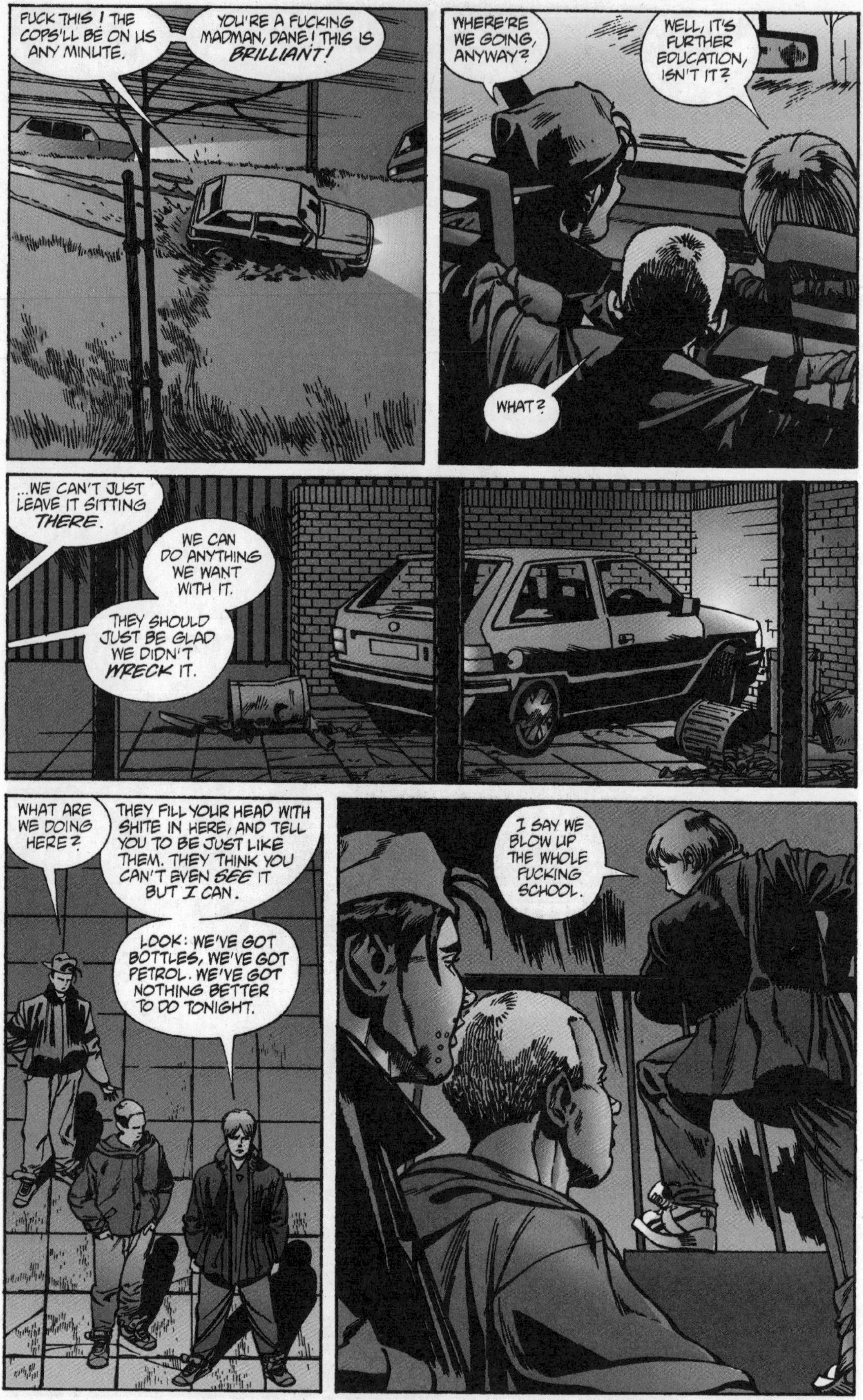
FUCK THIS ! THE COPS'LL BE ON US ANY MINUTE.
YOU'RE A FUCKING MADMAN, DANE! THIS IS BRILLIANT!
WHERE'RE WE GOING, ANYWAY?
WELL, IT'S FURTHER EDUCATION, ISN'T IT?
WHAT?
...WE CAN'T JUST LEAVE IT SITTING THERE.
WE CAN DO ANYTHING WE WANT WITH IT.
THEY SHOULD JUST BE GLAD WE DIDN'T WRECK IT.
WHAT ARE WE DOING HERE?
THEY FILL YOUR HEAD WITH SHITE IN HERE, AND TELL YOU TO BE JUST LIKE THEM. THEY THINK YOU CAN'T EVEN SEE IT BUT I CAN.
LOOK: WE'VE GOT BOTTLES, WE'VE GOT PETROL. WE'VE GOT NOTHING BETTER TO DO TONIGHT.
I SAY WE BLOW UP THE WHOLE FUCKING SCHOOL.

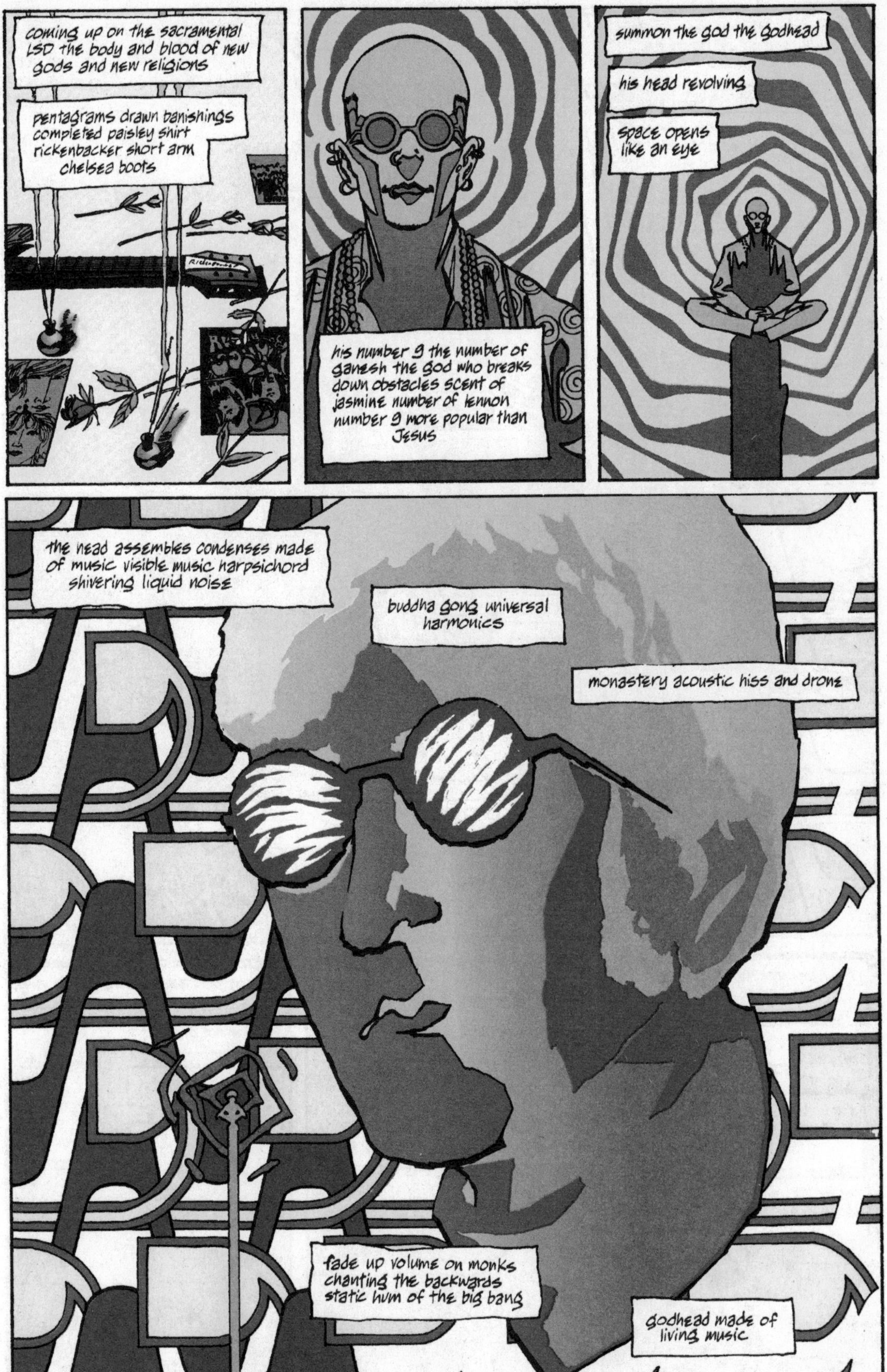
coming up on the sacramental LSD the body and blood of new gods and new religions
pentagrams drawn banishings completed paisley shirt rickenbacker short arm chelsea boots
his number 9 the number of ganesh the god who breaks down obstacles scent of jasmine number of lennon number 9 more popular than Jesus
summon the god the godhead
his head revolving
space opens like an eye
the head assembles condenses made of music visible music harpsichord shivering liquid noise
buddha gong universal harmonics
monastery acoustic hiss and drone
fade up volume on monks chanting the backwards static hum of the big bang
godhead made of living music

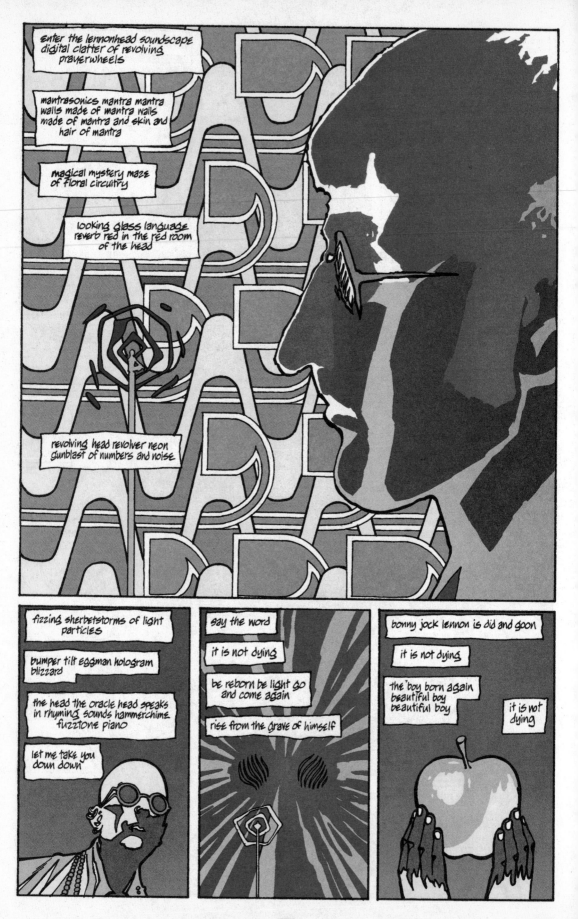

enter the lennonhead soundscape digital clatter of revolving prayerwheels

mantrasonics mantra mantra walls made of mantra walls made of mantra and skin and hair of mantra

magical mystery maze of floral circuitry

looking glass language reverb red in the red room of the head

revolving head revolver neon gunblast of numbers and noise.

fizzing sherbetstorms of light particles

bumper tilt eggman hologram blizzard

the head the oracle head speaks in rhyming sounds hammerchime fuzztone piano

let me take you down down

say the word

it is not dying

be reborn be light go and come again

rise from the grave of himself

bonny jock lennon is did and goon

it is not dying

the 'boy born again beautiful boy beautiful boy

it is not dying

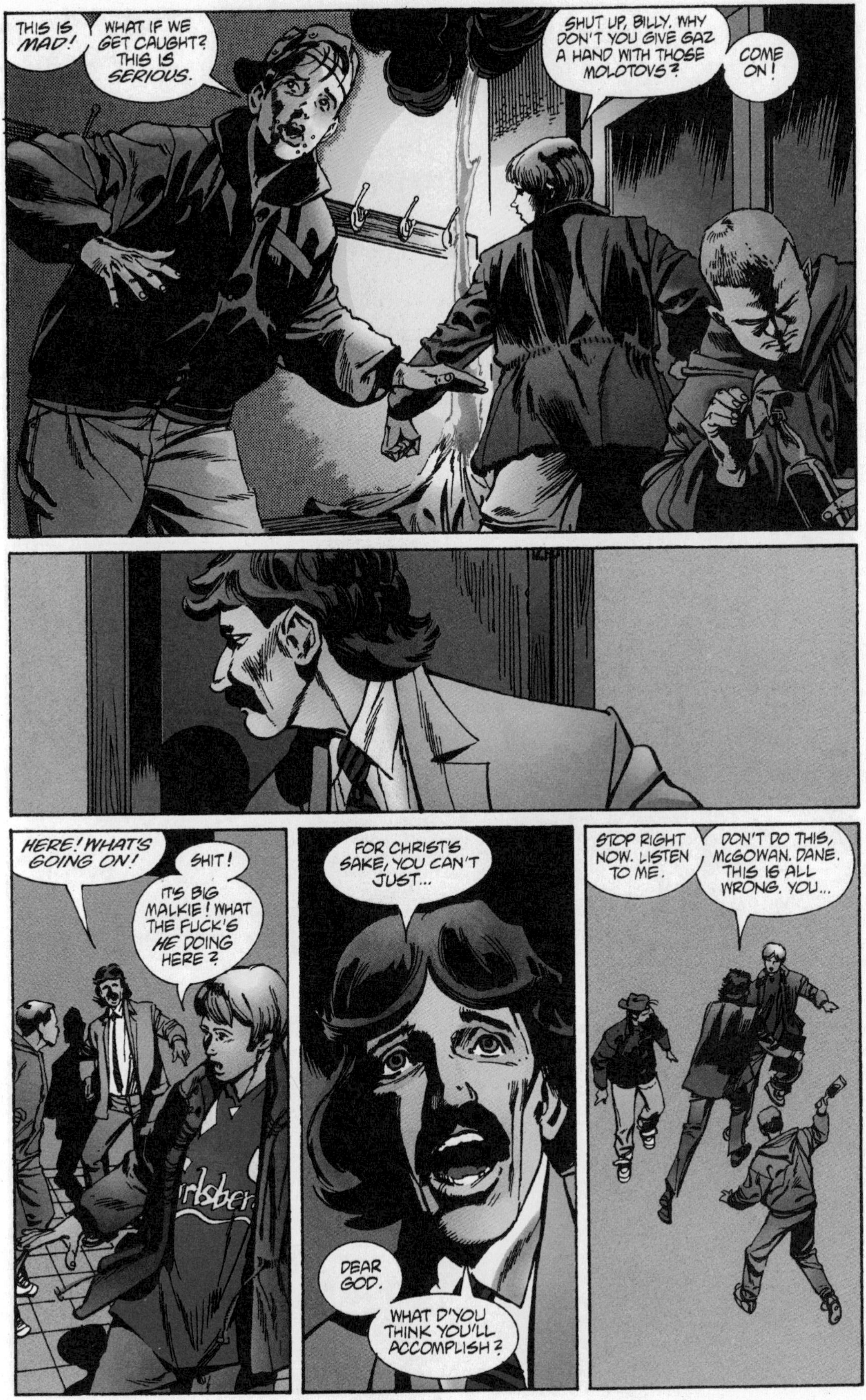
THIS IS MAD!
WHAT IF WE GET CAUGHT? THIS IS SERIOUS.
SHUT UP, BILLY. WHY DON'T YOU GIVE GAZ A HAND WITH THOSE MOLOTOVS?
COME ON!
HERE! WHAT'S GOING ON!
SHIT!
IT'S BIG MALKIE! WHAT THE FUCK'S HE DOING HERE?
FOR CHRIST'S SAKE, YOU CAN'T JUST...
DEAR GOD.
WHAT D'YOU THINK YOU'LL ACCOMPLISH?
STOP RIGHT NOW. LISTEN TO ME.
DON'T DO THIS, McGOWAN. DANE. THIS IS ALL WRONG. YOU...

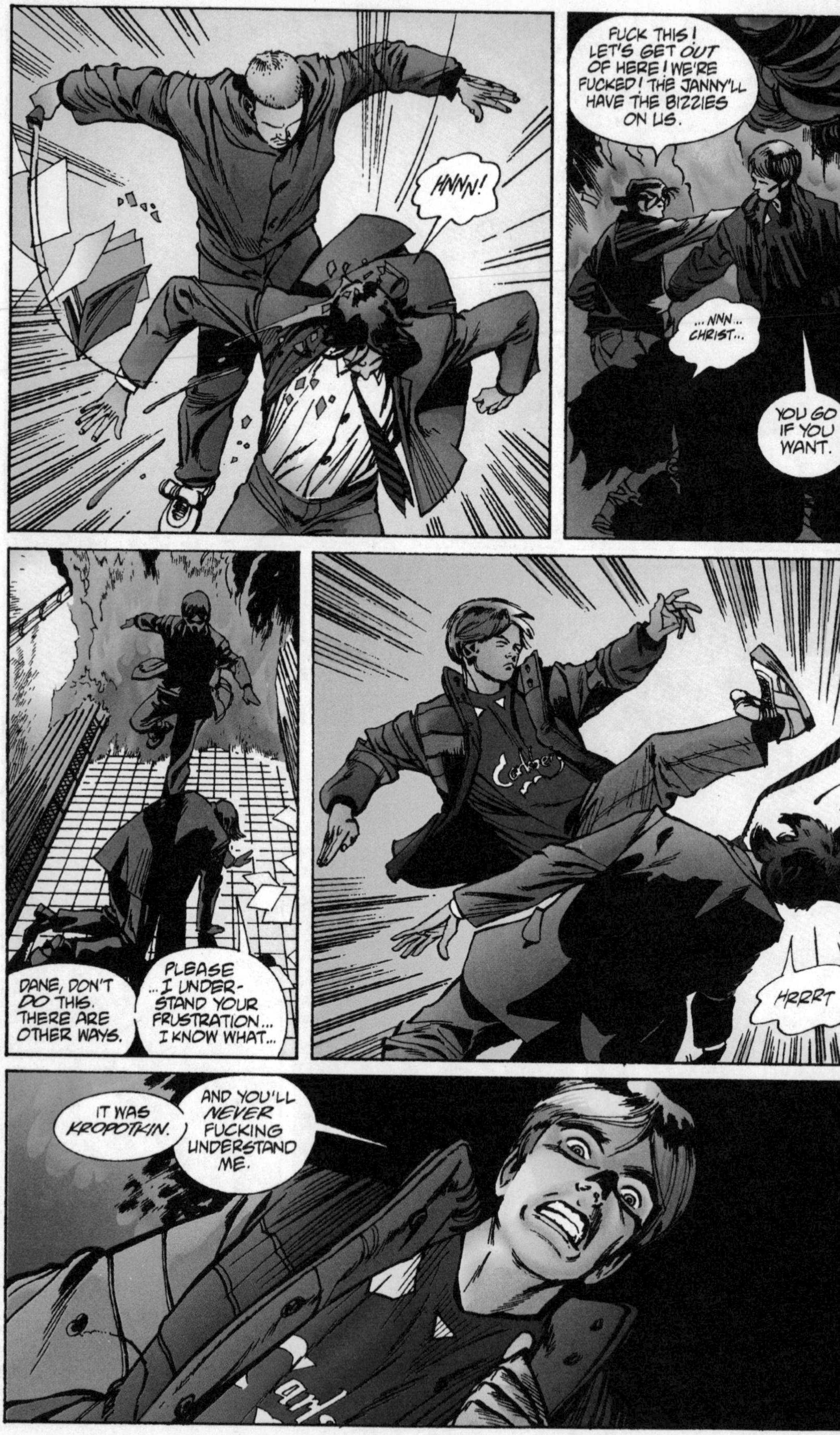
HNNN!
FUCK THIS! LET'S GET OUT OF HERE! WE'RE FUCKED! THE JANNY'LL HAVE THE BIZZIES ON US.
...NNN... CHRIST...
YOU GO IF YOU WANT.
DANE, DON'T DO THIS. THERE ARE OTHER WAYS.
PLEASE ...I UNDERSTAND YOUR FRUSTRATION... I KNOW WHAT...
HRRRT
IT WAS KROPOTKIN.
AND YOU'LL NEVER FUCKING UNDERSTAND ME.

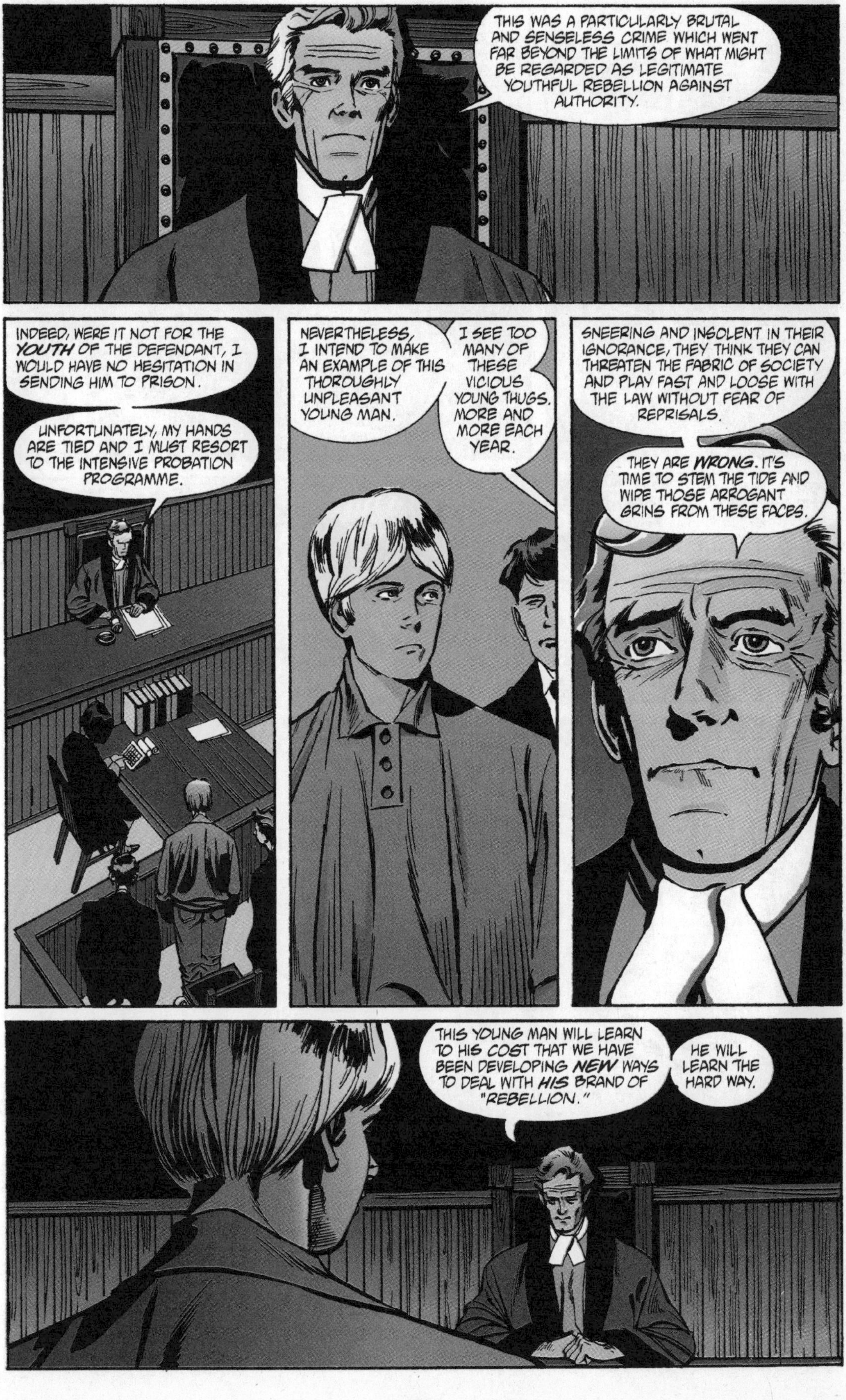
THIS WAS A PARTICULARLY BRUTAL AND SENSELESS CRIME WHICH WENT FAR BEYOND THE LIMITS OF WHAT MIGHT BE REGARDED AS LEGITIMATE YOUTHFUL REBELLION AGAINST AUTHORITY.
INDEED, WERE IT NOT FOR THE YOUTH OF THE DEFENDANT, I WOULD HAVE NO HESITATION IN SENDING HIM TO PRISON.
UNFORTUNATELY, MY HANDS ARE TIED AND I MUST RESORT TO THE INTENSIVE PROBATION PROGRAMME.
NEVERTHELESS, I INTEND TO MAKE AN EXAMPLE OF THIS THOROUGHLY UNPLEASANT YOUNG MAN.
I SEE TOO MANY OF THESE VICIOUS YOUNG THUGS. MORE AND MORE EACH YEAR.
SNEERING AND INSOLENT IN THEIR IGNORANCE, THEY THINK THEY CAN THREATEN THE FABRIC OF SOCIETY AND PLAY FAST AND LOOSE WITH THE LAW WITHOUT FEAR OF REPRISALS.
THEY ARE WRONG. IT'S TIME TO STEM THE TIDE AND WIPE THOSE ARROGANT GRINS FROM THESE FACES.
THIS YOUNG MAN WILL LEARN TO HIS COST THAT WE HAVE BEEN DEVELOPING NEW WAYS TO DEAL WITH HIS BRAND OF "REBELLION."
HE WILL LEARN THE HARD WAY.

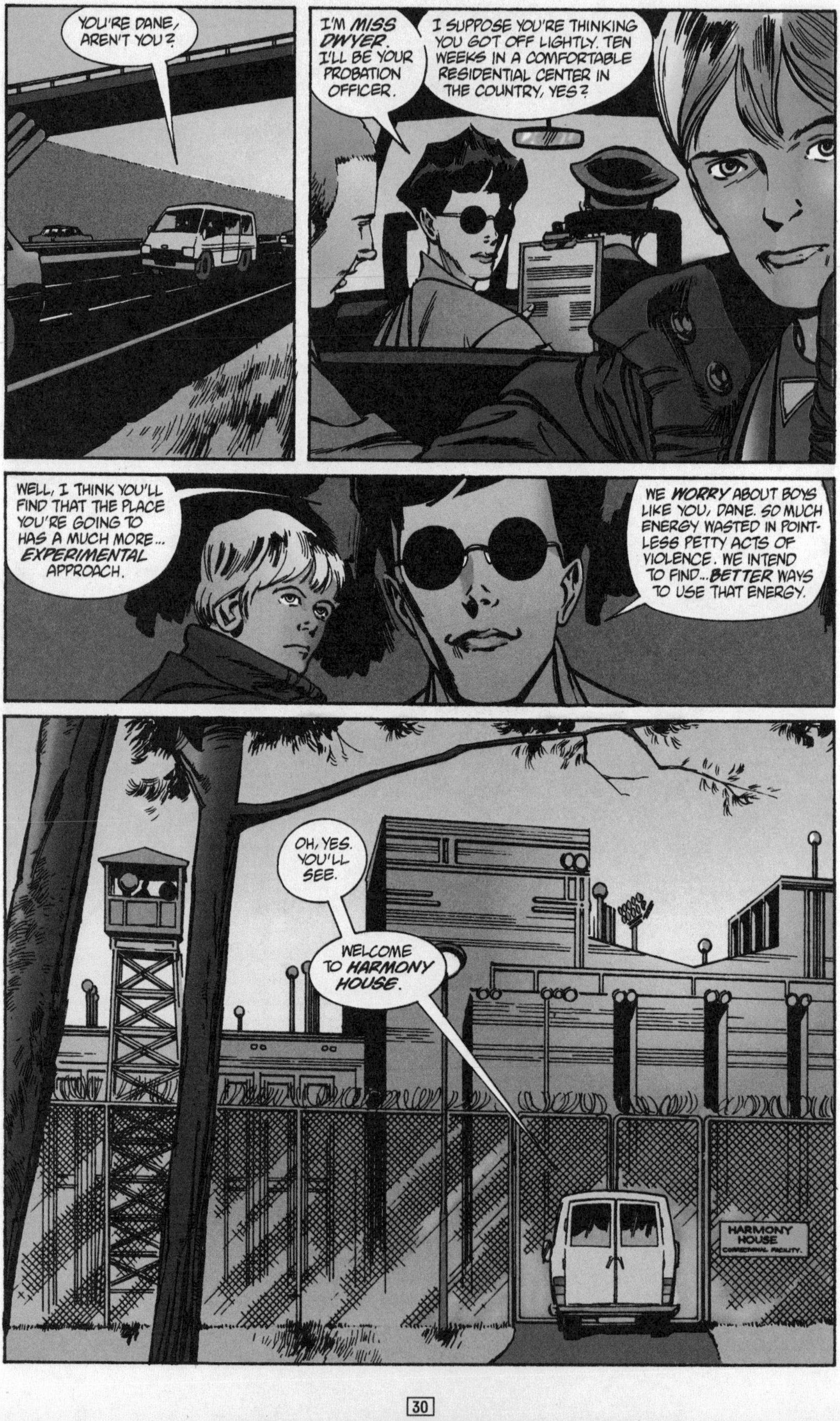
YOU'RE DANE, AREN'T YOU?
I'M MISS DWYER. I'LL BE YOUR PROBATION OFFICER.
I SUPPOSE YOU'RE THINKING YOU GOT OFF LIGHTLY. TEN WEEKS IN A COMFORTABLE RESIDENTIAL CENTER IN THE COUNTRY, YES?
WELL, I THINK YOU'LL FIND THAT THE PLACE YOU'RE GOING TO HAS A MUCH MORE... EXPERIMENTAL APPROACH.
WE WORRY ABOUT BOYS LIKE YOU, DANE. SO MUCH ENERGY WASTED IN POINTLESS PETTY ACTS OF VIOLENCE. WE INTEND TO FIND... BETTER WAYS TO USE THAT ENERGY.
OH, YES. YOU'LL SEE.
WELCOME TO HARMONY HOUSE.
HARMONY HOUSE

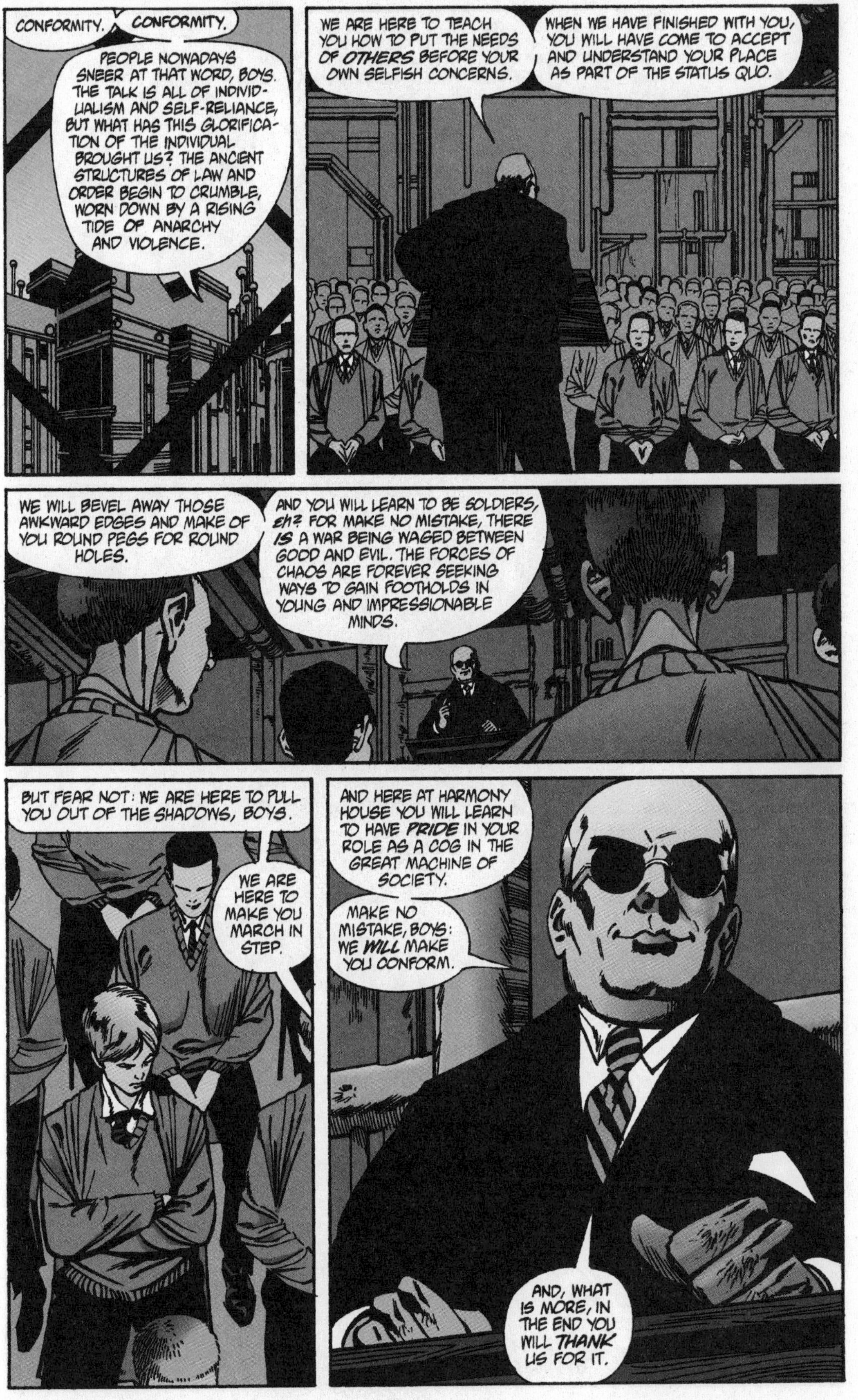
CONFORMITY.
CONFORMITY.
PEOPLE NOWADAYS SNEER AT THAT WORD, BOYS. THE TALK IS ALL OF INDIVIDUALISM AND SELF-RELIANCE, BUT WHAT HAS THIS GLORIFICATION OF THE INDIVIDUAL BROUGHT US? THE ANCIENT STRUCTURES OF LAW AND ORDER BEGIN TO CRUMBLE, WORN DOWN BY A RISING TIDE OF ANARCHY AND VIOLENCE.
WE ARE HERE TO TEACH YOU HOW TO PUT THE NEEDS OF OTHERS BEFORE YOUR OWN SELFISH CONCERNS.
WHEN WE HAVE FINISHED WITH YOU, YOU WILL HAVE COME TO ACCEPT AND UNDERSTAND YOUR PLACE AS PART OF THE STATUS QUO.
WE WILL BEVEL AWAY THOSE AWKWARD EDGES AND MAKE OF YOU ROUND PEGS FOR ROUND HOLES.
AND YOU WILL LEARN TO BE SOLDIERS, EH? FOR MAKE NO MISTAKE, THERE IS A WAR BEING WAGED BETWEEN GOOD AND EVIL. THE FORCES OF CHAOS ARE FOREVER SEEKING WAYS TO GAIN FOOTHOLDS IN YOUNG AND IMPRESSIONABLE MINDS.
BUT FEAR NOT: WE ARE HERE TO PULL YOU OUT OF THE SHADOWS, BOYS.
WE ARE HERE TO MAKE YOU MARCH IN STEP.
AND HERE AT HARMONY HOUSE YOU WILL LEARN TO HAVE PRIDE IN YOUR ROLE AS A COG IN THE GREAT MACHINE OF SOCIETY.
MAKE NO MISTAKE, BOYS: WE WILL MAKE YOU CONFORM.
AND, WHAT IS MORE, IN THE END YOU WILL THANK US FOR IT.

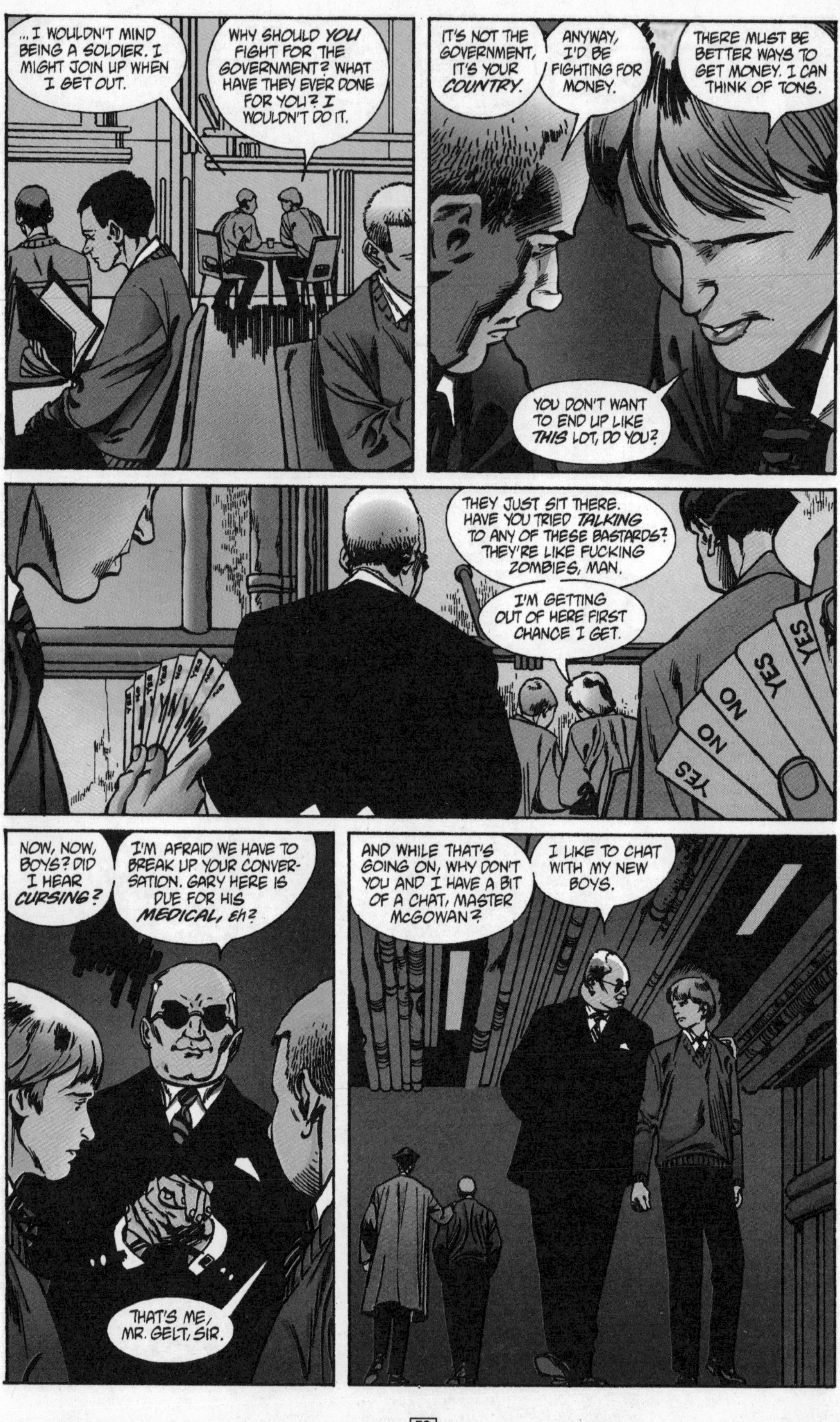
...I WOULDN'T MIND BEING A SOLDIER. I MIGHT JOIN UP WHEN I GET OUT.
WHY SHOULD YOU FIGHT FOR THE GOVERNMENT? WHAT HAVE THEY EVER DONE FOR YOU? I WOULDN'T DO IT.
IT'S NOT THE GOVERNMENT, IT'S YOUR COUNTRY.
ANYWAY, I'D BE FIGHTING FOR MONEY.
THERE MUST BE BETTER WAYS TO GET MONEY. I CAN THINK OF TONS.
YOU DON'T WANT TO END UP LIKE THIS LOT, DO YOU?
THEY JUST SIT THERE. HAVE YOU TRIED TALKING TO ANY OF THESE BASTARDS? THEY'RE LIKE FUCKING ZOMBIES, MAN.
I'M GETTING OUT OF HERE FIRST CHANCE I GET.
YES
YES
YES
NO
NO
YES
NOW, NOW, BOYS? DID I HEAR CURSING?
I'M AFRAID WE HAVE TO BREAK UP YOUR CONVERSATION. GARY HERE IS DUE FOR HIS MEDICAL, Eh?
THAT'S ME, MR. GELT, SIR.
AND WHILE THAT'S GOING ON, WHY DON'T YOU AND I HAVE A BIT OF A CHAT, MASTER McGOWAN?
I LIKE TO CHAT WITH MY NEW BOYS.

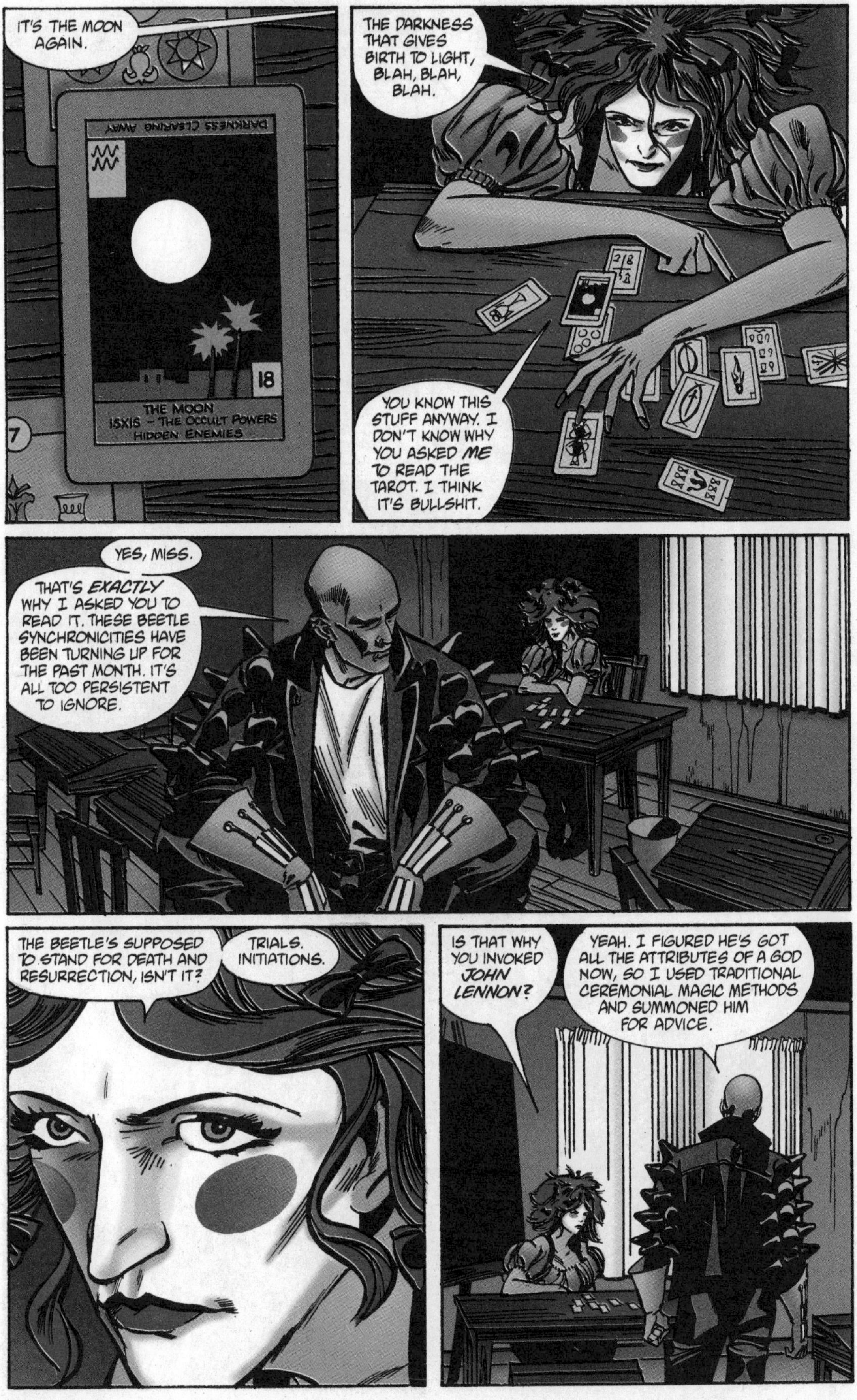
IT'S THE MOON AGAIN.
DARKNESS CLEARING AWAY
18
THE MOON
ISXIS - THE OCCULT POWERS
HIDDEN ENEMIES
THE DARKNESS THAT GIVES BIRTH TO LIGHT, BLAH, BLAH, BLAH.
YOU KNOW THIS STUFF ANYWAY. I DON'T KNOW WHY YOU ASKED *ME* TO READ THE TAROT. I THINK IT'S BULLSHIT.
YES, MISS.
THAT'S *EXACTLY* WHY I ASKED YOU TO READ IT. THESE BEETLE SYNCHRONICITIES HAVE BEEN TURNING UP FOR THE PAST MONTH. IT'S ALL TOO PERSISTENT TO IGNORE.
THE BEETLE'S SUPPOSED TO STAND FOR DEATH AND RESURRECTION, ISN'T IT?
TRIALS. INITIATIONS.
IS THAT WHY YOU INVOKED *JOHN LENNON*?
YEAH. I FIGURED HE'S GOT ALL THE ATTRIBUTES OF A GOD NOW, SO I USED TRADITIONAL CEREMONIAL MAGIC METHODS AND SUMMONED HIM FOR ADVICE.

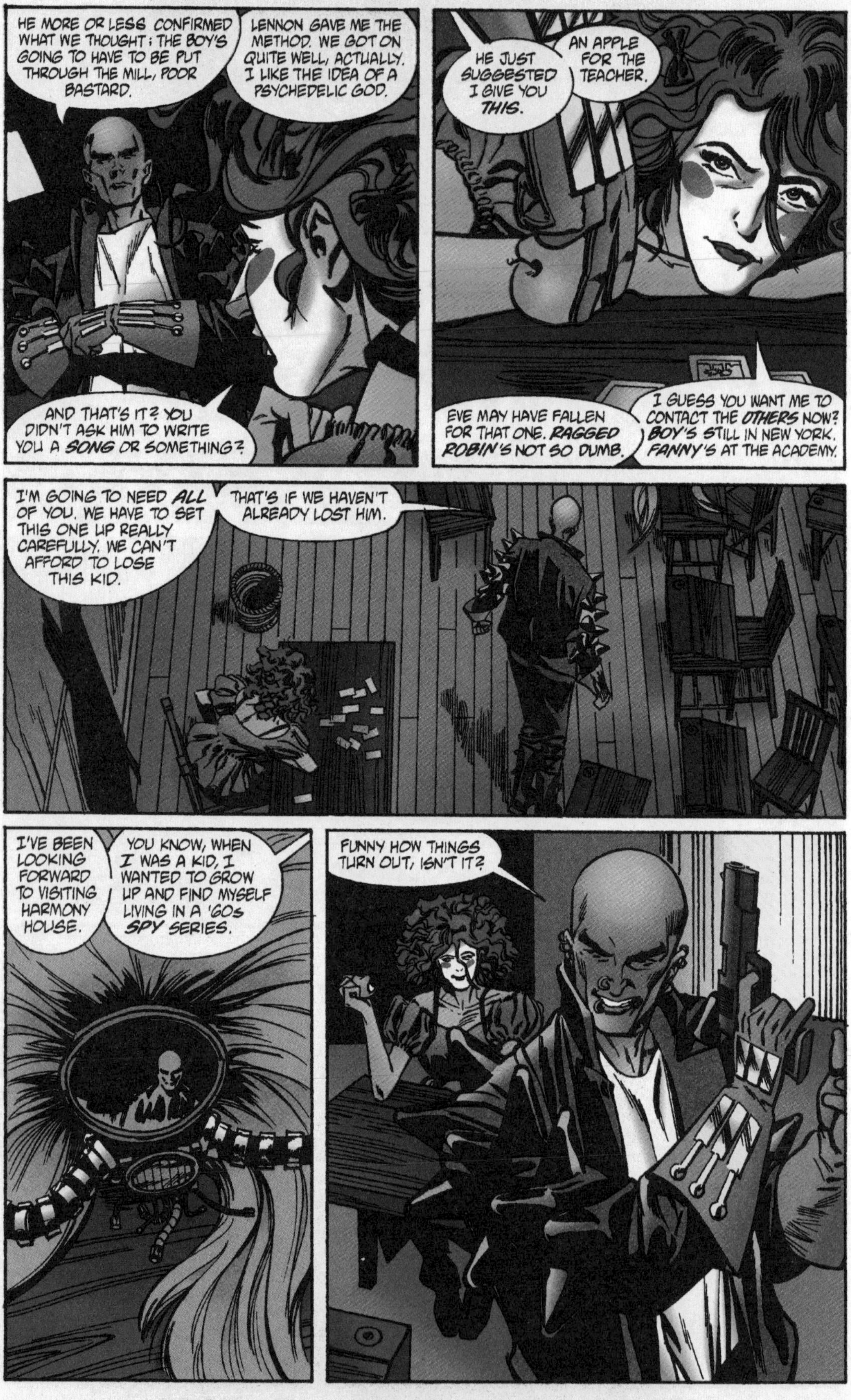
HE MORE OR LESS CONFIRMED WHAT WE THOUGHT; THE BOY'S GOING TO HAVE TO BE PUT THROUGH THE MILL, POOR BASTARD.
LENNON GAVE ME THE METHOD. WE GOT ON QUITE WELL, ACTUALLY. I LIKE THE IDEA OF A PSYCHEDELIC GOD.
AND THAT'S IT? YOU DIDN'T ASK HIM TO WRITE YOU A SONG OR SOMETHING?
HE JUST SUGGESTED I GIVE YOU THIS.
AN APPLE FOR THE TEACHER.
EVE MAY HAVE FALLEN FOR THAT ONE. RAGGED ROBIN'S NOT SO DUMB.
I GUESS YOU WANT ME TO CONTACT THE OTHERS NOW? BOY'S STILL IN NEW YORK. FANNY'S AT THE ACADEMY.
I'M GOING TO NEED ALL OF YOU. WE HAVE TO SET THIS ONE UP REALLY CAREFULLY. WE CAN'T AFFORD TO LOSE THIS KID.
THAT'S IF WE HAVEN'T ALREADY LOST HIM.
I'VE BEEN LOOKING FORWARD TO VISITING HARMONY HOUSE.
YOU KNOW, WHEN I WAS A KID, I WANTED TO GROW UP AND FIND MYSELF LIVING IN A '60s SPY SERIES.
FUNNY HOW THINGS TURN OUT, ISN'T IT?

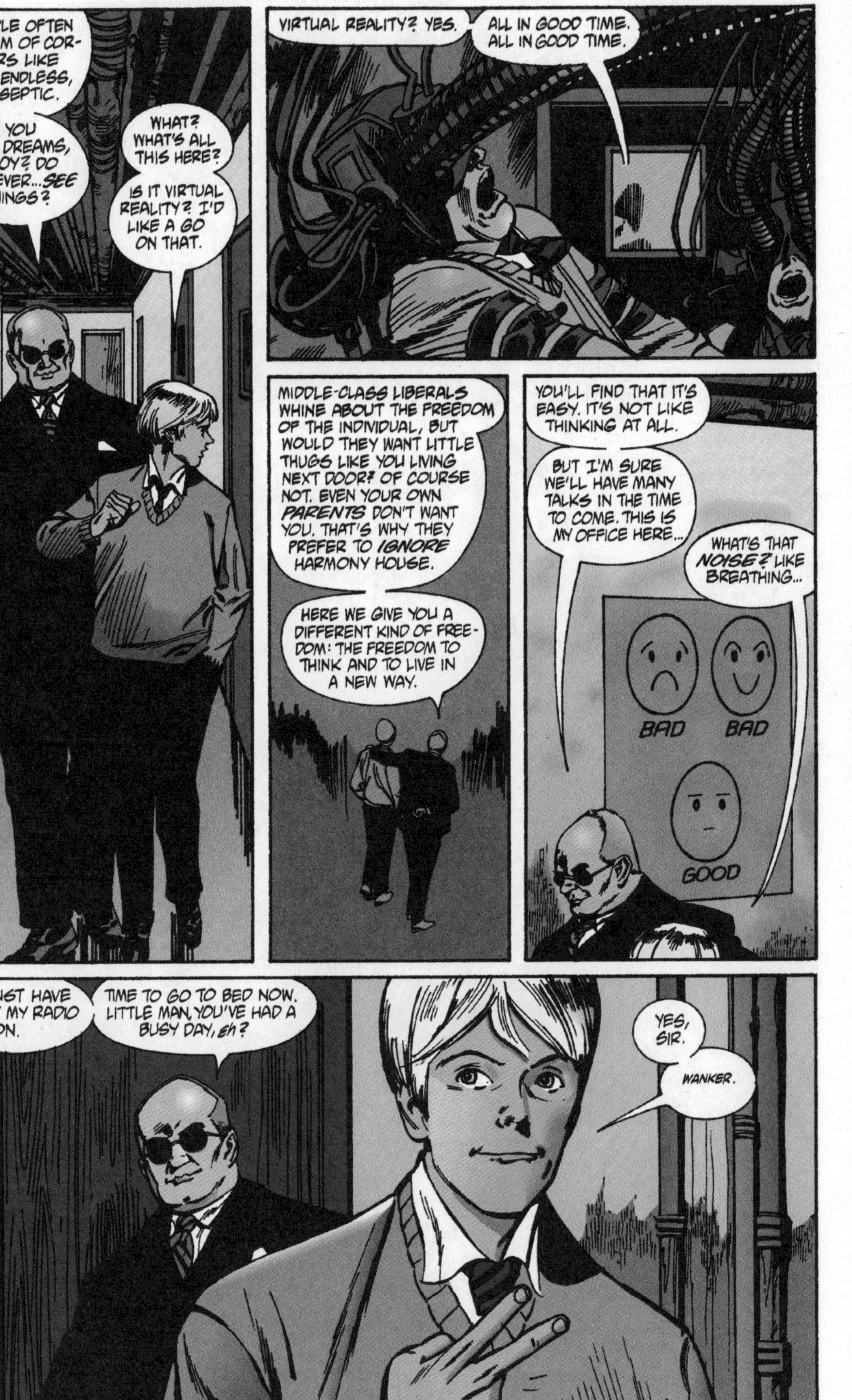
PEOPLE OFTEN DREAM OF CORRIDORS LIKE THIS: ENDLESS, ANTISEPTIC.
DO YOU HAVE DREAMS, MY BOY? DO YOU EVER... SEE THINGS?
WHAT? WHAT'S ALL THIS HERE?
IS IT VIRTUAL REALITY? I'D LIKE A GO ON THAT.
VIRTUAL REALITY? YES.
ALL IN GOOD TIME. ALL IN GOOD TIME.
MIDDLE-CLASS LIBERALS WHINE ABOUT THE FREEDOM OF THE INDIVIDUAL, BUT WOULD THEY WANT LITTLE THUGS LIKE YOU LIVING NEXT DOOR? OF COURSE NOT. EVEN YOUR OWN PARENTS DON'T WANT YOU. THAT'S WHY THEY PREFER TO IGNORE HARMONY HOUSE.
HERE WE GIVE YOU A DIFFERENT KIND OF FREEDOM: THE FREEDOM TO THINK AND TO LIVE IN A NEW WAY.
YOU'LL FIND THAT IT'S EASY. IT'S NOT LIKE THINKING AT ALL.
BUT I'M SURE WE'LL HAVE MANY TALKS IN THE TIME TO COME. THIS IS MY OFFICE HERE...
WHAT'S THAT NOISE? LIKE BREATHING...
BAD
BAD
GOOD
I MUST HAVE LEFT MY RADIO ON.
TIME TO GO TO BED NOW. LITTLE MAN, YOU'VE HAD A BUSY DAY, eh?
YES, SIR.
WANKER.

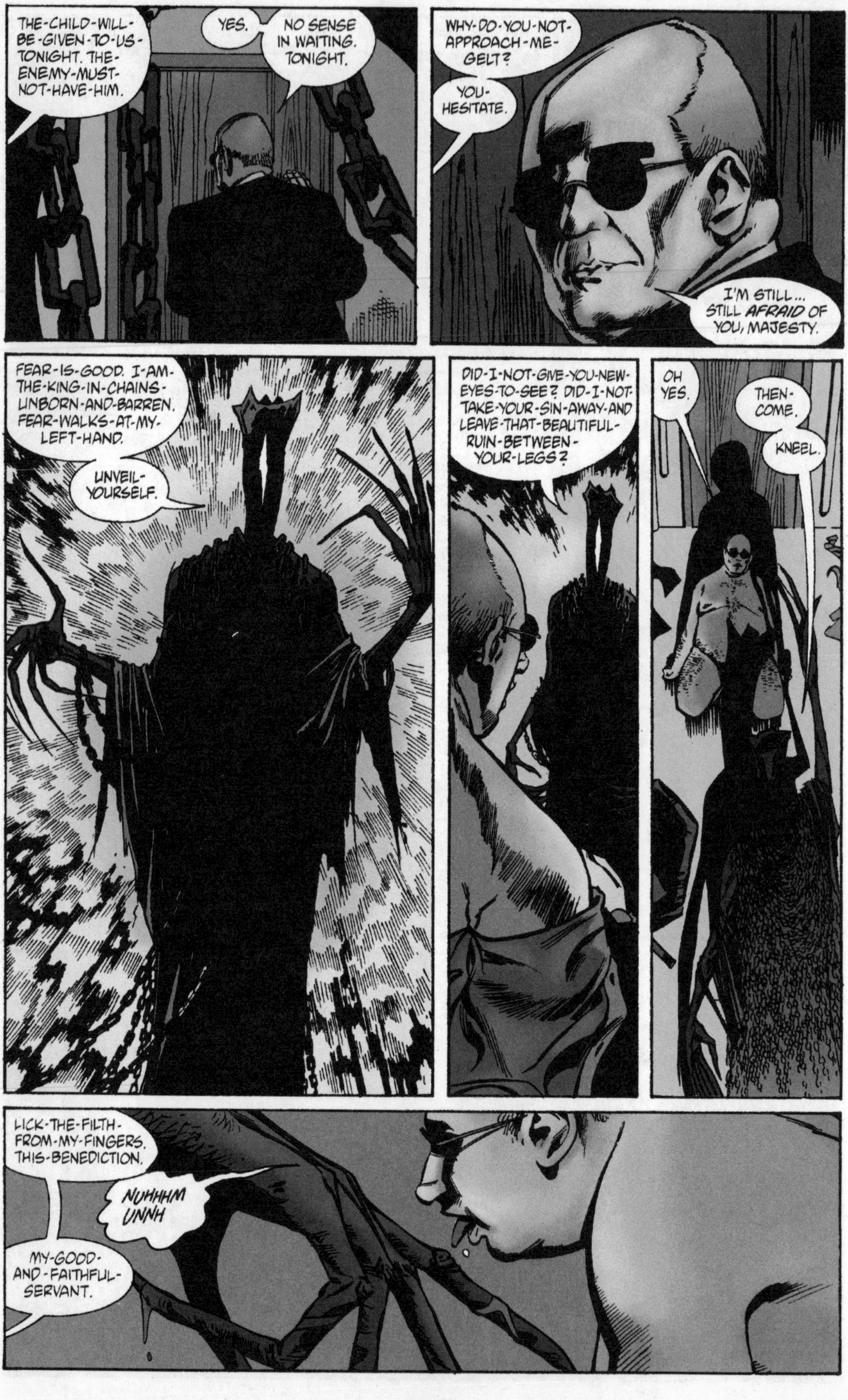
THE-CHILD-WILL-BE-GIVEN-TO-US-TONIGHT. THE-ENEMY-MUST-NOT-HAVE-HIM.
YES.
NO SENSE IN WAITING. TONIGHT.
WHY-DO-YOU-NOT-APPROACH-ME-GELT?
YOU-HESITATE.
I'M STILL... STILL AFRAID OF YOU, MAJESTY.
FEAR-IS-GOOD. I-AM-THE-KING-IN-CHAINS-UNBORN-AND-BARREN. FEAR-WALKS-AT-MY-LEFT-HAND.
UNVEIL-YOURSELF.
DID-I-NOT-GIVE-YOU-NEW-EYES-TO-SEE? DID-I-NOT-TAKE-YOUR-SIN-AWAY-AND-LEAVE-THAT-BEAUTIFUL-RUIN-BETWEEN-YOUR-LEGS?
OH YES.
THEN-COME.
KNEEL.
LICK-THE-FILTH-FROM-MY-FINGERS. THIS-BENEDICTION.
NUHHHM UNNH
MY-GOOD-AND-FAITHFUL-SERVANT.

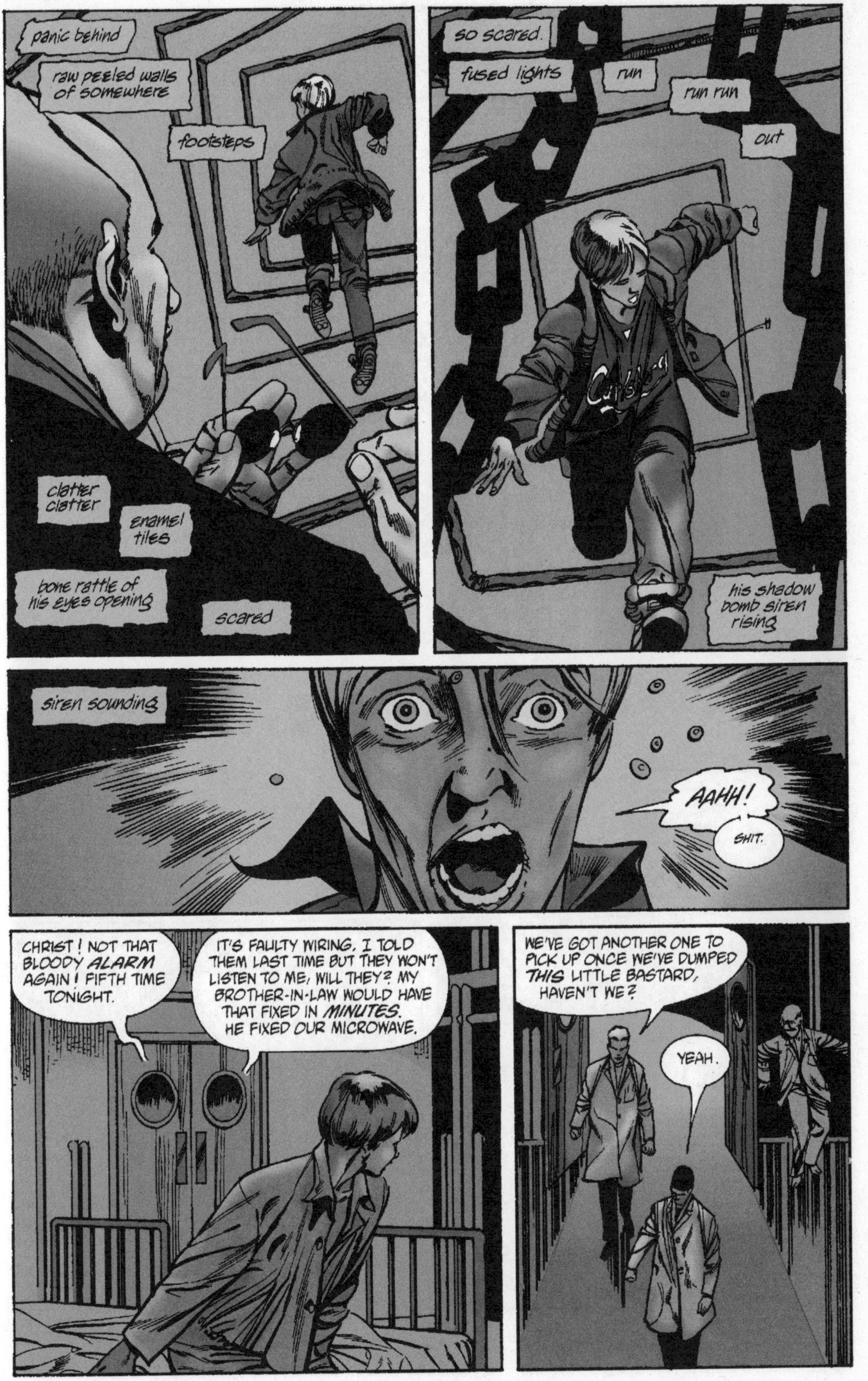
panic behind
raw peeled walls of somewhere
footsteps
clatter clatter
enamel tiles
bone rattle of his eyes opening
scared
so scared.
fused lights
run
run run
out
his shadow bomb siren rising
siren sounding
AAHH!
SHIT.
CHRIST! NOT THAT BLOODY ALARM AGAIN! FIFTH TIME TONIGHT.
IT'S FAULTY WIRING. I TOLD THEM LAST TIME BUT THEY WON'T LISTEN TO ME, WILL THEY? MY BROTHER-IN-LAW WOULD HAVE THAT FIXED IN MINUTES. HE FIXED OUR MICROWAVE.
WE'VE GOT ANOTHER ONE TO PICK UP ONCE WE'VE DUMPED THIS LITTLE BASTARD, HAVEN'T WE?
YEAH.

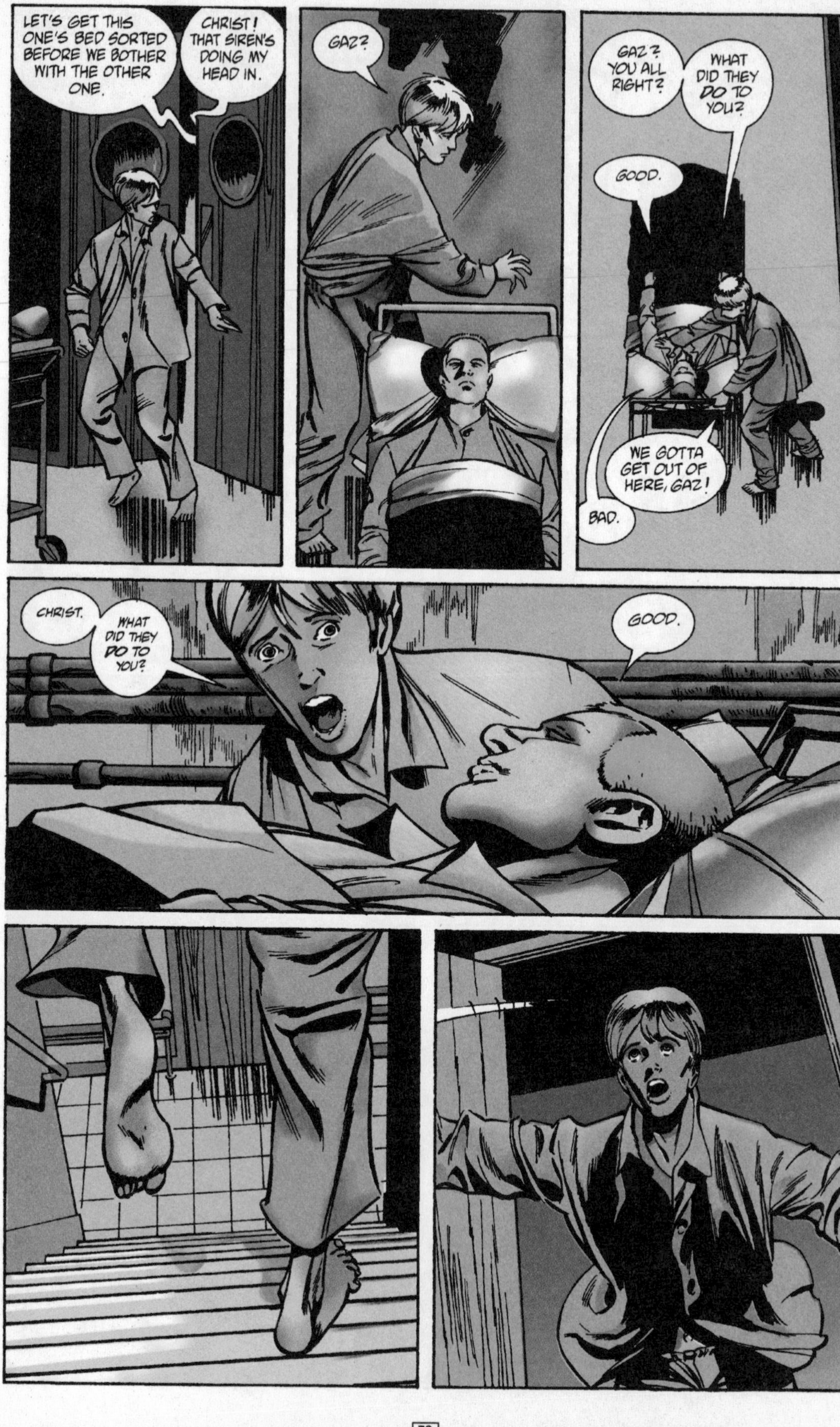
LET'S GET THIS ONE'S BED SORTED BEFORE WE BOTHER WITH THE OTHER ONE.
CHRIST! THAT SIREN'S DOING MY HEAD IN.
GAZ?
GAZ? YOU ALL RIGHT?
WHAT DID THEY DO TO YOU?
GOOD.
WE GOTTA GET OUT OF HERE, GAZ!
BAD.
CHRIST.
WHAT DID THEY DO TO YOU?
GOOD.

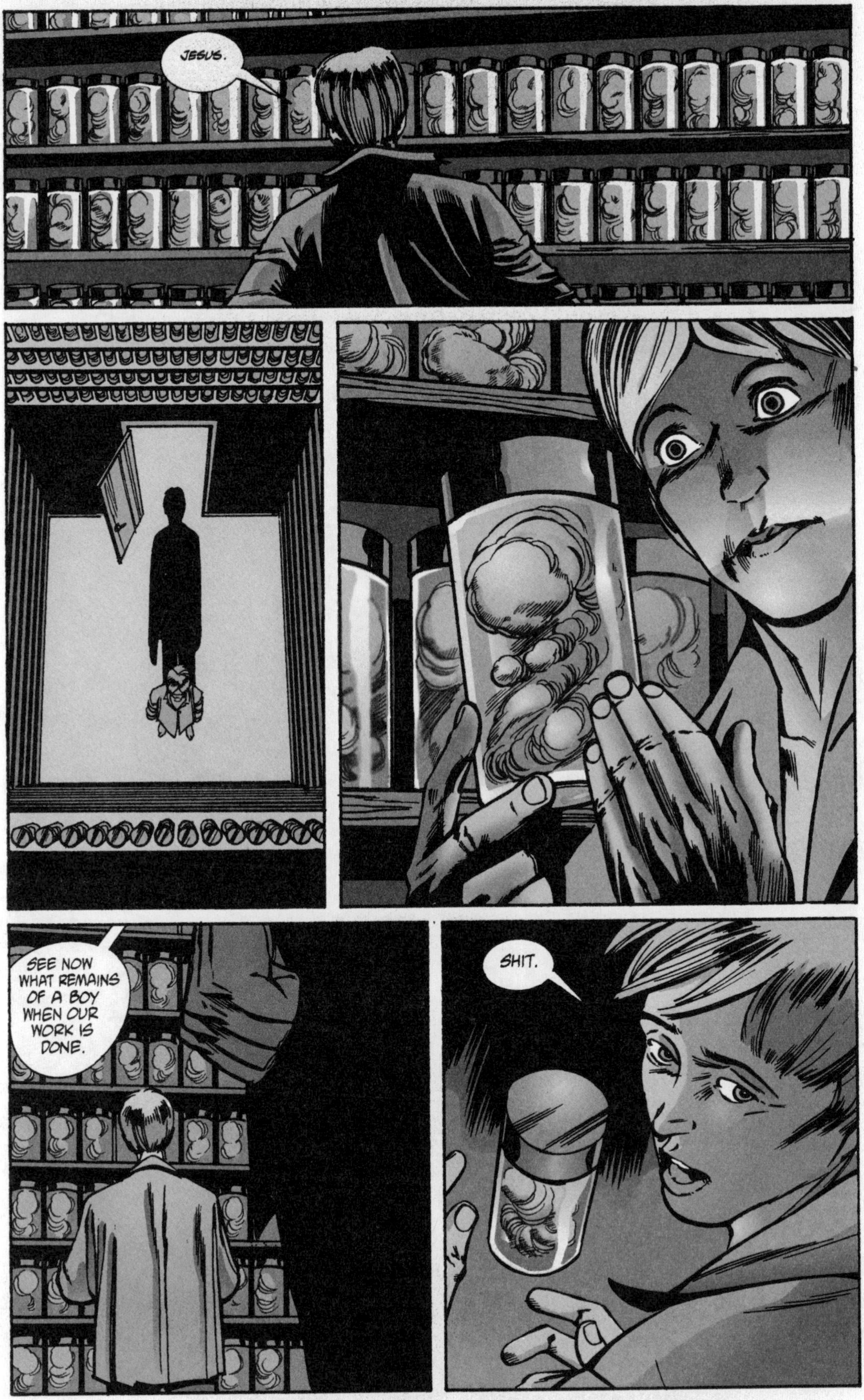
JESUS.
SEE NOW WHAT REMAINS OF A BOY WHEN OUR WORK IS DONE.
SHIT.

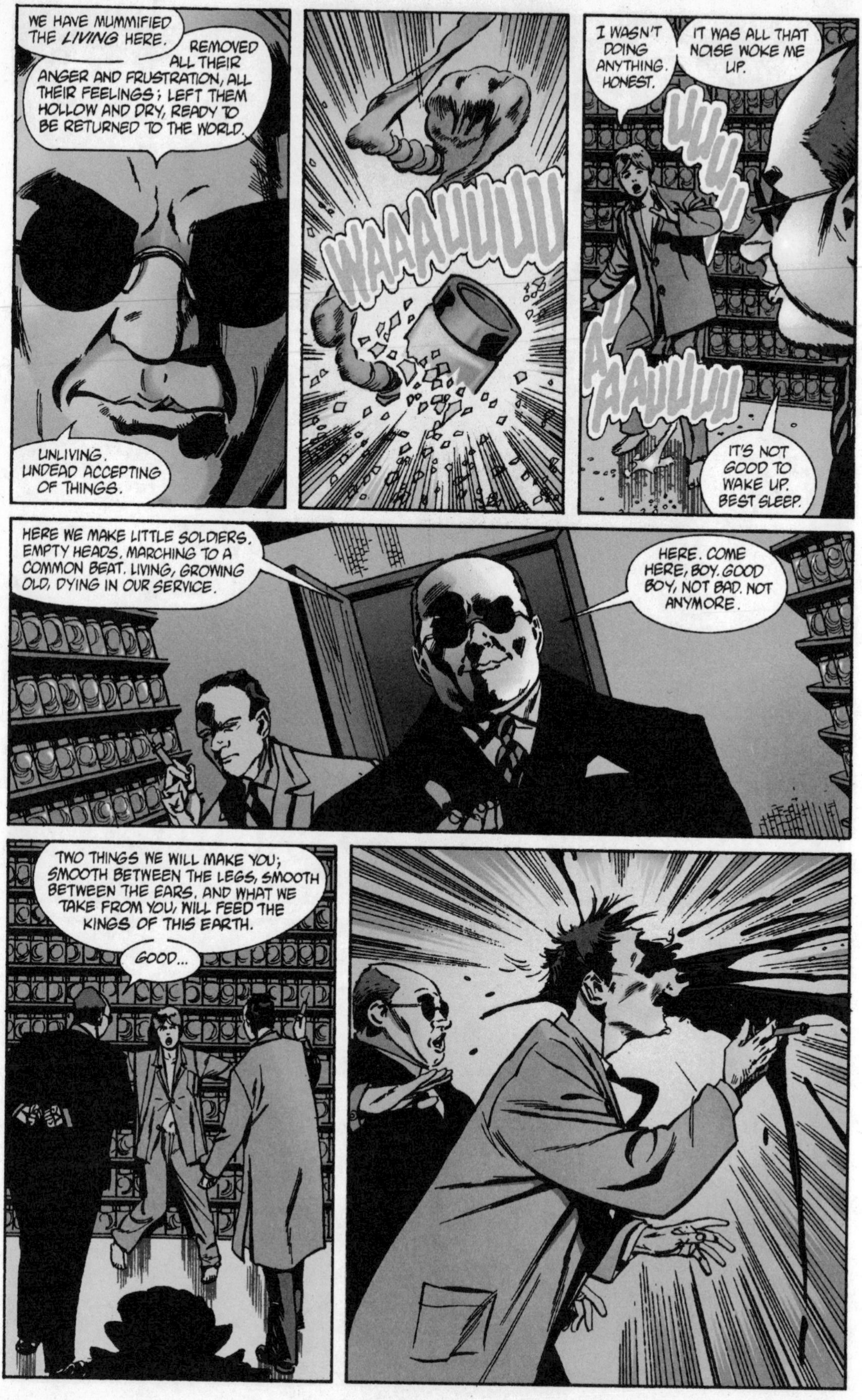
WE HAVE MUMMIFIED THE *LIVING* HERE.
REMOVED ALL THEIR ANGER AND FRUSTRATION, ALL THEIR FEELINGS; LEFT THEM HOLLOW AND DRY, READY TO BE RETURNED TO THE WORLD.
UNLIVING. UNDEAD ACCEPTING OF THINGS.
WAAAUUUUU
I WASN'T DOING ANYTHING. HONEST.
IT WAS ALL THAT NOISE WOKE ME UP.
UUUU
AAAUUUU
IT'S NOT GOOD TO WAKE UP. BEST SLEEP.
HERE WE MAKE LITTLE SOLDIERS. EMPTY HEADS, MARCHING TO A COMMON BEAT. LIVING, GROWING OLD, DYING IN OUR SERVICE.
HERE. COME HERE, BOY. GOOD BOY, NOT BAD. NOT ANYMORE.
TWO THINGS WE WILL MAKE YOU; SMOOTH BETWEEN THE LEGS, SMOOTH BETWEEN THE EARS, AND WHAT WE TAKE FROM YOU, WILL FEED THE KINGS OF THIS EARTH.
GOOD...

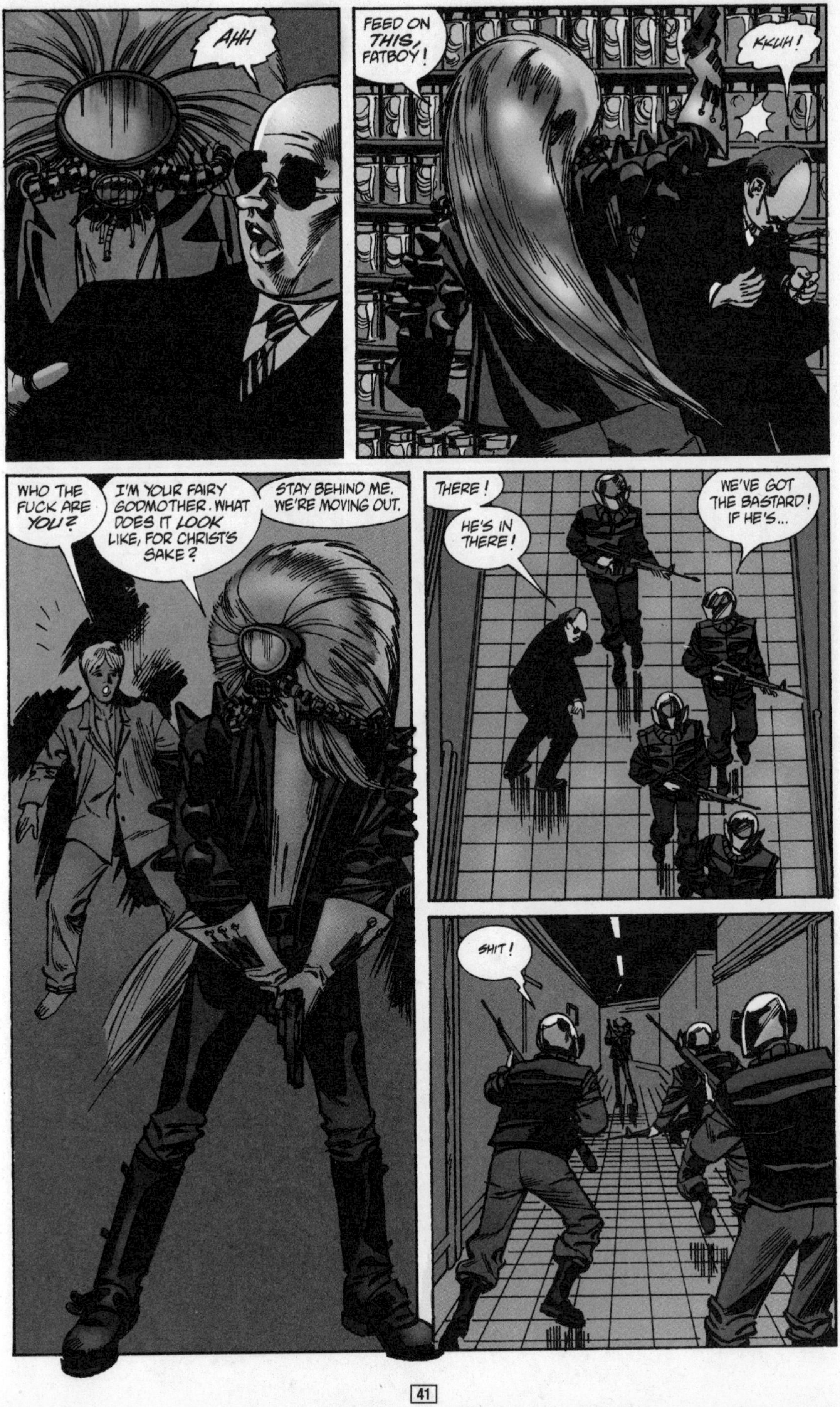
AHH
FEED ON THIS, FATBOY!
KKUH!
WHO THE FUCK ARE YOU?
I'M YOUR FAIRY GODMOTHER. WHAT DOES IT LOOK LIKE, FOR CHRIST'S SAKE?
STAY BEHIND ME. WE'RE MOVING OUT.
THERE!
HE'S IN THERE!
WE'VE GOT THE BASTARD! IF HE'S...
SHIT!

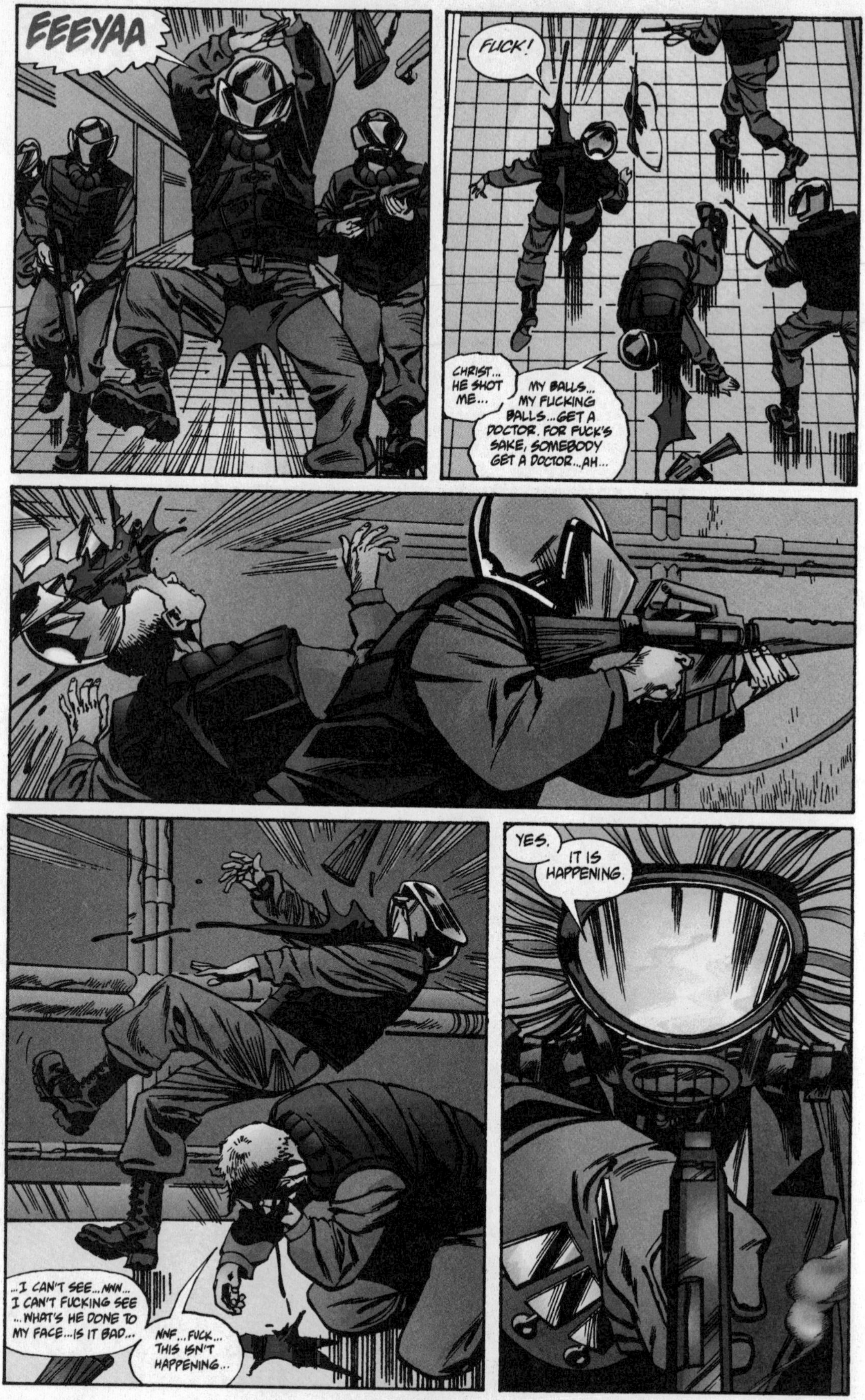
EEEYAA
FUCK!
CHRIST... HE SHOT ME...
MY BALLS... MY FUCKING BALLS...GET A DOCTOR. FOR FUCK'S SAKE, SOMEBODY GET A DOCTOR...AH...
YES.
IT IS HAPPENING.
...I CAN'T SEE...NNN... I CAN'T FUCKING SEE ...WHAT'S HE DONE TO MY FACE...IS IT BAD...
NNF...FUCK... THIS ISN'T HAPPENING...

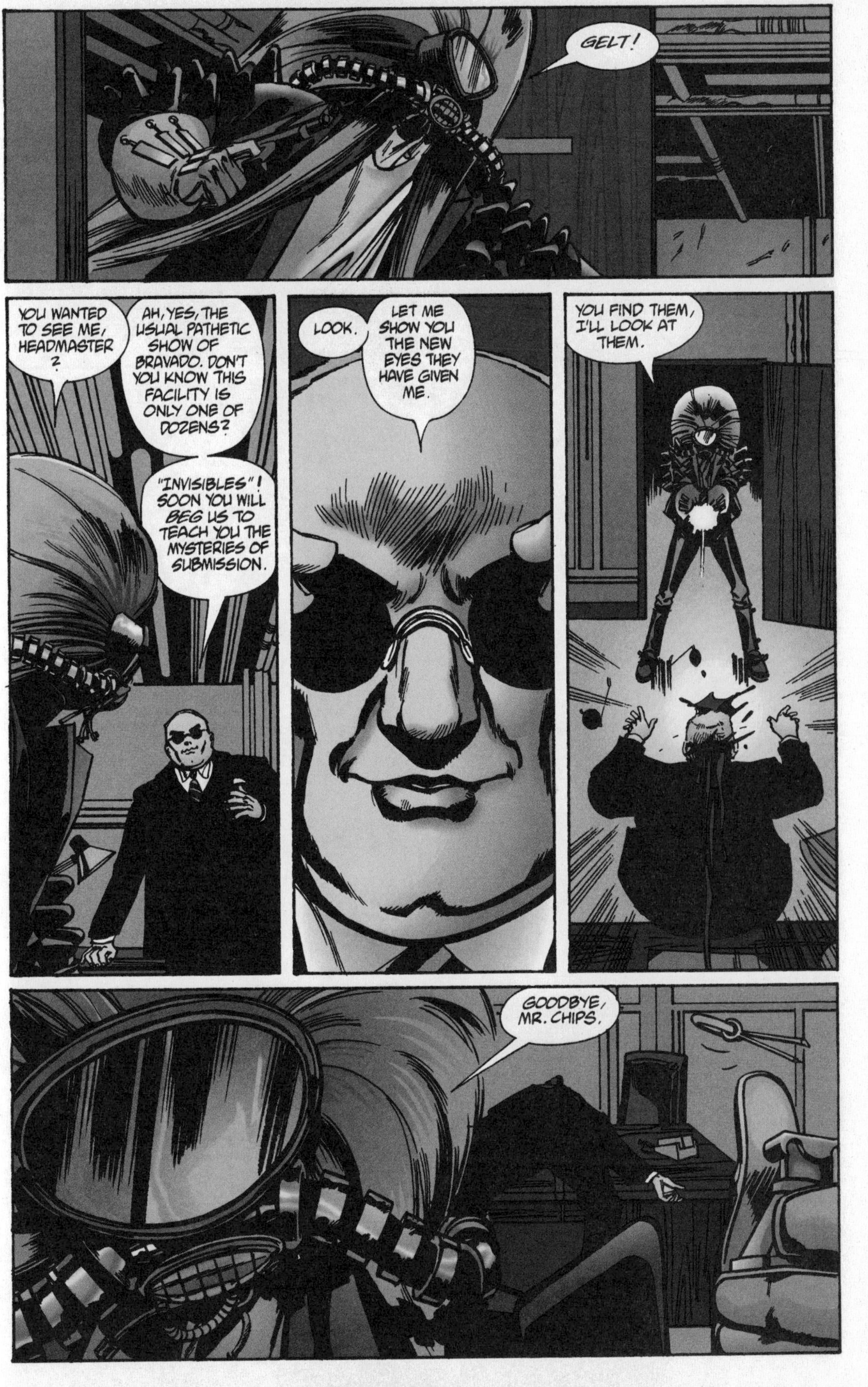
GELT!
YOU WANTED TO SEE ME, HEADMASTER?
AH, YES, THE USUAL PATHETIC SHOW OF BRAVADO. DON'T YOU KNOW THIS FACILITY IS ONLY ONE OF DOZENS?
"INVISIBLES"! SOON YOU WILL *BEG* US TO TEACH YOU THE MYSTERIES OF SUBMISSION.
LOOK.
LET ME SHOW YOU THE NEW EYES THEY HAVE GIVEN ME.
YOU FIND THEM, I'LL LOOK AT THEM.
GOODBYE, MR. CHIPS.

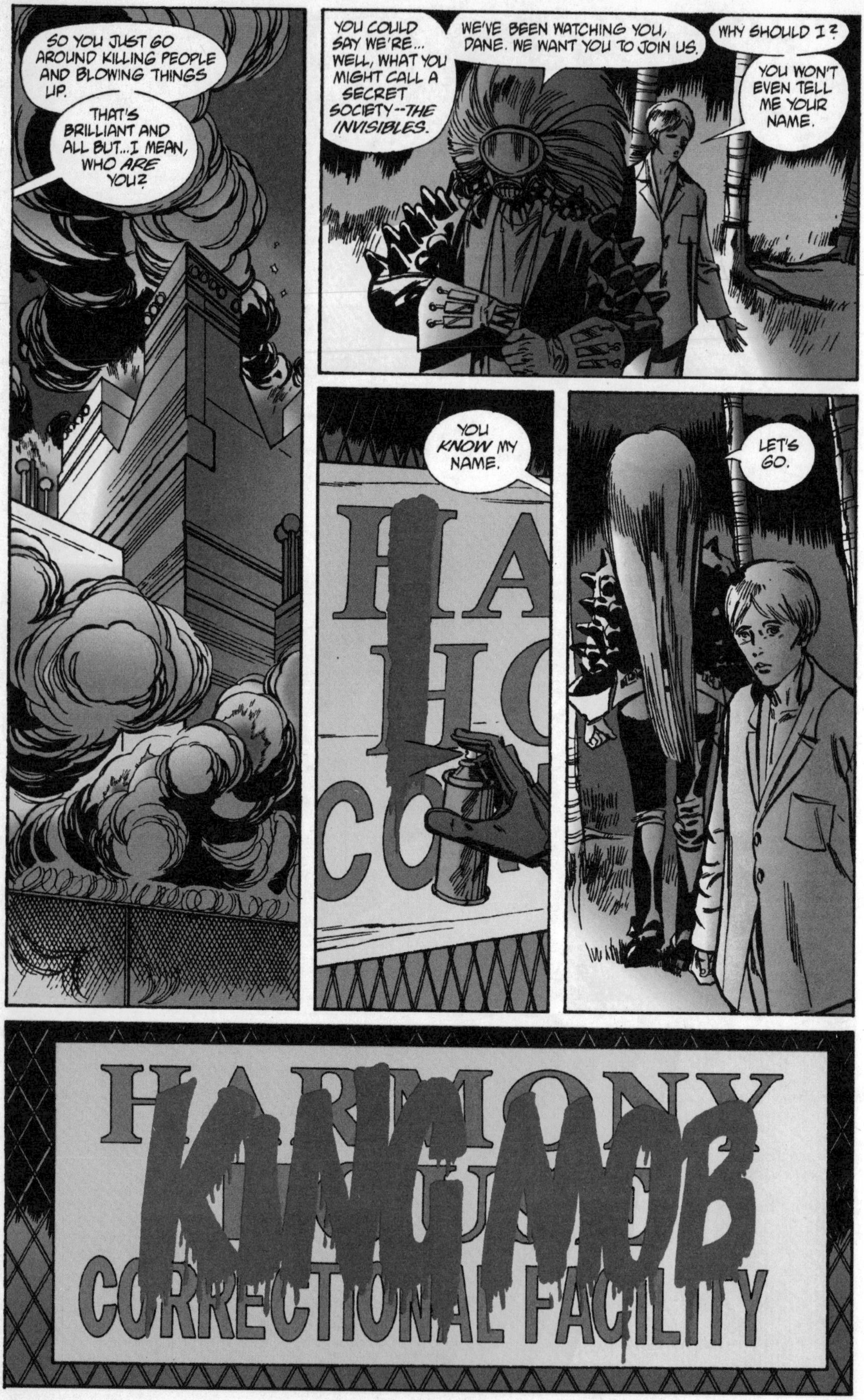

SO YOU JUST GO AROUND KILLING PEOPLE AND BLOWING THINGS UP.
THAT'S BRILLIANT AND ALL BUT...I MEAN, WHO ARE YOU?
YOU COULD SAY WE'RE... WELL, WHAT YOU MIGHT CALL A SECRET SOCIETY--THE INVISIBLES.
WE'VE BEEN WATCHING YOU, DANE. WE WANT YOU TO JOIN US.
WHY SHOULD I?
YOU WON'T EVEN TELL ME YOUR NAME.
YOU KNOW MY NAME.
LET'S GO.
HARMONY
CORRECTIONAL FACILITY
KING MOB

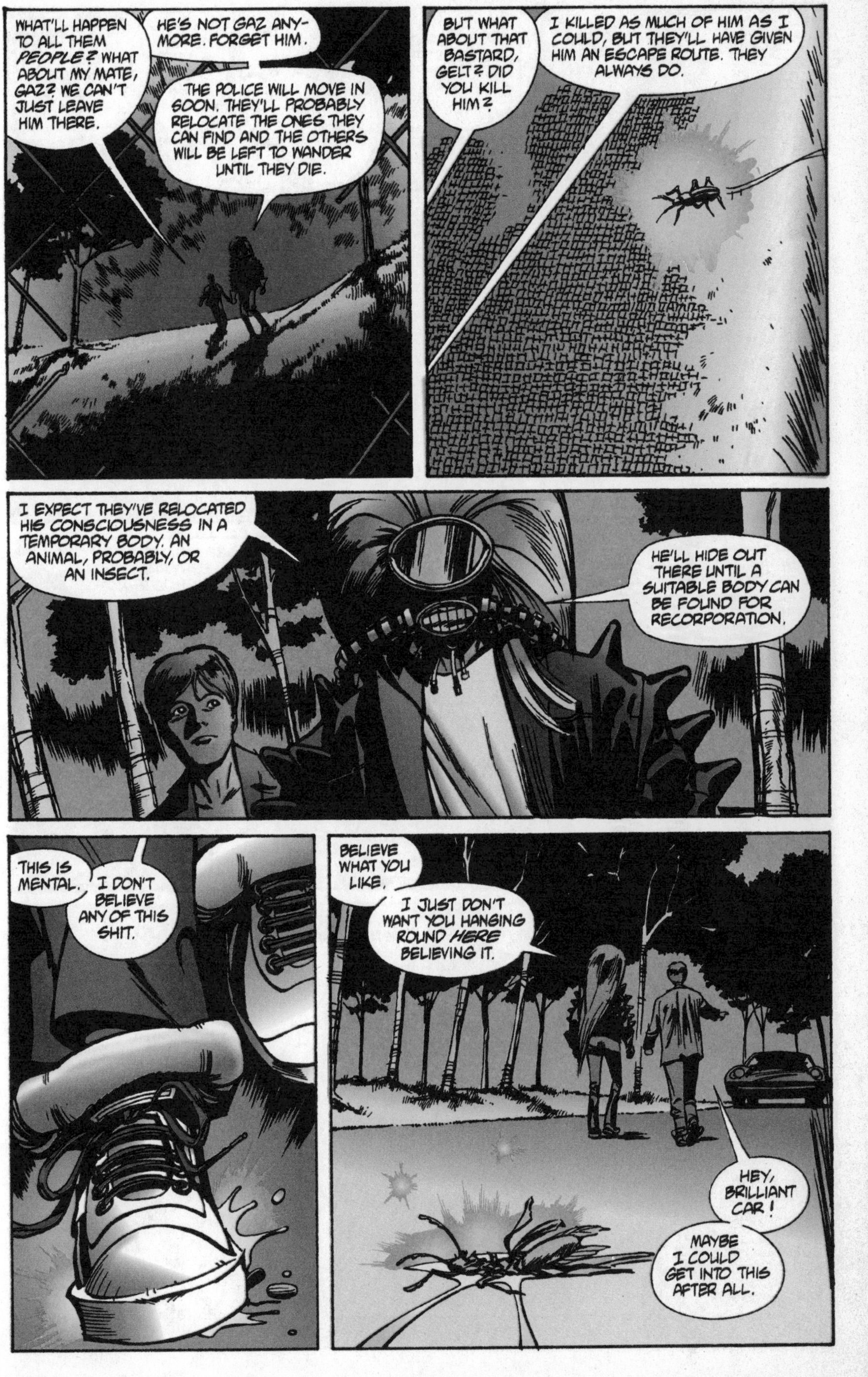
WHAT'LL HAPPEN TO ALL THEM *PEOPLE*? WHAT ABOUT MY MATE, GAZ? WE CAN'T JUST LEAVE HIM THERE.
HE'S NOT GAZ ANYMORE. FORGET HIM.
THE POLICE WILL MOVE IN SOON. THEY'LL PROBABLY RELOCATE THE ONES THEY CAN FIND AND THE OTHERS WILL BE LEFT TO WANDER UNTIL THEY DIE.
BUT WHAT ABOUT THAT BASTARD, GELT? DID YOU KILL HIM?
I KILLED AS MUCH OF HIM AS I COULD, BUT THEY'LL HAVE GIVEN HIM AN ESCAPE ROUTE. THEY ALWAYS DO.
I EXPECT THEY'VE RELOCATED HIS CONSCIOUSNESS IN A TEMPORARY BODY. AN ANIMAL, PROBABLY, OR AN INSECT.
HE'LL HIDE OUT THERE UNTIL A SUITABLE BODY CAN BE FOUND FOR RECORPORATION.
THIS IS MENTAL.
I DON'T BELIEVE ANY OF THIS SHIT.
BELIEVE WHAT YOU LIKE.
I JUST DON'T WANT YOU HANGING ROUND *HERE* BELIEVING IT.
HEY, BRILLIANT CAR!
MAYBE I COULD GET INTO THIS AFTER ALL.

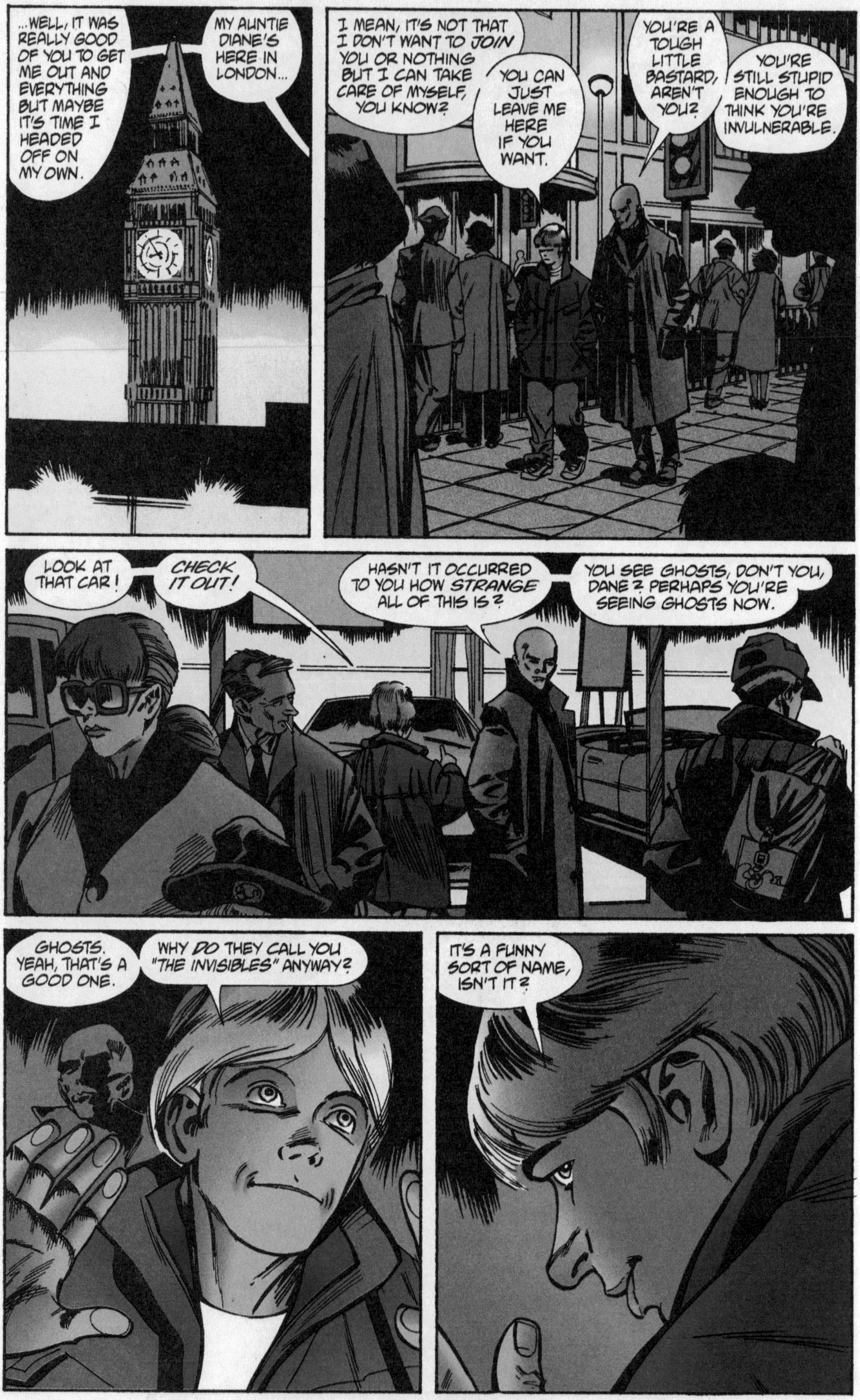
...WELL, IT WAS REALLY GOOD OF YOU TO GET ME OUT AND EVERYTHING BUT MAYBE IT'S TIME I HEADED OFF ON MY OWN.
MY AUNTIE DIANE'S HERE IN LONDON...
I MEAN, IT'S NOT THAT I DON'T WANT TO JOIN YOU OR NOTHING BUT I CAN TAKE CARE OF MYSELF, YOU KNOW?
YOU CAN JUST LEAVE ME HERE IF YOU WANT.
YOU'RE A TOUGH LITTLE BASTARD, AREN'T YOU?
YOU'RE STILL STUPID ENOUGH TO THINK YOU'RE INVULNERABLE.
LOOK AT THAT CAR!
CHECK IT OUT!
HASN'T IT OCCURRED TO YOU HOW STRANGE ALL OF THIS IS?
YOU SEE GHOSTS, DON'T YOU, DANE? PERHAPS YOU'RE SEEING GHOSTS NOW.
GHOSTS. YEAH, THAT'S A GOOD ONE.
WHY DO THEY CALL YOU "THE INVISIBLES" ANYWAY?
IT'S A FUNNY SORT OF NAME, ISN'T IT?

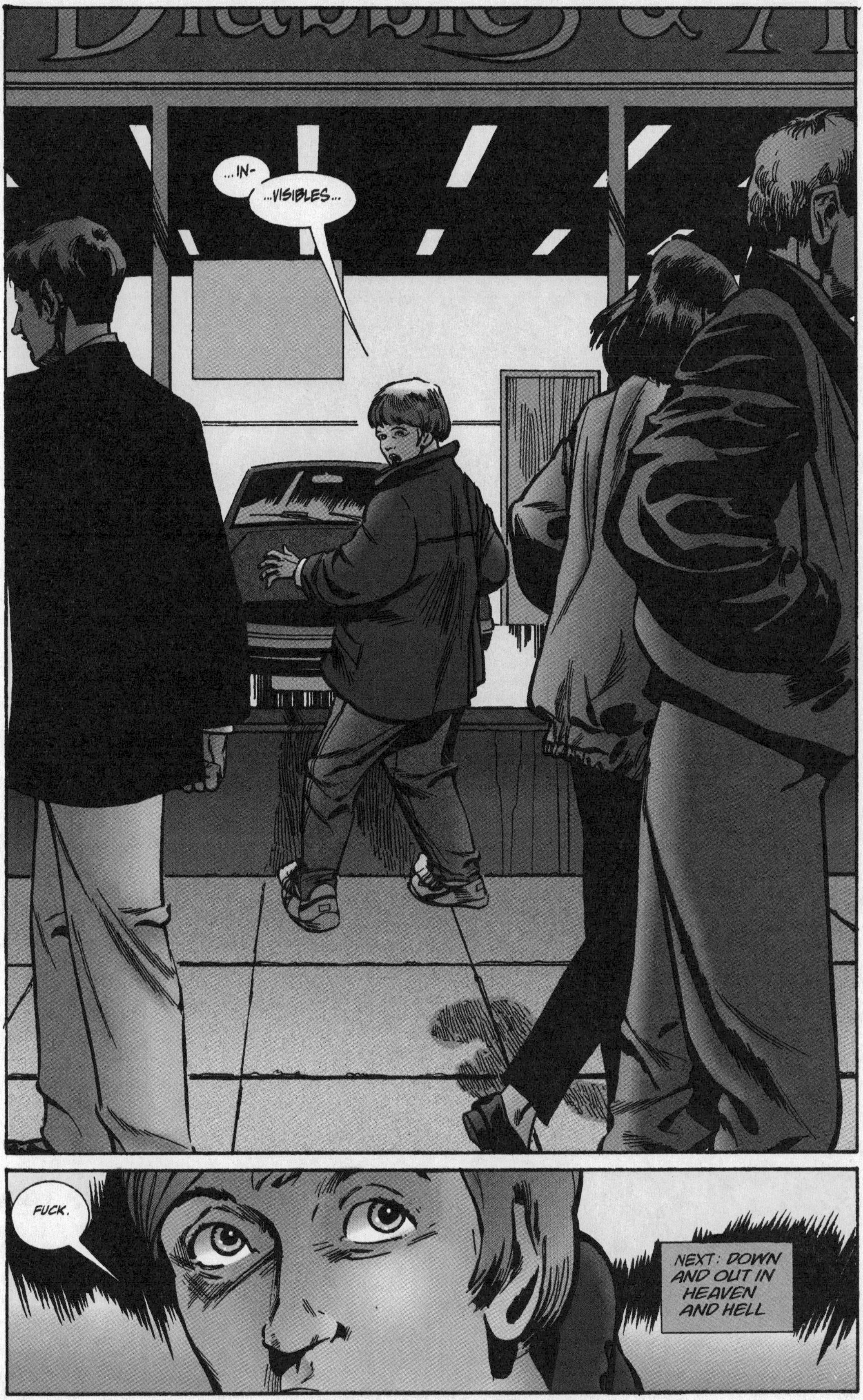
...IN-
...VISIBLES...
FUCK.
NEXT: DOWN AND OUT IN HEAVEN AND HELL

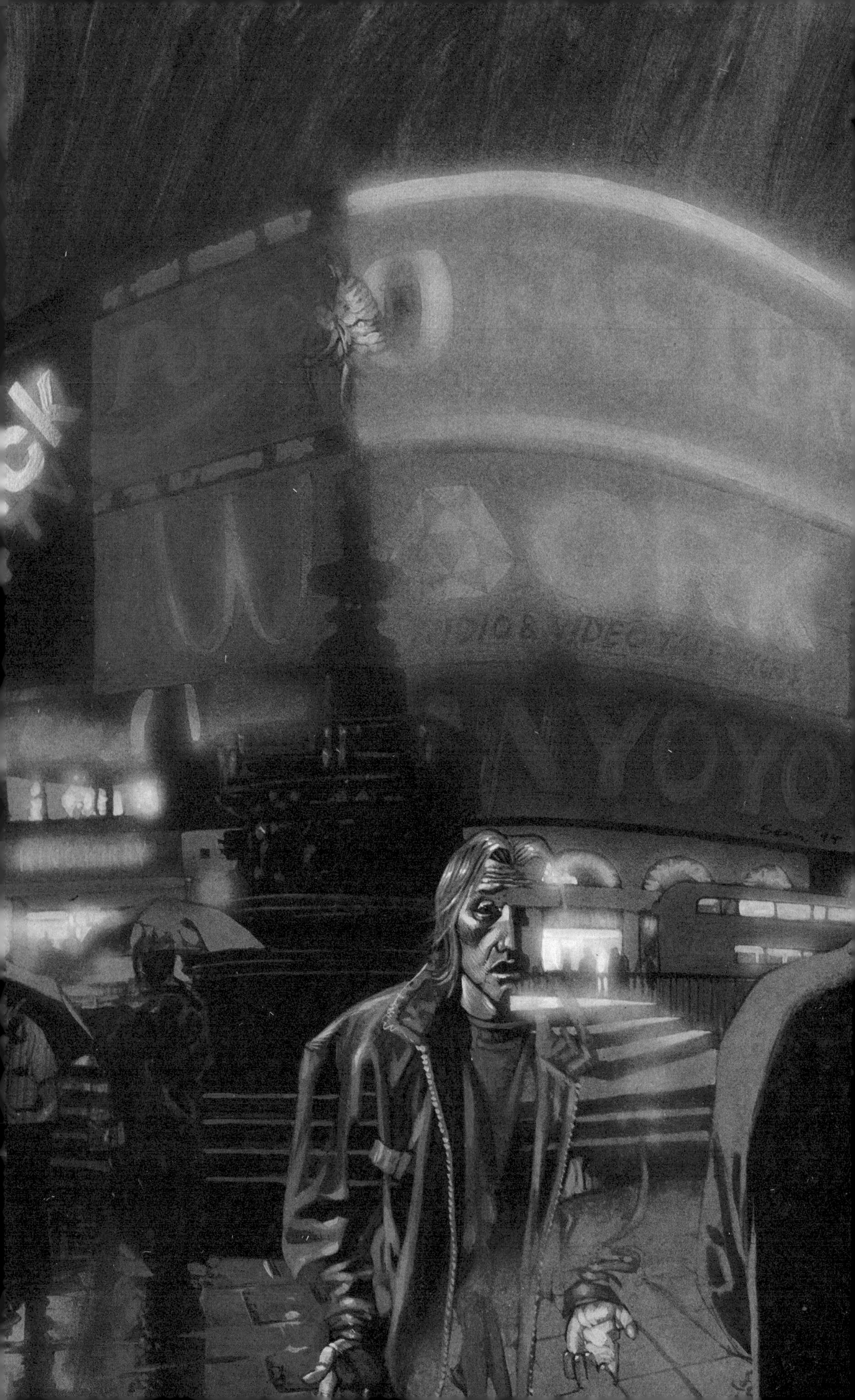

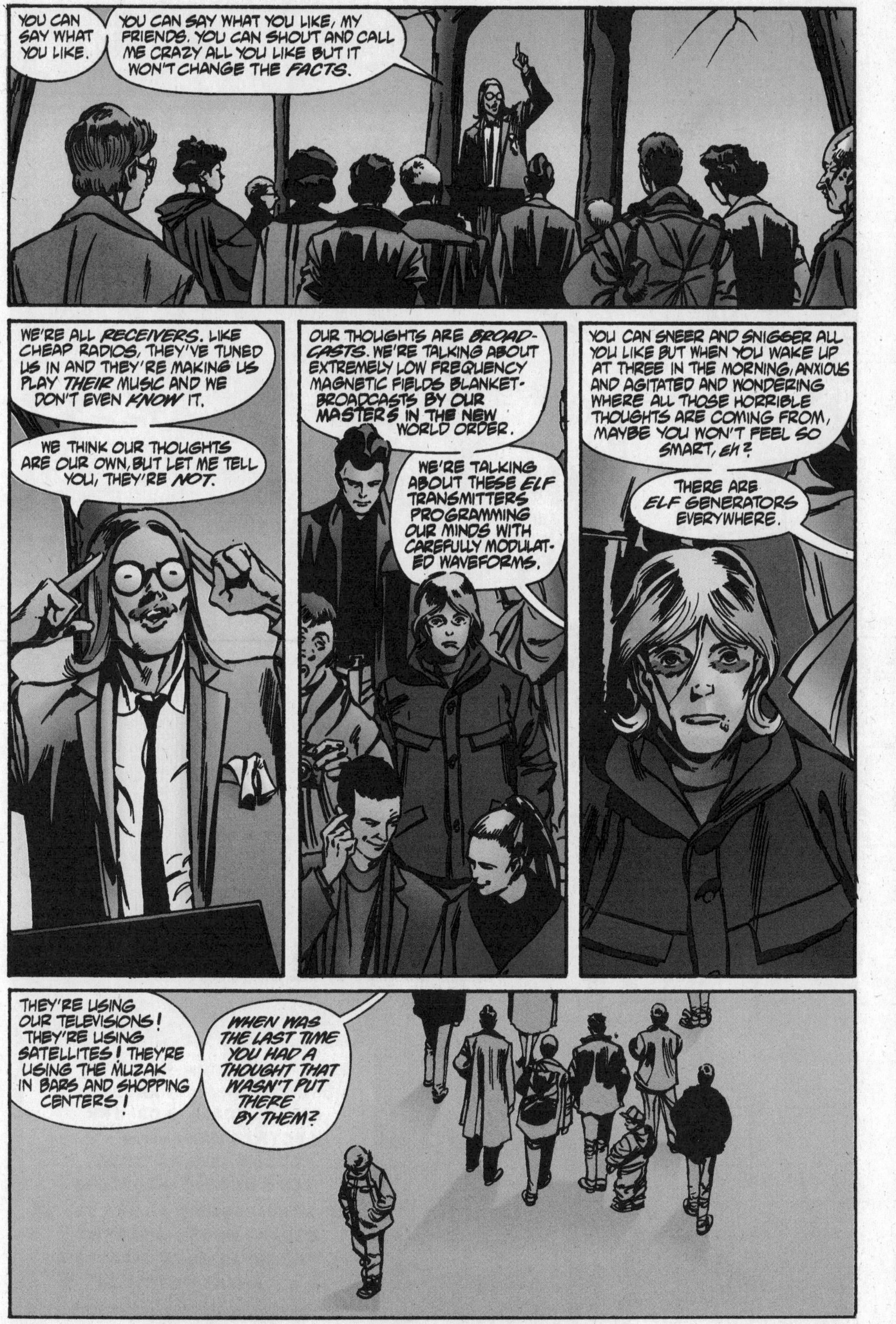
YOU CAN SAY WHAT YOU LIKE.
YOU CAN SAY WHAT YOU LIKE, MY FRIENDS. YOU CAN SHOUT AND CALL ME CRAZY ALL YOU LIKE BUT IT WON'T CHANGE THE *FACTS*.
WE'RE ALL *RECEIVERS*. LIKE CHEAP RADIOS, THEY'VE TUNED US IN AND THEY'RE MAKING US PLAY *THEIR* MUSIC AND WE DON'T EVEN *KNOW* IT.
WE THINK OUR THOUGHTS ARE OUR OWN, BUT LET ME TELL YOU, THEY'RE *NOT*.
OUR THOUGHTS ARE *BROADCASTS*. WE'RE TALKING ABOUT EXTREMELY LOW FREQUENCY MAGNETIC FIELDS BLANKET-BROADCASTS BY OUR *MASTERS* IN THE NEW WORLD ORDER.
WE'RE TALKING ABOUT THESE *ELF* TRANSMITTERS PROGRAMMING OUR MINDS WITH CAREFULLY MODULATED WAVEFORMS.
YOU CAN SNEER AND SNIGGER ALL YOU LIKE BUT WHEN YOU WAKE UP AT THREE IN THE MORNING, ANXIOUS AND AGITATED AND WONDERING WHERE ALL THOSE HORRIBLE THOUGHTS ARE COMING FROM, MAYBE YOU WON'T FEEL SO SMART, *EH*?
THERE ARE *ELF* GENERATORS EVERYWHERE.
THEY'RE USING OUR TELEVISIONS! THEY'RE USING SATELLITES! THEY'RE USING THE MUZAK IN BARS AND SHOPPING CENTERS!
WHEN WAS THE LAST TIME YOU HAD A THOUGHT THAT WASN'T PUT THERE BY THEM?

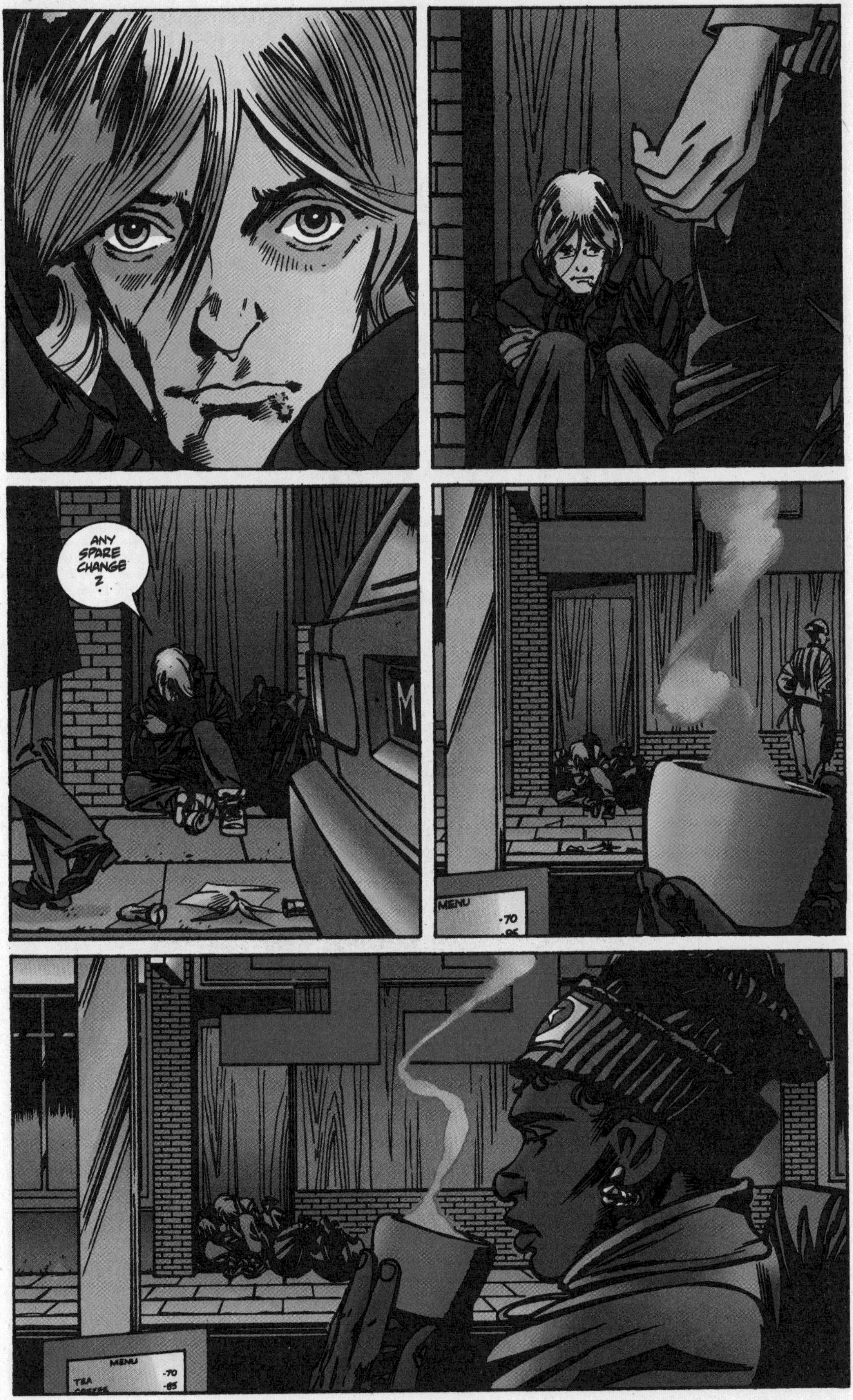
ANY SPARE CHANGE ?
MENU
·70
MENU
TEA ·70
·85

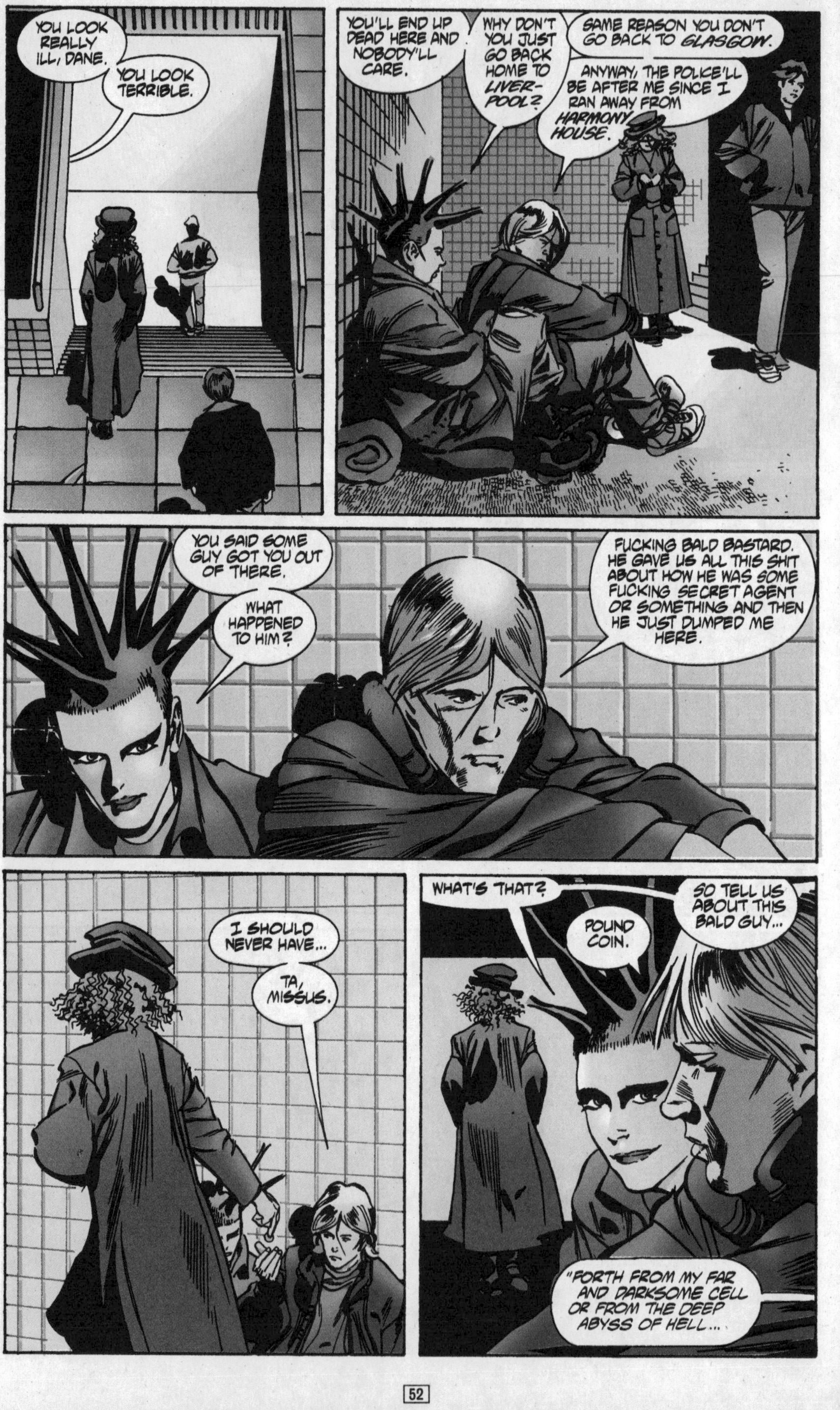
YOU LOOK REALLY ILL, DANE.
YOU LOOK TERRIBLE.
YOU'LL END UP DEAD HERE AND NOBODY'LL CARE.
WHY DON'T YOU JUST GO BACK HOME TO LIVER-POOL?
SAME REASON YOU DON'T GO BACK TO GLASGOW.
ANYWAY, THE POLICE'LL BE AFTER ME SINCE I RAN AWAY FROM HARMONY HOUSE.
YOU SAID SOME GUY GOT YOU OUT OF THERE.
WHAT HAPPENED TO HIM?
FUCKING BALD BASTARD. HE GAVE US ALL THIS SHIT ABOUT HOW HE WAS SOME FUCKING SECRET AGENT OR SOMETHING AND THEN HE JUST DUMPED ME HERE.
I SHOULD NEVER HAVE...
TA, MISSUS.
WHAT'S THAT?
POUND COIN.
SO TELL US ABOUT THIS BALD GUY...
"FORTH FROM MY FAR AND DARKSOME CELL OR FROM THE DEEP ABYSS OF HELL...

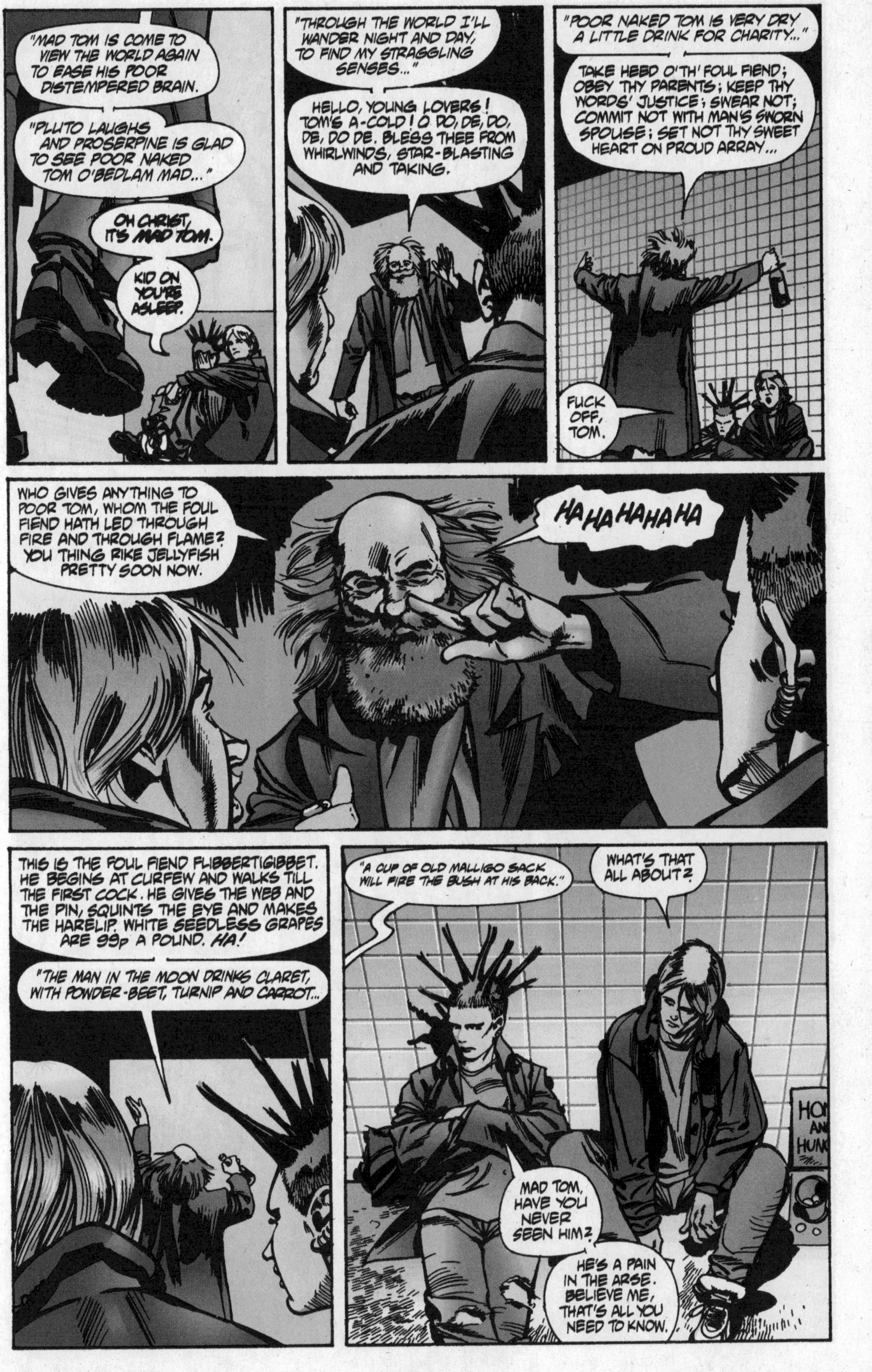
"MAD TOM IS COME TO VIEW THE WORLD AGAIN TO EASE HIS POOR DISTEMPERED BRAIN.
"PLUTO LAUGHS AND PROSERPINE IS GLAD TO SEE POOR NAKED TOM O'BEDLAM MAD..."
OH CHRIST, IT'S MAD TOM.
KID ON YOU'RE ASLEEP.
"THROUGH THE WORLD I'LL WANDER NIGHT AND DAY, TO FIND MY STRAGGLING SENSES..."
HELLO, YOUNG LOVERS! TOM'S A-COLD! O, DO, DE, DO, DE, DO DE. BLESS THEE FROM WHIRLWINDS, STAR-BLASTING AND TAKING.
"POOR NAKED TOM IS VERY DRY A LITTLE DRINK FOR CHARITY..."
TAKE HEED O'TH' FOUL FIEND; OBEY THY PARENTS; KEEP THY WORDS' JUSTICE; SWEAR NOT; COMMIT NOT WITH MAN'S SWORN SPOUSE; SET NOT THY SWEET HEART ON PROUD ARRAY...
FUCK OFF, TOM.
WHO GIVES ANYTHING TO POOR TOM, WHOM THE FOUL FIEND HATH LED THROUGH FIRE AND THROUGH FLAME? YOU THING RIKE JELLYFISH PRETTY SOON NOW.
HAHAHAHAHAHA
THIS IS THE FOUL FIEND FLIBBERTIGIBBET. HE BEGINS AT CURFEW AND WALKS TILL THE FIRST COCK. HE GIVES THE WEB AND THE PIN, SQUINTS THE EYE AND MAKES THE HARELIP. WHITE SEEDLESS GRAPES ARE 99p A POUND. HA!
"THE MAN IN THE MOON DRINKS CLARET, WITH POWDER-BEET, TURNIP AND CARROT...
"A CUP OF OLD MALLIGO SACK WILL FIRE THE BUSH AT HIS BACK."
WHAT'S THAT ALL ABOUT?
MAD TOM, HAVE YOU NEVER SEEN HIM?
HE'S A PAIN IN THE ARSE. BELIEVE ME, THAT'S ALL YOU NEED TO KNOW.

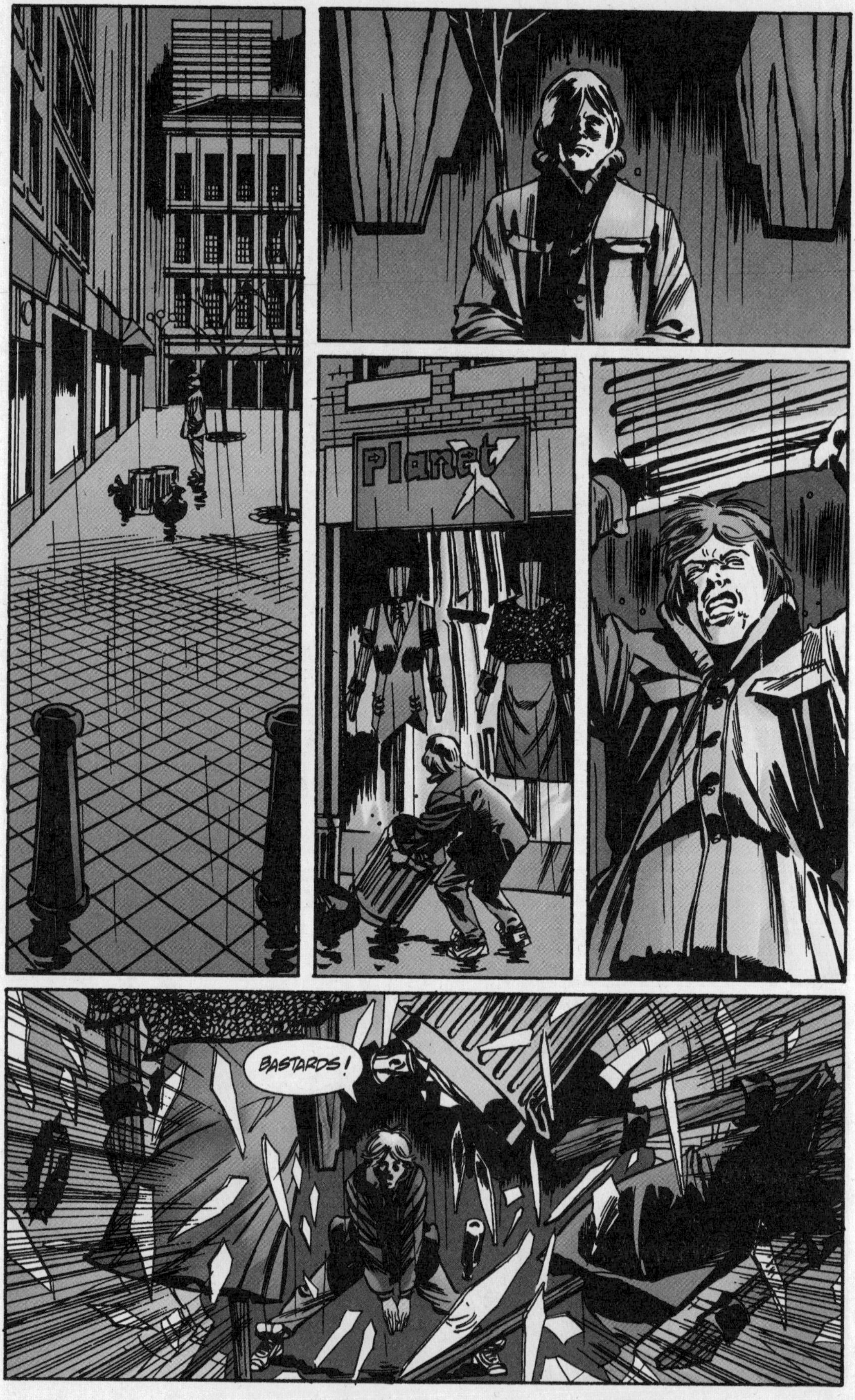
Planet X
BASTARDS!

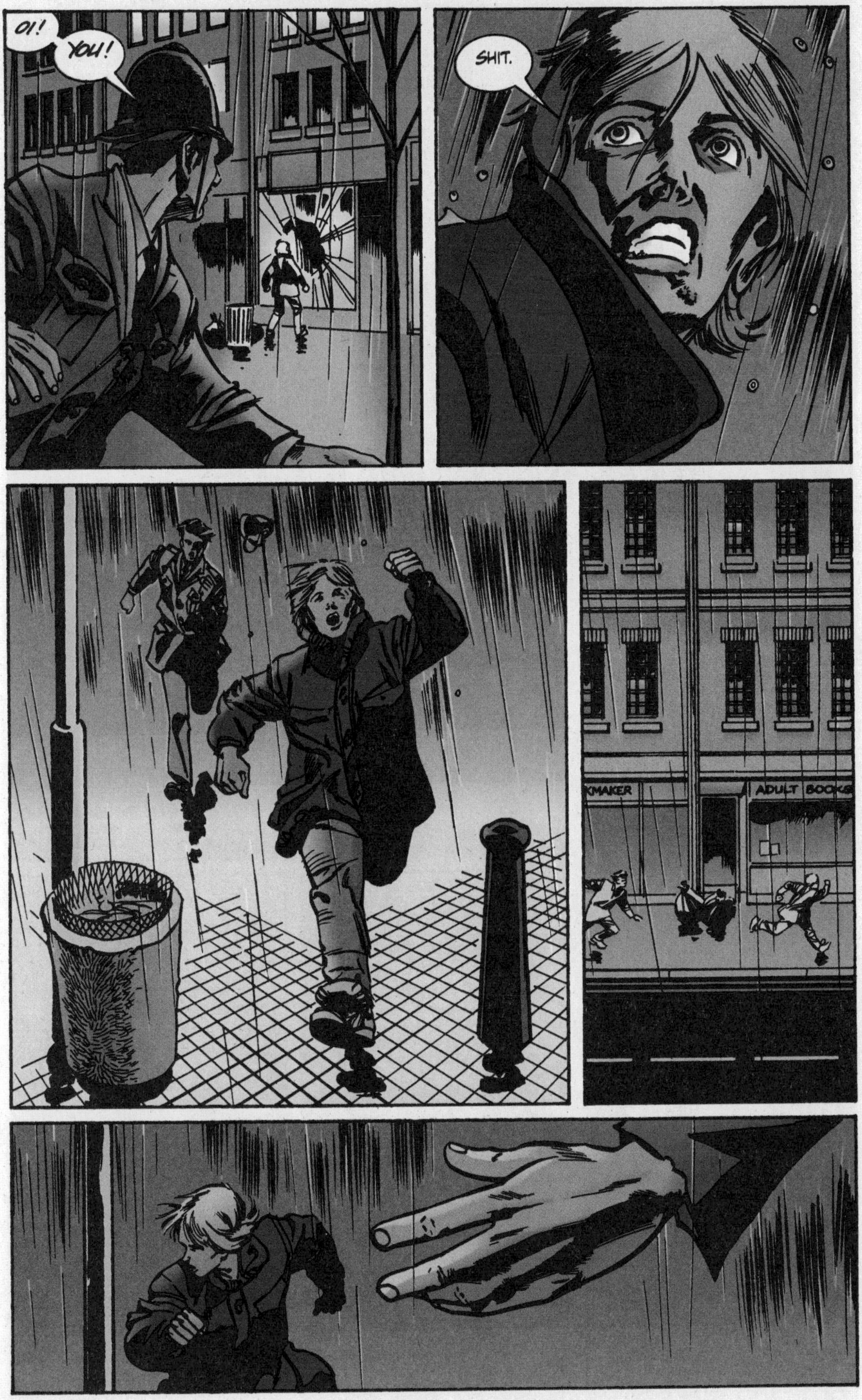
OI!
YOU!
SHIT.
KMAKER
ADULT BOOKS

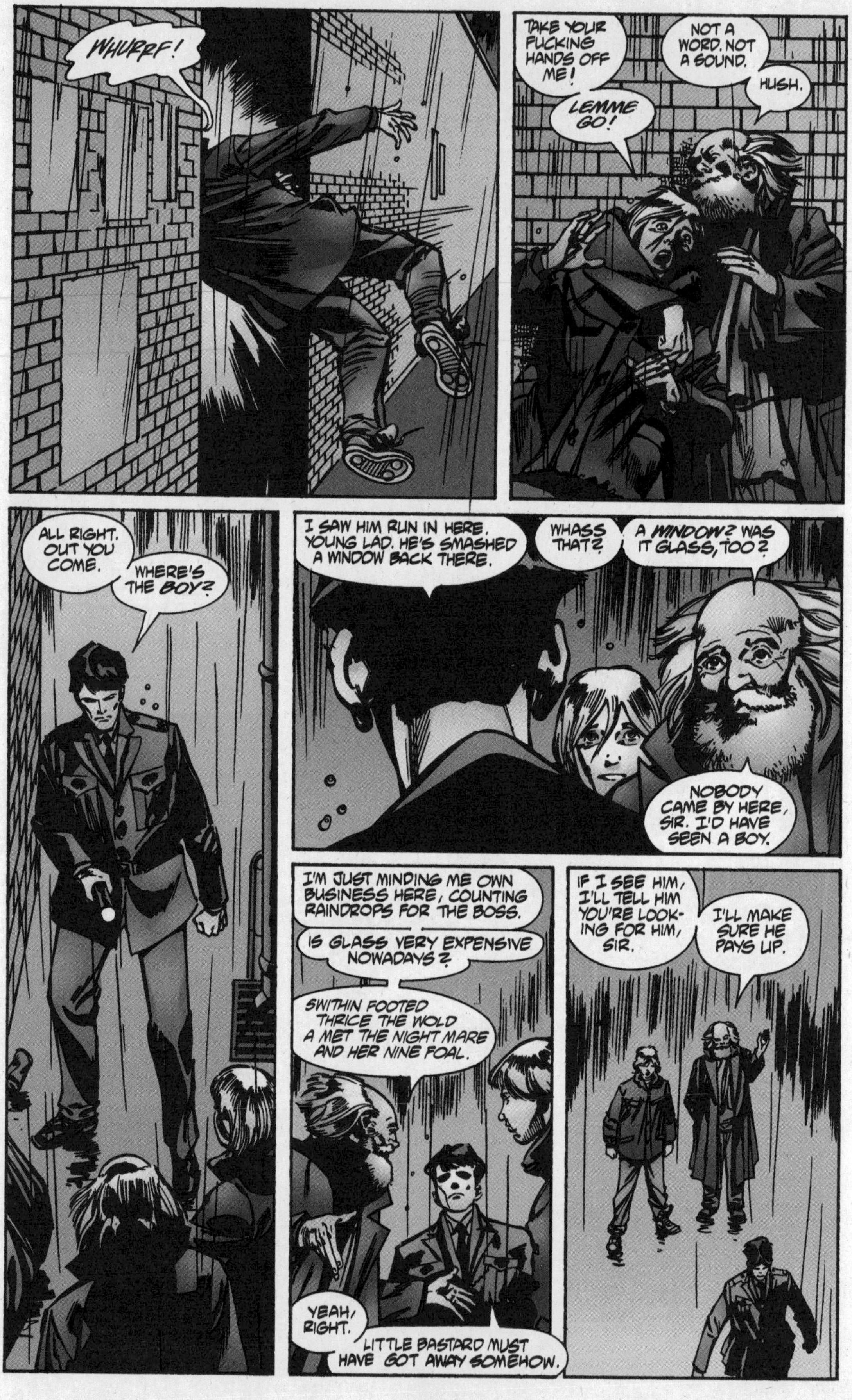
WHURRF!
TAKE YOUR FUCKING HANDS OFF ME!
LEMME GO!
NOT A WORD. NOT A SOUND.
HUSH.
ALL RIGHT. OUT YOU COME.
WHERE'S THE BOY?
I SAW HIM RUN IN HERE, YOUNG LAD. HE'S SMASHED A WINDOW BACK THERE.
WHASS THAT?
A WINDOW? WAS IT GLASS, TOO?
NOBODY CAME BY HERE, SIR. I'D HAVE SEEN A BOY.
I'M JUST MINDING ME OWN BUSINESS HERE, COUNTING RAINDROPS FOR THE BOSS.
IS GLASS VERY EXPENSIVE NOWADAYS?
SWITHIN FOOTED THRICE THE WOLD A MET THE NIGHT MARE AND HER NINE FOAL.
YEAH, RIGHT.
LITTLE BASTARD MUST HAVE GOT AWAY SOMEHOW.
IF I SEE HIM, I'LL TELL HIM YOU'RE LOOKING FOR HIM, SIR.
I'LL MAKE SURE HE PAYS UP.

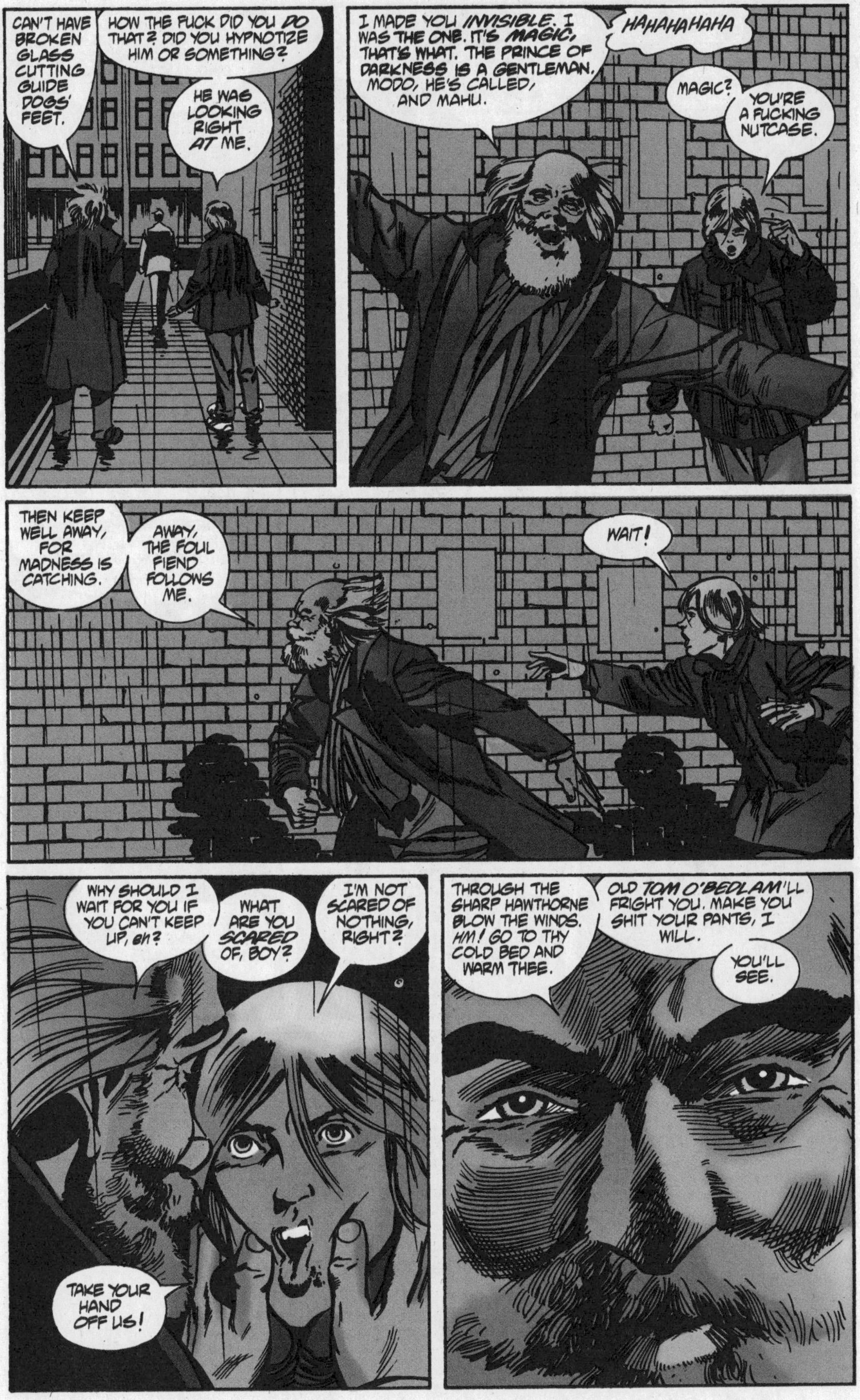
CAN'T HAVE BROKEN GLASS CUTTING GUIDE DOGS' FEET.
HOW THE FUCK DID YOU DO THAT? DID YOU HYPNOTIZE HIM OR SOMETHING?
HE WAS LOOKING RIGHT AT ME.
I MADE YOU INVISIBLE. I WAS THE ONE. IT'S MAGIC, THAT'S WHAT. THE PRINCE OF DARKNESS IS A GENTLEMAN. MODO, HE'S CALLED, AND MAHU.
HAHAHAHAHA
MAGIC?
YOU'RE A FUCKING NUTCASE.
THEN KEEP WELL AWAY, FOR MADNESS IS CATCHING.
AWAY, THE FOUL FIEND FOLLOWS ME.
WAIT!
WHY SHOULD I WAIT FOR YOU IF YOU CAN'T KEEP UP, eh?
WHAT ARE YOU SCARED OF, BOY?
I'M NOT SCARED OF NOTHING, RIGHT?
TAKE YOUR HAND OFF US!
THROUGH THE SHARP HAWTHORNE BLOW THE WINDS. HM! GO TO THY COLD BED AND WARM THEE.
OLD TOM O'BEDLAM'LL FRIGHT YOU. MAKE YOU SHIT YOUR PANTS, I WILL.
YOU'LL SEE.

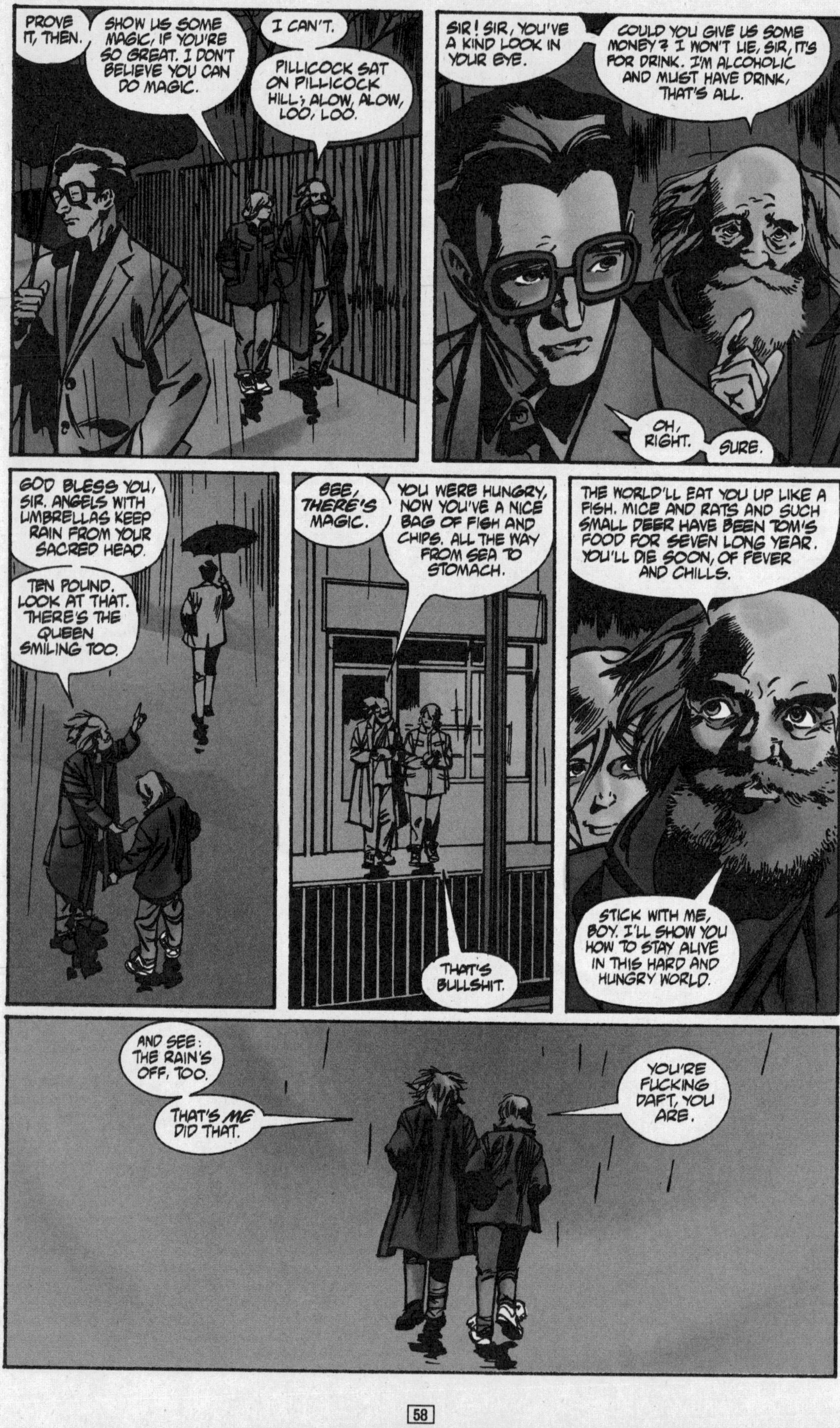
PROVE IT, THEN.
SHOW US SOME MAGIC, IF YOU'RE SO GREAT. I DON'T BELIEVE YOU CAN DO MAGIC.
I CAN'T.
PILLICOCK SAT ON PILLICOCK HILL; ALOW, ALOW, LOO, LOO.
SIR! SIR, YOU'VE A KIND LOOK IN YOUR EYE.
COULD YOU GIVE US SOME MONEY? I WON'T LIE, SIR, IT'S FOR DRINK. I'M ALCOHOLIC AND MUST HAVE DRINK, THAT'S ALL.
OH, RIGHT.
SURE.
GOD BLESS YOU, SIR. ANGELS WITH UMBRELLAS KEEP RAIN FROM YOUR SACRED HEAD.
TEN POUND. LOOK AT THAT. THERE'S THE QUEEN SMILING TOO.
SEE, *THERE'S* MAGIC.
YOU WERE HUNGRY, NOW YOU'VE A NICE BAG OF FISH AND CHIPS. ALL THE WAY FROM SEA TO STOMACH.
THAT'S BULLSHIT.
THE WORLD'LL EAT YOU UP LIKE A FISH. MICE AND RATS AND SUCH SMALL DEER HAVE BEEN TOM'S FOOD FOR SEVEN LONG YEAR. YOU'LL DIE SOON, OF FEVER AND CHILLS.
STICK WITH ME, BOY. I'LL SHOW YOU HOW TO STAY ALIVE IN THIS HARD AND HUNGRY WORLD.
AND SEE: THE RAIN'S OFF, TOO.
THAT'S *ME* DID THAT.
YOU'RE FUCKING DAFT, YOU ARE.

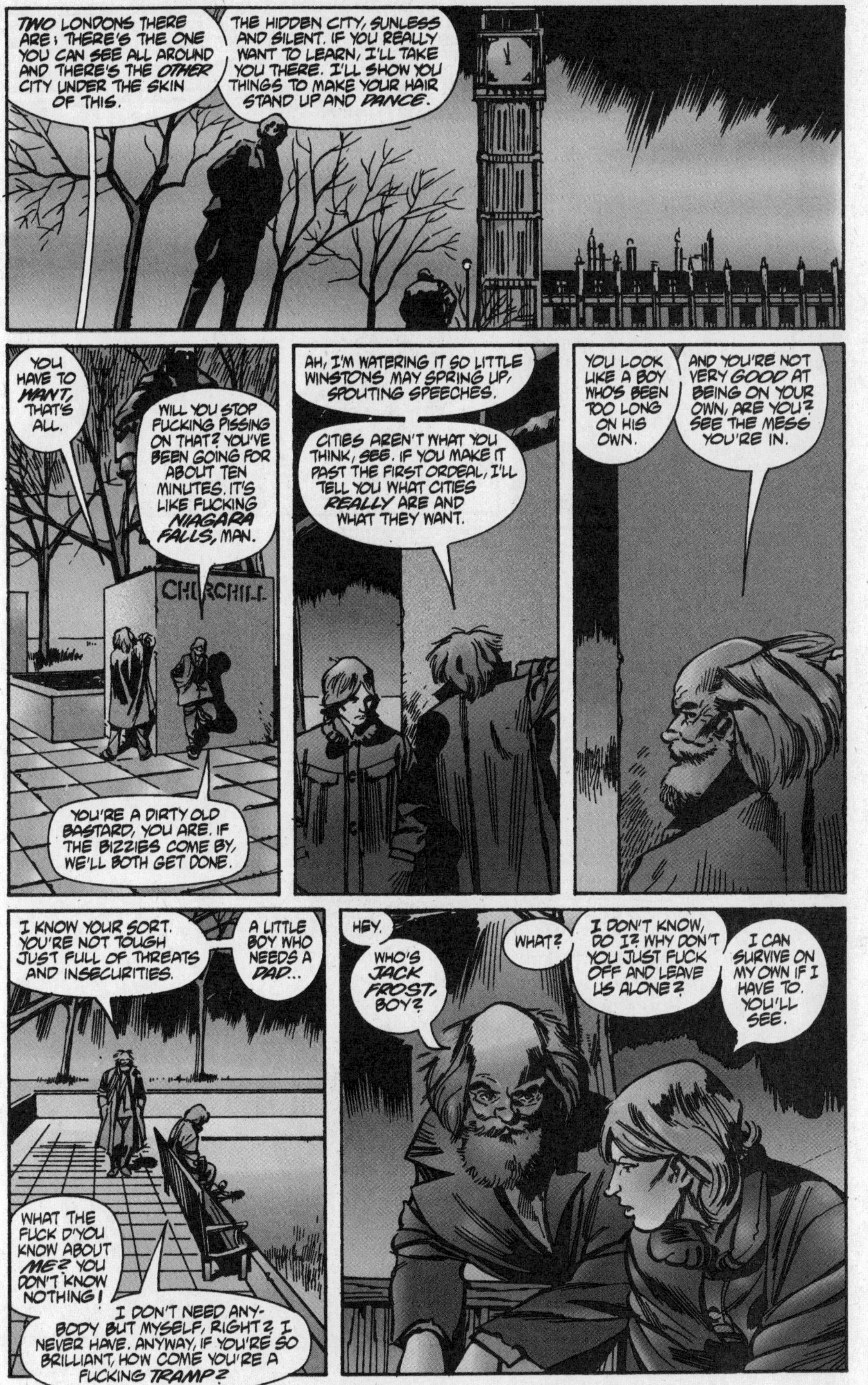
TWO LONDONS THERE ARE; THERE'S THE ONE YOU CAN SEE ALL AROUND AND THERE'S THE OTHER CITY UNDER THE SKIN OF THIS.
THE HIDDEN CITY, SUNLESS AND SILENT. IF YOU REALLY WANT TO LEARN, I'LL TAKE YOU THERE. I'LL SHOW YOU THINGS TO MAKE YOUR HAIR STAND UP AND DANCE.
YOU HAVE TO WANT, THAT'S ALL.
WILL YOU STOP FUCKING PISSING ON THAT? YOU'VE BEEN GOING FOR ABOUT TEN MINUTES. IT'S LIKE FUCKING NIAGARA FALLS, MAN.
CHURCHILL
YOU'RE A DIRTY OLD BASTARD, YOU ARE. IF THE BIZZIES COME BY, WE'LL BOTH GET DONE.
AH, I'M WATERING IT SO LITTLE WINSTONS MAY SPRING UP, SPOUTING SPEECHES.
CITIES AREN'T WHAT YOU THINK, SEE. IF YOU MAKE IT PAST THE FIRST ORDEAL, I'LL TELL YOU WHAT CITIES REALLY ARE AND WHAT THEY WANT.
YOU LOOK LIKE A BOY WHO'S BEEN TOO LONG ON HIS OWN.
AND YOU'RE NOT VERY GOOD AT BEING ON YOUR OWN, ARE YOU? SEE THE MESS YOU'RE IN.
I KNOW YOUR SORT. YOU'RE NOT TOUGH JUST FULL OF THREATS AND INSECURITIES.
A LITTLE BOY WHO NEEDS A DAD...
WHAT THE FUCK D'YOU KNOW ABOUT ME? YOU DON'T KNOW NOTHING!
I DON'T NEED ANYBODY BUT MYSELF, RIGHT? I NEVER HAVE. ANYWAY, IF YOU'RE SO BRILLIANT, HOW COME YOU'RE A FUCKING TRAMP?
HEY.
WHO'S JACK FROST, BOY?
WHAT?
I DON'T KNOW, DO I? WHY DON'T YOU JUST FUCK OFF AND LEAVE US ALONE?
I CAN SURVIVE ON MY OWN IF I HAVE TO. YOU'LL SEE.

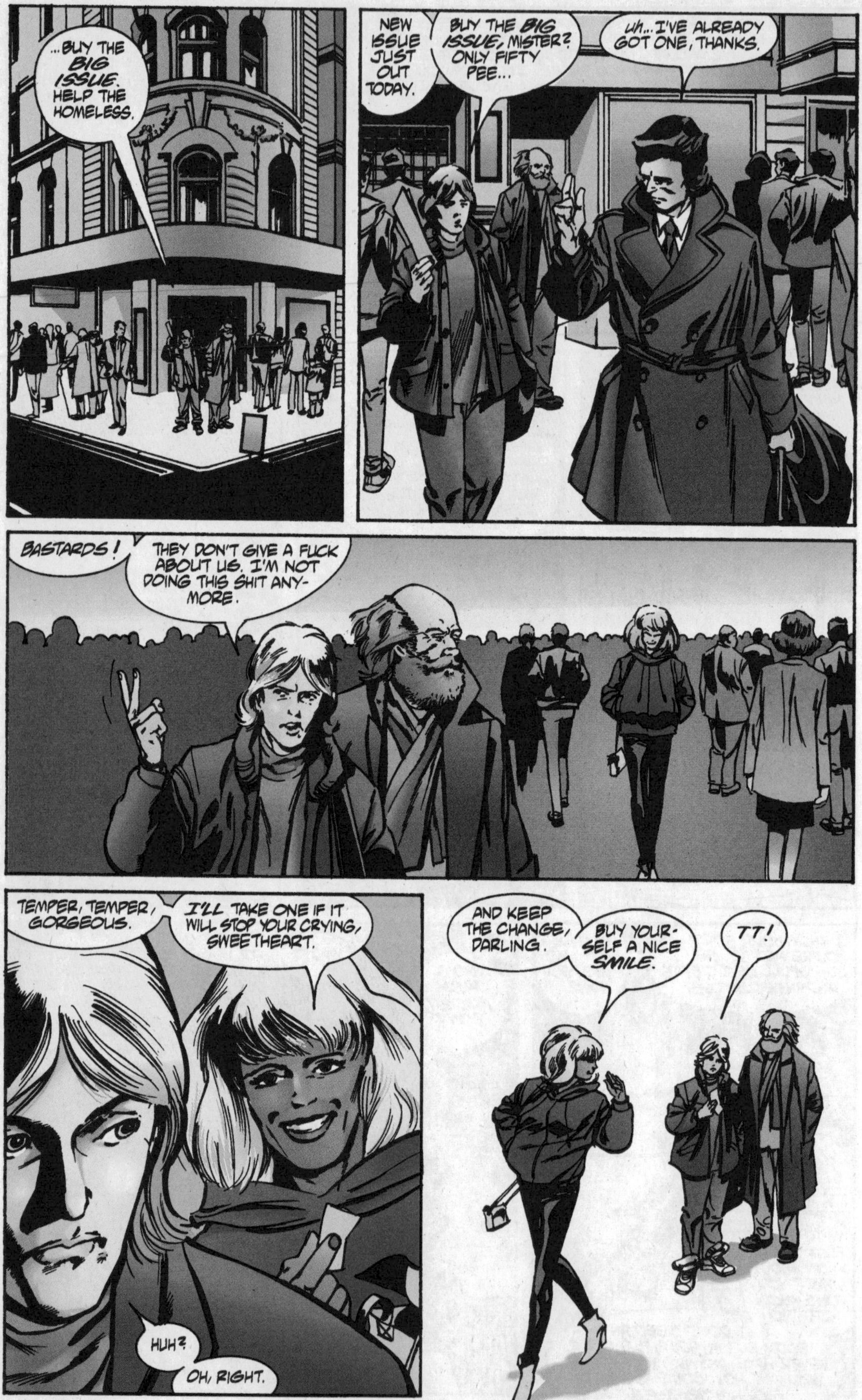
...BUY THE BIG ISSUE. HELP THE HOMELESS.
NEW ISSUE JUST OUT TODAY.
BUY THE BIG ISSUE, MISTER? ONLY FIFTY PEE...
uh... I'VE ALREADY GOT ONE, THANKS.
BASTARDS!
THEY DON'T GIVE A FUCK ABOUT US. I'M NOT DOING THIS SHIT ANYMORE.
TEMPER, TEMPER, GORGEOUS.
I'LL TAKE ONE IF IT WILL STOP YOUR CRYING, SWEETHEART.
HUH?
OH, RIGHT.
AND KEEP THE CHANGE, DARLING.
BUY YOURSELF A NICE SMILE.
TT!

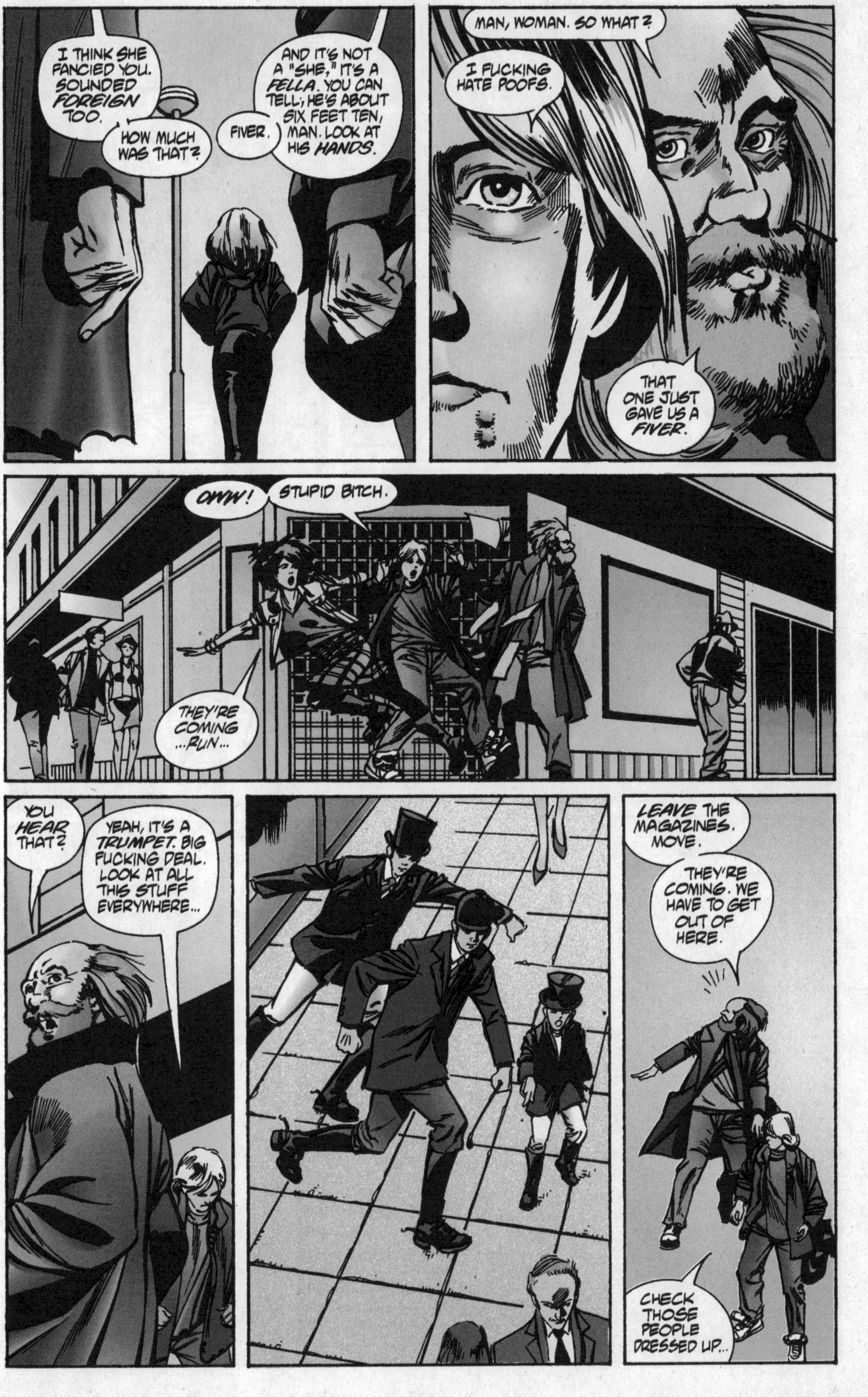
I THINK SHE FANCIED YOU. SOUNDED *FOREIGN* TOO.
HOW MUCH WAS THAT?
FIVER.
AND IT'S NOT A "SHE," IT'S A *FELLA*. YOU CAN TELL; HE'S ABOUT SIX FEET TEN, MAN. LOOK AT HIS *HANDS*.
MAN, WOMAN. SO WHAT?
I FUCKING HATE POOFS.
THAT ONE JUST GAVE US A *FIVER*.
OWW!
STUPID BITCH.
THEY'RE COMING ...RUN...
YOU *HEAR* THAT?
YEAH, IT'S A *TRUMPET*. BIG FUCKING DEAL. LOOK AT ALL THIS STUFF EVERYWHERE...
LEAVE THE MAGAZINES. MOVE.
THEY'RE COMING. WE HAVE TO GET OUT OF HERE.
CHECK THOSE PEOPLE DRESSED UP...

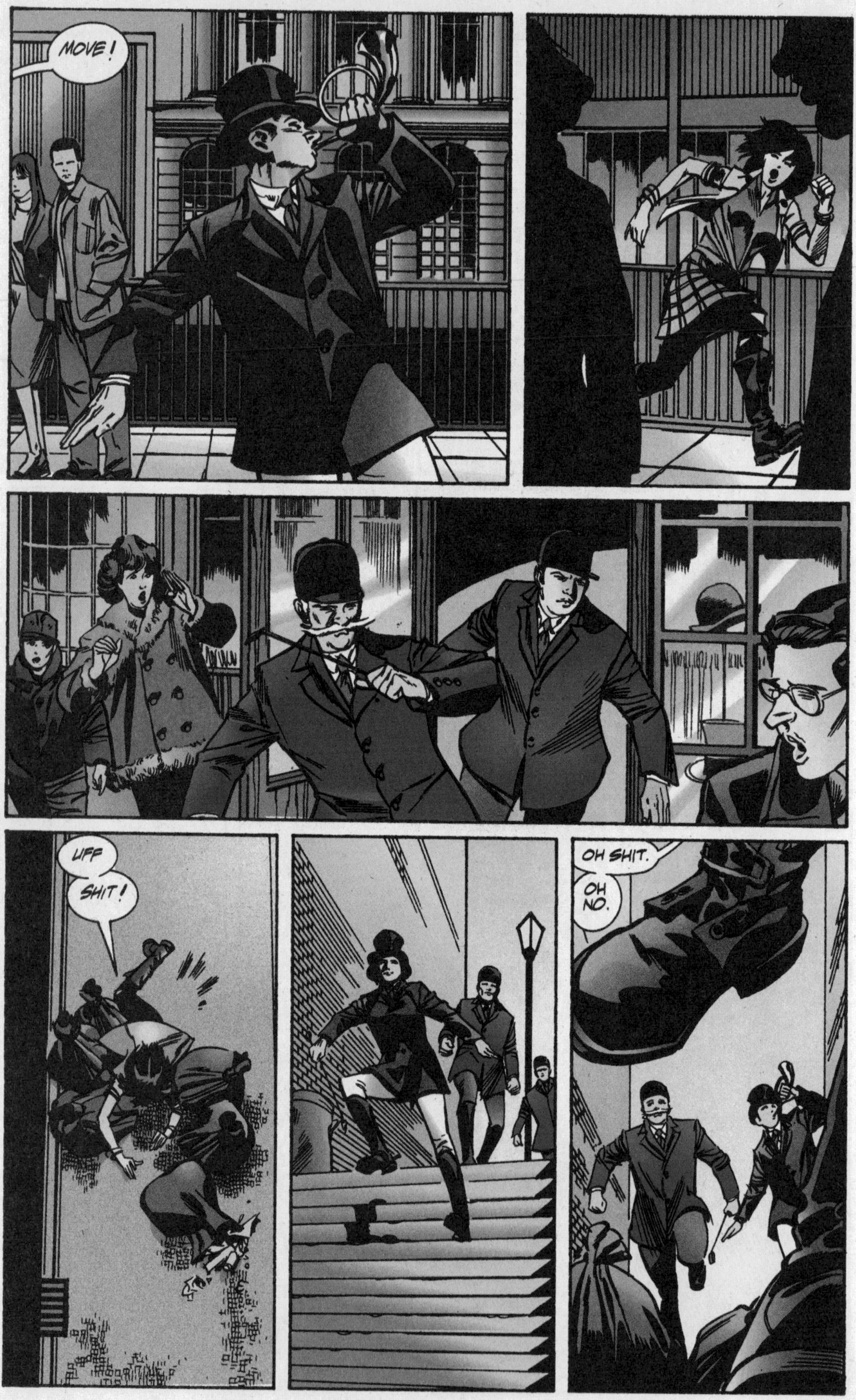

MOVE!
UFF
SHIT!
OH SHIT.
OH NO.

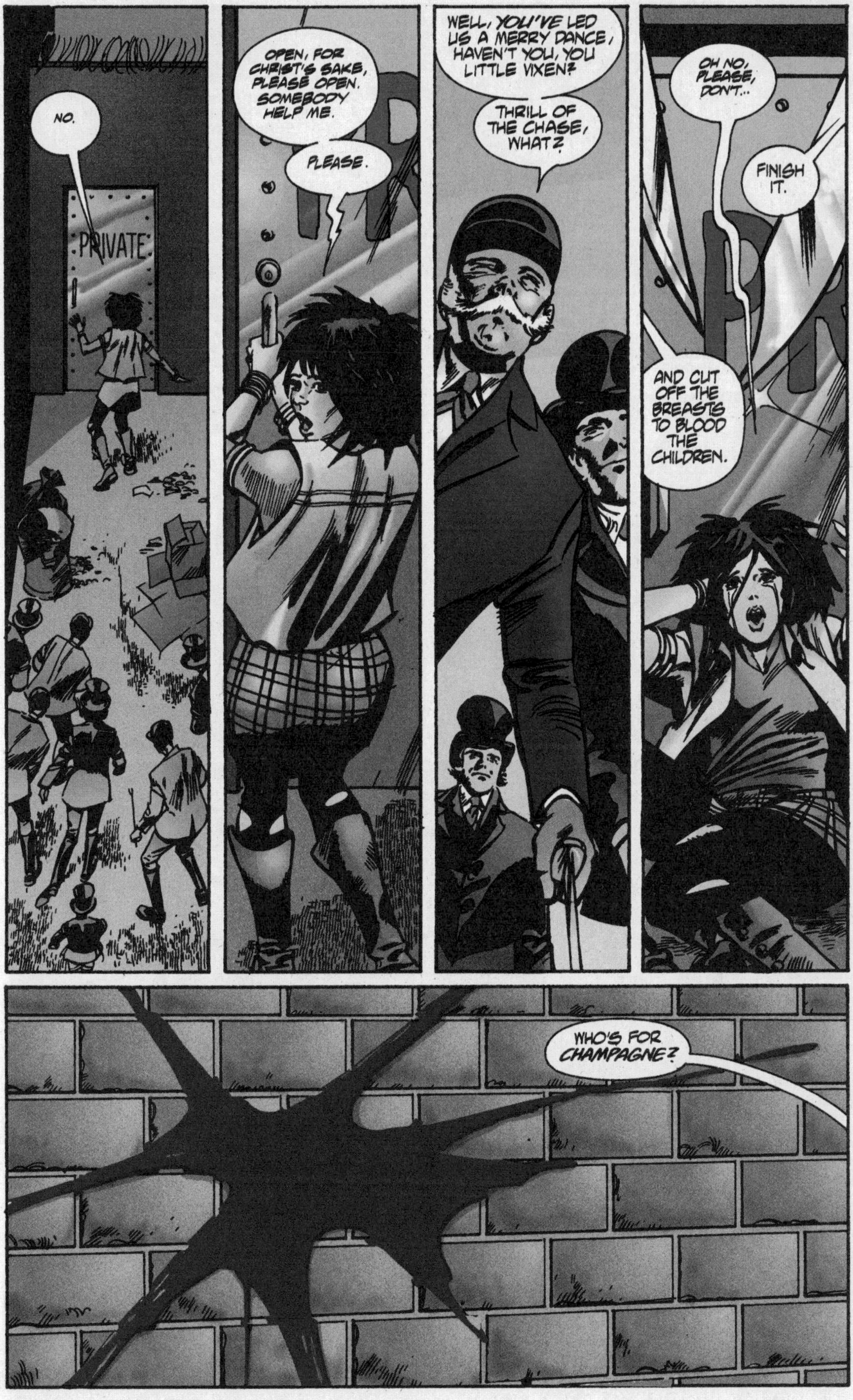
NO.
PRIVATE
OPEN, FOR CHRIST'S SAKE, PLEASE OPEN. SOMEBODY HELP ME.
PLEASE.
WELL, YOU'VE LED US A MERRY DANCE, HAVEN'T YOU, YOU LITTLE VIXEN?
THRILL OF THE CHASE, WHAT?
OH NO, PLEASE, DON'T...
FINISH IT.
AND CUT OFF THE BREASTS TO BLOOD THE CHILDREN.
WHO'S FOR CHAMPAGNE?

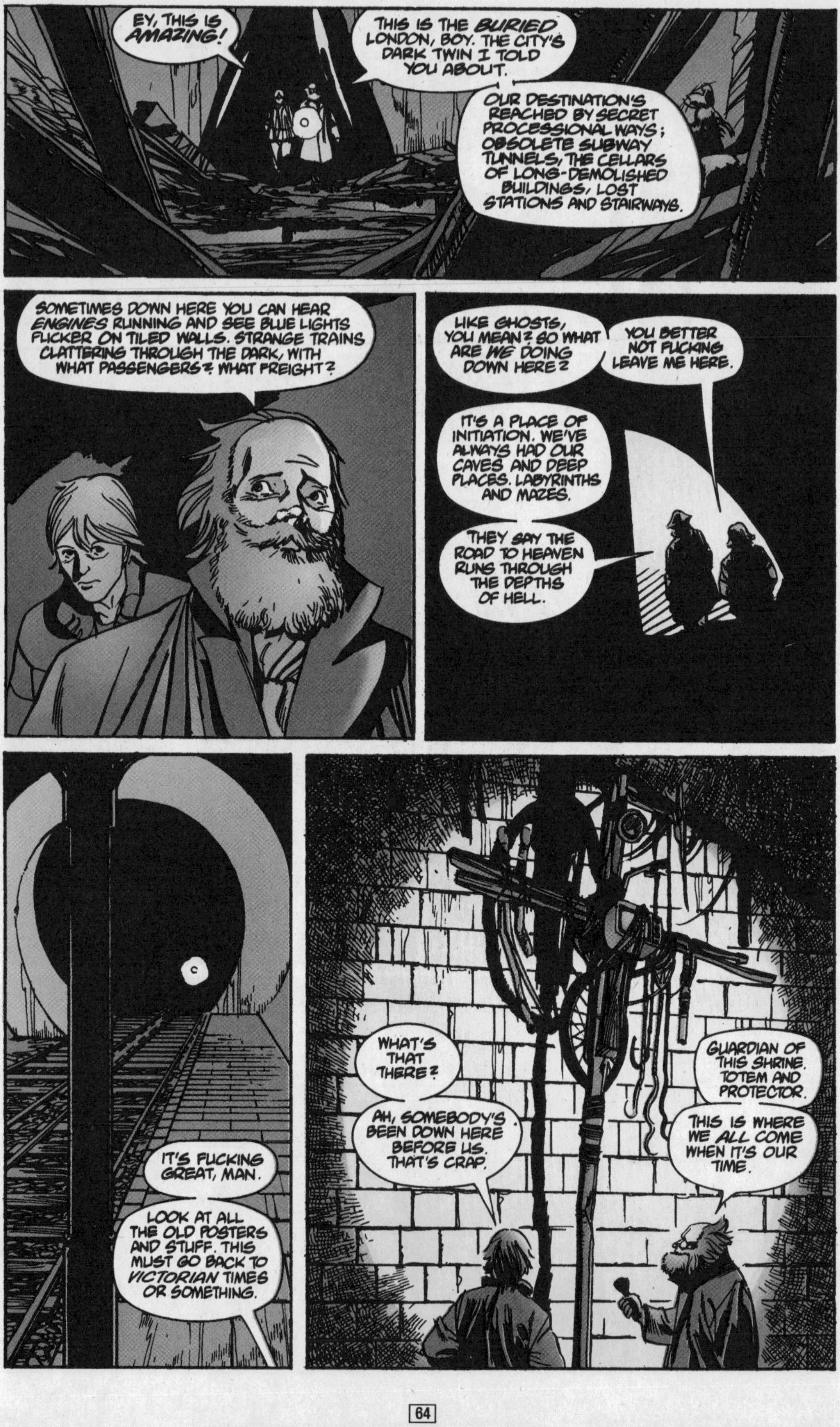
EY, THIS IS AMAZING!
THIS IS THE BURIED LONDON, BOY. THE CITY'S DARK TWIN I TOLD YOU ABOUT.
OUR DESTINATION'S REACHED BY SECRET PROCESSIONAL WAYS; OBSOLETE SUBWAY TUNNELS, THE CELLARS OF LONG-DEMOLISHED BUILDINGS, LOST STATIONS AND STAIRWAYS.
SOMETIMES DOWN HERE YOU CAN HEAR ENGINES RUNNING AND SEE BLUE LIGHTS FLICKER ON TILED WALLS. STRANGE TRAINS CLATTERING THROUGH THE DARK, WITH WHAT PASSENGERS? WHAT FREIGHT?
LIKE GHOSTS, YOU MEAN? SO WHAT ARE WE DOING DOWN HERE?
YOU BETTER NOT FUCKING LEAVE ME HERE.
IT'S A PLACE OF INITIATION. WE'VE ALWAYS HAD OUR CAVES AND DEEP PLACES. LABYRINTHS AND MAZES.
THEY SAY THE ROAD TO HEAVEN RUNS THROUGH THE DEPTHS OF HELL.
IT'S FUCKING GREAT, MAN.
LOOK AT ALL THE OLD POSTERS AND STUFF. THIS MUST GO BACK TO VICTORIAN TIMES OR SOMETHING.
WHAT'S THAT THERE?
AH, SOMEBODY'S BEEN DOWN HERE BEFORE US. THAT'S CRAP.
GUARDIAN OF THIS SHRINE. TOTEM AND PROTECTOR.
THIS IS WHERE WE ALL COME WHEN IT'S OUR TIME.

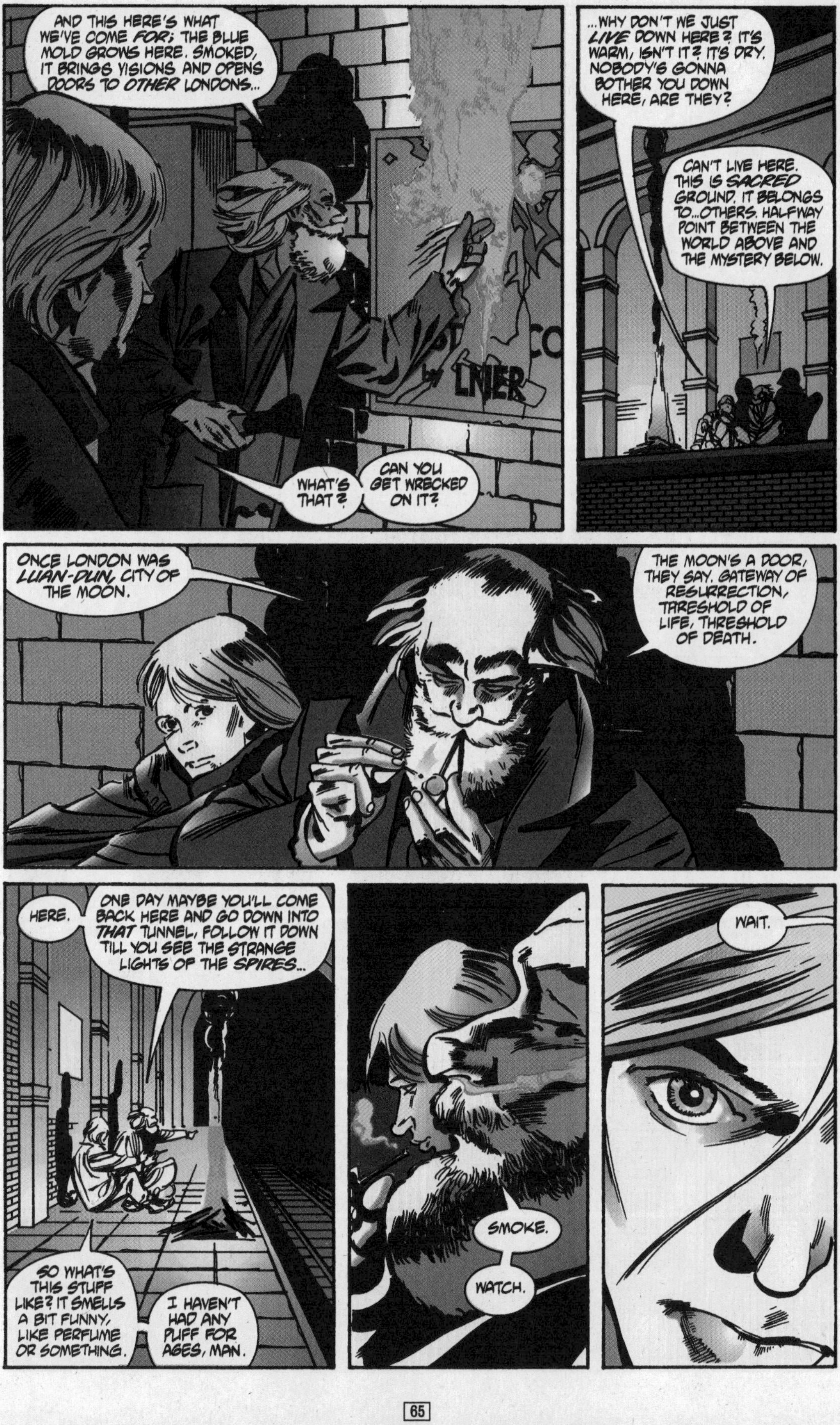
AND THIS HERE'S WHAT WE'VE COME FOR; THE BLUE MOLD GROWS HERE. SMOKED, IT BRINGS VISIONS AND OPENS DOORS TO OTHER LONDONS...
WHAT'S THAT?
CAN YOU GET WRECKED ON IT?
...WHY DON'T WE JUST LIVE DOWN HERE? IT'S WARM, ISN'T IT? IT'S DRY. NOBODY'S GONNA BOTHER YOU DOWN HERE, ARE THEY?
CAN'T LIVE HERE. THIS IS SACRED GROUND. IT BELONGS TO...OTHERS. HALFWAY POINT BETWEEN THE WORLD ABOVE AND THE MYSTERY BELOW.
ONCE LONDON WAS LUAN-DUN, CITY OF THE MOON.
THE MOON'S A DOOR, THEY SAY. GATEWAY OF RESURRECTION, THRESHOLD OF LIFE, THRESHOLD OF DEATH.
HERE.
ONE DAY MAYBE YOU'LL COME BACK HERE AND GO DOWN INTO THAT TUNNEL, FOLLOW IT DOWN TILL YOU SEE THE STRANGE LIGHTS OF THE SPIRES...
SO WHAT'S THIS STUFF LIKE? IT SMELLS A BIT FUNNY, LIKE PERFUME OR SOMETHING.
I HAVEN'T HAD ANY PUFF FOR AGES, MAN.
SMOKE.
WATCH.
WAIT.

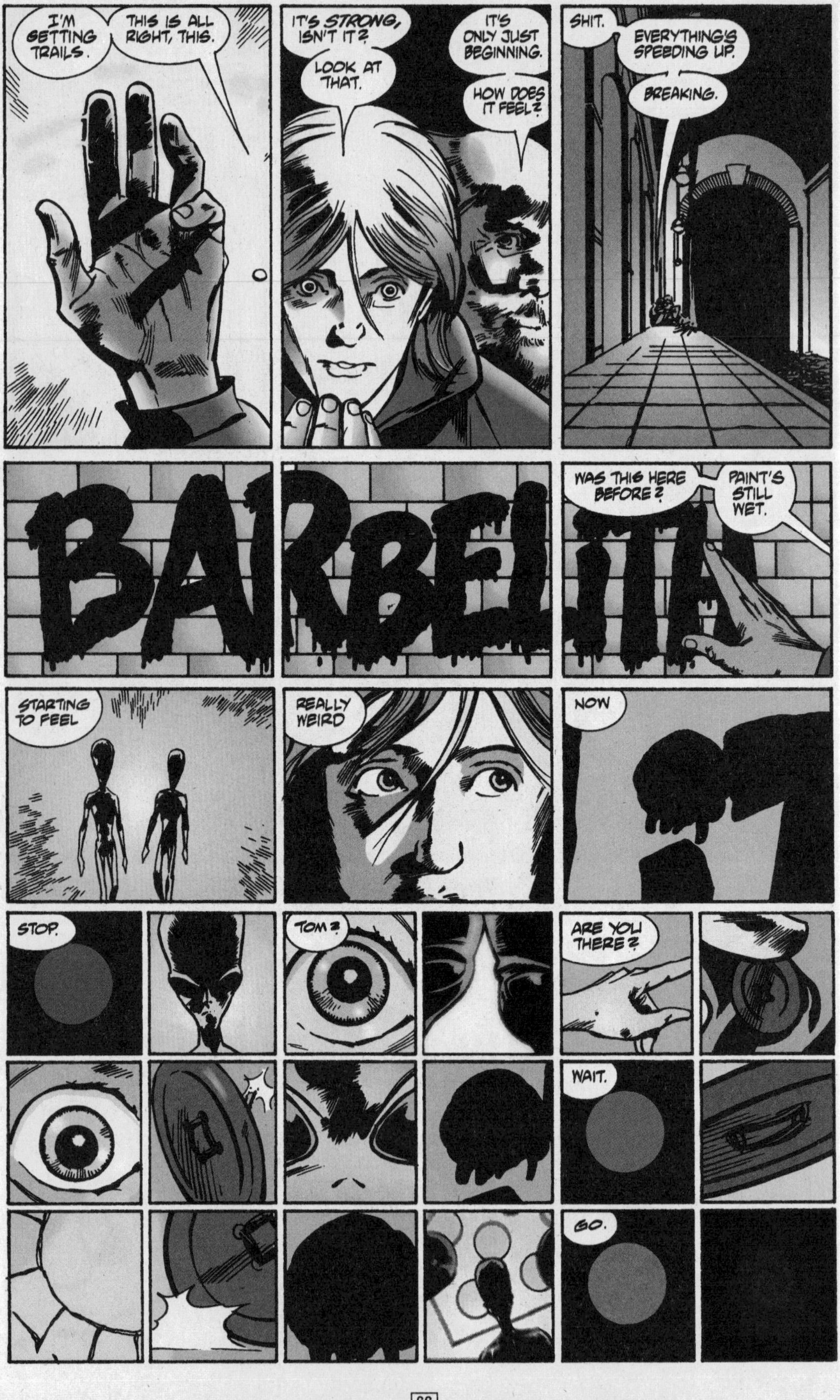
I'M GETTING TRAILS.
THIS IS ALL RIGHT, THIS.
IT'S STRONG, ISN'T IT?
LOOK AT THAT.
IT'S ONLY JUST BEGINNING.
HOW DOES IT FEEL?
SHIT.
EVERYTHING'S SPEEDING UP.
BREAKING.
BARBELITH
WAS THIS HERE BEFORE?
PAINT'S STILL WET.
STARTING TO FEEL
REALLY WEIRD
NOW
STOP.
TOM?
ARE YOU THERE?
WAIT.
GO.

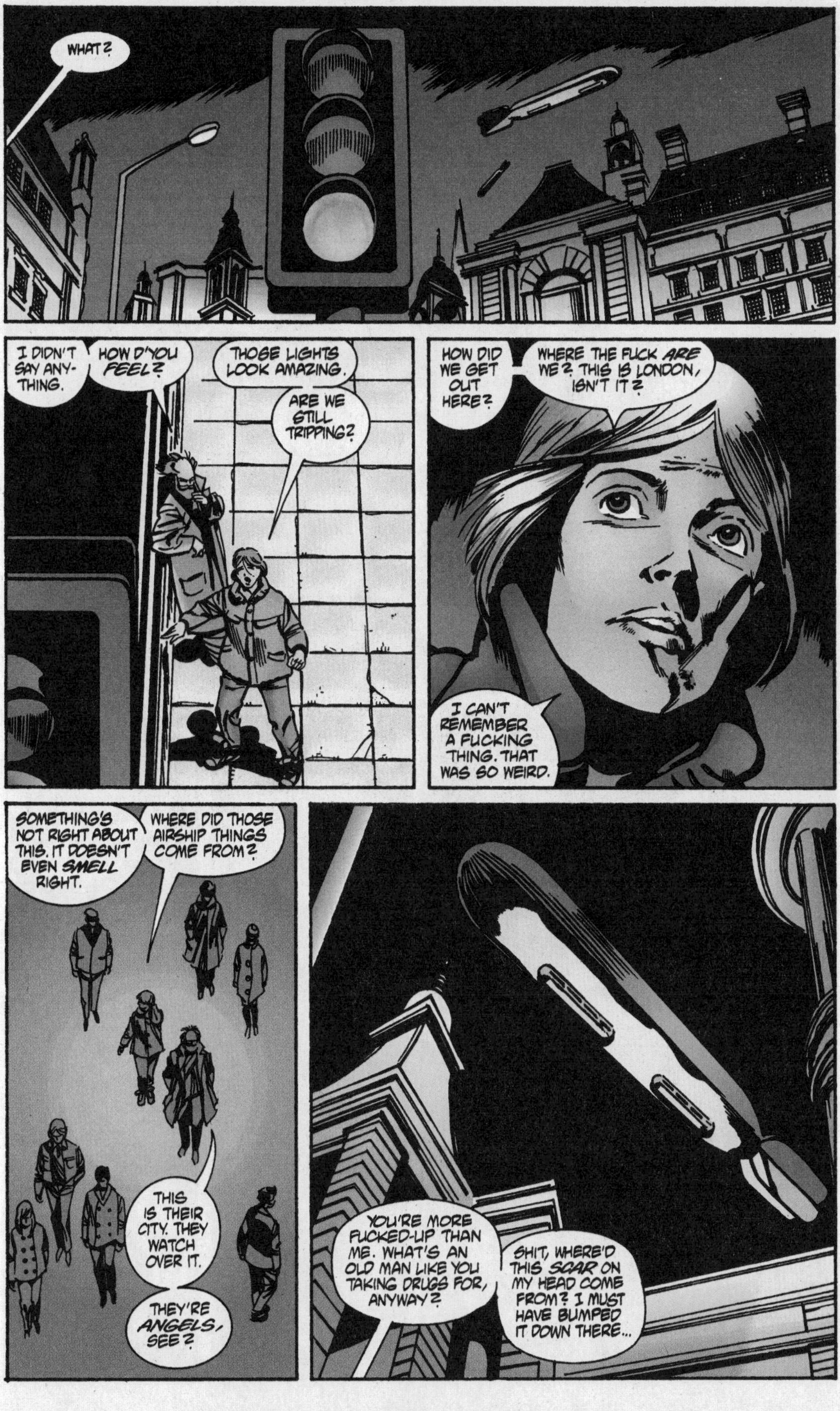
WHAT?
I DIDN'T SAY ANYTHING.
HOW D'YOU *FEEL*?
THOSE LIGHTS LOOK AMAZING.
ARE WE STILL TRIPPING?
HOW DID WE GET OUT HERE?
WHERE THE FUCK *ARE* WE? THIS IS LONDON, ISN'T IT?
I CAN'T REMEMBER A FUCKING THING. THAT WAS SO WEIRD.
SOMETHING'S NOT RIGHT ABOUT THIS. IT DOESN'T EVEN *SMELL* RIGHT.
WHERE DID THOSE AIRSHIP THINGS COME FROM?
THIS IS THEIR CITY. THEY WATCH OVER IT.
THEY'RE *ANGELS*, SEE?
YOU'RE MORE FUCKED-UP THAN ME. WHAT'S AN OLD MAN LIKE YOU TAKING DRUGS FOR, ANYWAY?
SHIT, WHERE'D THIS *SCAR* ON MY HEAD COME FROM? I MUST HAVE BUMPED IT DOWN THERE...

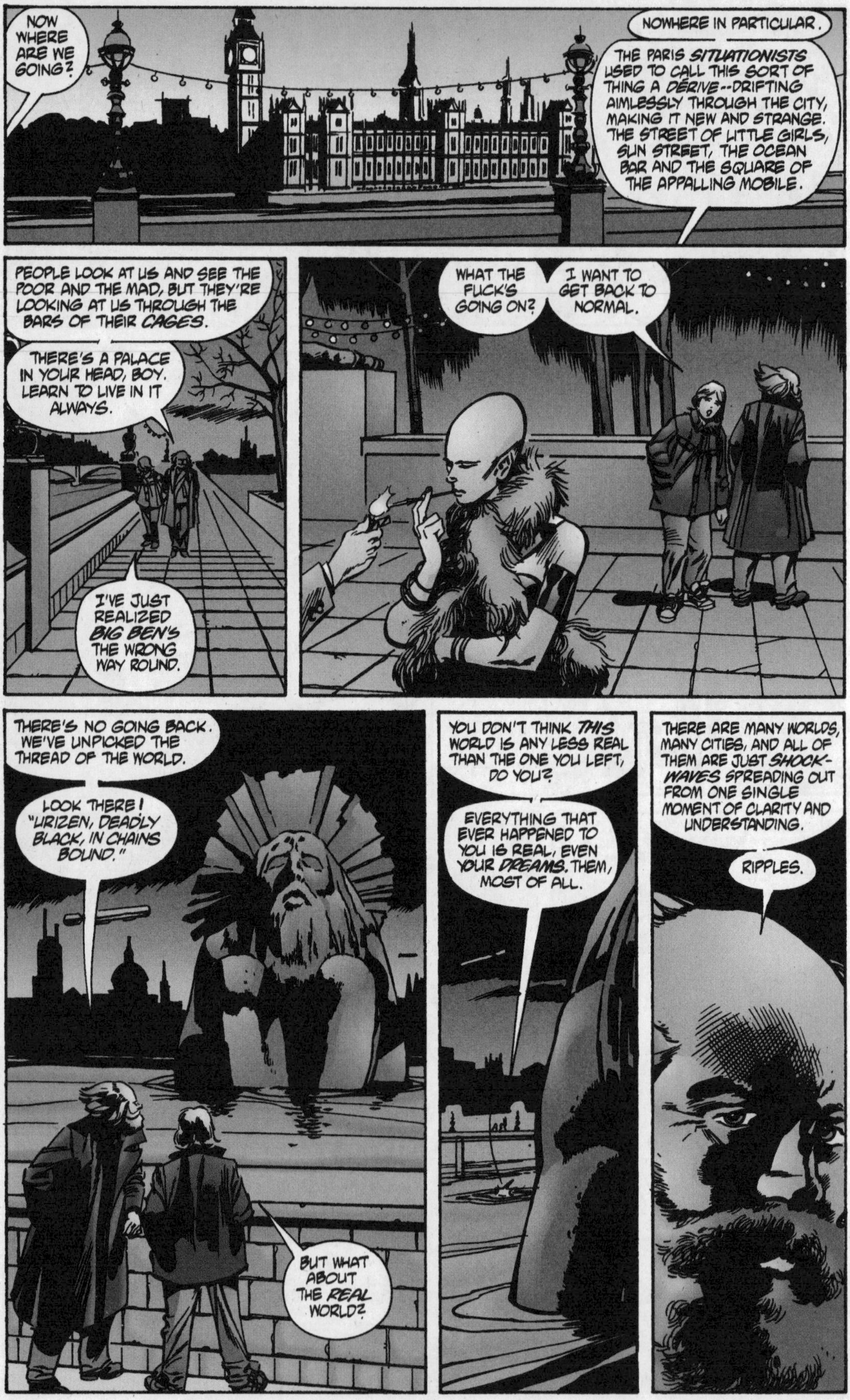
NOW WHERE ARE WE GOING?
NOWHERE IN PARTICULAR.
THE PARIS SITUATIONISTS USED TO CALL THIS SORT OF THING A DÉRIVE--DRIFTING AIMLESSLY THROUGH THE CITY, MAKING IT NEW AND STRANGE. THE STREET OF LITTLE GIRLS, SUN STREET, THE OCEAN BAR AND THE SQUARE OF THE APPALLING MOBILE.
PEOPLE LOOK AT US AND SEE THE POOR AND THE MAD, BUT THEY'RE LOOKING AT US THROUGH THE BARS OF THEIR CAGES.
THERE'S A PALACE IN YOUR HEAD, BOY. LEARN TO LIVE IN IT ALWAYS.
I'VE JUST REALIZED BIG BEN'S THE WRONG WAY ROUND.
WHAT THE FUCK'S GOING ON?
I WANT TO GET BACK TO NORMAL.
THERE'S NO GOING BACK. WE'VE UNPICKED THE THREAD OF THE WORLD.
LOOK THERE! "URIZEN, DEADLY BLACK, IN CHAINS BOUND."
BUT WHAT ABOUT THE REAL WORLD?
YOU DON'T THINK THIS WORLD IS ANY LESS REAL THAN THE ONE YOU LEFT, DO YOU?
EVERYTHING THAT EVER HAPPENED TO YOU IS REAL, EVEN YOUR DREAMS. THEM, MOST OF ALL.
THERE ARE MANY WORLDS, MANY CITIES, AND ALL OF THEM ARE JUST SHOCK-WAVES SPREADING OUT FROM ONE SINGLE MOMENT OF CLARITY AND UNDERSTANDING.
RIPPLES.

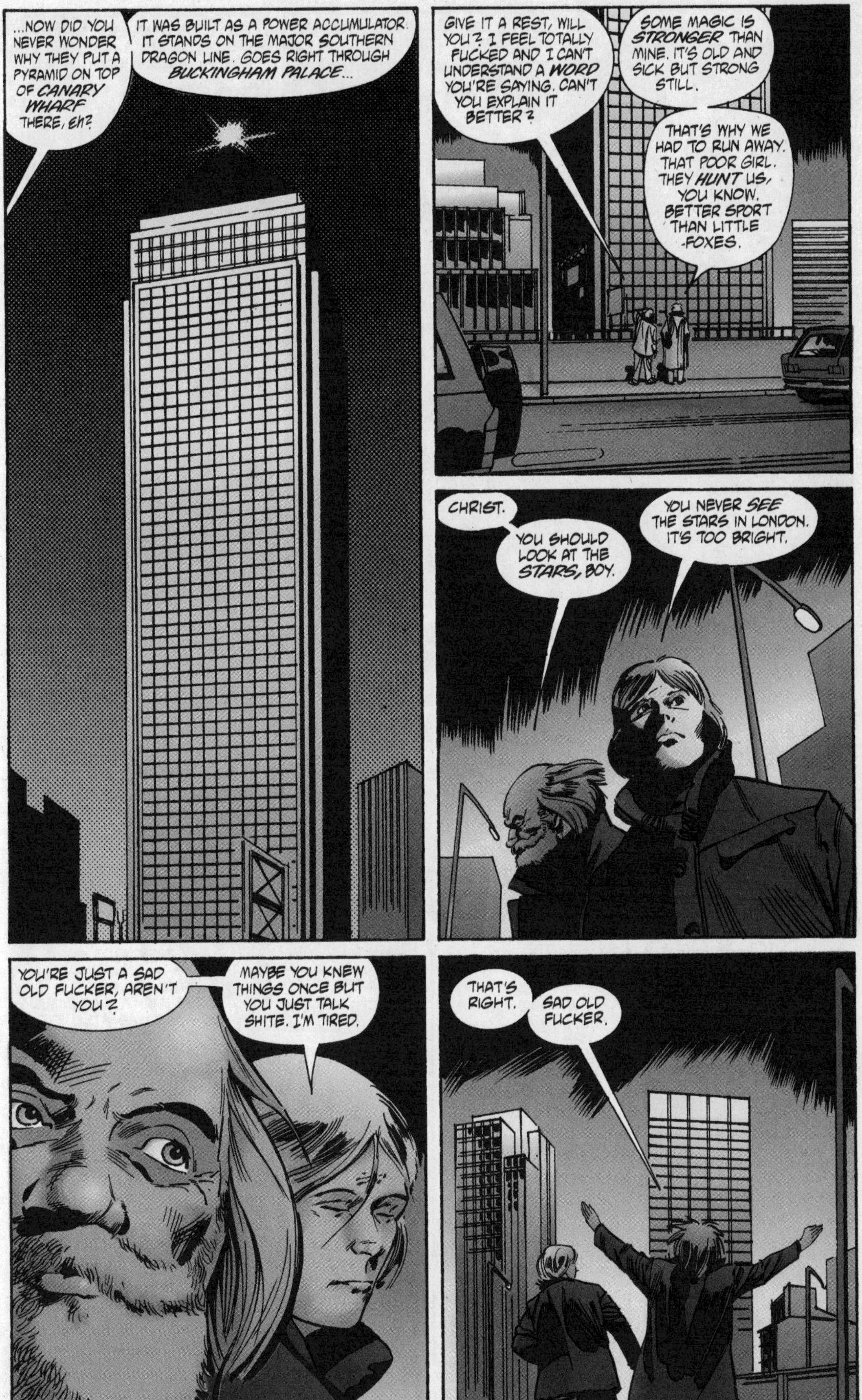
...NOW DID YOU NEVER WONDER WHY THEY PUT A PYRAMID ON TOP OF CANARY WHARF THERE, EH?
IT WAS BUILT AS A POWER ACCUMULATOR. IT STANDS ON THE MAJOR SOUTHERN DRAGON LINE. GOES RIGHT THROUGH BUCKINGHAM PALACE...
GIVE IT A REST, WILL YOU? I FEEL TOTALLY FUCKED AND I CAN'T UNDERSTAND A WORD YOU'RE SAYING. CAN'T YOU EXPLAIN IT BETTER?
SOME MAGIC IS STRONGER THAN MINE. IT'S OLD AND SICK BUT STRONG STILL.
THAT'S WHY WE HAD TO RUN AWAY. THAT POOR GIRL. THEY HUNT US, YOU KNOW. BETTER SPORT THAN LITTLE FOXES.
CHRIST.
YOU SHOULD LOOK AT THE STARS, BOY.
YOU NEVER SEE THE STARS IN LONDON. IT'S TOO BRIGHT.
YOU'RE JUST A SAD OLD FUCKER, AREN'T YOU?
MAYBE YOU KNEW THINGS ONCE BUT YOU JUST TALK SHITE. I'M TIRED.
THAT'S RIGHT.
SAD OLD FUCKER.

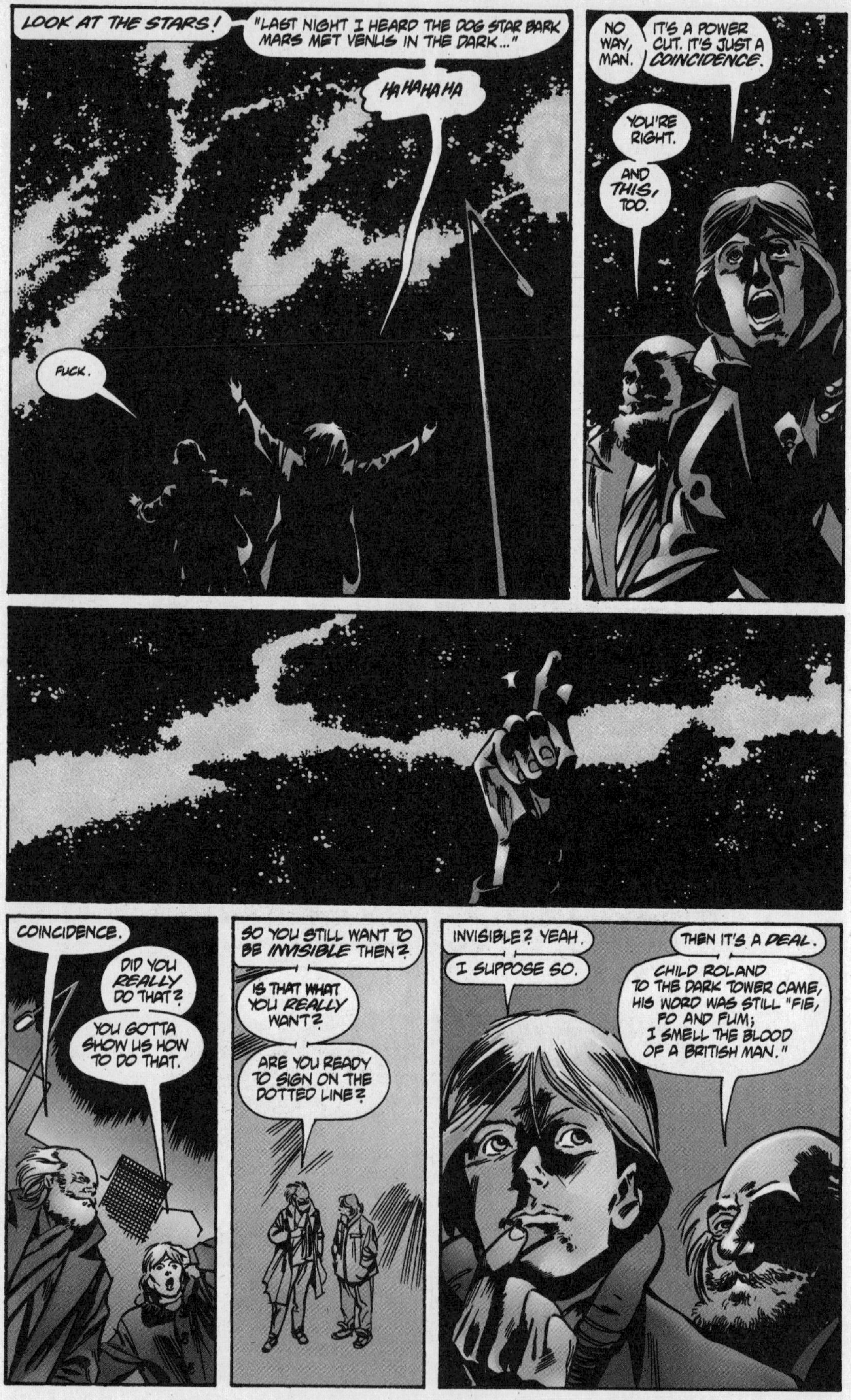
LOOK AT THE STARS!
"LAST NIGHT I HEARD THE DOG STAR BARK MARS MET VENUS IN THE DARK..."
HA HA HA HA HA
FUCK.
NO WAY, MAN.
IT'S A POWER CUT. IT'S JUST A COINCIDENCE.
YOU'RE RIGHT.
AND THIS, TOO.
COINCIDENCE.
DID YOU REALLY DO THAT?
YOU GOTTA SHOW US HOW TO DO THAT.
SO YOU STILL WANT TO BE INVISIBLE THEN?
IS THAT WHAT YOU REALLY WANT?
ARE YOU READY TO SIGN ON THE DOTTED LINE?
INVISIBLE? YEAH.
I SUPPOSE SO.
THEN IT'S A DEAL.
CHILD ROLAND TO THE DARK TOWER CAME, HIS WORD WAS STILL "FIE, FO AND FUM; I SMELL THE BLOOD OF A BRITISH MAN."

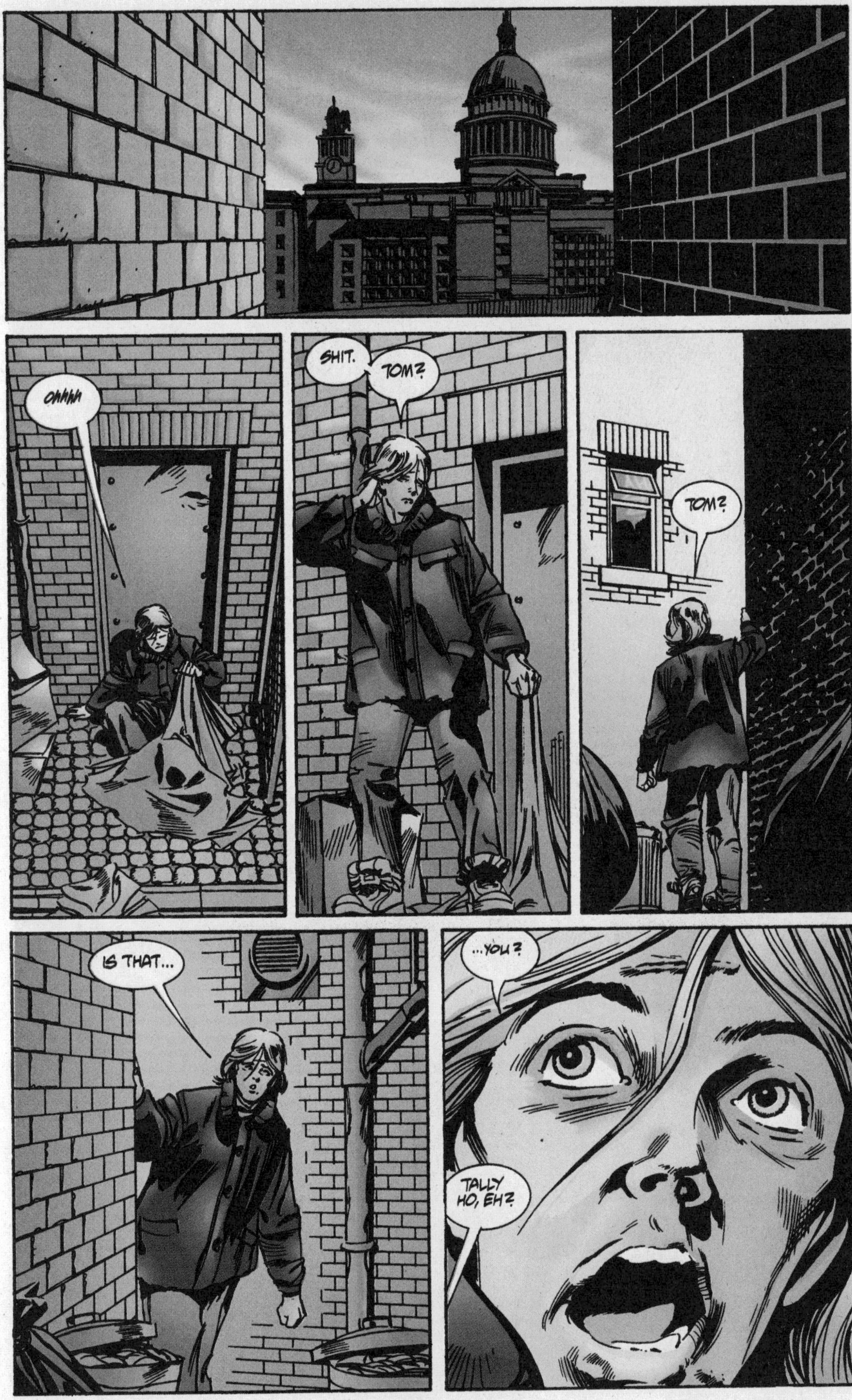
OHHHH
SHIT.
TOM?
TOM?
IS THAT...
...YOU?
TALLY HO, EH?

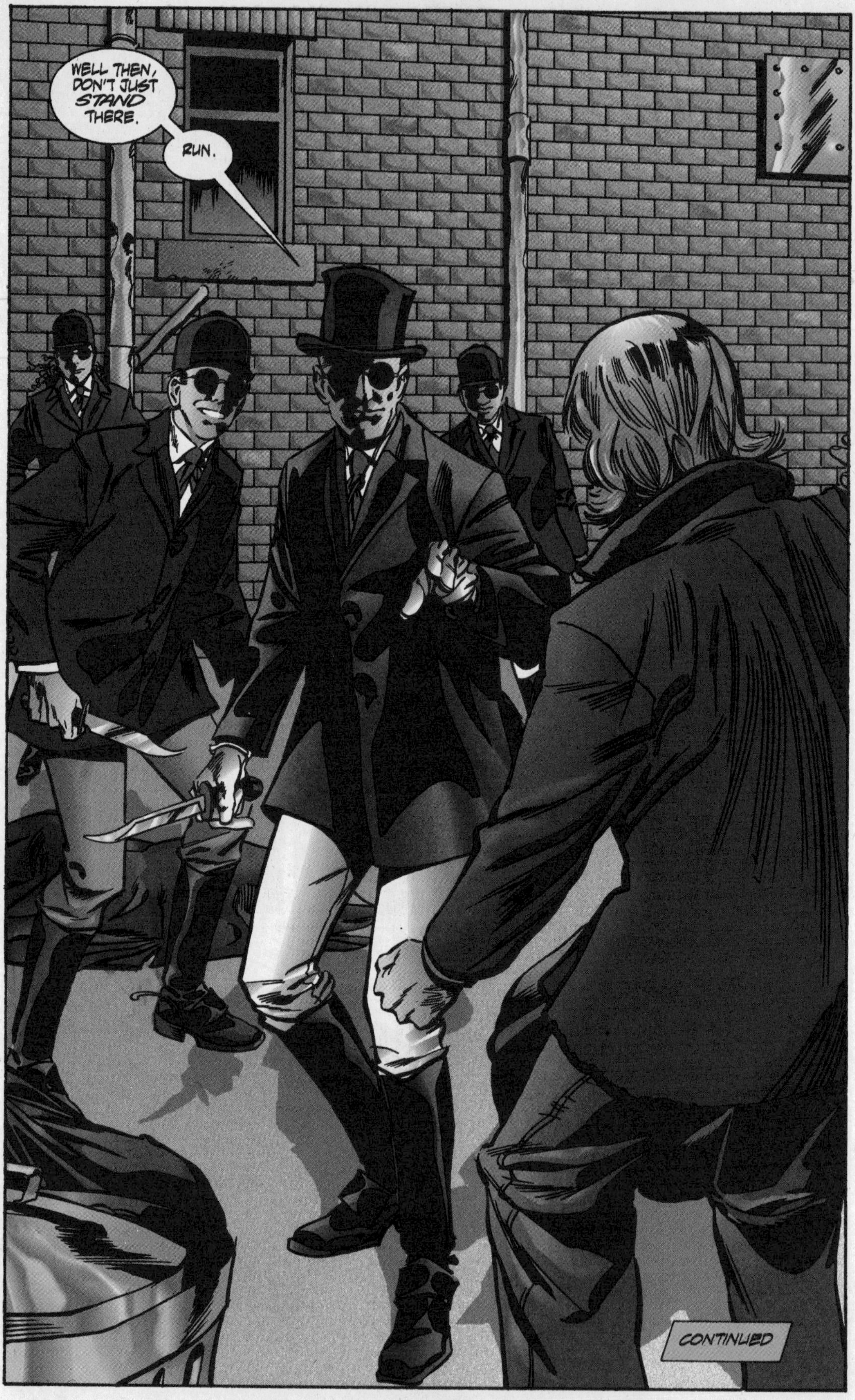
WELL THEN, DON'T JUST STAND THERE.
RUN.
CONTINUED

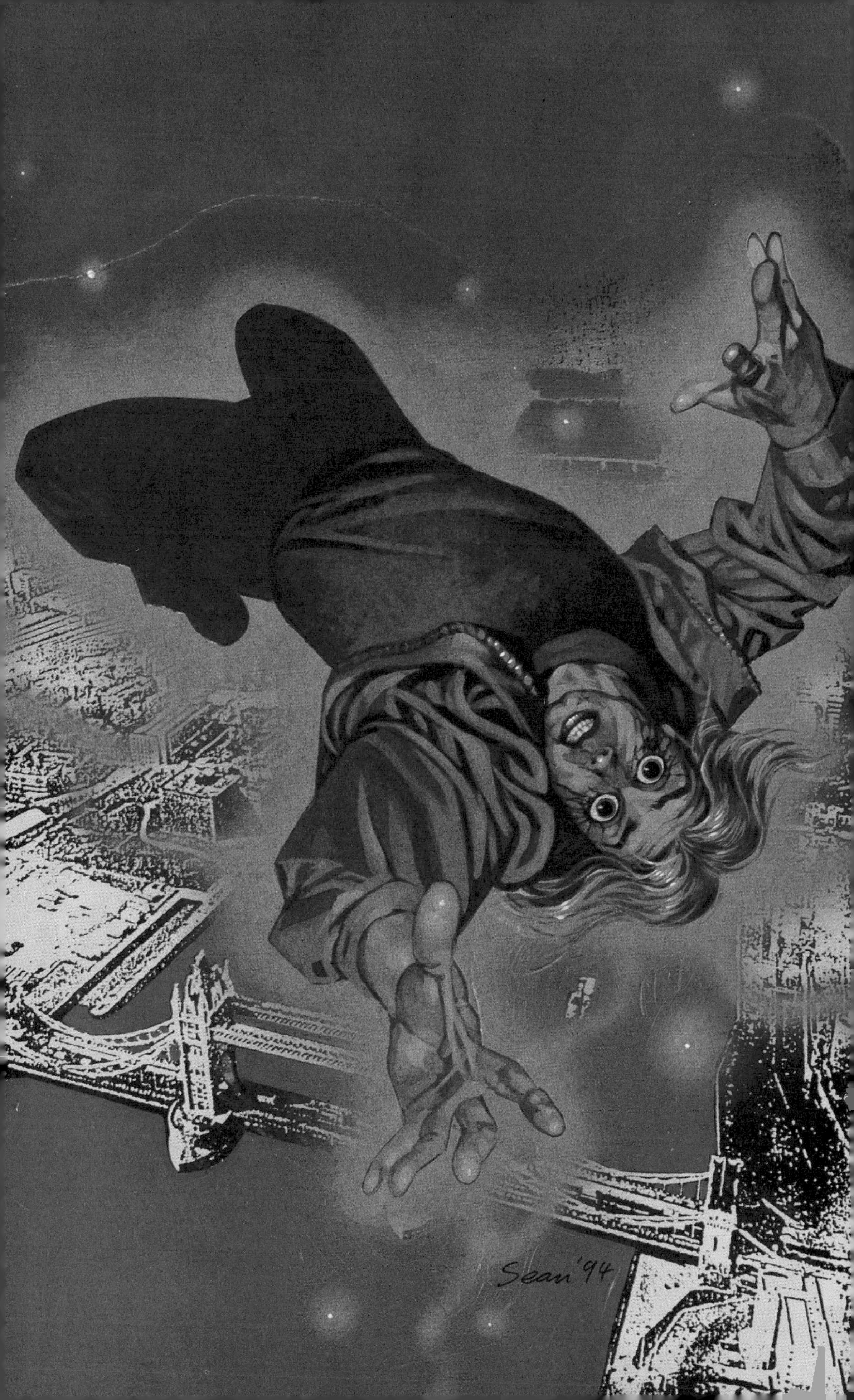
Sean '94

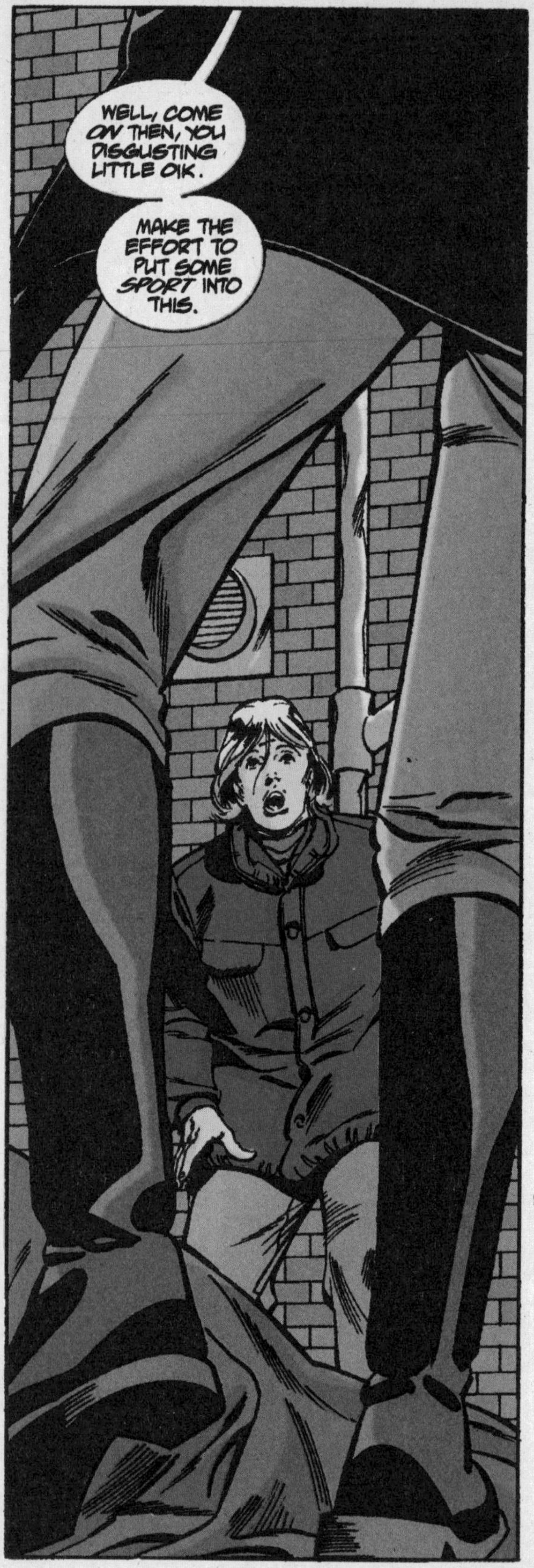
WELL, COME ON THEN, YOU DISGUSTING LITTLE OIK.
MAKE THE EFFORT TO PUT SOME SPORT INTO THIS.

DOWN AND OUT IN HEAVEN AND HELL

PART 2

GRANT MORRISON → WRITER
STEVE YEOWELL → ARTIST
DANIEL VOZZO → COLORS
ELECTRIC CRAYON → COLOR SEPARATIONS
CLEM ROBINS → LETTERS
JULIE ROTTENBERG → ASST. EDITOR
STUART MOORE → EDITOR

THE INVISIBLES CREATED BY
GRANT MORRISON

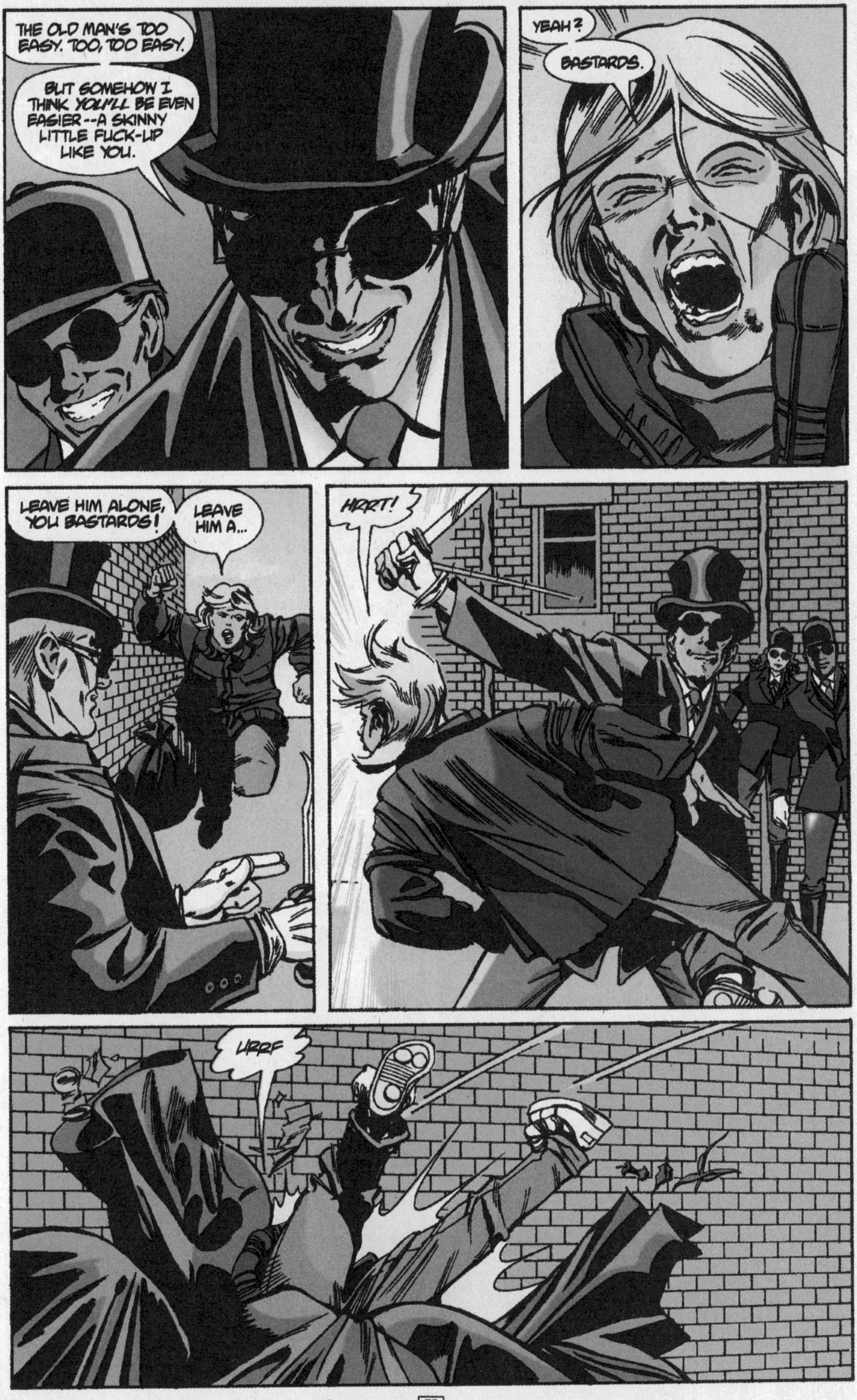
THE OLD MAN'S TOO EASY. TOO, TOO EASY.
BUT SOMEHOW I THINK YOU'LL BE EVEN EASIER--A SKINNY LITTLE FUCK-UP LIKE YOU.
YEAH?
BASTARDS.
LEAVE HIM ALONE, YOU BASTARDS!
LEAVE HIM A...
HRRT!
URRF

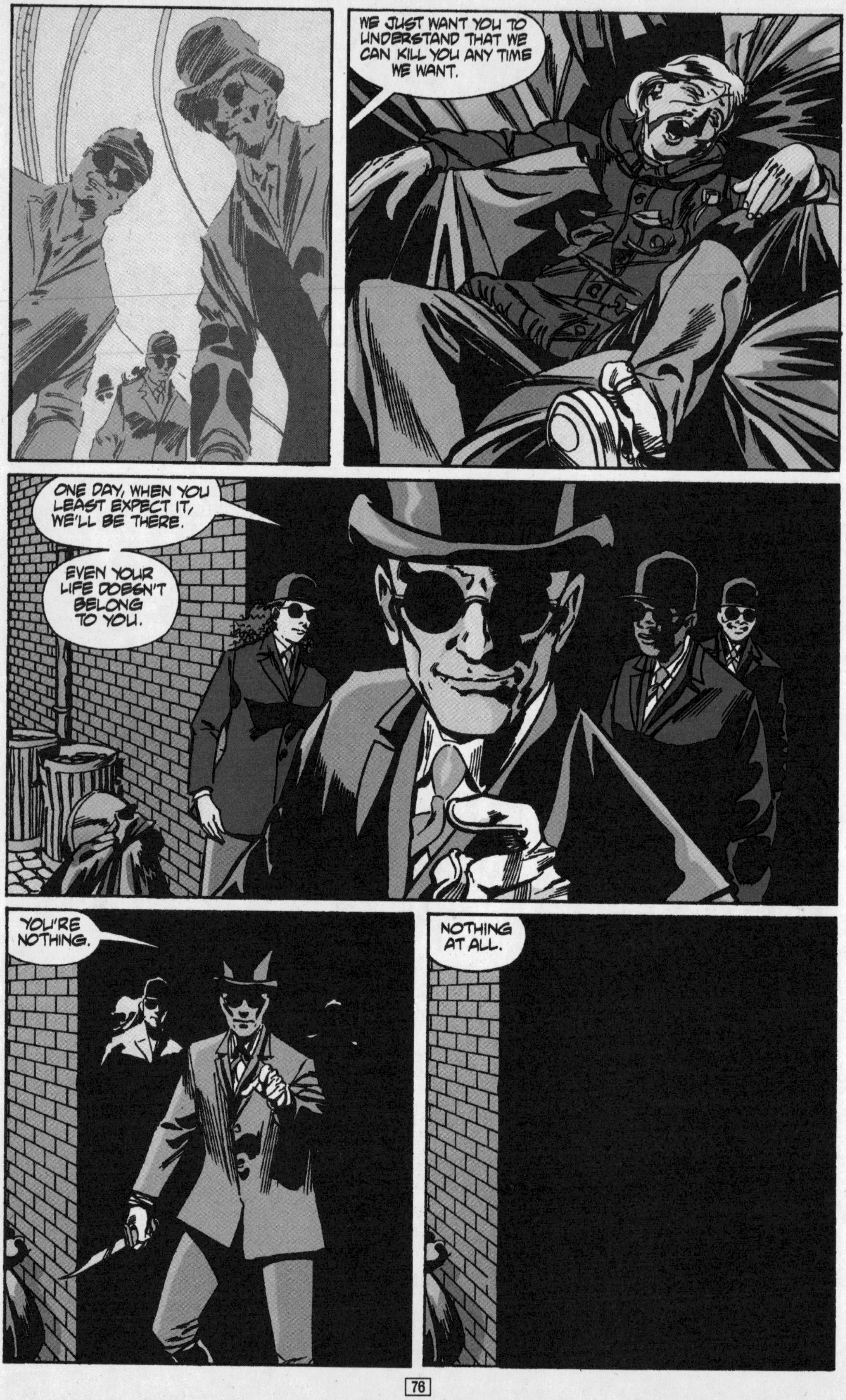
WE JUST WANT YOU TO UNDERSTAND THAT WE CAN KILL YOU ANY TIME WE WANT.
ONE DAY, WHEN YOU LEAST EXPECT IT, WE'LL BE THERE.
EVEN YOUR LIFE DOESN'T BELONG TO YOU.
YOU'RE NOTHING.
NOTHING AT ALL.

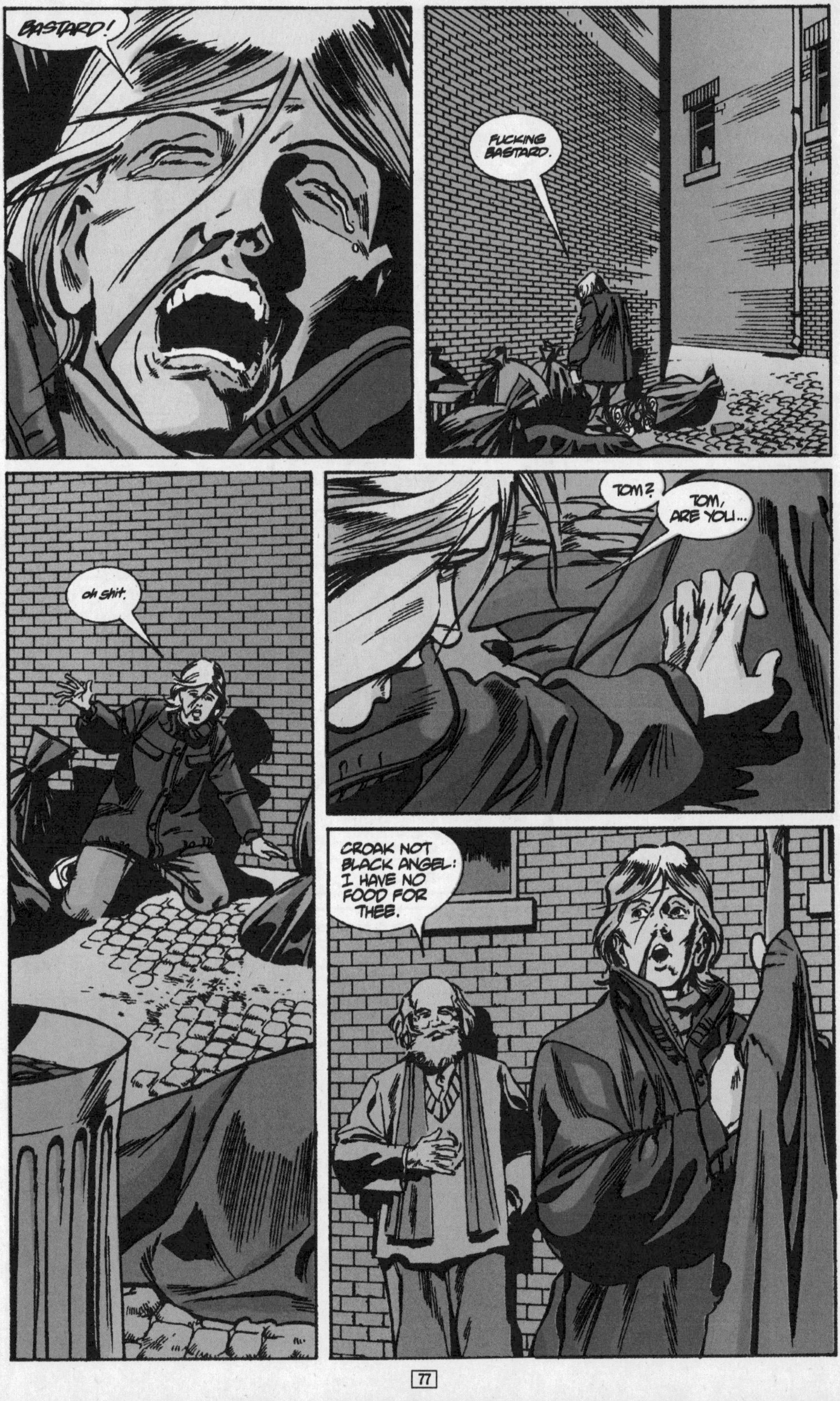
BASTARD!
FUCKING BASTARD.
oh shit.
TOM?
TOM, ARE YOU...
CROAK NOT BLACK ANGEL: I HAVE NO FOOD FOR THEE.

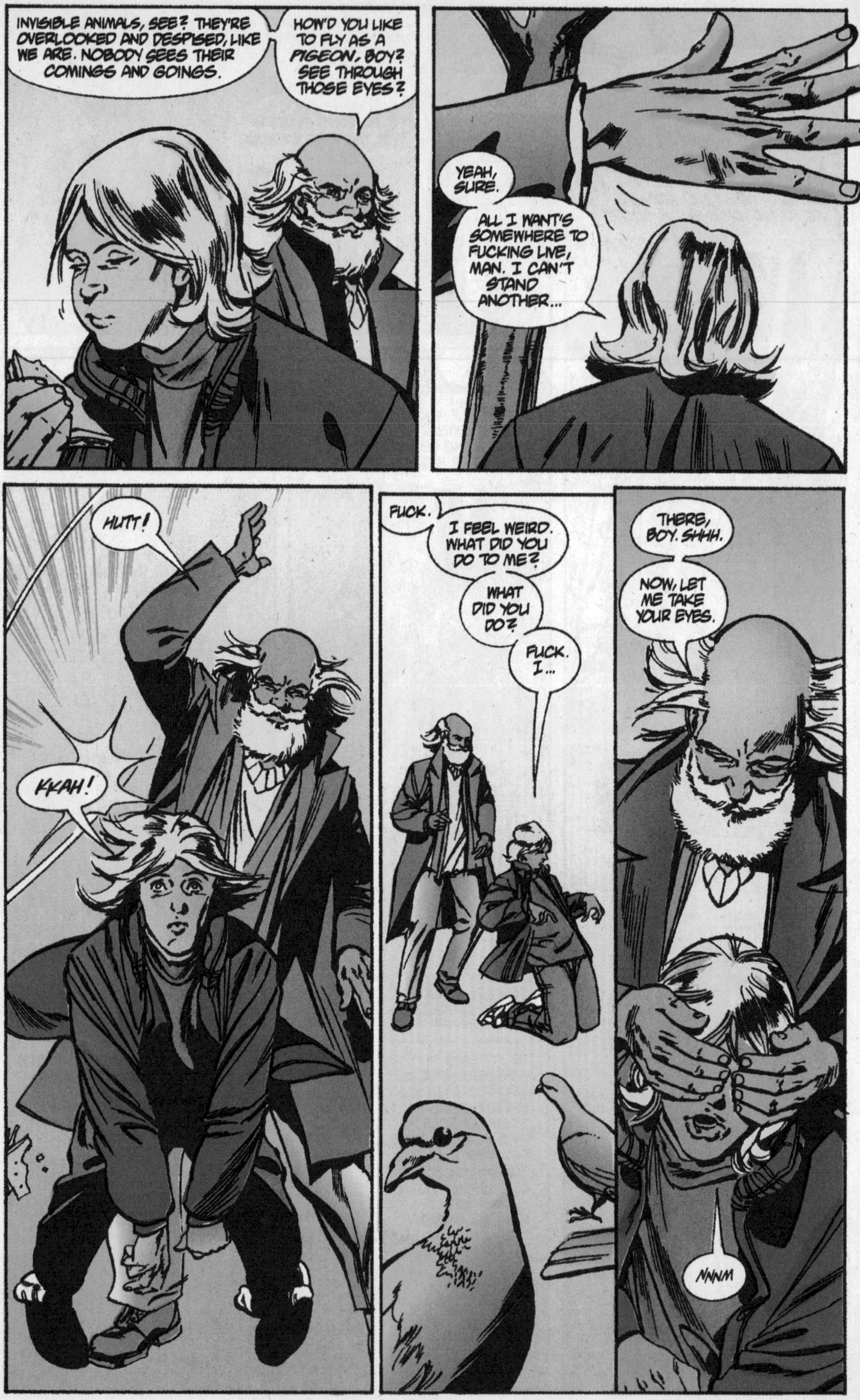

INVISIBLE ANIMALS, SEE? THEY'RE OVERLOOKED AND DESPISED, LIKE WE ARE. NOBODY SEES THEIR COMINGS AND GOINGS.
HOW'D YOU LIKE TO FLY AS A PIGEON, BOY? SEE THROUGH THOSE EYES?
YEAH, SURE.
ALL I WANT'S SOMEWHERE TO FUCKING LIVE, MAN. I CAN'T STAND ANOTHER...
HUTT!
KKAH!
FUCK.
I FEEL WEIRD. WHAT DID YOU DO TO ME?
WHAT DID YOU DO?
FUCK. I...
THERE, BOY. SHHH.
NOW, LET ME TAKE YOUR EYES.
NNNM

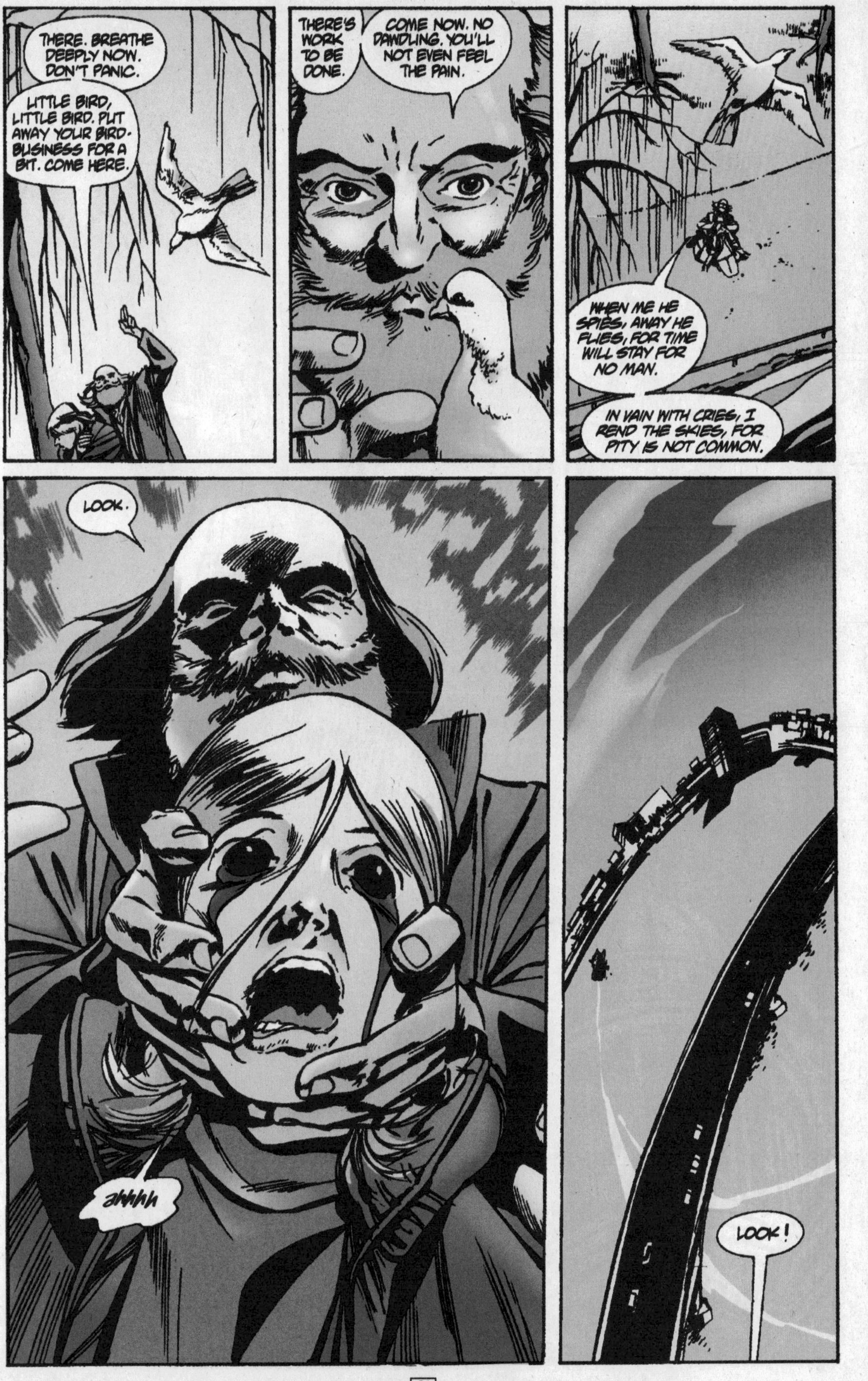

THERE. BREATHE DEEPLY NOW. DON'T PANIC.
LITTLE BIRD, LITTLE BIRD. PUT AWAY YOUR BIRD-BUSINESS FOR A BIT. COME HERE.
THERE'S WORK TO BE DONE.
COME NOW. NO DANDLING. YOU'LL NOT EVEN FEEL THE PAIN.
WHEN ME HE SPIES, AWAY HE FLIES, FOR TIME WILL STAY FOR NO MAN.
IN VAIN WITH CRIES, I REND THE SKIES, FOR PITY IS NOT COMMON.
LOOK.
ahhhh
LOOK!

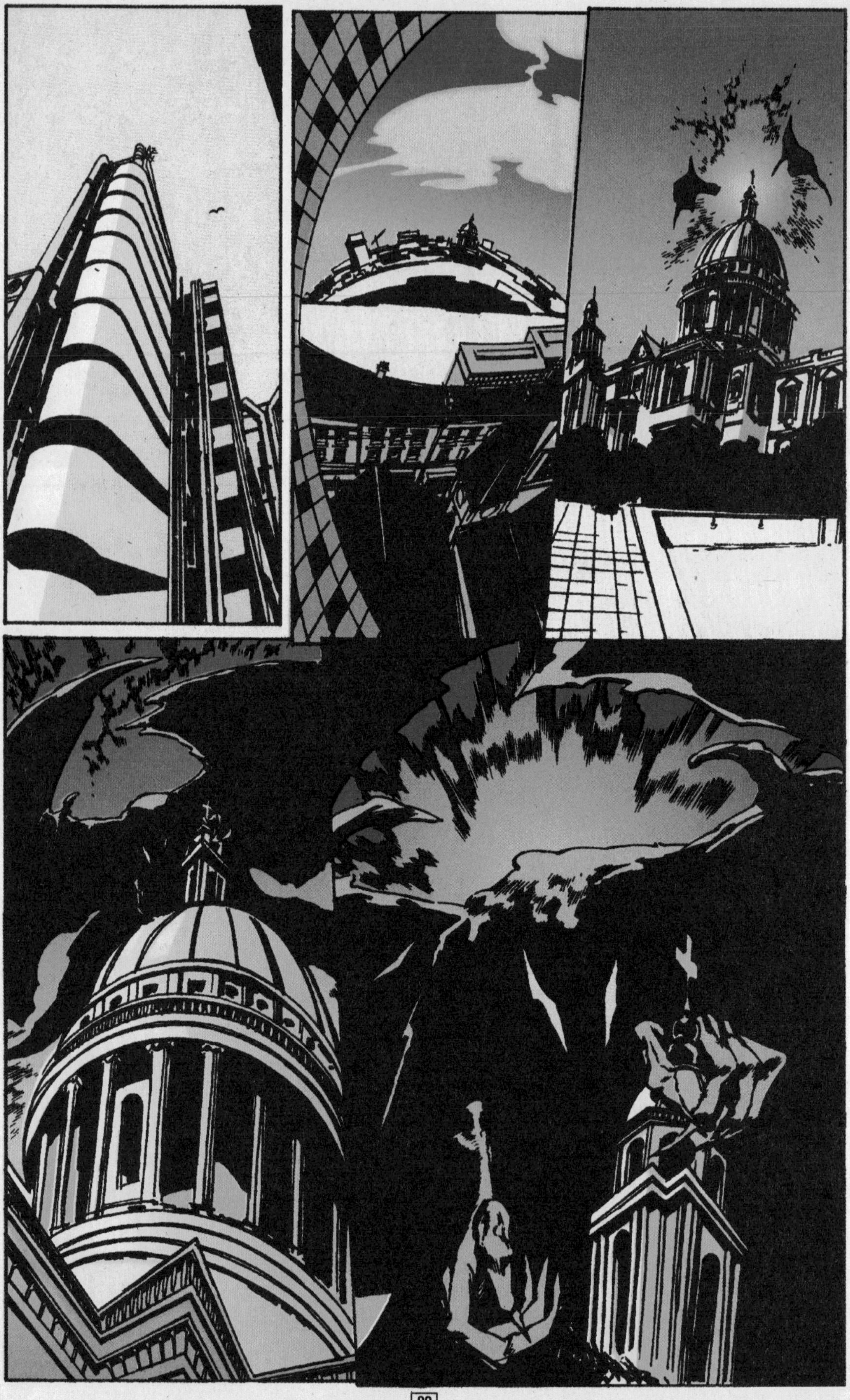

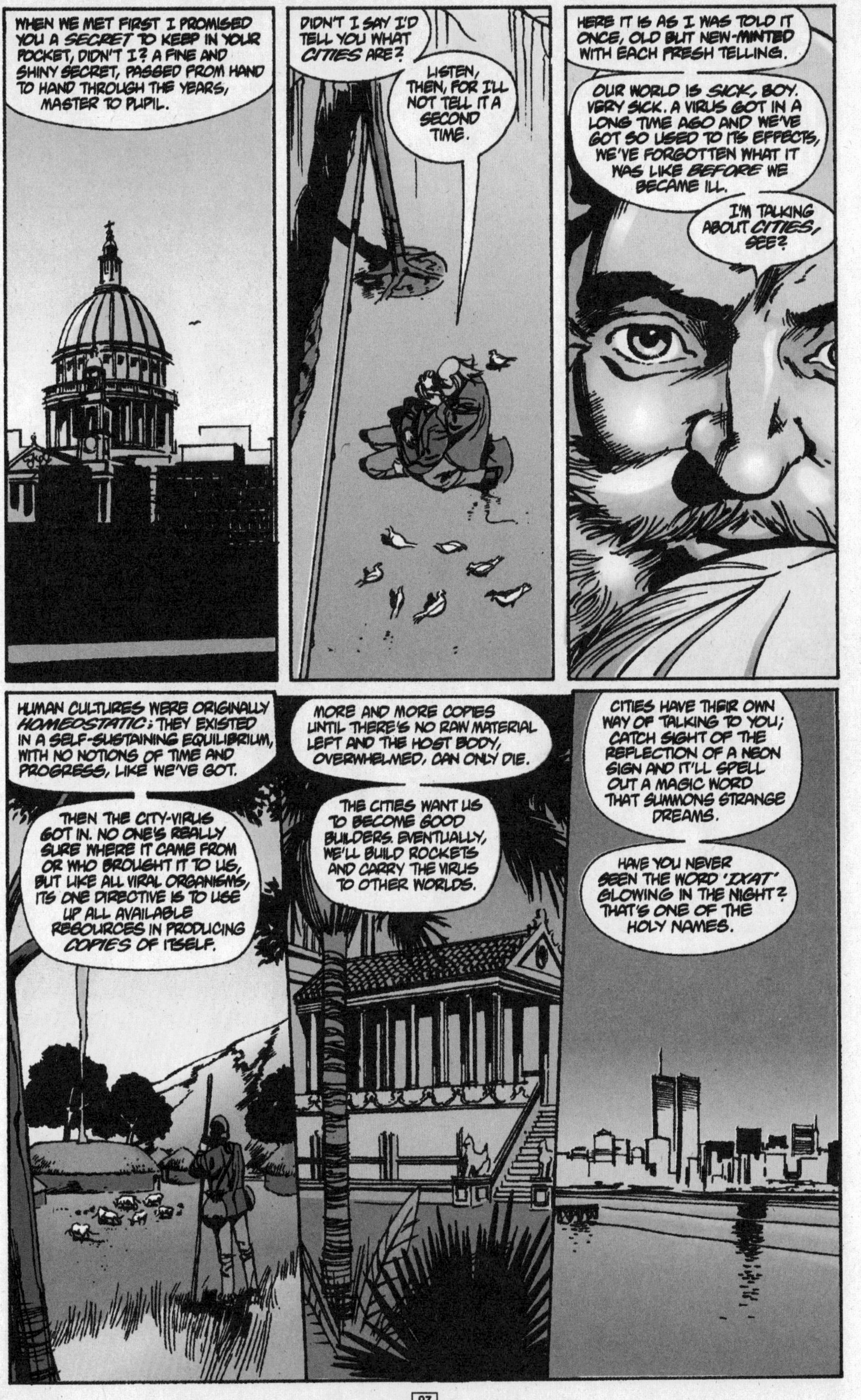
WHEN WE MET FIRST I PROMISED YOU A *SECRET* TO KEEP IN YOUR POCKET, DIDN'T I? A FINE AND SHINY SECRET, PASSED FROM HAND TO HAND THROUGH THE YEARS, MASTER TO PUPIL.
DIDN'T I SAY I'D TELL YOU WHAT *CITIES* ARE?
LISTEN, THEN, FOR I'LL NOT TELL IT A SECOND TIME.
HERE IT IS AS I WAS TOLD IT ONCE, OLD BUT NEW-*MINTED* WITH EACH FRESH TELLING.
OUR WORLD IS *SICK*, BOY. VERY SICK. A VIRUS GOT IN A LONG TIME AGO AND WE'VE GOT SO USED TO ITS EFFECTS, WE'VE FORGOTTEN WHAT IT WAS LIKE *BEFORE* WE BECAME ILL.
I'M TALKING ABOUT *CITIES*, SEE?
HUMAN CULTURES WERE ORIGINALLY *HOMEOSTATIC*; THEY EXISTED IN A SELF-SUSTAINING EQUILIBRIUM, WITH NO NOTIONS OF TIME AND PROGRESS, LIKE WE'VE GOT.
THEN THE CITY-VIRUS GOT IN. NO ONE'S REALLY SURE WHERE IT CAME FROM OR WHO BROUGHT IT TO US, BUT LIKE ALL VIRAL ORGANISMS, ITS ONE DIRECTIVE IS TO USE UP ALL AVAILABLE RESOURCES IN PRODUCING *COPIES* OF ITSELF.
MORE AND MORE COPIES UNTIL THERE'S NO RAW MATERIAL LEFT AND THE HOST BODY, OVERWHELMED, CAN ONLY DIE.
THE CITIES WANT US TO BECOME GOOD BUILDERS. EVENTUALLY, WE'LL BUILD ROCKETS AND CARRY THE VIRUS TO OTHER WORLDS.
CITIES HAVE THEIR OWN WAY OF TALKING TO YOU; CATCH SIGHT OF THE REFLECTION OF A NEON SIGN AND IT'LL SPELL OUT A MAGIC WORD THAT SUMMONS STRANGE DREAMS.
HAVE YOU NEVER SEEN THE WORD '*IXAT*' GLOWING IN THE NIGHT? THAT'S ONE OF THE HOLY NAMES.

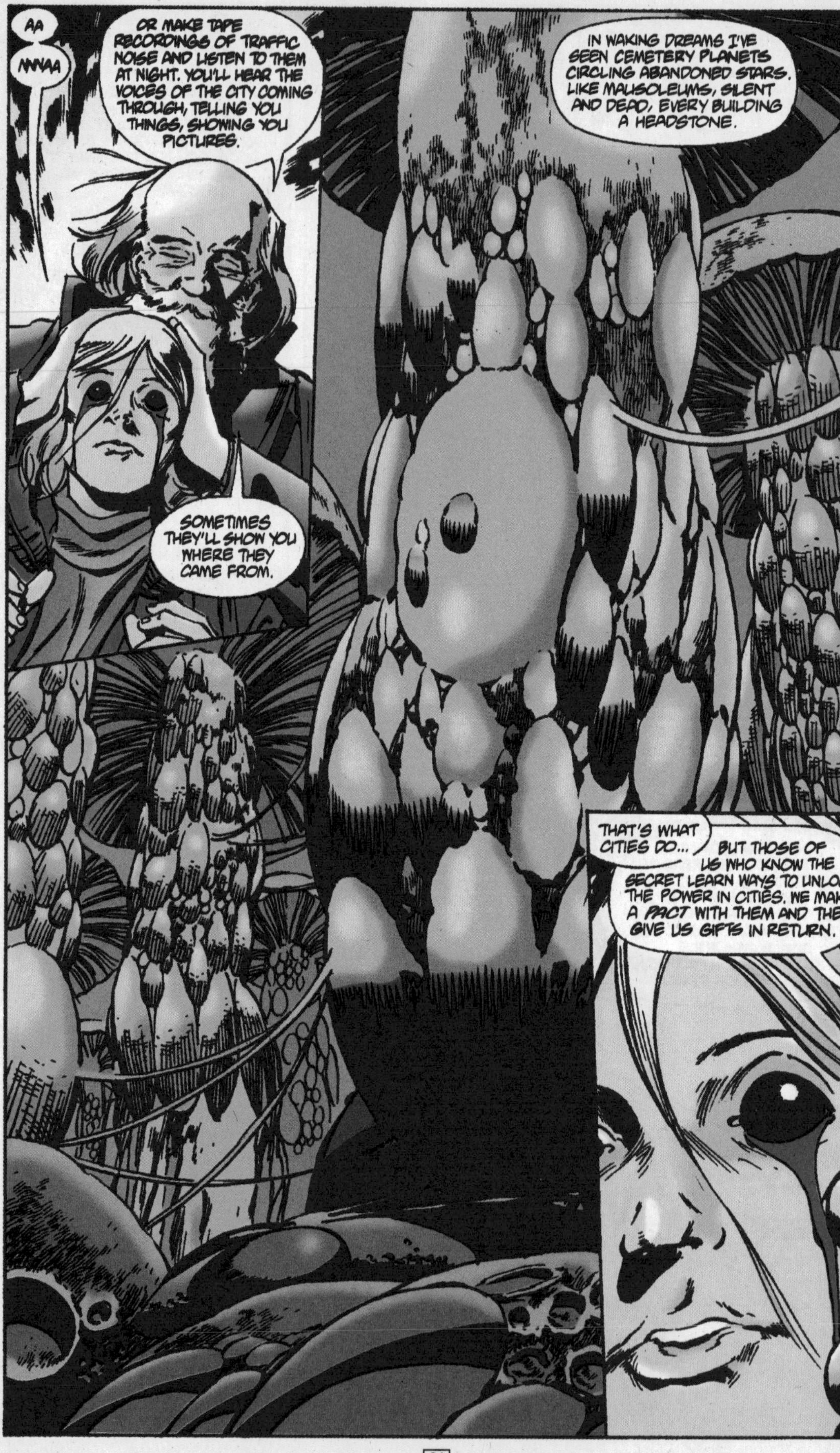
AA
NNNAA
OR MAKE TAPE RECORDINGS OF TRAFFIC NOISE AND LISTEN TO THEM AT NIGHT. YOU'LL HEAR THE VOICES OF THE CITY COMING THROUGH, TELLING YOU THINGS, SHOWING YOU PICTURES.
SOMETIMES THEY'LL SHOW YOU WHERE THEY CAME FROM.
IN WAKING DREAMS I'VE SEEN CEMETERY PLANETS CIRCLING ABANDONED STARS. LIKE MAUSOLEUMS, SILENT AND DEAD, EVERY BUILDING A HEADSTONE.
THAT'S WHAT CITIES DO...
BUT THOSE OF US WHO KNOW THE SECRET LEARN WAYS TO UNLOCK THE POWER IN CITIES. WE MAKE A *PACT* WITH THEM AND THEY GIVE US GIFTS IN RETURN.

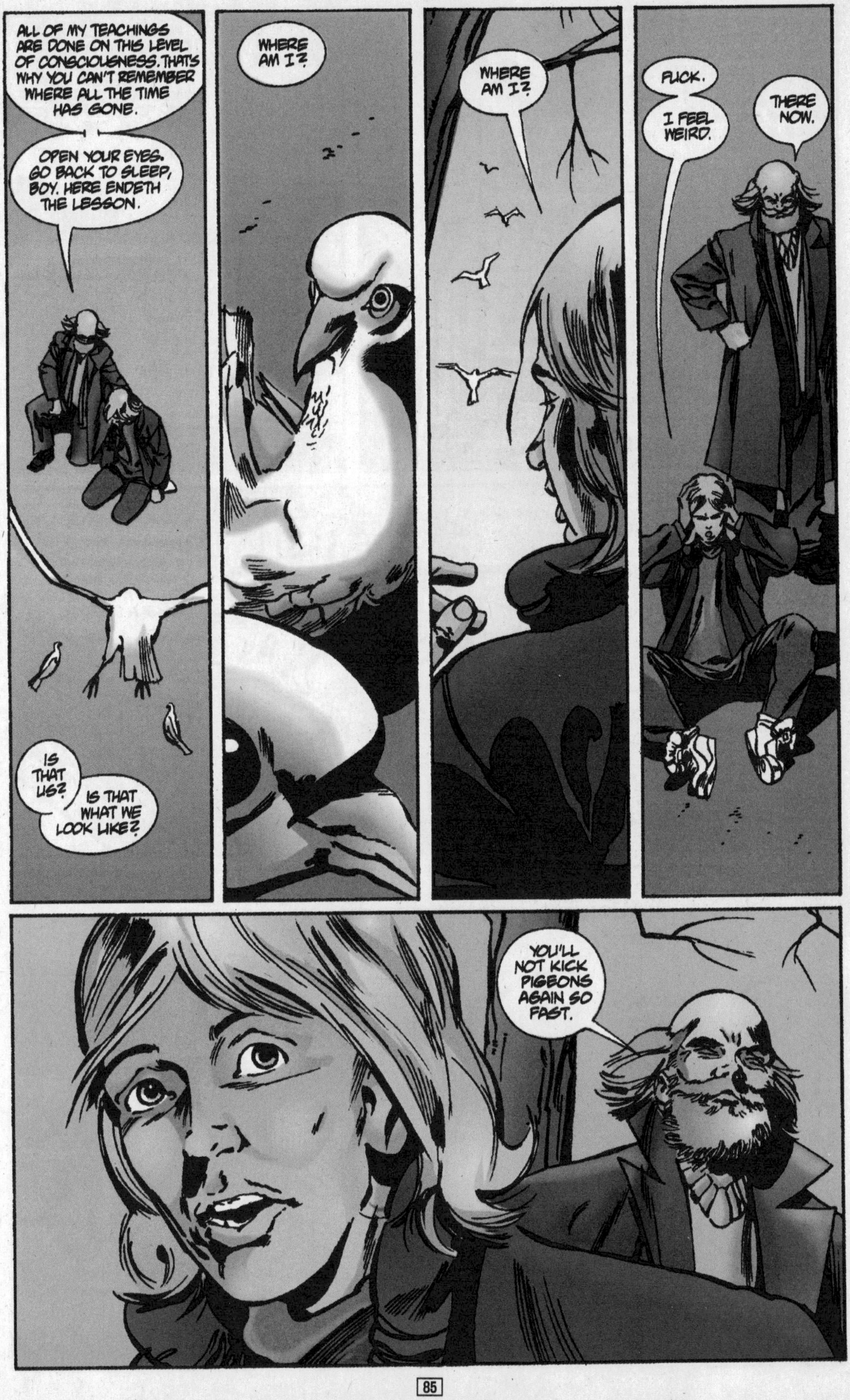
ALL OF MY TEACHINGS ARE DONE ON THIS LEVEL OF CONSCIOUSNESS. THAT'S WHY YOU CAN'T REMEMBER WHERE ALL THE TIME HAS GONE.
OPEN YOUR EYES. GO BACK TO SLEEP, BOY. HERE ENDETH THE LESSON.
IS THAT US?
IS THAT WHAT WE LOOK LIKE?
WHERE AM I?
WHERE AM I?
FUCK.
I FEEL WEIRD.
THERE NOW.
YOU'LL NOT KICK PIGEONS AGAIN SO FAST.

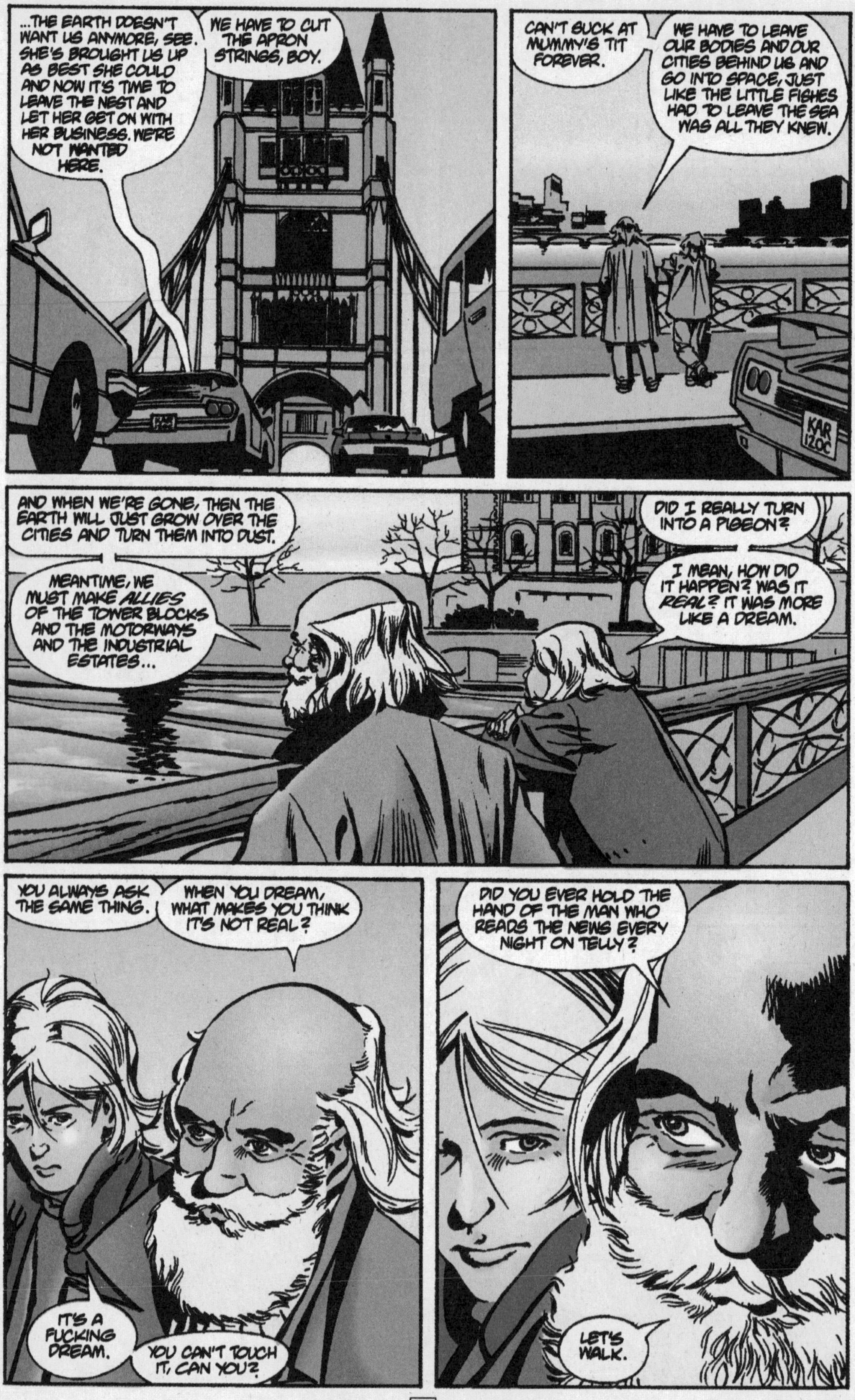
...THE EARTH DOESN'T WANT US ANYMORE, SEE. SHE'S BROUGHT US UP AS BEST SHE COULD AND NOW IT'S TIME TO LEAVE THE NEST AND LET HER GET ON WITH HER BUSINESS. WE'RE NOT WANTED HERE.
WE HAVE TO CUT THE APRON STRINGS, BOY.
CAN'T SUCK AT MUMMY'S TIT FOREVER.
WE HAVE TO LEAVE OUR BODIES AND OUR CITIES BEHIND US AND GO INTO SPACE, JUST LIKE THE LITTLE FISHES HAD TO LEAVE THE SEA WAS ALL THEY KNEW.
KAR 120C
AND WHEN WE'RE GONE, THEN THE EARTH WILL JUST GROW OVER THE CITIES AND TURN THEM INTO DUST.
MEANTIME, WE MUST MAKE ALLIES OF THE TOWER BLOCKS AND THE MOTORWAYS AND THE INDUSTRIAL ESTATES...
DID I REALLY TURN INTO A PIGEON?
I MEAN, HOW DID IT HAPPEN? WAS IT REAL? IT WAS MORE LIKE A DREAM.
YOU ALWAYS ASK THE SAME THING.
WHEN YOU DREAM, WHAT MAKES YOU THINK IT'S NOT REAL?
IT'S A FUCKING DREAM.
YOU CAN'T TOUCH IT, CAN YOU?
DID YOU EVER HOLD THE HAND OF THE MAN WHO READS THE NEWS EVERY NIGHT ON TELLY?
LET'S WALK.

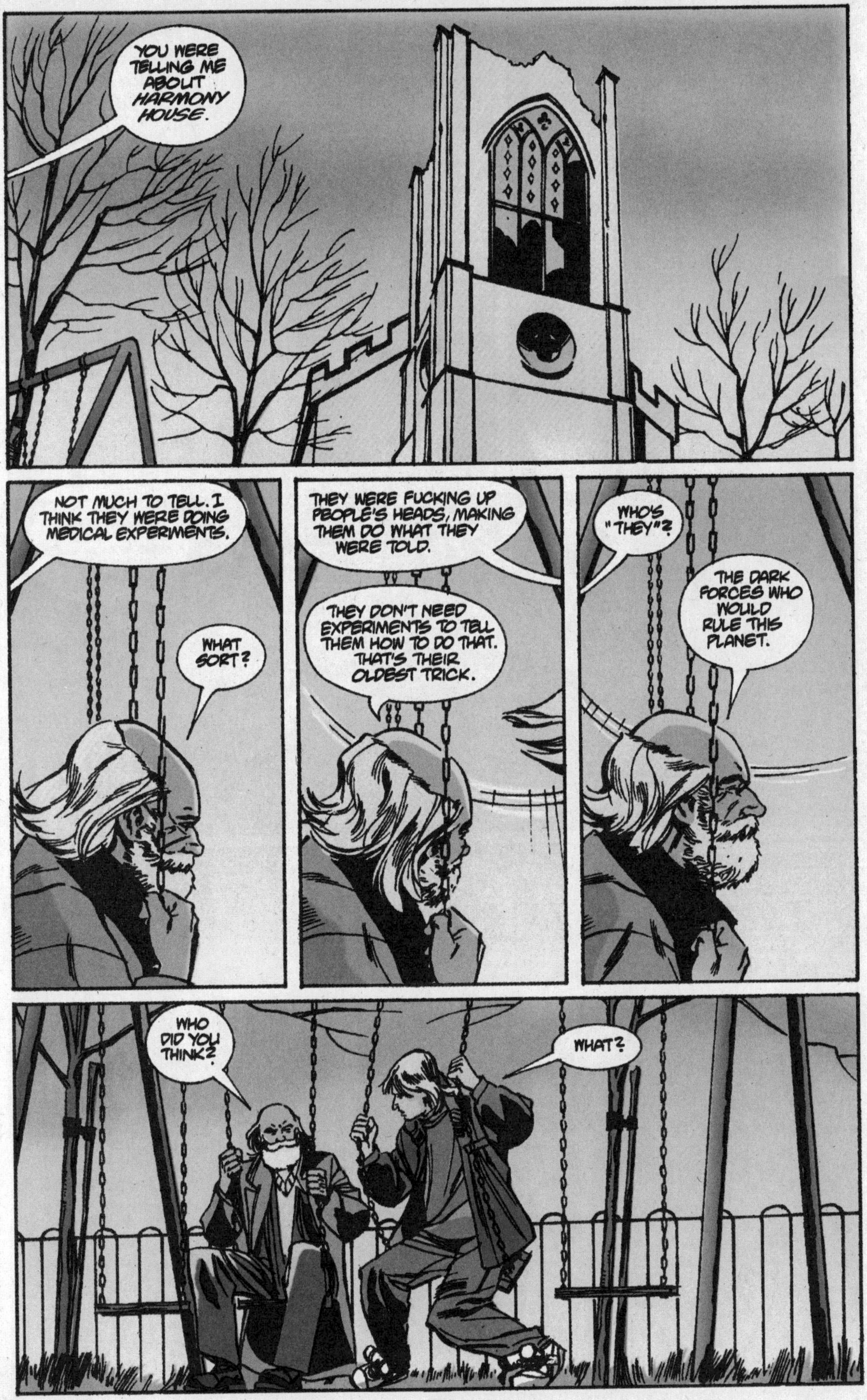
YOU WERE TELLING ME ABOUT HARMONY HOUSE.
NOT MUCH TO TELL. I THINK THEY WERE DOING MEDICAL EXPERIMENTS.
WHAT SORT?
THEY WERE FUCKING UP PEOPLE'S HEADS, MAKING THEM DO WHAT THEY WERE TOLD.
THEY DON'T NEED EXPERIMENTS TO TELL THEM HOW TO DO THAT. THAT'S THEIR OLDEST TRICK.
WHO'S "THEY"?
THE DARK FORCES WHO WOULD RULE THIS PLANET.
WHO DID YOU THINK?
WHAT?

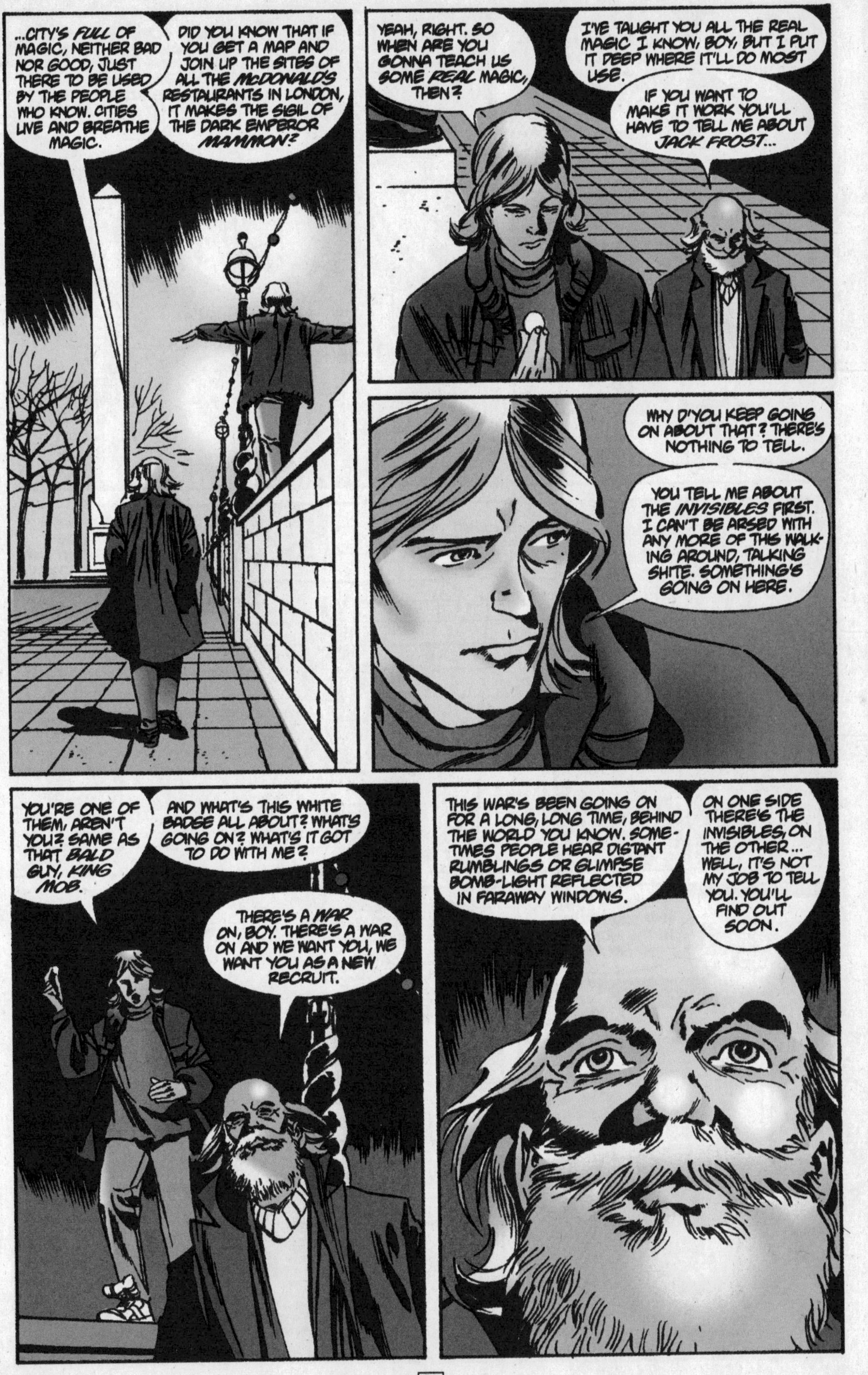
...CITY'S FULL OF MAGIC, NEITHER BAD NOR GOOD, JUST THERE TO BE USED BY THE PEOPLE WHO KNOW. CITIES LIVE AND BREATHE MAGIC.
DID YOU KNOW THAT IF YOU GET A MAP AND JOIN UP THE SITES OF ALL THE McDONALD'S RESTAURANTS IN LONDON, IT MAKES THE SIGIL OF THE DARK EMPEROR MAMMON?
YEAH, RIGHT. SO WHEN ARE YOU GONNA TEACH US SOME REAL MAGIC, THEN?
I'VE TAUGHT YOU ALL THE REAL MAGIC I KNOW, BOY, BUT I PUT IT DEEP WHERE IT'LL DO MOST USE.
IF YOU WANT TO MAKE IT WORK YOU'LL HAVE TO TELL ME ABOUT JACK FROST...
WHY D'YOU KEEP GOING ON ABOUT THAT? THERE'S NOTHING TO TELL.
YOU TELL ME ABOUT THE INVISIBLES FIRST. I CAN'T BE ARSED WITH ANY MORE OF THIS WALKING AROUND, TALKING SHITE. SOMETHING'S GOING ON HERE.
YOU'RE ONE OF THEM, AREN'T YOU? SAME AS THAT BALD GUY, KING MOB.
AND WHAT'S THIS WHITE BADGE ALL ABOUT? WHAT'S GOING ON? WHAT'S IT GOT TO DO WITH ME?
THERE'S A WAR ON, BOY. THERE'S A WAR ON AND WE WANT YOU, WE WANT YOU AS A NEW RECRUIT.
THIS WAR'S BEEN GOING ON FOR A LONG, LONG TIME, BEHIND THE WORLD YOU KNOW. SOMETIMES PEOPLE HEAR DISTANT RUMBLINGS OR GLIMPSE BOMB-LIGHT REFLECTED IN FARAWAY WINDOWS.
ON ONE SIDE THERE'S THE INVISIBLES, ON THE OTHER... WELL, IT'S NOT MY JOB TO TELL YOU. YOU'LL FIND OUT SOON.

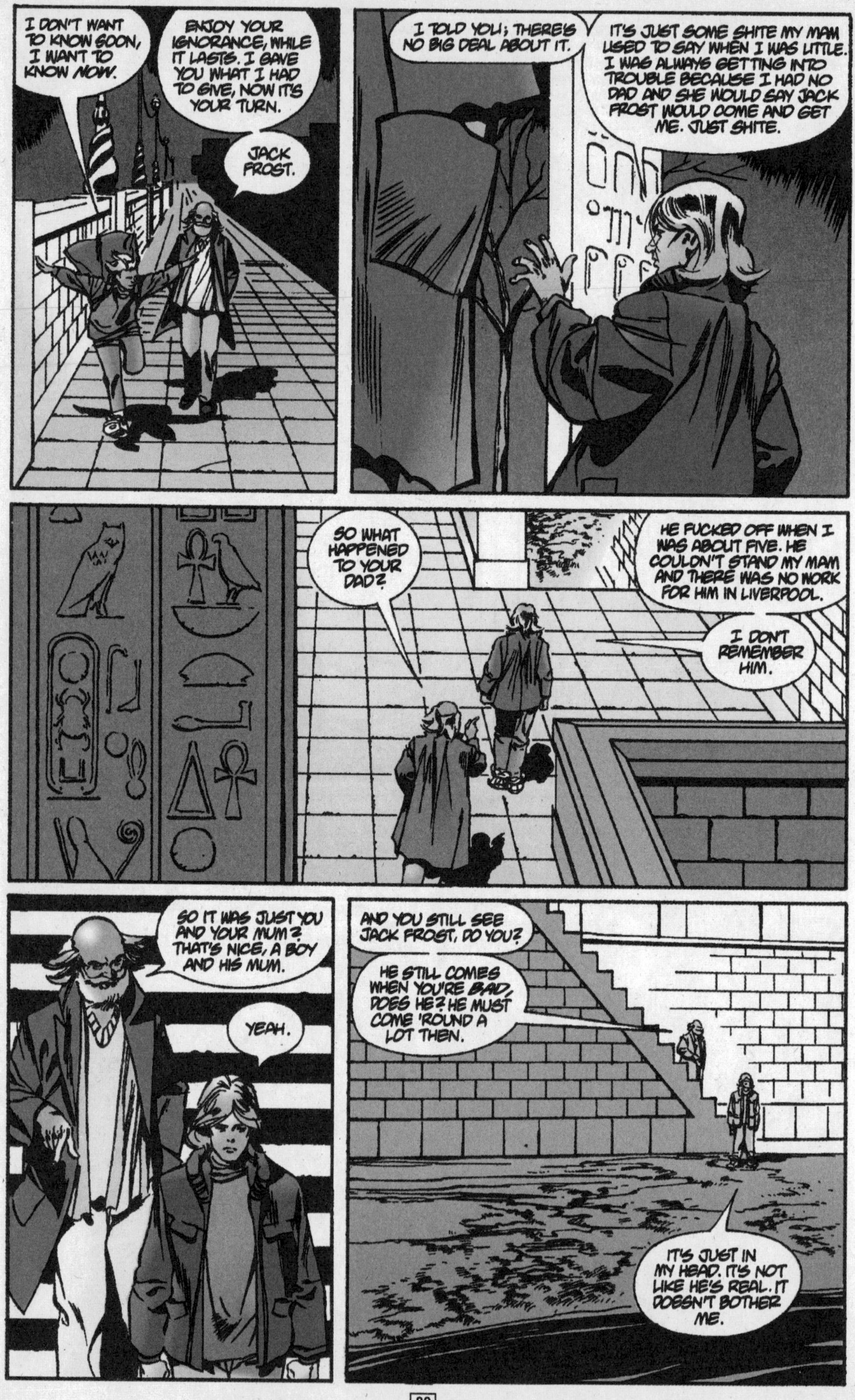
I DON'T WANT TO KNOW SOON, I WANT TO KNOW NOW.
ENJOY YOUR IGNORANCE, WHILE IT LASTS. I GAVE YOU WHAT I HAD TO GIVE, NOW IT'S YOUR TURN.
JACK FROST.
I TOLD YOU; THERE'S NO BIG DEAL ABOUT IT.
IT'S JUST SOME SHITE MY MAM USED TO SAY WHEN I WAS LITTLE. I WAS ALWAYS GETTING INTO TROUBLE BECAUSE I HAD NO DAD AND SHE WOULD SAY JACK FROST WOULD COME AND GET ME. JUST SHITE.
SO WHAT HAPPENED TO YOUR DAD?
HE FUCKED OFF WHEN I WAS ABOUT FIVE. HE COULDN'T STAND MY MAM AND THERE WAS NO WORK FOR HIM IN LIVERPOOL.
I DON'T REMEMBER HIM.
SO IT WAS JUST YOU AND YOUR MUM? THAT'S NICE, A BOY AND HIS MUM.
YEAH.
AND YOU STILL SEE JACK FROST, DO YOU?
HE STILL COMES WHEN YOU'RE BAD, DOES HE? HE MUST COME 'ROUND A LOT THEN.
IT'S JUST IN MY HEAD. IT'S NOT LIKE HE'S REAL. IT DOESN'T BOTHER ME.

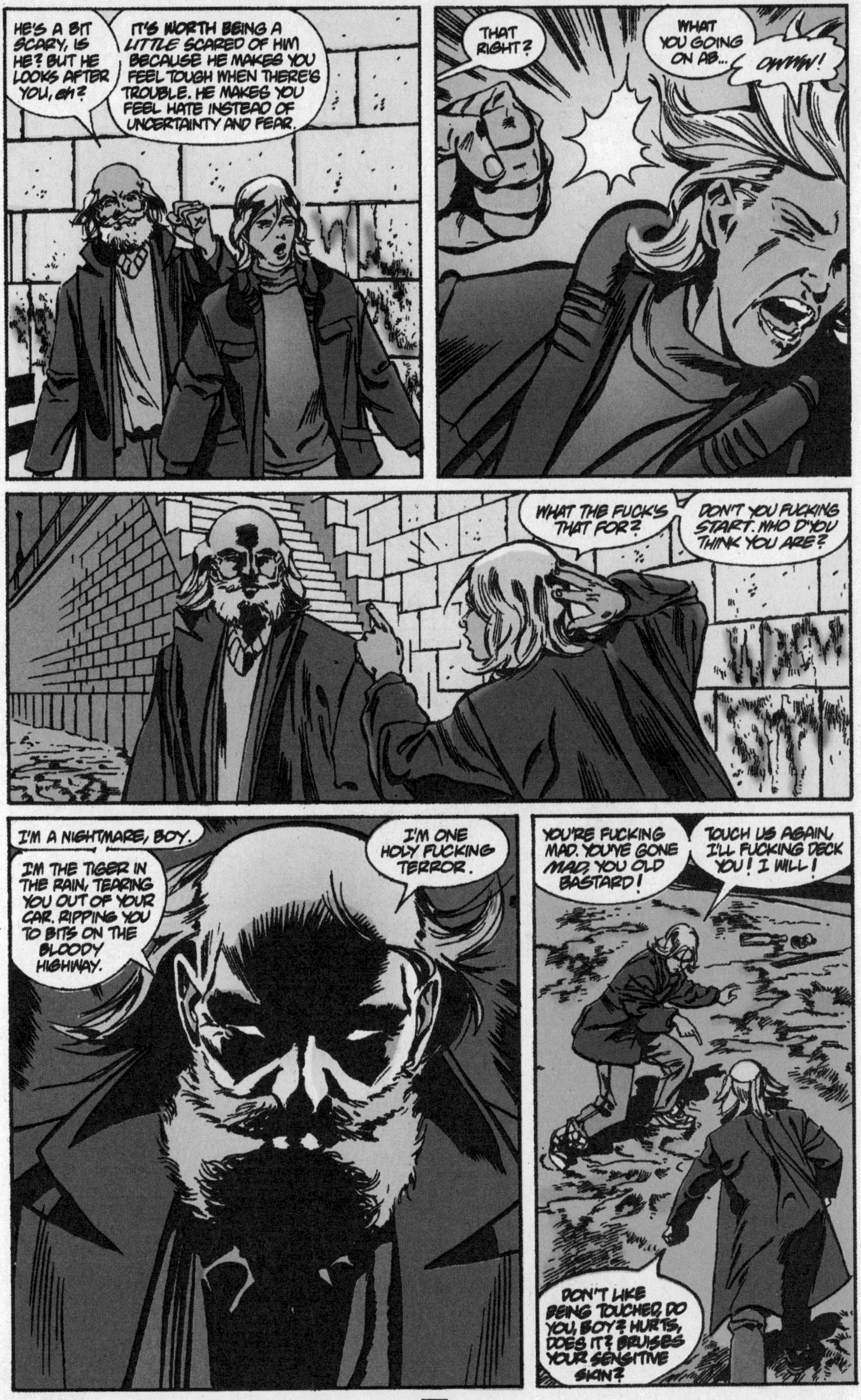

HE'S A BIT SCARY, IS HE? BUT HE LOOKS AFTER YOU, eh?
IT'S WORTH BEING A LITTLE SCARED OF HIM BECAUSE HE MAKES YOU FEEL TOUGH WHEN THERE'S TROUBLE. HE MAKES YOU FEEL HATE INSTEAD OF UNCERTAINTY AND FEAR.
THAT RIGHT?
WHAT YOU GOING ON AB...
OWWW!
WHAT THE FUCK'S THAT FOR?
DON'T YOU FUCKING START. WHO D'YOU THINK YOU ARE?
I'M A NIGHTMARE, BOY.
I'M THE TIGER IN THE RAIN, TEARING YOU OUT OF YOUR CAR. RIPPING YOU TO BITS ON THE BLOODY HIGHWAY.
I'M ONE HOLY FUCKING TERROR.
YOU'RE FUCKING MAD. YOU'VE GONE MAD, YOU OLD BASTARD!
TOUCH US AGAIN, I'LL FUCKING DECK YOU! I WILL!
DON'T LIKE BEING TOUCHED, DO YOU, BOY? HURTS, DOES IT? BRUISES YOUR SENSITIVE SKIN?

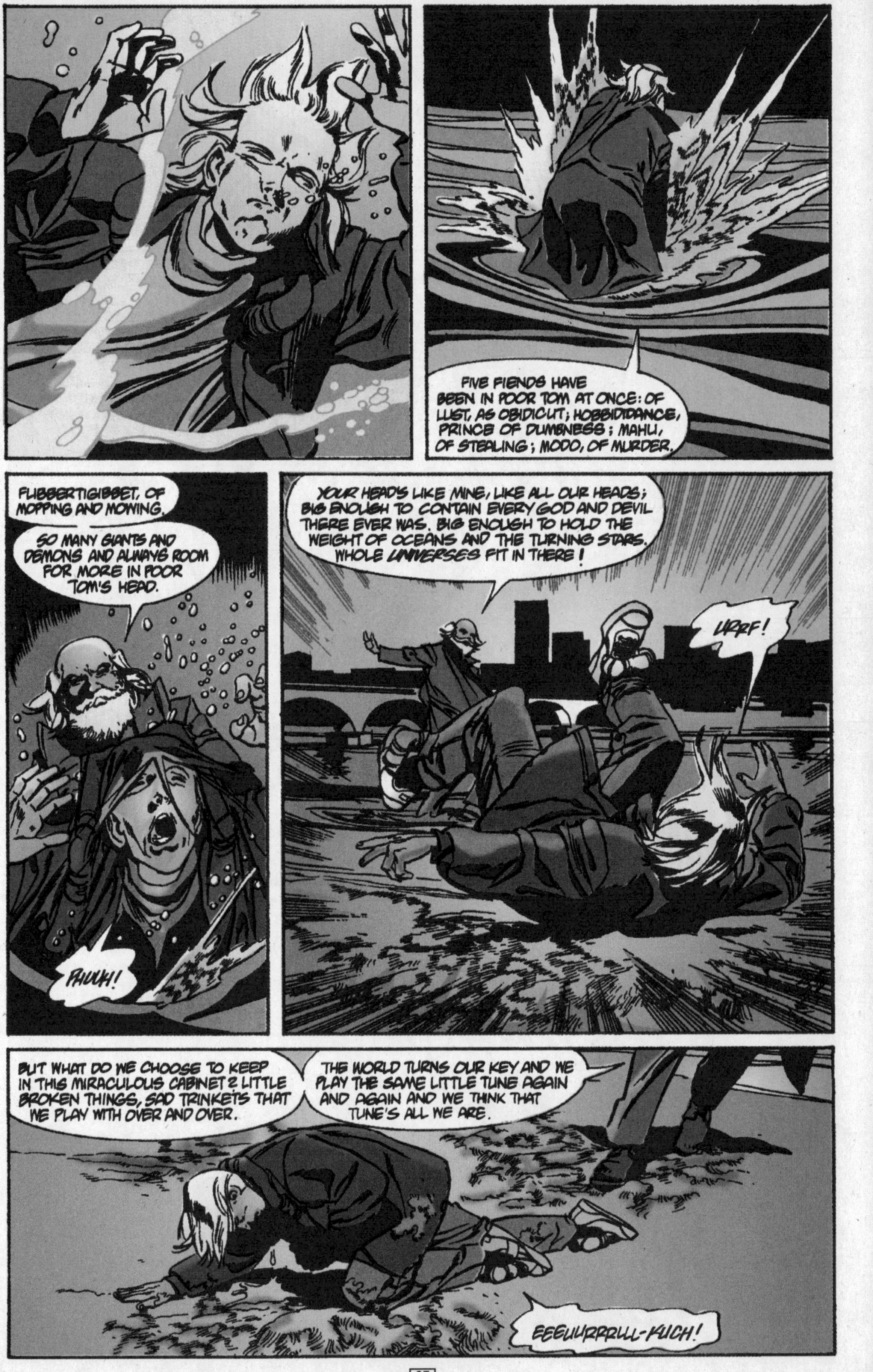
FIVE FIENDS HAVE BEEN IN POOR TOM AT ONCE: OF LUST, AS OBIDICUT; HOBBIDIDANCE, PRINCE OF DUMBNESS; MAHU, OF STEALING; MODO, OF MURDER.
FLIBBERTIGIBBET, OF MOPPING AND MOWING.
SO MANY GIANTS AND DEMONS AND ALWAYS ROOM FOR MORE IN POOR TOM'S HEAD.
PHUUH!
YOUR HEAD'S LIKE MINE, LIKE ALL OUR HEADS; BIG ENOUGH TO CONTAIN EVERY GOD AND DEVIL THERE EVER WAS. BIG ENOUGH TO HOLD THE WEIGHT OF OCEANS AND THE TURNING STARS. WHOLE *UNIVERSES* FIT IN THERE!
URRF!
BUT WHAT DO WE CHOOSE TO KEEP IN THIS MIRACULOUS CABINET? LITTLE BROKEN THINGS, SAD TRINKETS THAT WE PLAY WITH OVER AND OVER.
THE WORLD TURNS OUR KEY AND WE PLAY THE SAME LITTLE TUNE AGAIN AND AGAIN AND WE THINK THAT TUNE'S ALL WE ARE.
EEEUURRRLLL-KUCH!

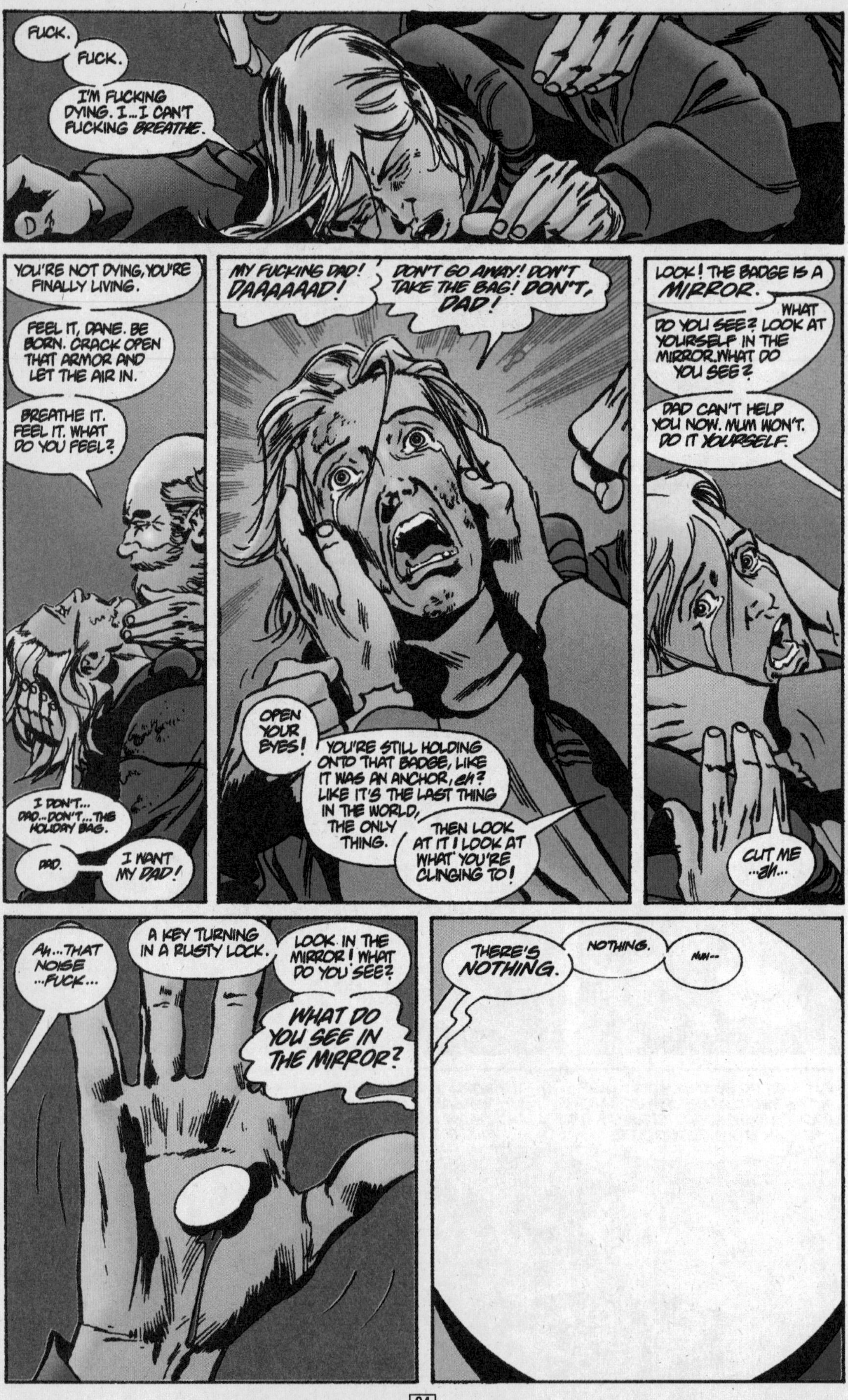
FUCK.
FUCK.
I'M FUCKING DYING. I...I CAN'T FUCKING BREATHE.
YOU'RE NOT DYING, YOU'RE FINALLY LIVING.
FEEL IT, DANE. BE BORN. CRACK OPEN THAT ARMOR AND LET THE AIR IN.
BREATHE IT. FEEL IT. WHAT DO YOU FEEL?
I DON'T... DAD...DON'T...THE HOLIDAY BAG.
DAD.
I WANT MY DAD!
MY FUCKING DAD! DAAAAAAD!
DON'T GO AWAY! DON'T TAKE THE BAG! DON'T, DAD!
OPEN YOUR EYES!
YOU'RE STILL HOLDING ONTO THAT BADGE, LIKE IT WAS AN ANCHOR, eh? LIKE IT'S THE LAST THING IN THE WORLD, THE ONLY THING.
THEN LOOK AT IT! LOOK AT WHAT YOU'RE CLINGING TO!
LOOK! THE BADGE IS A MIRROR.
WHAT DO YOU SEE? LOOK AT YOURSELF IN THE MIRROR. WHAT DO YOU SEE?
DAD CAN'T HELP YOU NOW. MUM WON'T. DO IT YOURSELF.
CUT ME ...ah...
Ah...THAT NOISE ...FUCK...
A KEY TURNING IN A RUSTY LOCK.
LOOK IN THE MIRROR! WHAT DO YOU SEE?
WHAT DO YOU SEE IN THE MIRROR?
THERE'S NOTHING.
NOTHING.
NUH--

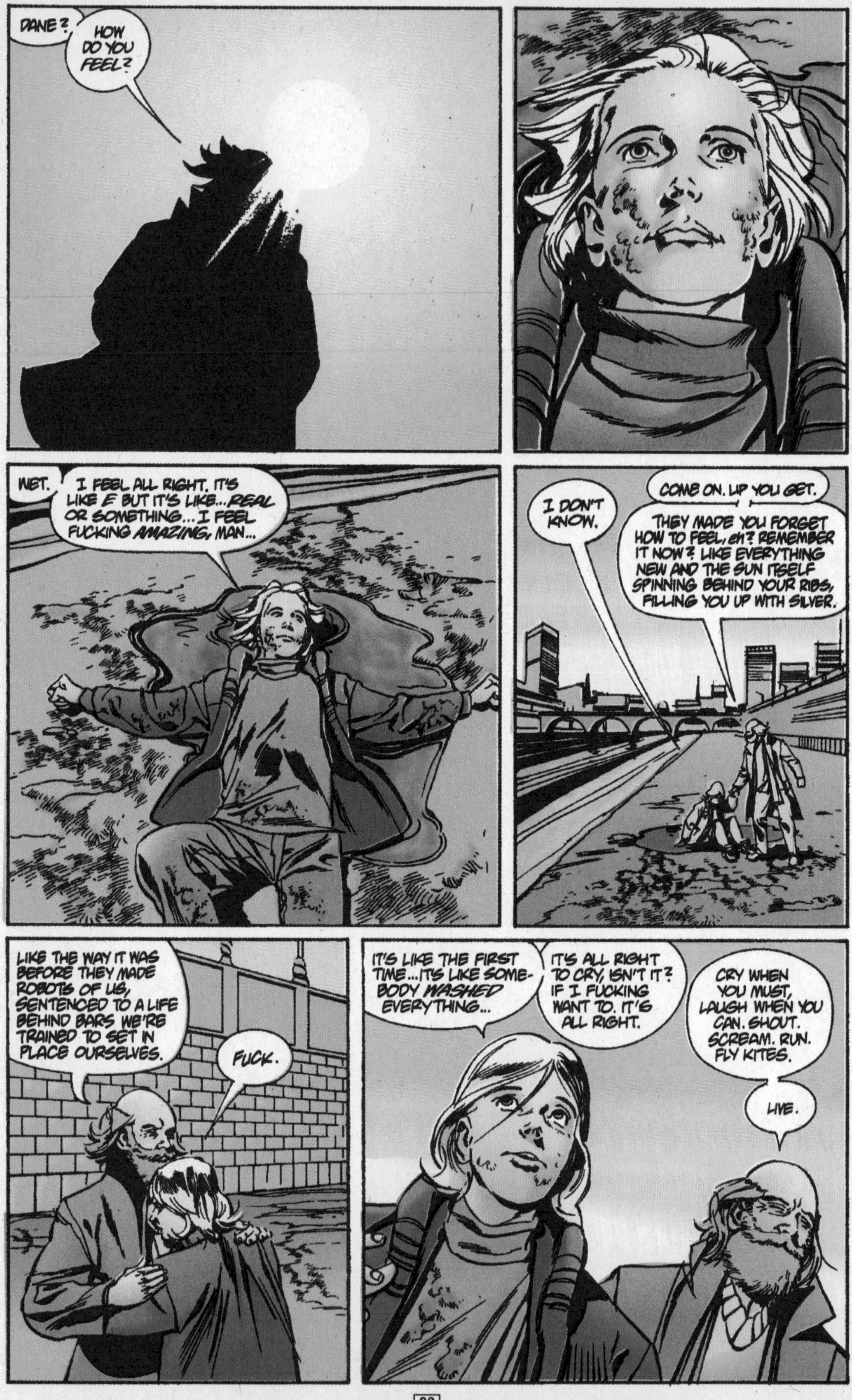
DANE?
HOW DO YOU FEEL?
WET.
I FEEL ALL RIGHT. IT'S LIKE E BUT IT'S LIKE... REAL OR SOMETHING... I FEEL FUCKING AMAZING, MAN...
COME ON. UP YOU GET.
I DON'T KNOW.
THEY MADE YOU FORGET HOW TO FEEL, eh? REMEMBER IT NOW? LIKE EVERYTHING NEW AND THE SUN ITSELF SPINNING BEHIND YOUR RIBS, FILLING YOU UP WITH SILVER.
LIKE THE WAY IT WAS BEFORE THEY MADE ROBOTS OF US, SENTENCED TO A LIFE BEHIND BARS WE'RE TRAINED TO SET IN PLACE OURSELVES.
FUCK.
IT'S LIKE THE FIRST TIME... IT'S LIKE SOMEBODY WASHED EVERYTHING...
IT'S ALL RIGHT TO CRY, ISN'T IT? IF I FUCKING WANT TO. IT'S ALL RIGHT.
CRY WHEN YOU MUST, LAUGH WHEN YOU CAN. SHOUT. SCREAM. RUN. FLY KITES.
LIVE.

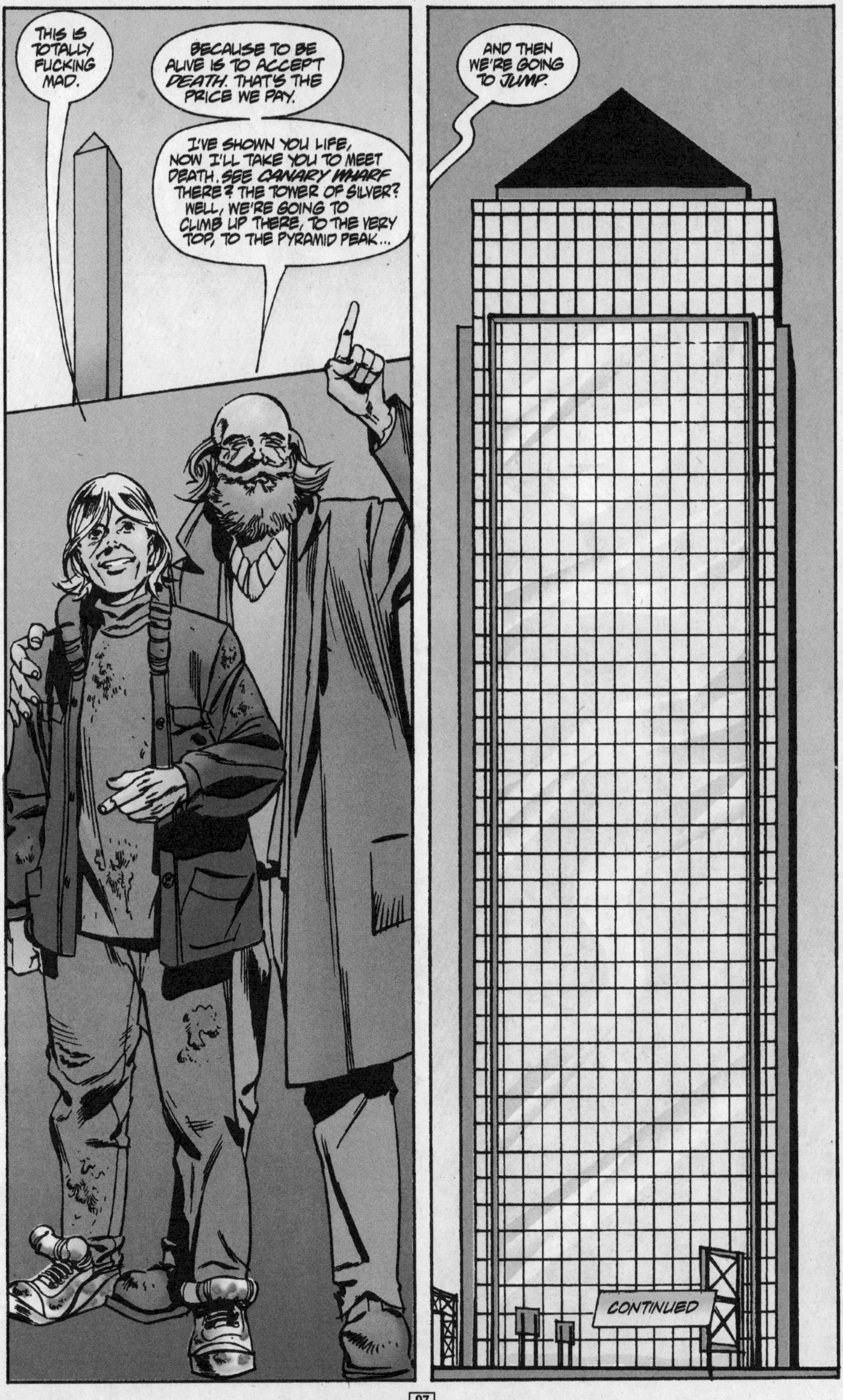
THIS IS TOTALLY FUCKING MAD.
BECAUSE TO BE ALIVE IS TO ACCEPT DEATH. THAT'S THE PRICE WE PAY.
I'VE SHOWN YOU LIFE, NOW I'LL TAKE YOU TO MEET DEATH. SEE CANARY WHARF THERE? THE TOWER OF SILVER? WELL, WE'RE GOING TO CLIMB UP THERE, TO THE VERY TOP, TO THE PYRAMID PEAK...
AND THEN WE'RE GOING TO JUMP.
CONTINUED

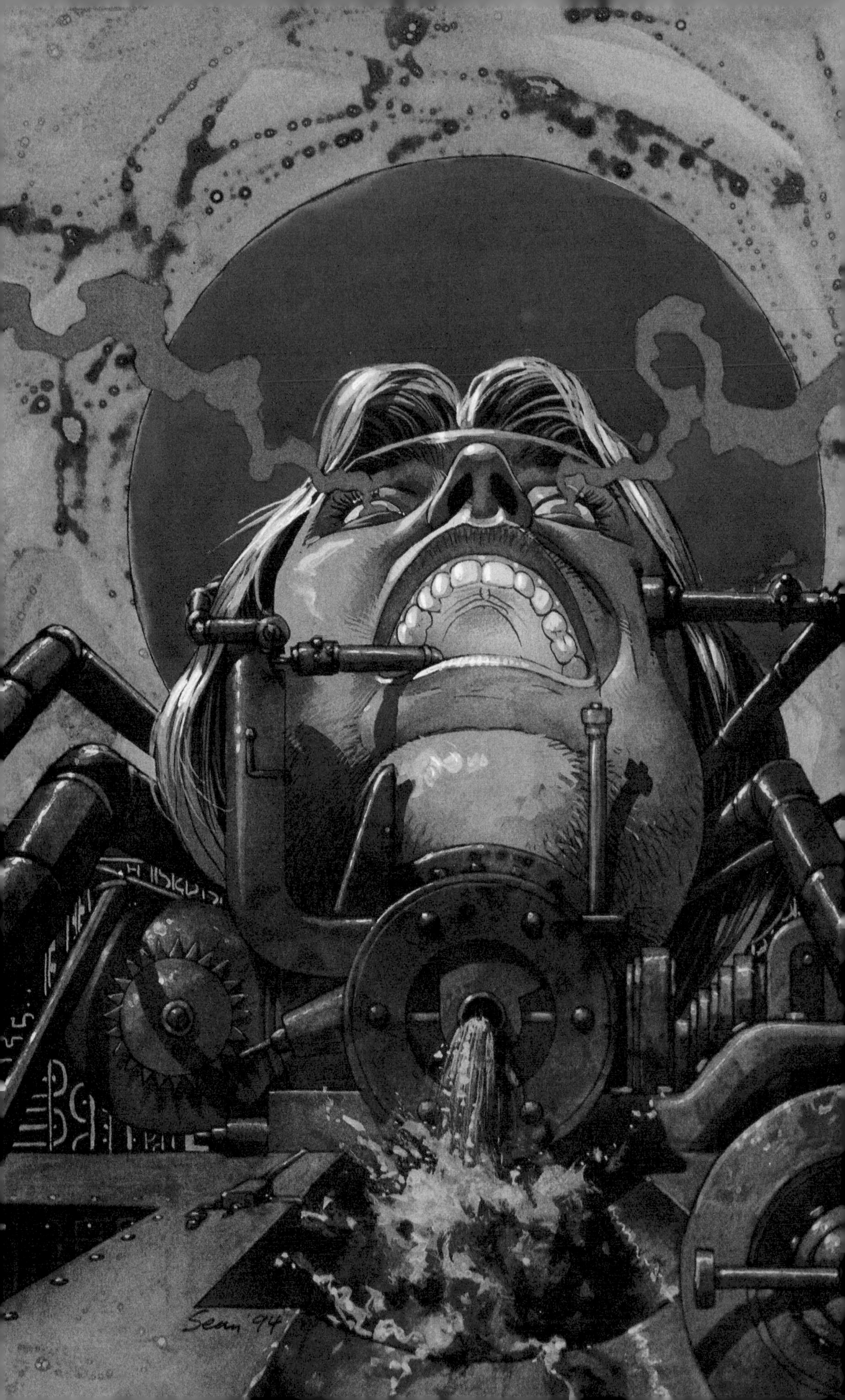
Sean '94

DOWN AND OUT IN HEAVEN AND HELL

PART 3

THE INVISIBLES CREATED BY
GRANT MORRISON

GRANT MORRISON → WRITER

STEVE YEOWELL → ARTIST

DANIEL VOZZO → COLORS

CLEM ROBINS → LETTERS

STUART MOORE → EDITOR

JULIE ROTTENBERG → ASST. EDITOR

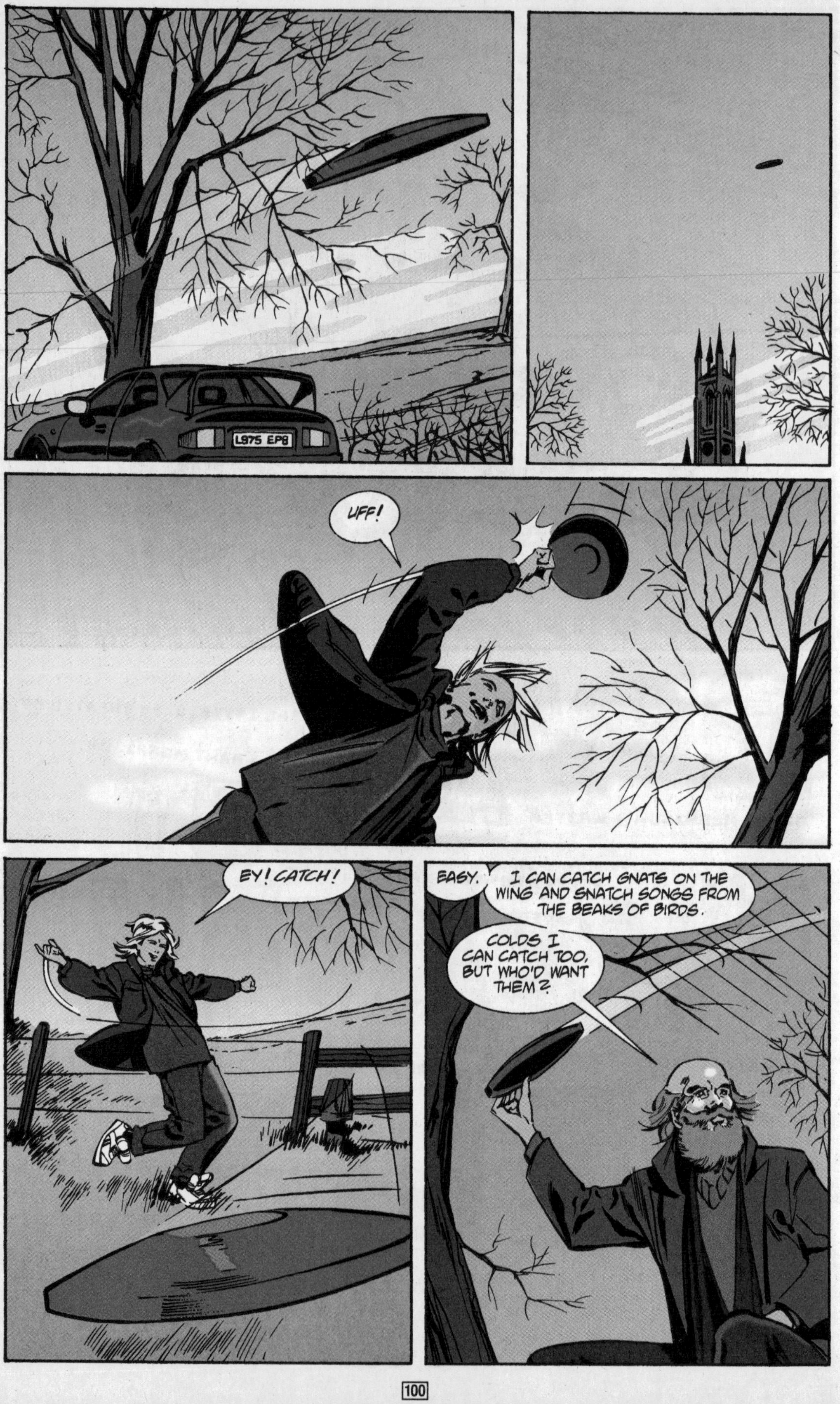
L975 EP8
UFF!
EY! CATCH!
EASY.
I CAN CATCH GNATS ON THE WING AND SNATCH SONGS FROM THE BEAKS OF BIRDS.
COLDS I CAN CATCH TOO, BUT WHO'D WANT THEM?

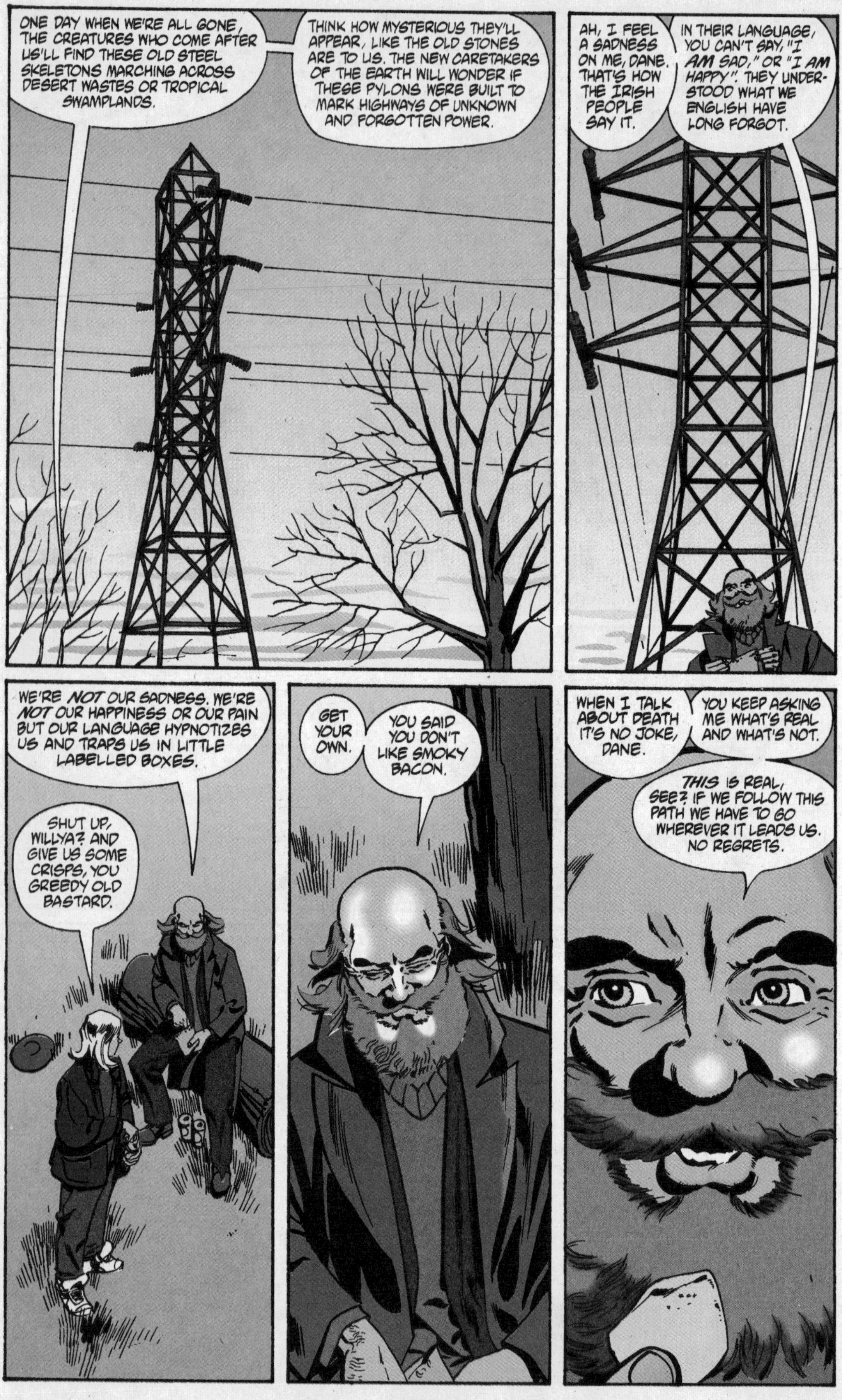

ONE DAY WHEN WE'RE ALL GONE, THE CREATURES WHO COME AFTER US'LL FIND THESE OLD STEEL SKELETONS MARCHING ACROSS DESERT WASTES OR TROPICAL SWAMPLANDS.
THINK HOW MYSTERIOUS THEY'LL APPEAR, LIKE THE OLD STONES ARE TO US. THE NEW CARETAKERS OF THE EARTH WILL WONDER IF THESE PYLONS WERE BUILT TO MARK HIGHWAYS OF UNKNOWN AND FORGOTTEN POWER.
AH, I FEEL A SADNESS ON ME, DANE. THAT'S HOW THE IRISH PEOPLE SAY IT.
IN THEIR LANGUAGE, YOU CAN'T SAY, "I AM SAD," OR "I AM HAPPY". THEY UNDERSTOOD WHAT WE ENGLISH HAVE LONG FORGOT.
WE'RE NOT OUR SADNESS. WE'RE NOT OUR HAPPINESS OR OUR PAIN BUT OUR LANGUAGE HYPNOTIZES US AND TRAPS US IN LITTLE LABELLED BOXES.
SHUT UP, WILLYA? AND GIVE US SOME CRISPS, YOU GREEDY OLD BASTARD.
GET YOUR OWN.
YOU SAID YOU DON'T LIKE SMOKY BACON.
WHEN I TALK ABOUT DEATH IT'S NO JOKE, DANE.
YOU KEEP ASKING ME WHAT'S REAL AND WHAT'S NOT.
THIS IS REAL, SEE? IF WE FOLLOW THIS PATH WE HAVE TO GO WHEREVER IT LEADS US. NO REGRETS.

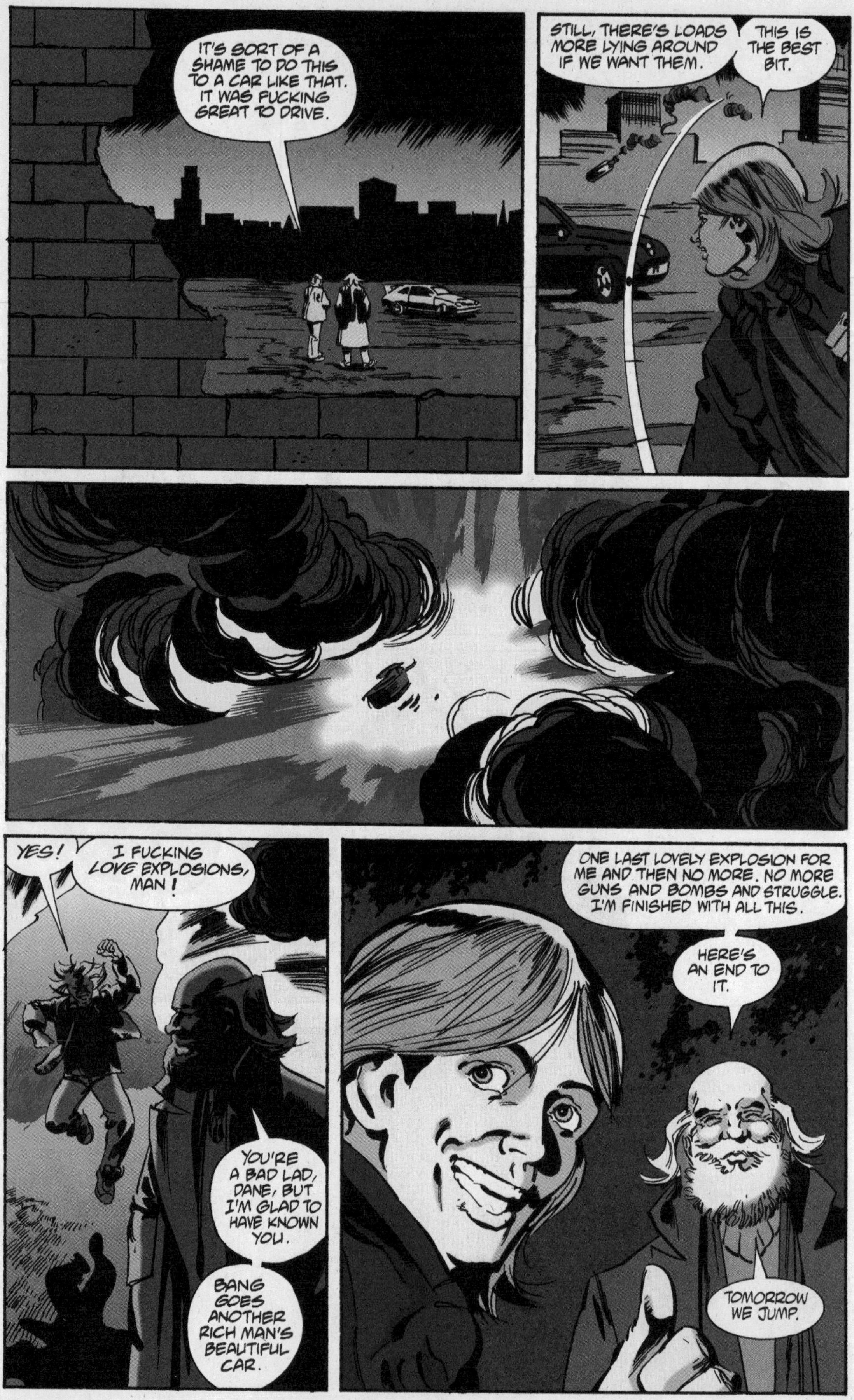
IT'S SORT OF A SHAME TO DO THIS TO A CAR LIKE THAT. IT WAS FUCKING GREAT TO DRIVE.
STILL, THERE'S LOADS MORE LYING AROUND IF WE WANT THEM.
THIS IS THE BEST BIT.
YES!
I FUCKING LOVE EXPLOSIONS, MAN!
YOU'RE A BAD LAD, DANE, BUT I'M GLAD TO HAVE KNOWN YOU.
BANG GOES ANOTHER RICH MAN'S BEAUTIFUL CAR.
ONE LAST LOVELY EXPLOSION FOR ME AND THEN NO MORE. NO MORE GUNS AND BOMBS AND STRUGGLE. I'M FINISHED WITH ALL THIS.
HERE'S AN END TO IT.
TOMORROW WE JUMP.

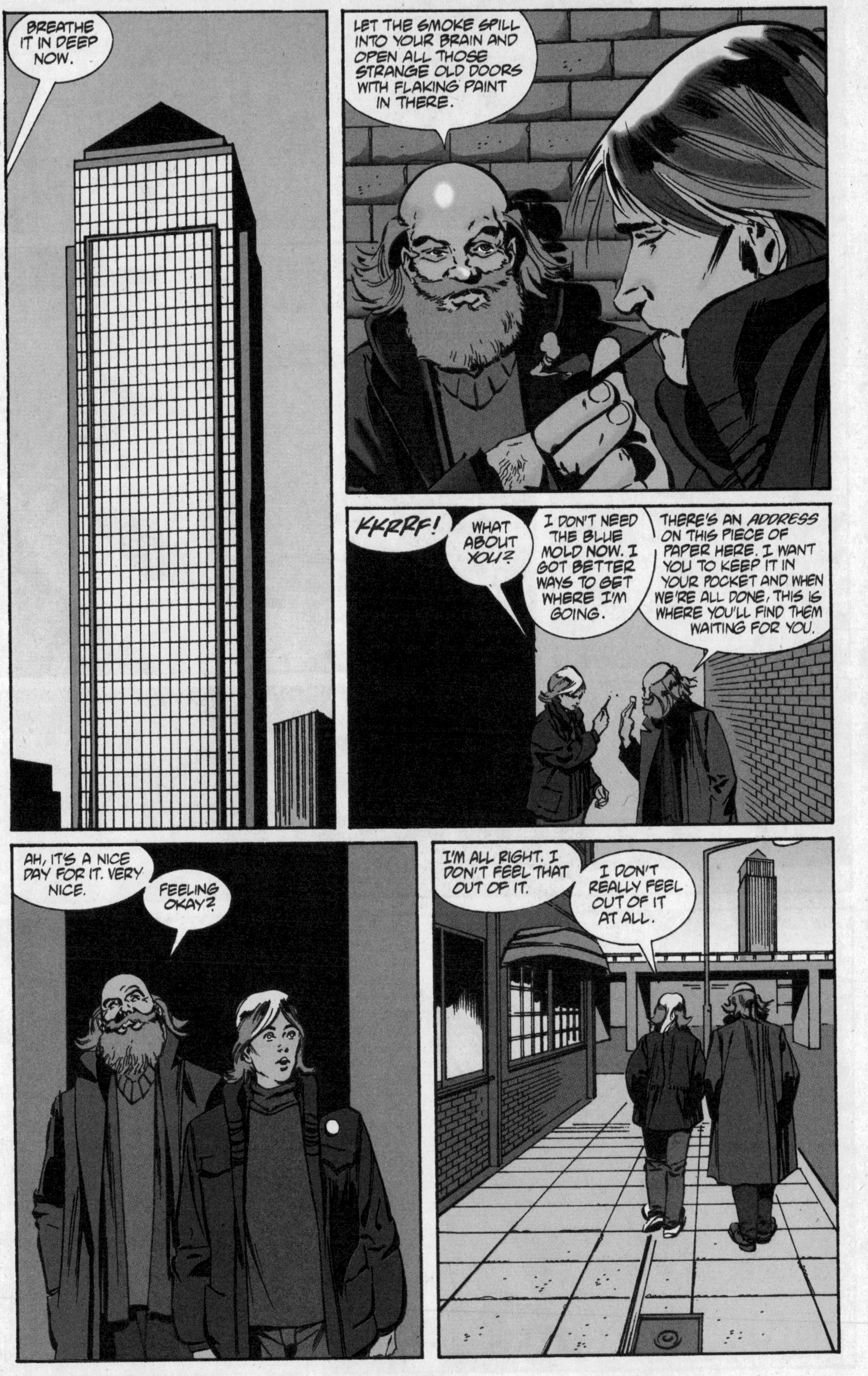
BREATHE IT IN DEEP NOW.
LET THE SMOKE SPILL INTO YOUR BRAIN AND OPEN ALL THOSE STRANGE OLD DOORS WITH FLAKING PAINT IN THERE.
KKRRF!
WHAT ABOUT YOU?
I DON'T NEED THE BLUE MOLD NOW. I GOT BETTER WAYS TO GET WHERE I'M GOING.
THERE'S AN ADDRESS ON THIS PIECE OF PAPER HERE. I WANT YOU TO KEEP IT IN YOUR POCKET AND WHEN WE'RE ALL DONE, THIS IS WHERE YOU'LL FIND THEM WAITING FOR YOU.
AH, IT'S A NICE DAY FOR IT. VERY NICE.
FEELING OKAY?
I'M ALL RIGHT. I DON'T FEEL THAT OUT OF IT.
I DON'T REALLY FEEL OUT OF IT AT ALL.

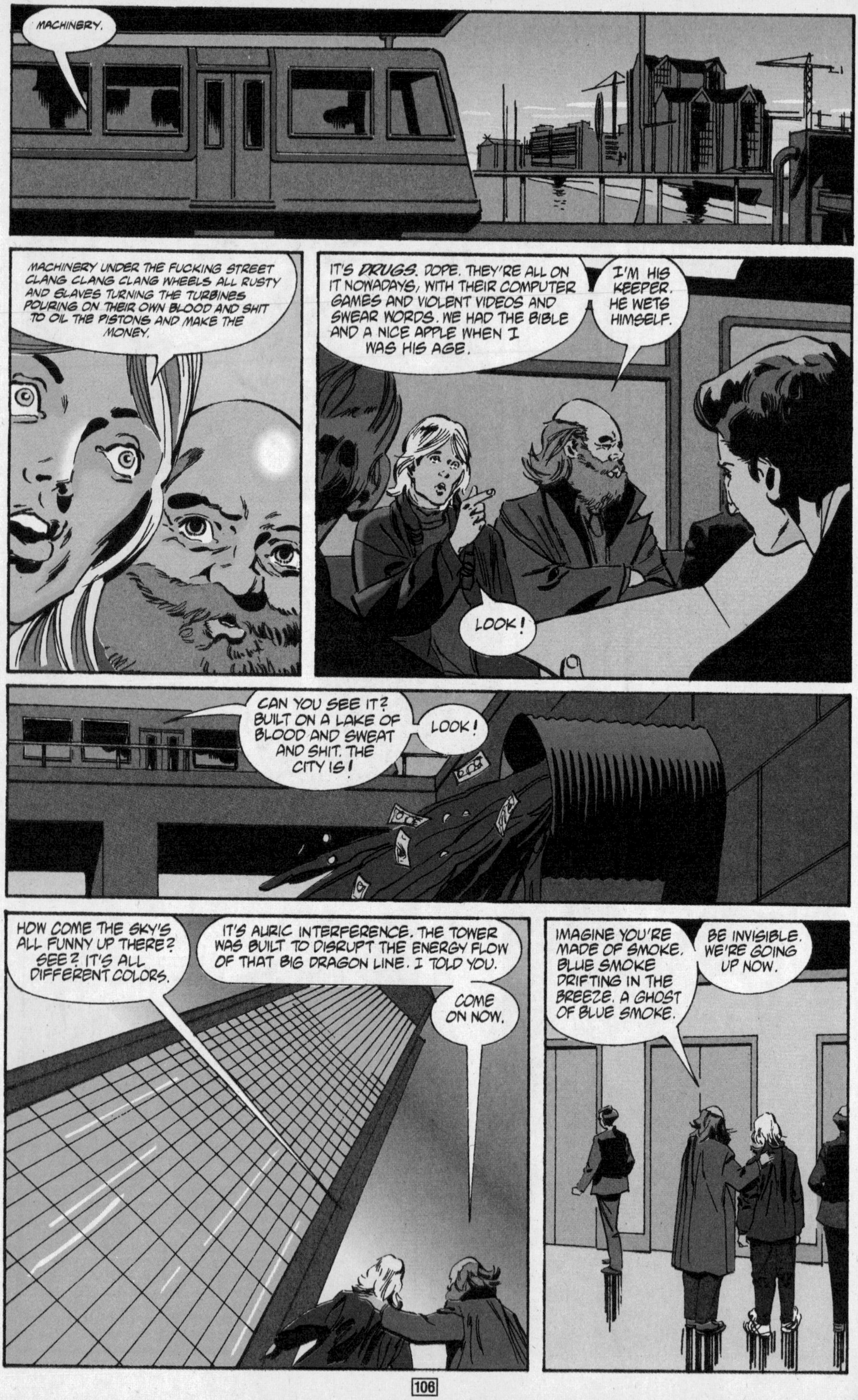
MACHINERY.
MACHINERY UNDER THE FUCKING STREET CLANG CLANG CLANG WHEELS ALL RUSTY AND SLAVES TURNING THE TURBINES POURING ON THEIR OWN BLOOD AND SHIT TO OIL THE PISTONS AND MAKE THE MONEY.
IT'S DRUGS. DOPE. THEY'RE ALL ON IT NOWADAYS, WITH THEIR COMPUTER GAMES AND VIOLENT VIDEOS AND SWEAR WORDS. WE HAD THE BIBLE AND A NICE APPLE WHEN I WAS HIS AGE.
I'M HIS KEEPER. HE WETS HIMSELF.
LOOK!
CAN YOU SEE IT? BUILT ON A LAKE OF BLOOD AND SWEAT AND SHIT. THE CITY IS!
LOOK!
HOW COME THE SKY'S ALL FUNNY UP THERE? SEE? IT'S ALL DIFFERENT COLORS.
IT'S AURIC INTERFERENCE. THE TOWER WAS BUILT TO DISRUPT THE ENERGY FLOW OF THAT BIG DRAGON LINE. I TOLD YOU.
COME ON NOW.
IMAGINE YOU'RE MADE OF SMOKE. BLUE SMOKE DRIFTING IN THE BREEZE. A GHOST OF BLUE SMOKE.
BE INVISIBLE. WE'RE GOING UP NOW.

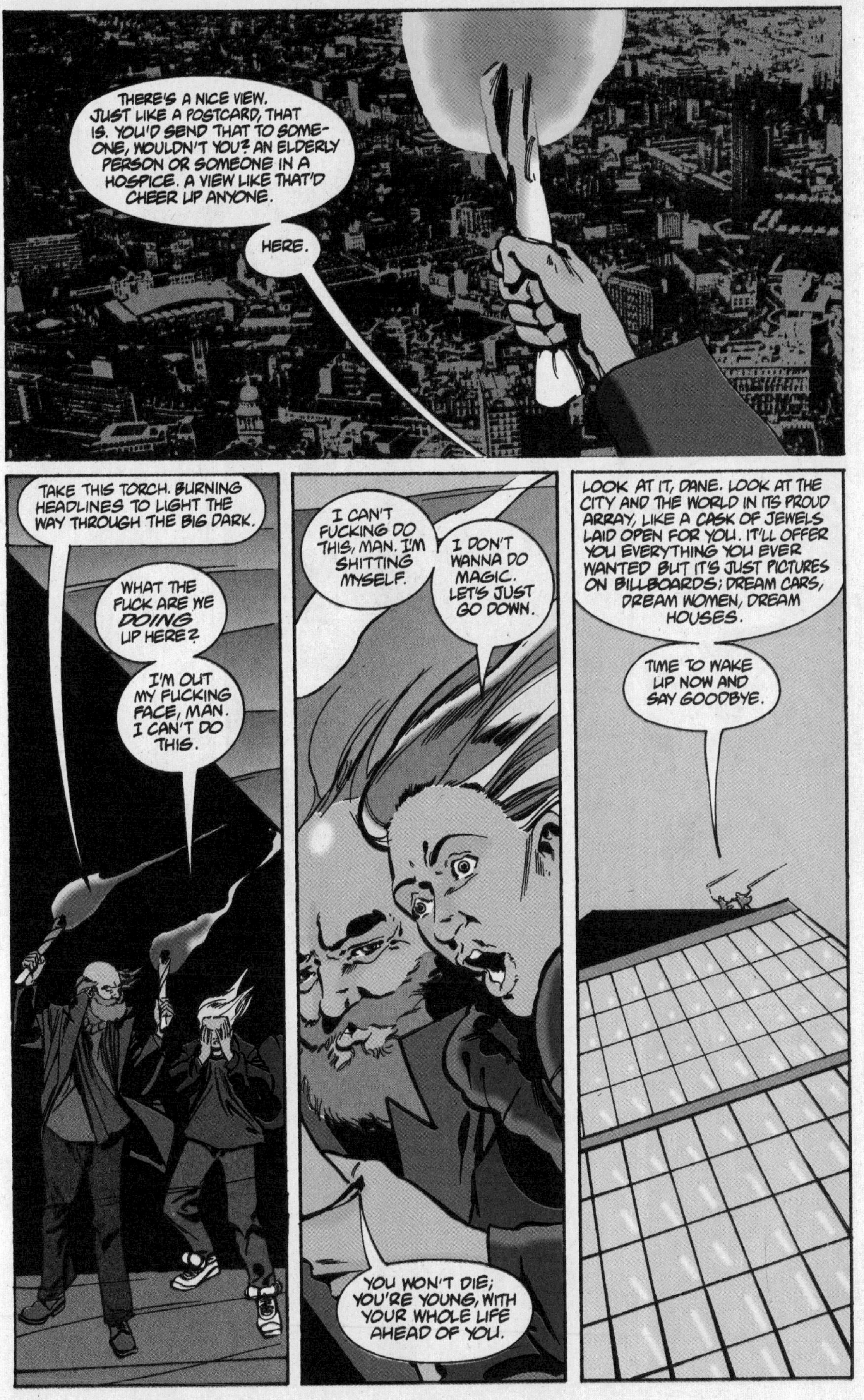
THERE'S A NICE VIEW. JUST LIKE A POSTCARD, THAT IS. YOU'D SEND THAT TO SOMEONE, WOULDN'T YOU? AN ELDERLY PERSON OR SOMEONE IN A HOSPICE. A VIEW LIKE THAT'D CHEER UP ANYONE.
HERE.
TAKE THIS TORCH. BURNING HEADLINES TO LIGHT THE WAY THROUGH THE BIG DARK.
WHAT THE FUCK ARE WE *DOING* UP HERE?
I'M OUT MY FUCKING FACE, MAN. I CAN'T DO THIS.
I CAN'T FUCKING DO THIS, MAN. I'M SHITTING MYSELF.
I DON'T WANNA DO MAGIC. LET'S JUST GO DOWN.
YOU WON'T DIE; YOU'RE YOUNG, WITH YOUR WHOLE LIFE AHEAD OF YOU.
LOOK AT IT, DANE. LOOK AT THE CITY AND THE WORLD IN ITS PROUD ARRAY, LIKE A CASK OF JEWELS LAID OPEN FOR YOU. IT'LL OFFER YOU EVERYTHING YOU EVER WANTED BUT IT'S JUST PICTURES ON BILLBOARDS; DREAM CARS, DREAM WOMEN, DREAM HOUSES.
TIME TO WAKE UP NOW AND SAY GOODBYE.

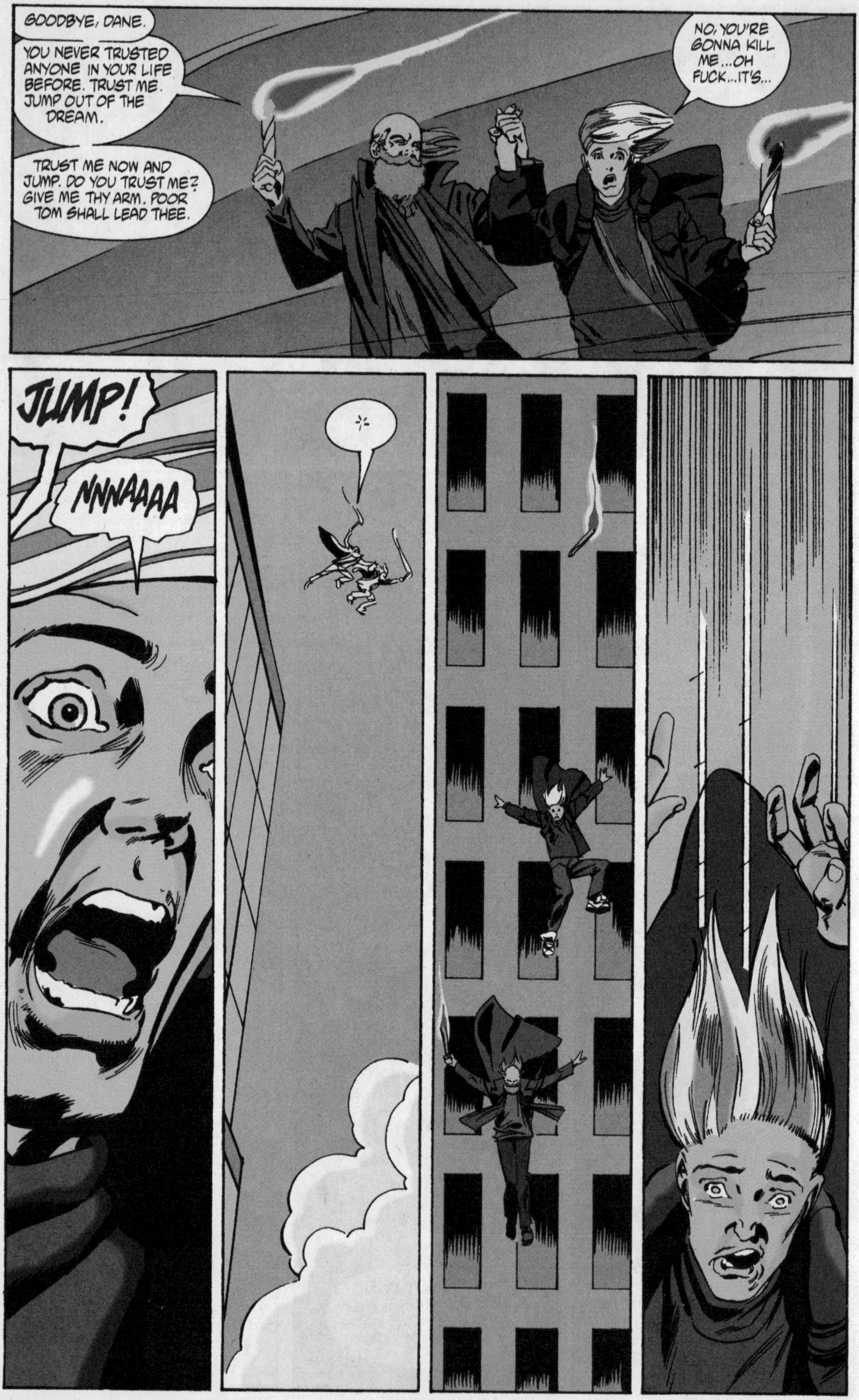
GOODBYE, DANE.
YOU NEVER TRUSTED ANYONE IN YOUR LIFE BEFORE. TRUST ME. JUMP OUT OF THE DREAM.
TRUST ME NOW AND JUMP. DO YOU TRUST ME? GIVE ME THY ARM. POOR TOM SHALL LEAD THEE.
NO, YOU'RE GONNA KILL ME...OH FUCK...IT'S...
JUMP!
NNNAAAA

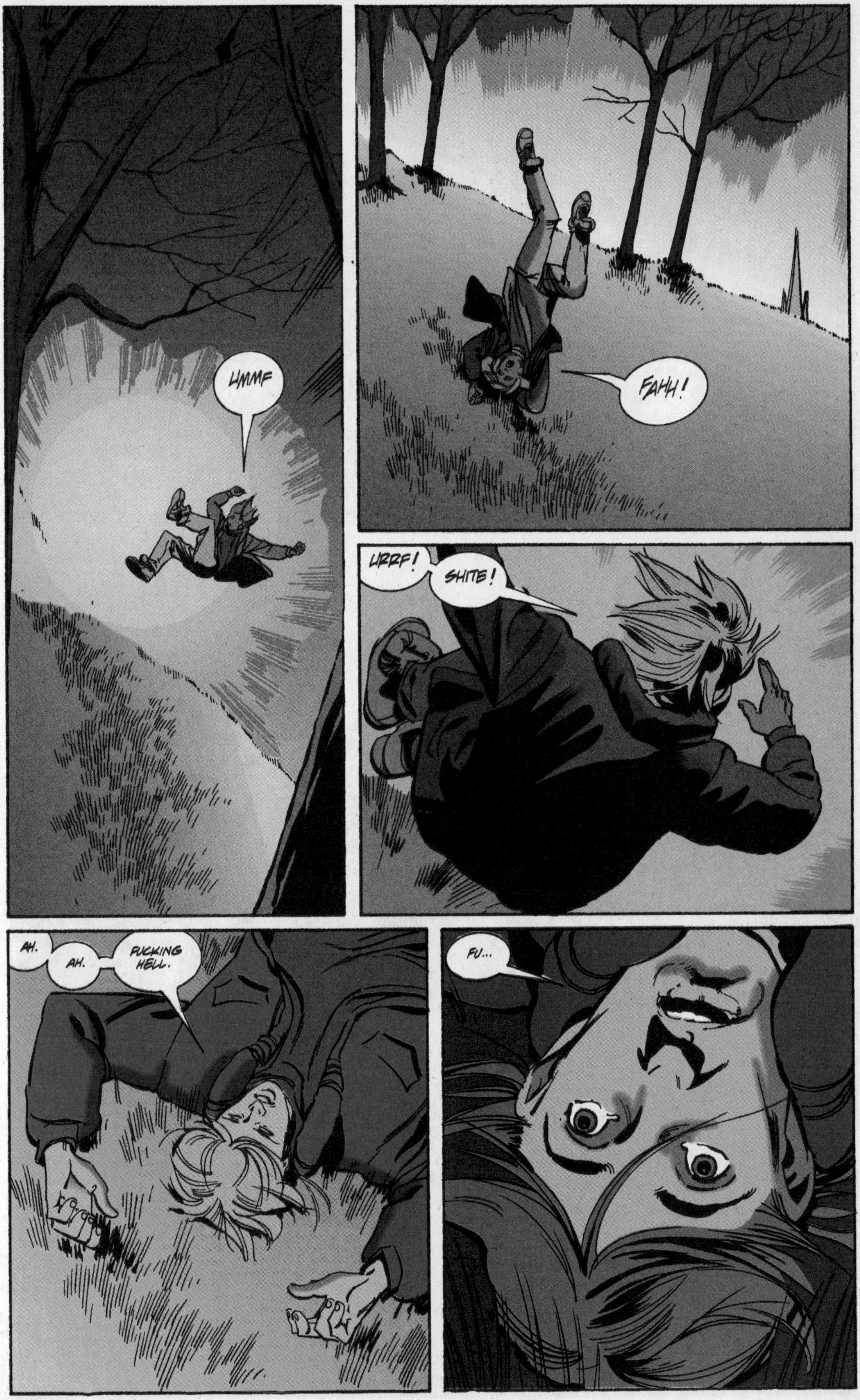
UMMF
FAHH!
URRF!
SHITE!
AH.
AH.
FUCKING HELL.
FU...

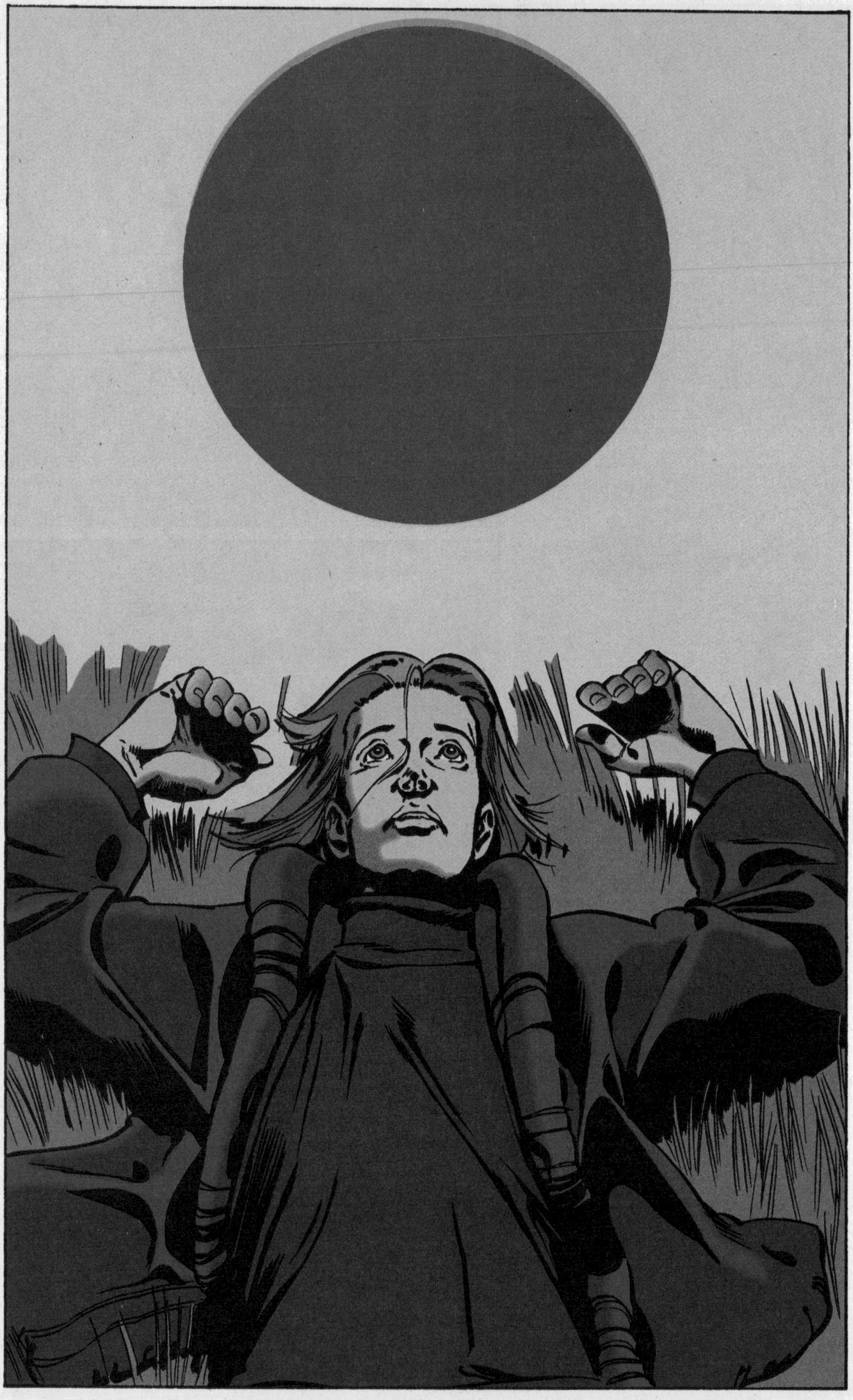

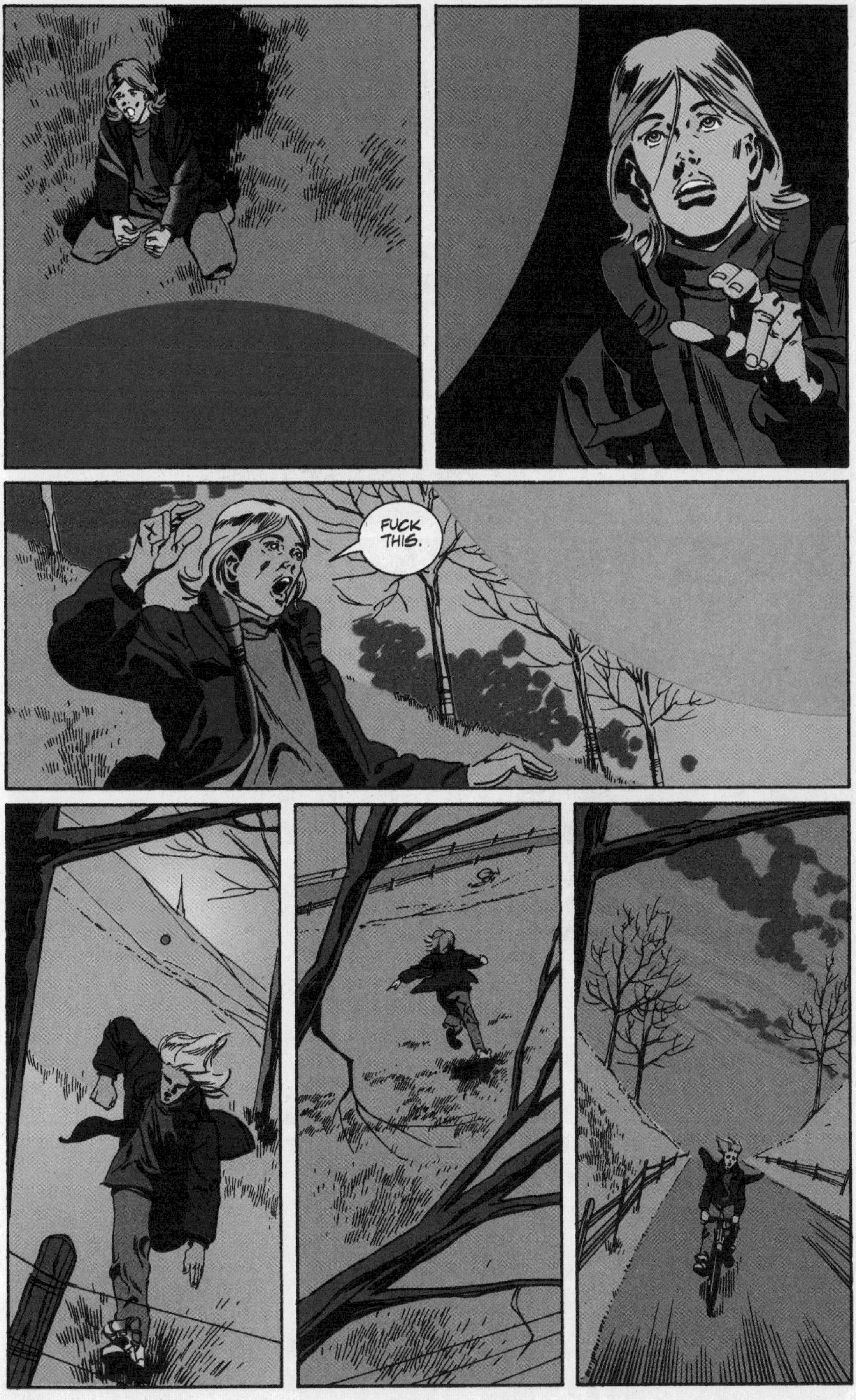
FUCK THIS.

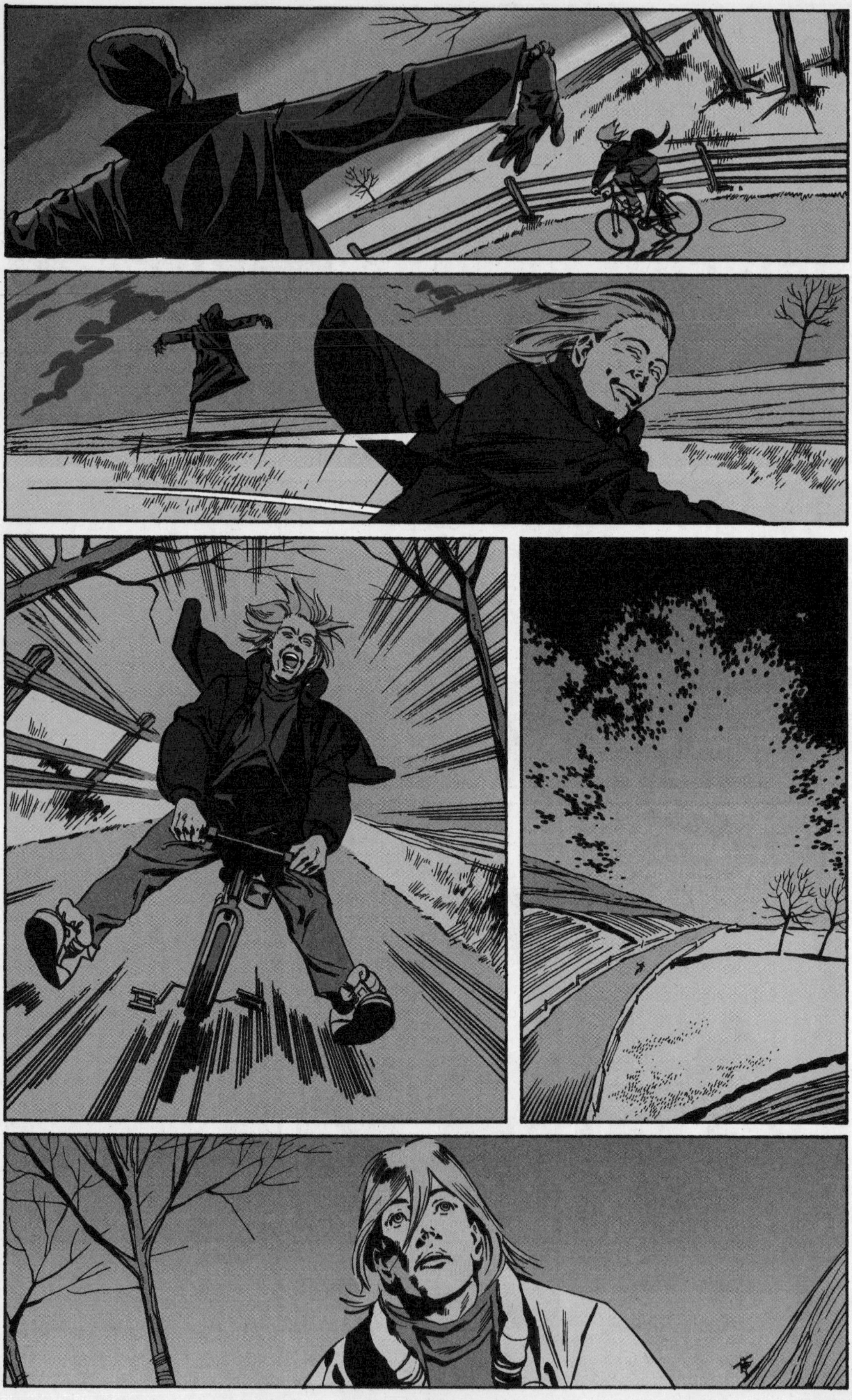

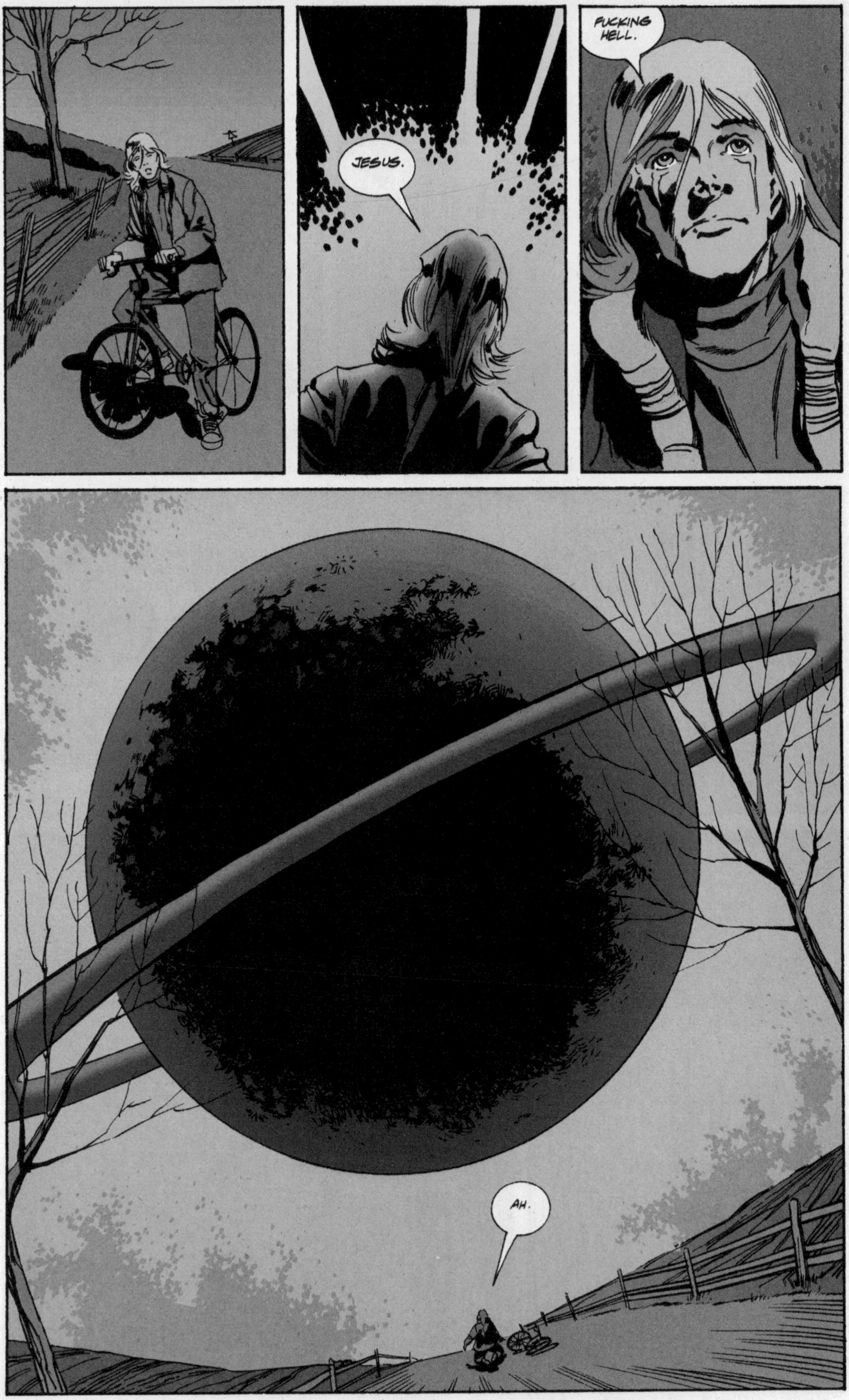
JESUS.
FUCKING HELL.
AH.

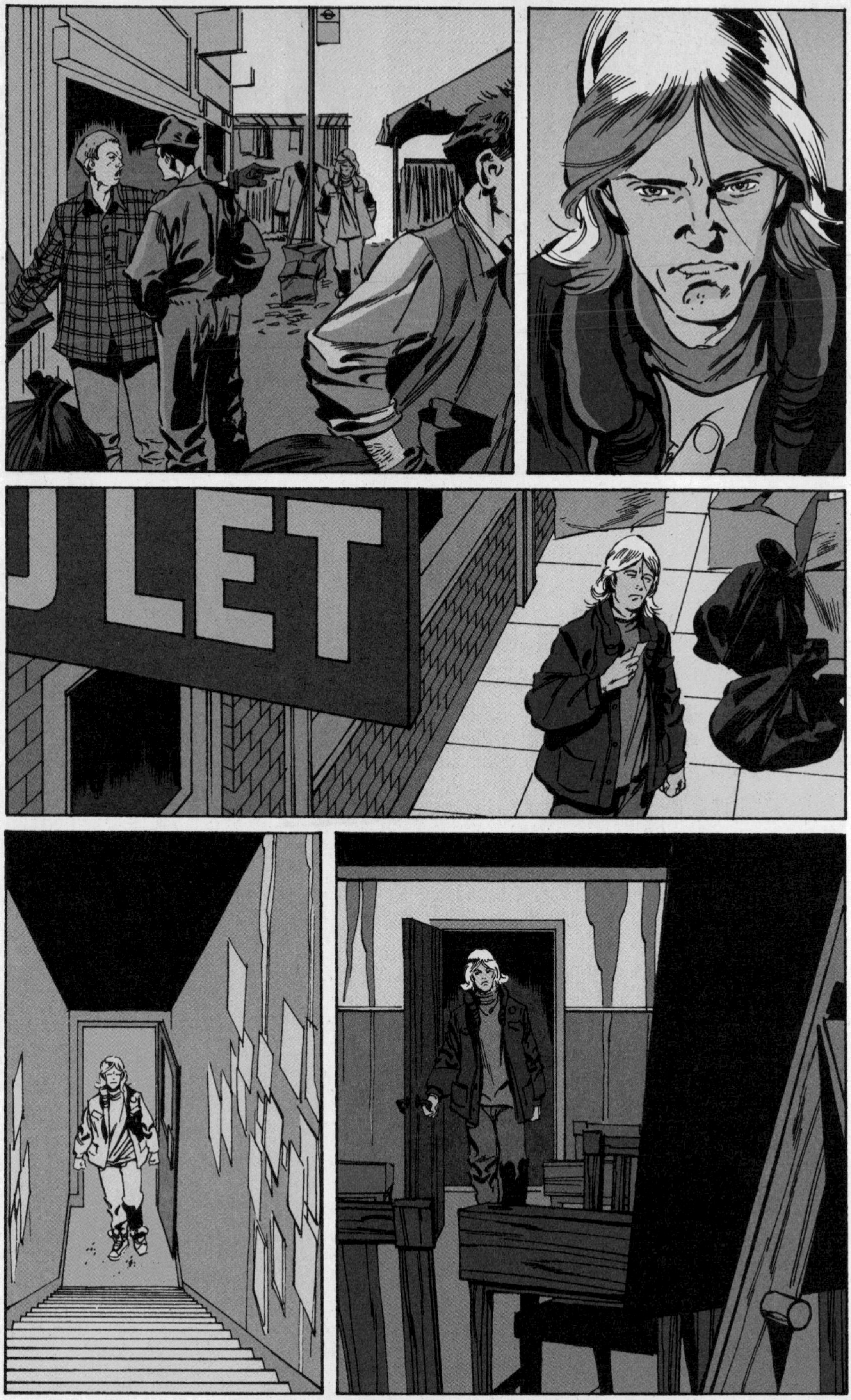
LET

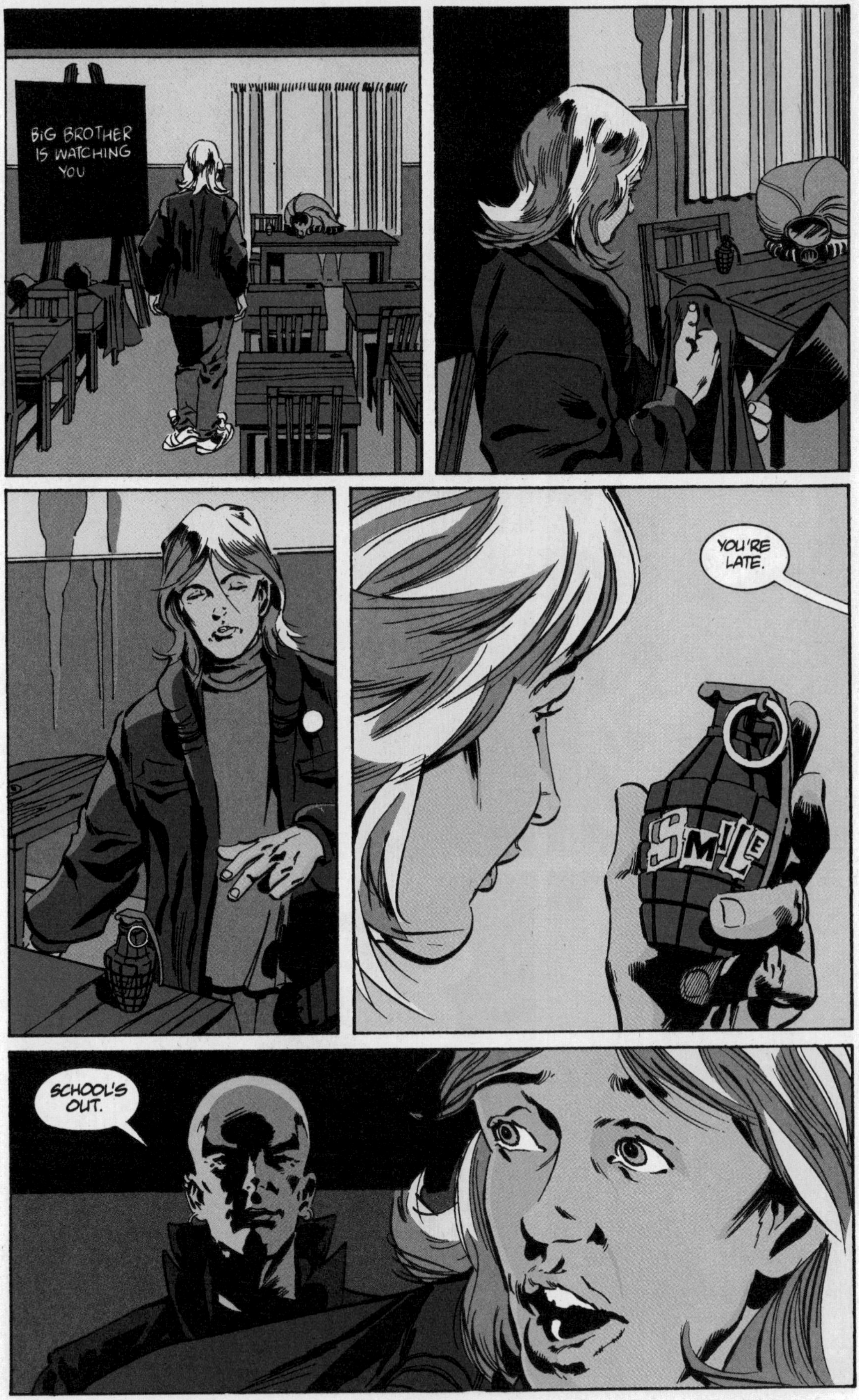
BIG BROTHER
IS WATCHING
YOU
YOU'RE LATE.
SMILE
SCHOOL'S OUT.

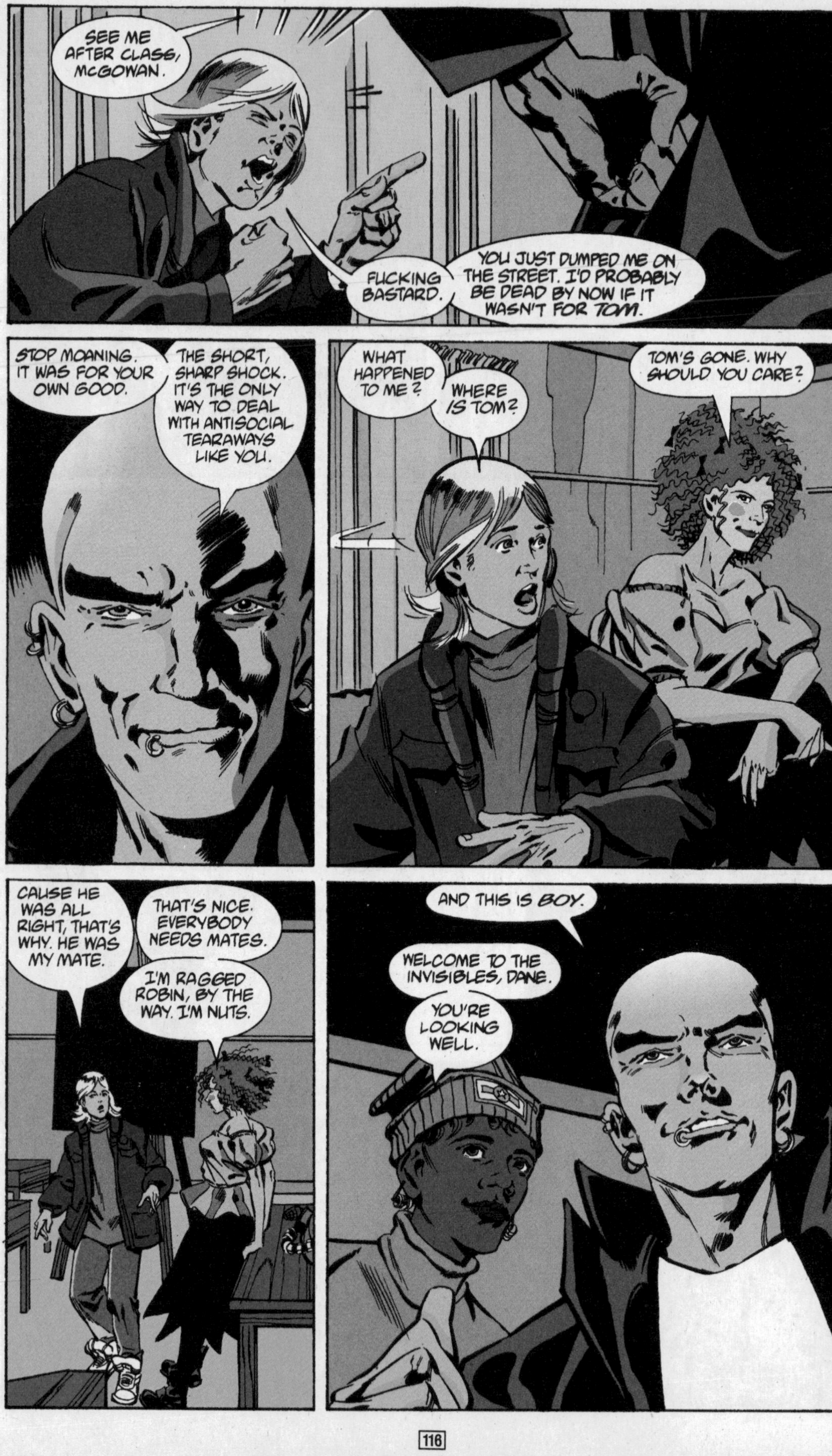
SEE ME AFTER CLASS, MCGOWAN.
FUCKING BASTARD.
YOU JUST DUMPED ME ON THE STREET. I'D PROBABLY BE DEAD BY NOW IF IT WASN'T FOR *TOM*.
STOP MOANING. IT WAS FOR YOUR OWN GOOD.
THE SHORT, SHARP SHOCK. IT'S THE ONLY WAY TO DEAL WITH ANTISOCIAL TEARAWAYS LIKE YOU.
WHAT HAPPENED TO ME?
WHERE *IS* TOM?
TOM'S GONE. WHY SHOULD YOU CARE?
CAUSE HE WAS ALL RIGHT, THAT'S WHY. HE WAS MY MATE.
THAT'S NICE. EVERYBODY NEEDS MATES.
I'M RAGGED ROBIN, BY THE WAY. I'M NUTS.
AND THIS IS *BOY*.
WELCOME TO THE INVISIBLES, DANE.
YOU'RE LOOKING WELL.

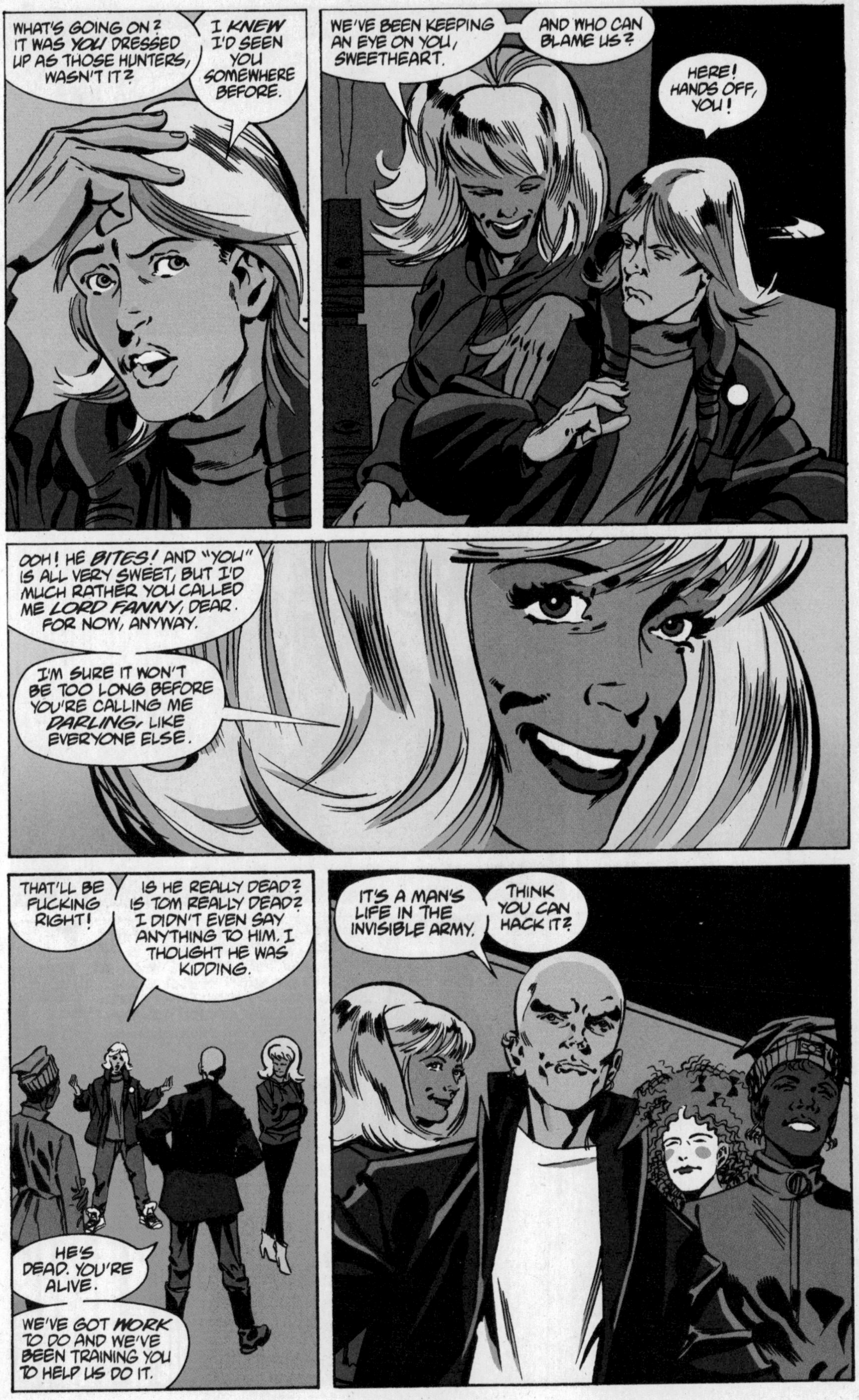

WHAT'S GOING ON? IT WAS YOU DRESSED UP AS THOSE HUNTERS, WASN'T IT?
I KNEW I'D SEEN YOU SOMEWHERE BEFORE.
WE'VE BEEN KEEPING AN EYE ON YOU, SWEETHEART.
AND WHO CAN BLAME US?
HERE! HANDS OFF, YOU!
OOH! HE BITES! AND "YOU" IS ALL VERY SWEET, BUT I'D MUCH RATHER YOU CALLED ME LORD FANNY, DEAR. FOR NOW, ANYWAY.
I'M SURE IT WON'T BE TOO LONG BEFORE YOU'RE CALLING ME DARLING, LIKE EVERYONE ELSE.
THAT'LL BE FUCKING RIGHT!
IS HE REALLY DEAD? IS TOM REALLY DEAD? I DIDN'T EVEN SAY ANYTHING TO HIM. I THOUGHT HE WAS KIDDING.
HE'S DEAD. YOU'RE ALIVE.
WE'VE GOT WORK TO DO AND WE'VE BEEN TRAINING YOU TO HELP US DO IT.
IT'S A MAN'S LIFE IN THE INVISIBLE ARMY.
THINK YOU CAN HACK IT?

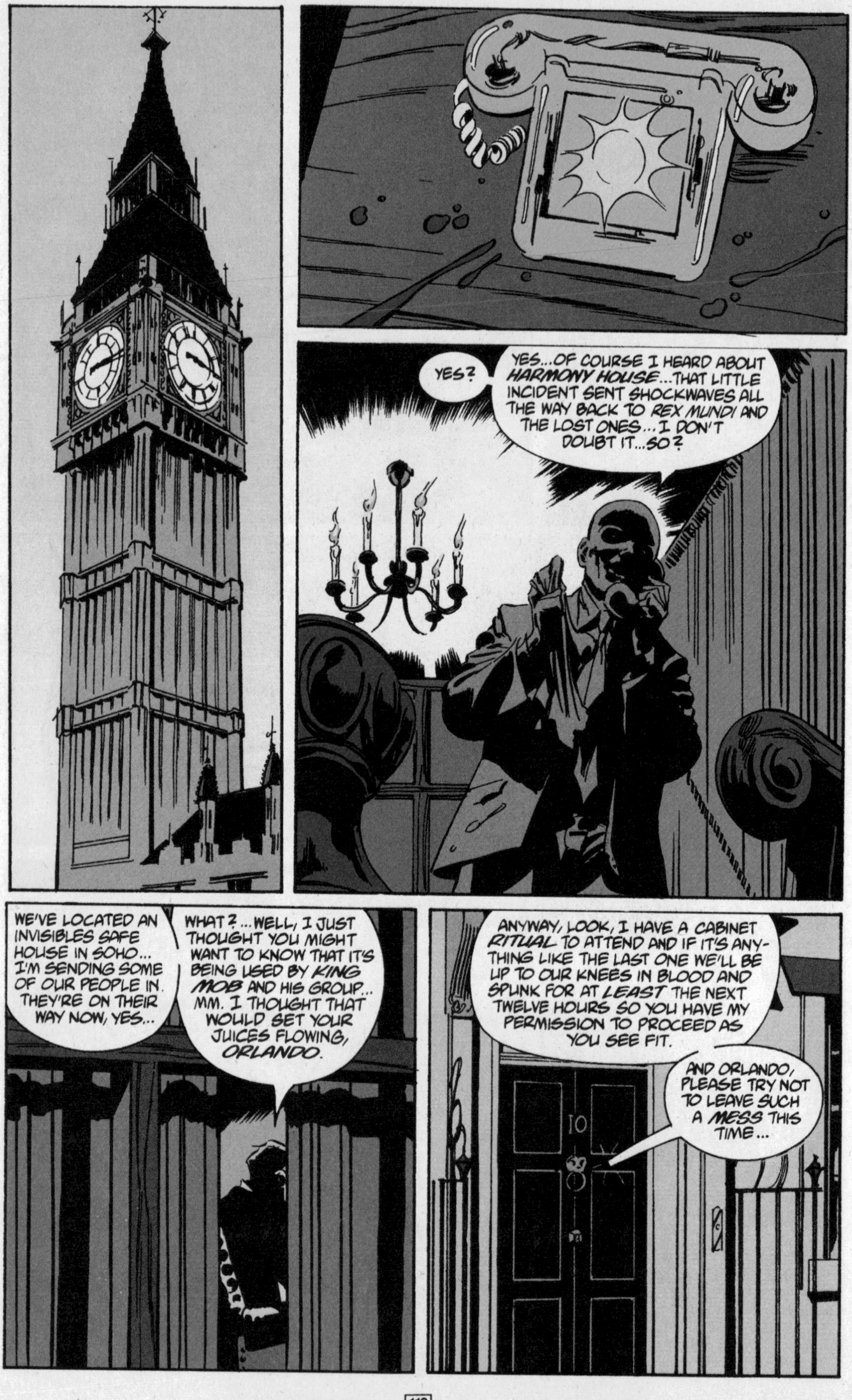
YES?
YES...OF COURSE I HEARD ABOUT HARMONY HOUSE...THAT LITTLE INCIDENT SENT SHOCKWAVES ALL THE WAY BACK TO REX MUNDI AND THE LOST ONES... I DON'T DOUBT IT...SO?
WE'VE LOCATED AN INVISIBLES SAFE HOUSE IN SOHO... I'M SENDING SOME OF OUR PEOPLE IN. THEY'RE ON THEIR WAY NOW, YES...
WHAT? ...WELL, I JUST THOUGHT YOU MIGHT WANT TO KNOW THAT IT'S BEING USED BY KING MOB AND HIS GROUP... MM. I THOUGHT THAT WOULD SET YOUR JUICES FLOWING, ORLANDO.
ANYWAY, LOOK, I HAVE A CABINET RITUAL TO ATTEND AND IF IT'S ANYTHING LIKE THE LAST ONE WE'LL BE UP TO OUR KNEES IN BLOOD AND SPUNK FOR AT LEAST THE NEXT TWELVE HOURS SO YOU HAVE MY PERMISSION TO PROCEED AS YOU SEE FIT.
AND ORLANDO, PLEASE TRY NOT TO LEAVE SUCH A MESS THIS TIME...
10

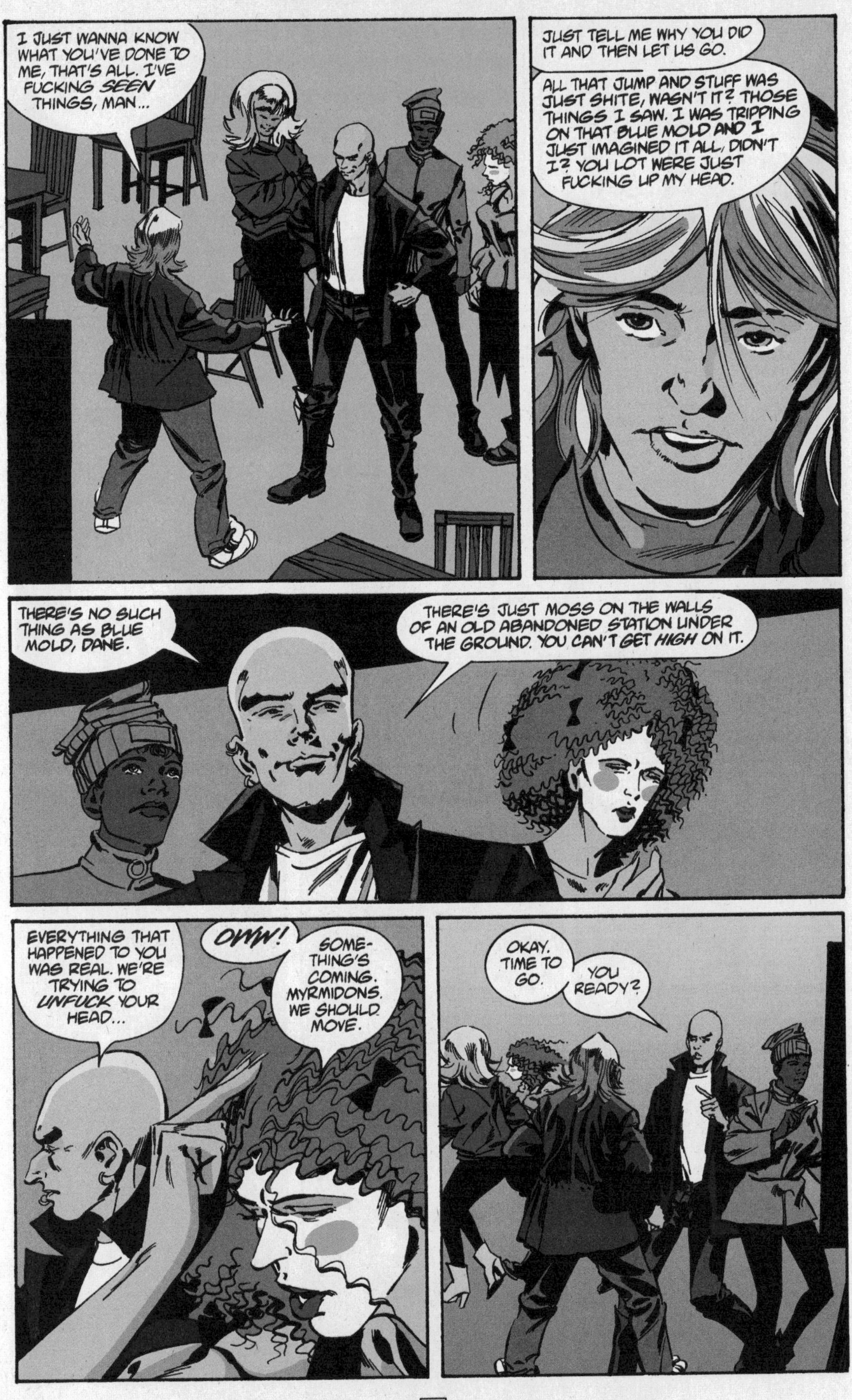
I JUST WANNA KNOW WHAT YOU'VE DONE TO ME, THAT'S ALL. I'VE FUCKING SEEN THINGS, MAN...
JUST TELL ME WHY YOU DID IT AND THEN LET US GO.
ALL THAT JUMP AND STUFF WAS JUST SHITE, WASN'T IT? THOSE THINGS I SAW. I WAS TRIPPING ON THAT BLUE MOLD AND I JUST IMAGINED IT ALL, DIDN'T I? YOU LOT WERE JUST FUCKING UP MY HEAD.
THERE'S NO SUCH THING AS BLUE MOLD, DANE.
THERE'S JUST MOSS ON THE WALLS OF AN OLD ABANDONED STATION UNDER THE GROUND. YOU CAN'T GET HIGH ON IT.
EVERYTHING THAT HAPPENED TO YOU WAS REAL. WE'RE TRYING TO UNFUCK YOUR HEAD...
OWW!
SOME-THING'S COMING. MYRMIDONS. WE SHOULD MOVE.
OKAY. TIME TO GO.
YOU READY?

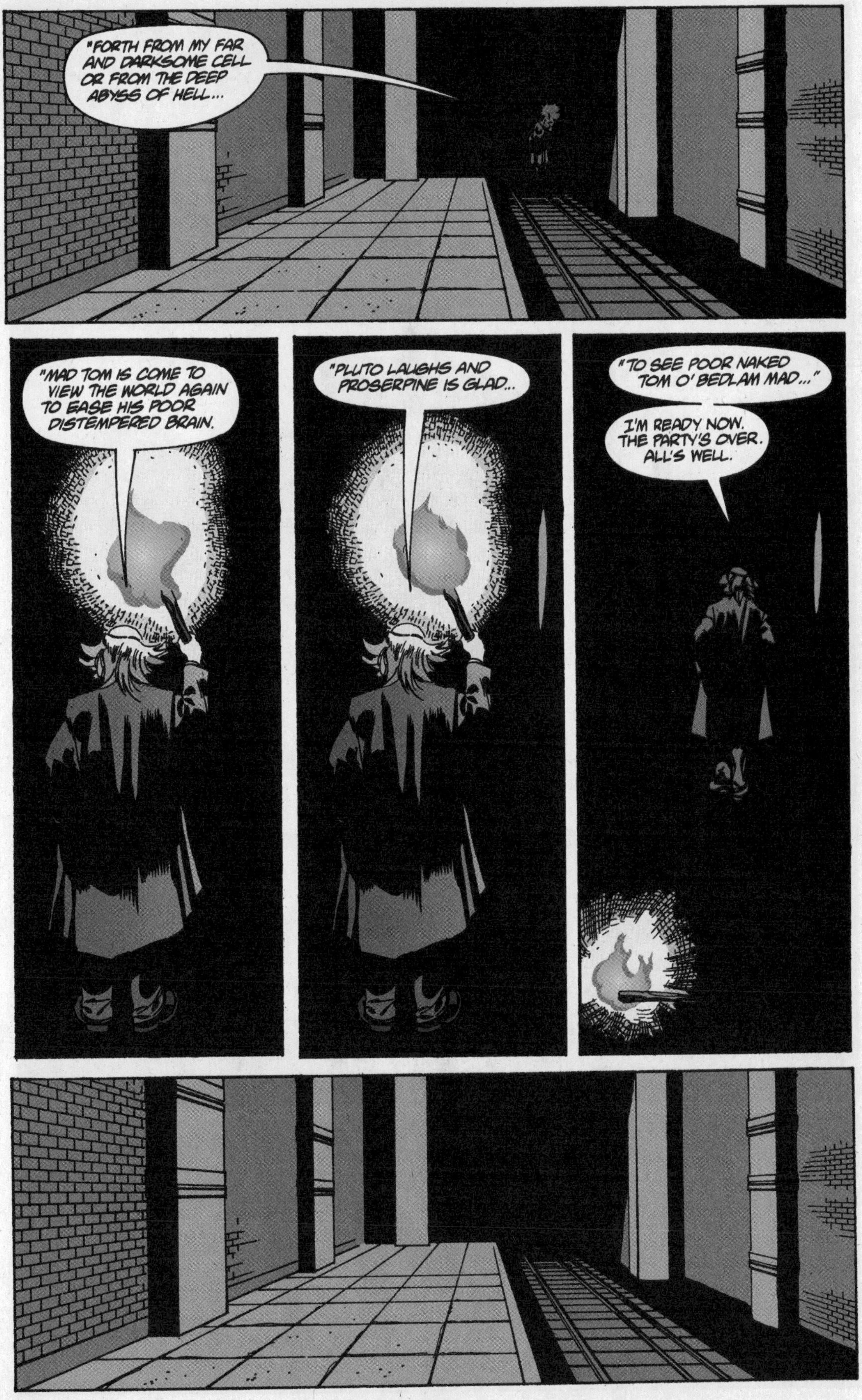
"FORTH FROM MY FAR AND DARKSOME CELL OR FROM THE DEEP ABYSS OF HELL...
"MAD TOM IS COME TO VIEW THE WORLD AGAIN TO EASE HIS POOR DISTEMPERED BRAIN.
"PLUTO LAUGHS AND PROSERPINE IS GLAD...
"TO SEE POOR NAKED TOM O' BEDLAM MAD..."
I'M READY NOW. THE PARTY'S OVER. ALL'S WELL.

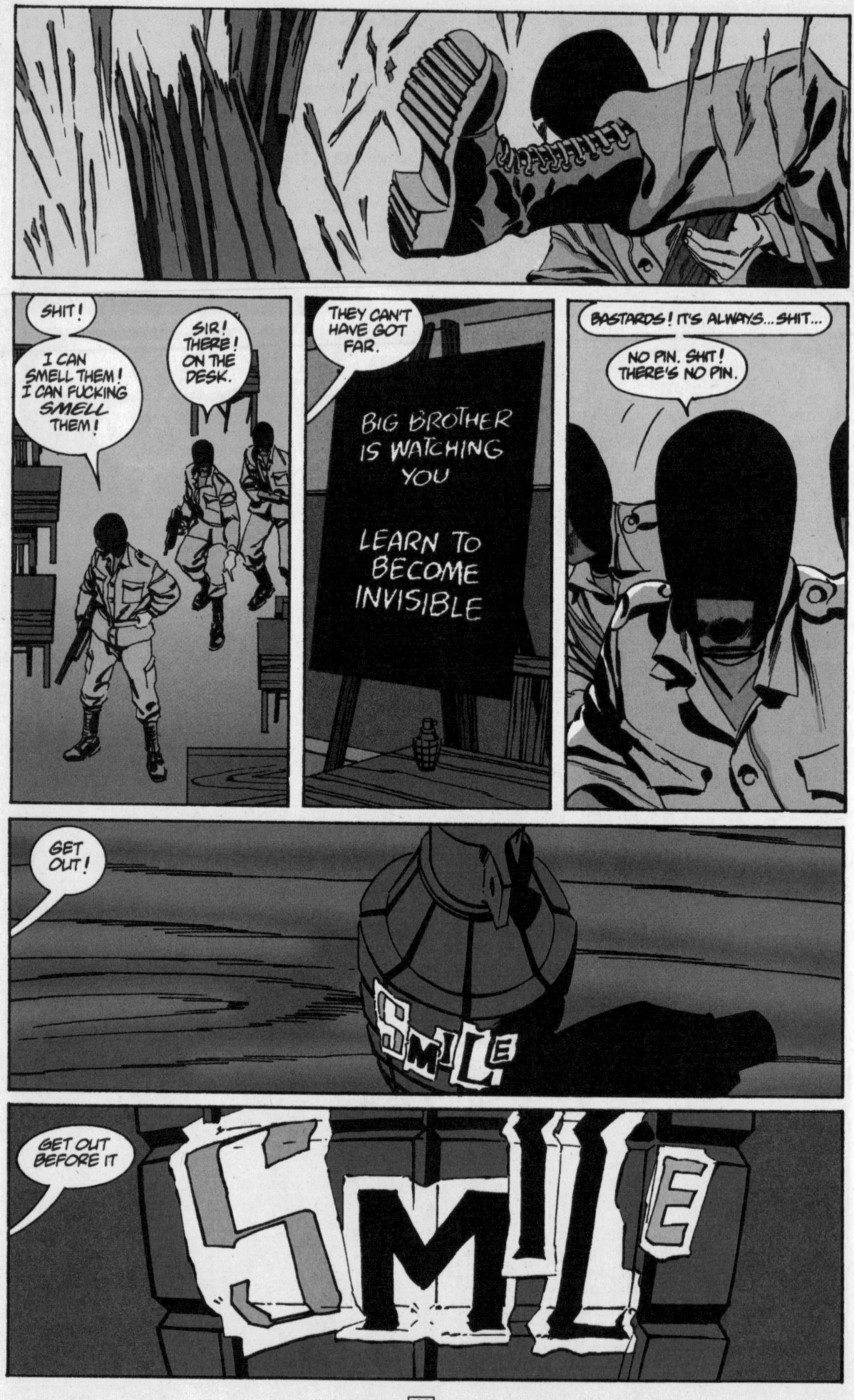
SHIT!
I CAN SMELL THEM! I CAN FUCKING SMELL THEM!
SIR! THERE! ON THE DESK.
THEY CAN'T HAVE GOT FAR.
BIG BROTHER IS WATCHING YOU
LEARN TO BECOME INVISIBLE
BASTARDS! IT'S ALWAYS...SHIT...
NO PIN. SHIT! THERE'S NO PIN.
GET OUT!
SMILE
GET OUT BEFORE IT
SMILE

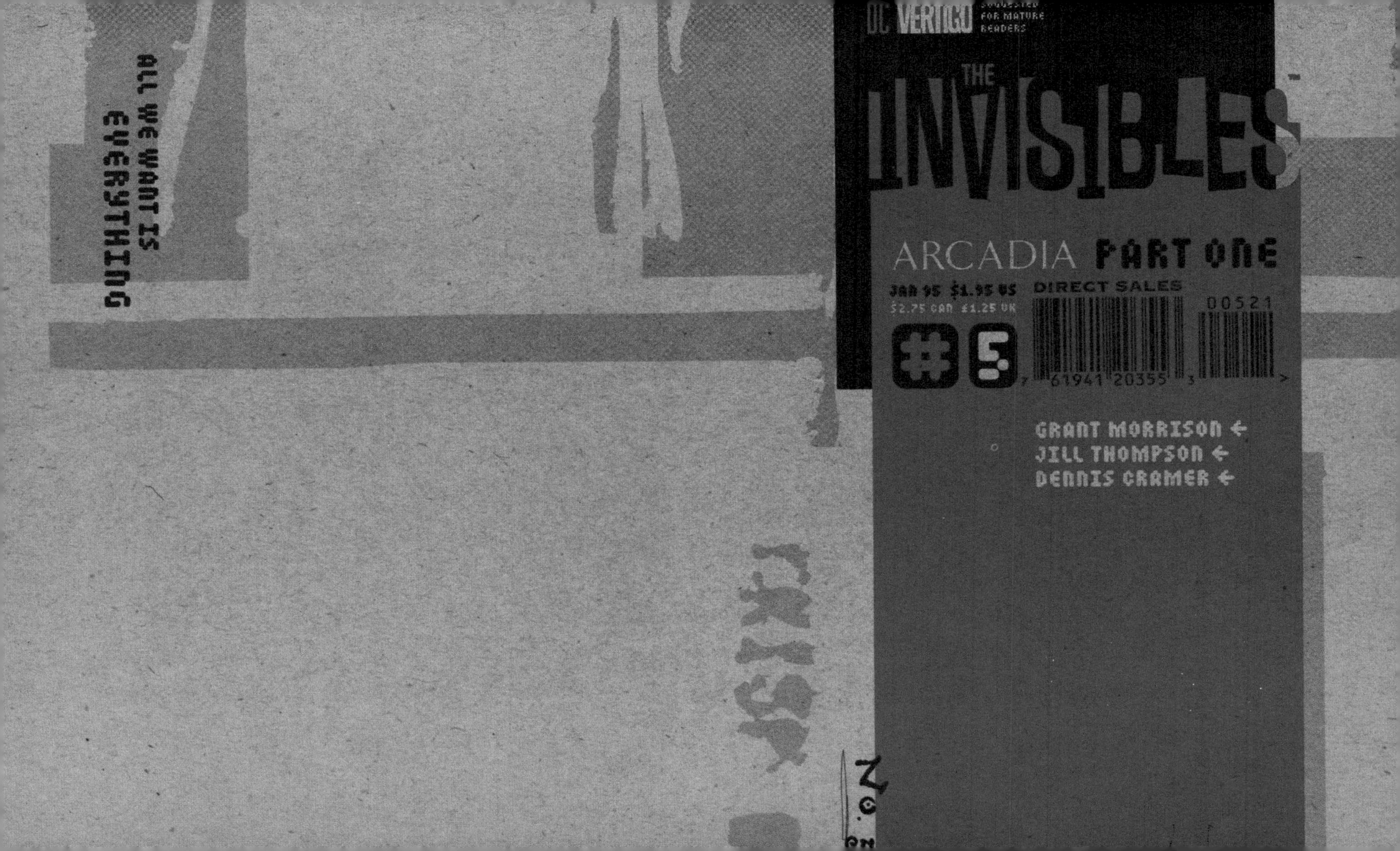

DC VERTIGO
FOR MATURE READERS
THE INVISIBLES
ARCADIA PART ONE
JAN 95 $1.95 US
$2.75 CAN £1.25 UK
DIRECT SALES
#5
GRANT MORRISON
JILL THOMPSON
DENNIS CRAMER
ALL WE WANT IS
EVERYTHING

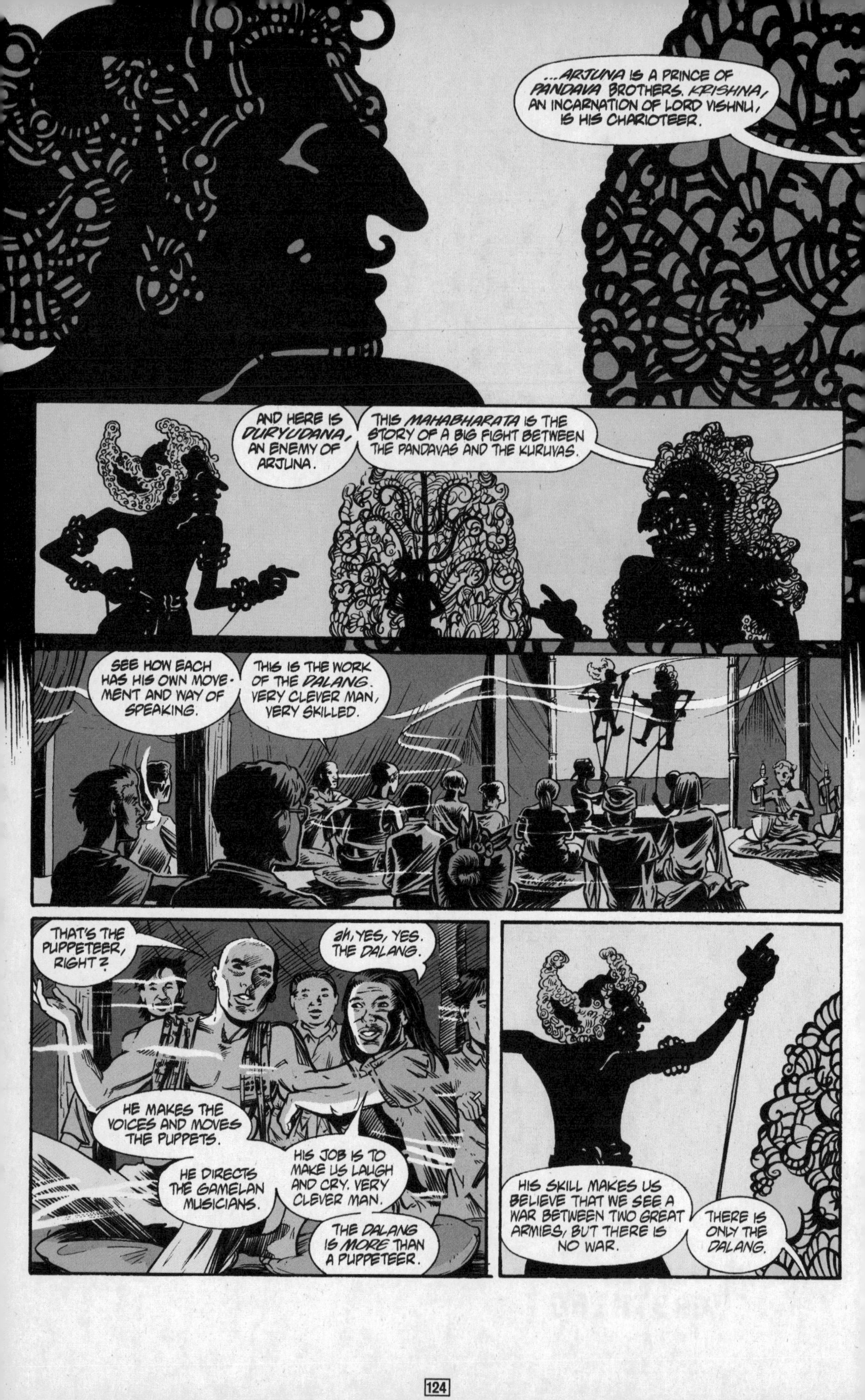
...ARJUNA IS A PRINCE OF PANDAVA BROTHERS. KRISHNA, AN INCARNATION OF LORD VISHNU, IS HIS CHARIOTEER.
AND HERE IS DURYUDANA, AN ENEMY OF ARJUNA.
THIS MAHABHARATA IS THE STORY OF A BIG FIGHT BETWEEN THE PANDAVAS AND THE KURUVAS.
SEE HOW EACH HAS HIS OWN MOVE-MENT AND WAY OF SPEAKING.
THIS IS THE WORK OF THE DALANG. VERY CLEVER MAN, VERY SKILLED.
THAT'S THE PUPPETEER, RIGHT?
AH, YES, YES. THE DALANG.
HE MAKES THE VOICES AND MOVES THE PUPPETS.
HE DIRECTS THE GAMELAN MUSICIANS.
HIS JOB IS TO MAKE US LAUGH AND CRY. VERY CLEVER MAN.
THE DALANG IS MORE THAN A PUPPETEER.
HIS SKILL MAKES US BELIEVE THAT WE SEE A WAR BETWEEN TWO GREAT ARMIES, BUT THERE IS NO WAR.
THERE IS ONLY THE DALANG.

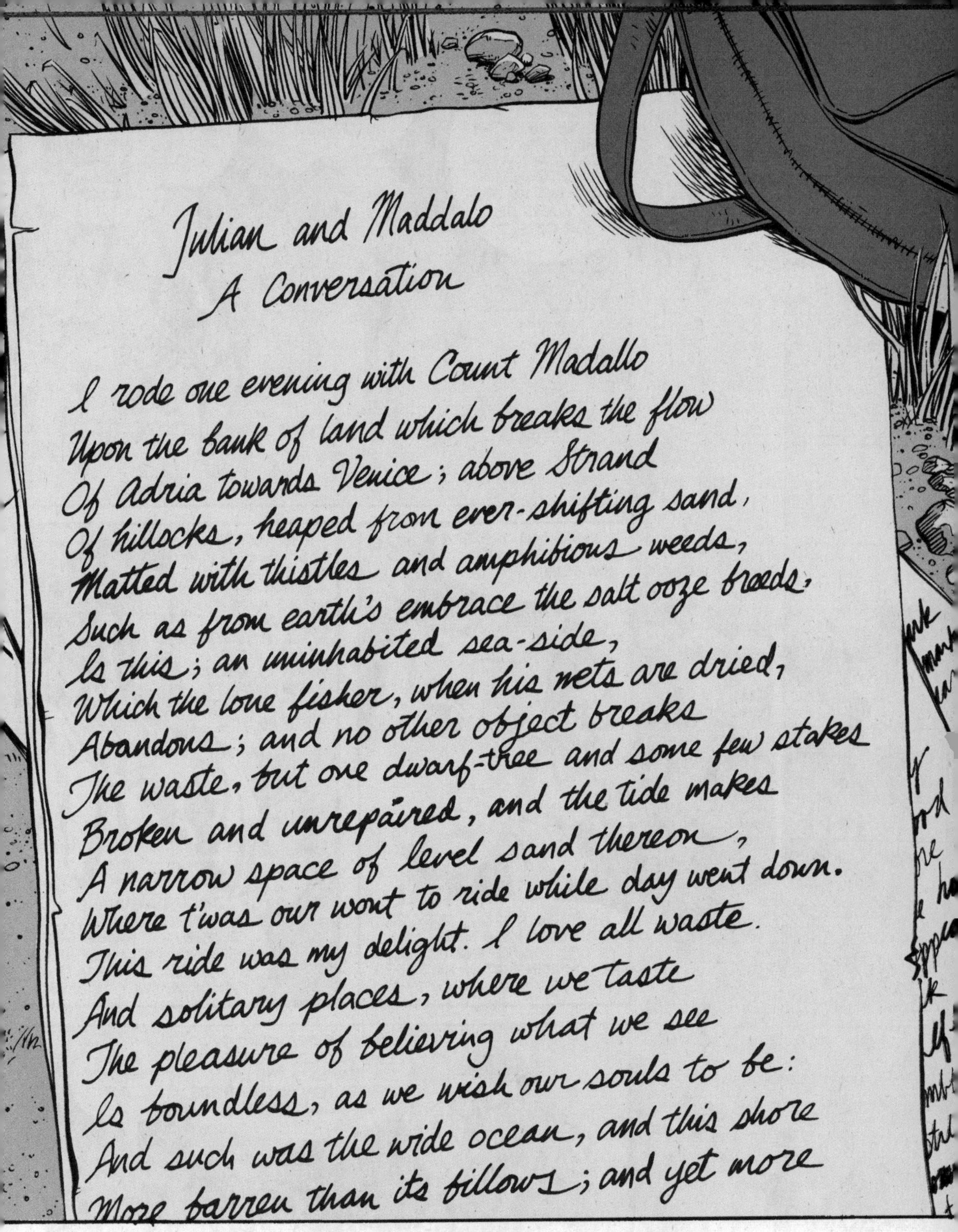
Julian and Maddalo
A Conversation
I rode one evening with Count Madallo
Upon the bank of land which breaks the flow
Of Adria towards Venice; above Strand
Of hillocks, heaped from ever-shifting sand,
Matted with thistles and amphibious weeds,
Such as from earth's embrace the salt ooze breeds,
Is this; an uninhabited sea-side,
Which the lone fisher, when his nets are dried,
Abandons; and no other object breaks
The waste, but one dwarf-tree and some few stakes
Broken and unrepaired, and the tide makes
A narrow space of level sand thereon,
Where t'was our wont to ride while day went down.
This ride was my delight. I love all waste
And solitary places, where we taste
The pleasure of believing what we see
Is boundless, as we wish our souls to be:
And such was the wide ocean, and this shore
More barren than its billows; and yet more

ARCADIA

PART 1 BLOODY POETRY

GRANT MORRISON → WRITER JILL THOMPSON → PENCILS DENNIS CRAMER → INKS

DANIEL VOZZO → COLORS CLEM ROBINS → LETTERS

JULIE ROTTENBERG → ASSISTANT EDITOR STUART MOORE → EDITOR

THE INVISIBLES CREATED BY GRANT MORRISON

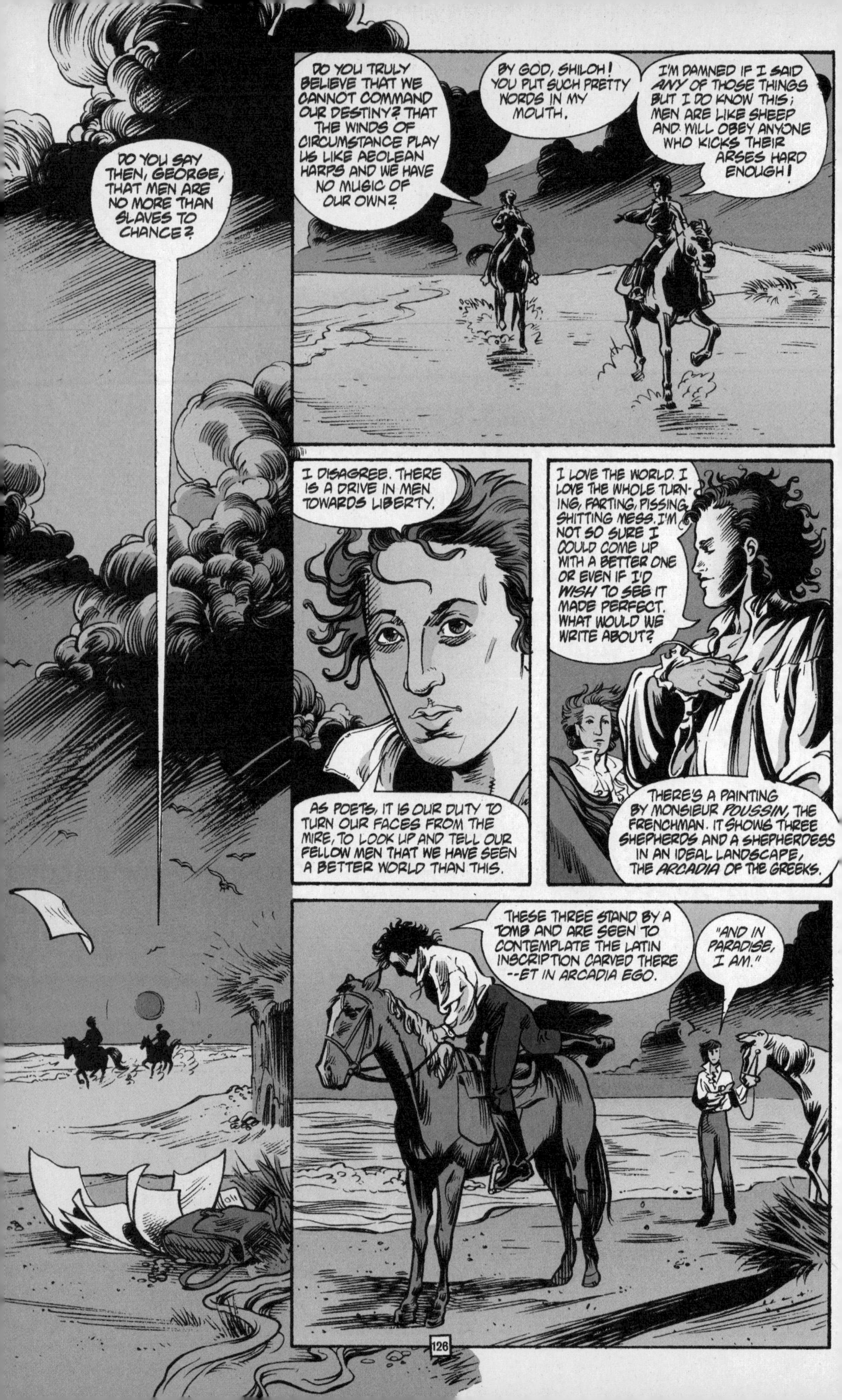
DO YOU SAY THEN, GEORGE, THAT MEN ARE NO MORE THAN SLAVES TO CHANCE?
DO YOU TRULY BELIEVE THAT WE CANNOT COMMAND OUR DESTINY? THAT THE WINDS OF CIRCUMSTANCE PLAY US LIKE AEOLEAN HARPS AND WE HAVE NO MUSIC OF OUR OWN?
BY GOD, SHILOH! YOU PUT SUCH PRETTY WORDS IN MY MOUTH.
I'M DAMNED IF I SAID ANY OF THOSE THINGS BUT I DO KNOW THIS; MEN ARE LIKE SHEEP AND WILL OBEY ANYONE WHO KICKS THEIR ARSES HARD ENOUGH!
I DISAGREE. THERE IS A DRIVE IN MEN TOWARDS LIBERTY.
AS POETS, IT IS OUR DUTY TO TURN OUR FACES FROM THE MIRE, TO LOOK UP AND TELL OUR FELLOW MEN THAT WE HAVE SEEN A BETTER WORLD THAN THIS.
I LOVE THE WORLD. I LOVE THE WHOLE TURNING, FARTING, PISSING, SHITTING MESS. I'M NOT SO SURE I COULD COME UP WITH A BETTER ONE OR EVEN IF I'D WISH TO SEE IT MADE PERFECT. WHAT WOULD WE WRITE ABOUT?
THERE'S A PAINTING BY MONSIEUR POUSSIN, THE FRENCHMAN. IT SHOWS THREE SHEPHERDS AND A SHEPHERDESS IN AN IDEAL LANDSCAPE, THE ARCADIA OF THE GREEKS.
THESE THREE STAND BY A TOMB AND ARE SEEN TO CONTEMPLATE THE LATIN INSCRIPTION CARVED THERE --ET IN ARCADIA EGO.
"AND IN PARADISE, I AM."

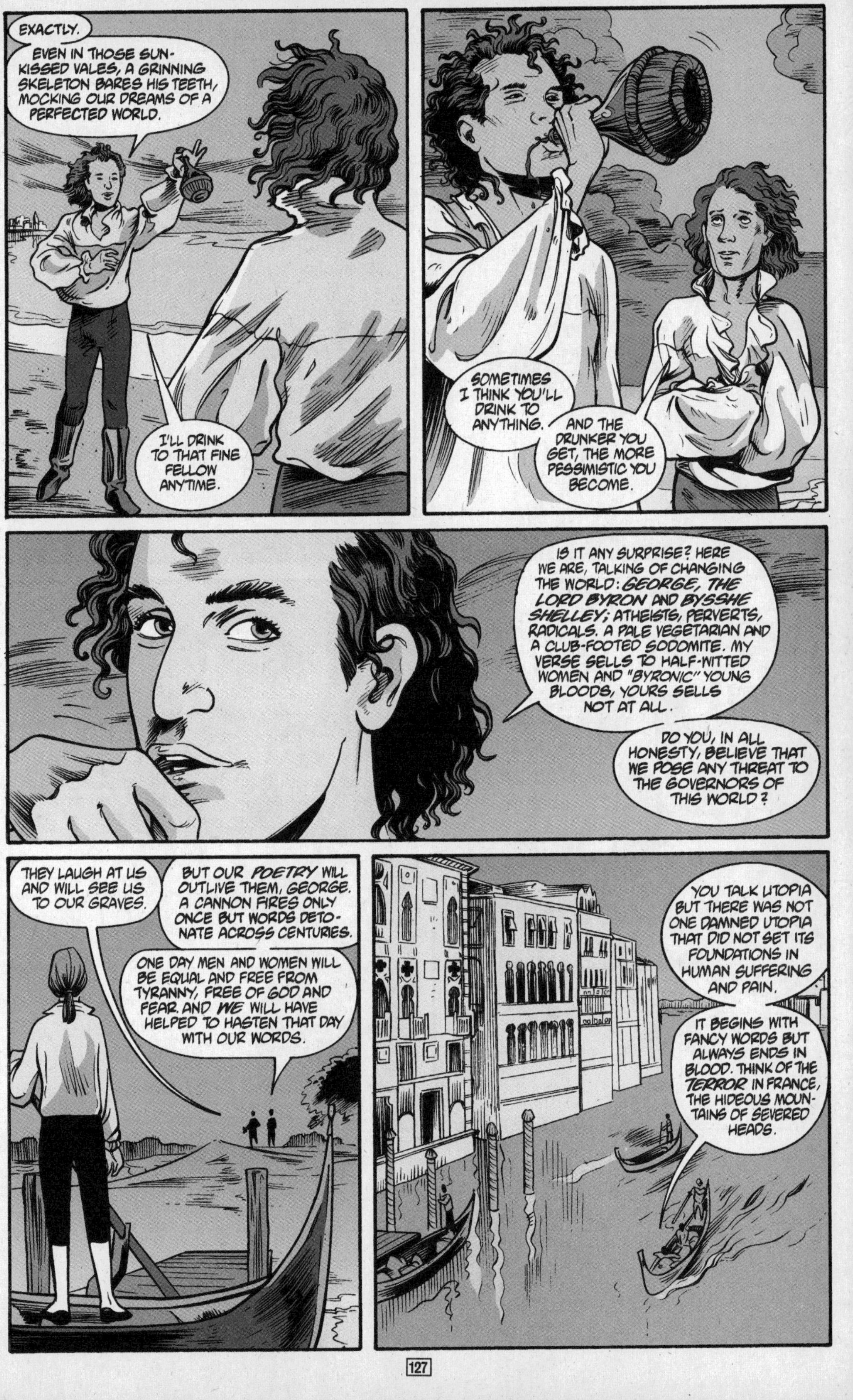
EXACTLY.
EVEN IN THOSE SUN-KISSED VALES, A GRINNING SKELETON BARES HIS TEETH, MOCKING OUR DREAMS OF A PERFECTED WORLD.
I'LL DRINK TO THAT FINE FELLOW ANYTIME.
SOMETIMES I THINK YOU'LL DRINK TO ANYTHING.
AND THE DRUNKER YOU GET, THE MORE PESSIMISTIC YOU BECOME.
IS IT ANY SURPRISE? HERE WE ARE, TALKING OF CHANGING THE WORLD: GEORGE, THE LORD BYRON AND BYSSHE SHELLEY; ATHEISTS, PERVERTS, RADICALS. A PALE VEGETARIAN AND A CLUB-FOOTED SODOMITE. MY VERSE SELLS TO HALF-WITTED WOMEN AND "BYRONIC" YOUNG BLOODS, YOURS SELLS NOT AT ALL.
DO YOU, IN ALL HONESTY, BELIEVE THAT WE POSE ANY THREAT TO THE GOVERNORS OF THIS WORLD?
THEY LAUGH AT US AND WILL SEE US TO OUR GRAVES.
BUT OUR POETRY WILL OUTLIVE THEM, GEORGE. A CANNON FIRES ONLY ONCE BUT WORDS DETONATE ACROSS CENTURIES.
ONE DAY MEN AND WOMEN WILL BE EQUAL AND FREE FROM TYRANNY, FREE OF GOD AND FEAR. AND WE WILL HAVE HELPED TO HASTEN THAT DAY WITH OUR WORDS.
YOU TALK UTOPIA BUT THERE WAS NOT ONE DAMNED UTOPIA THAT DID NOT SET ITS FOUNDATIONS IN HUMAN SUFFERING AND PAIN.
IT BEGINS WITH FANCY WORDS BUT ALWAYS ENDS IN BLOOD. THINK OF THE TERROR IN FRANCE, THE HIDEOUS MOUNTAINS OF SEVERED HEADS.

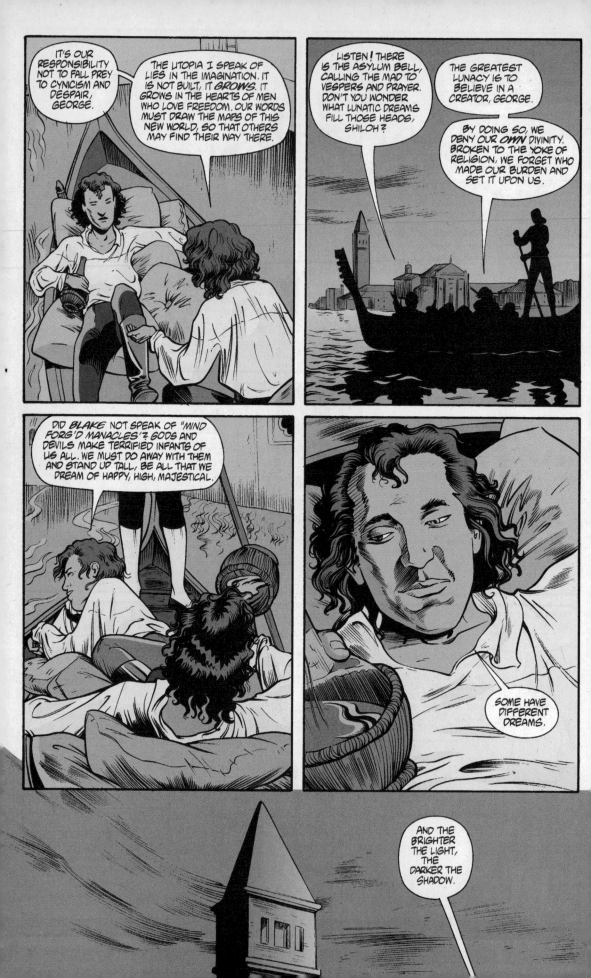

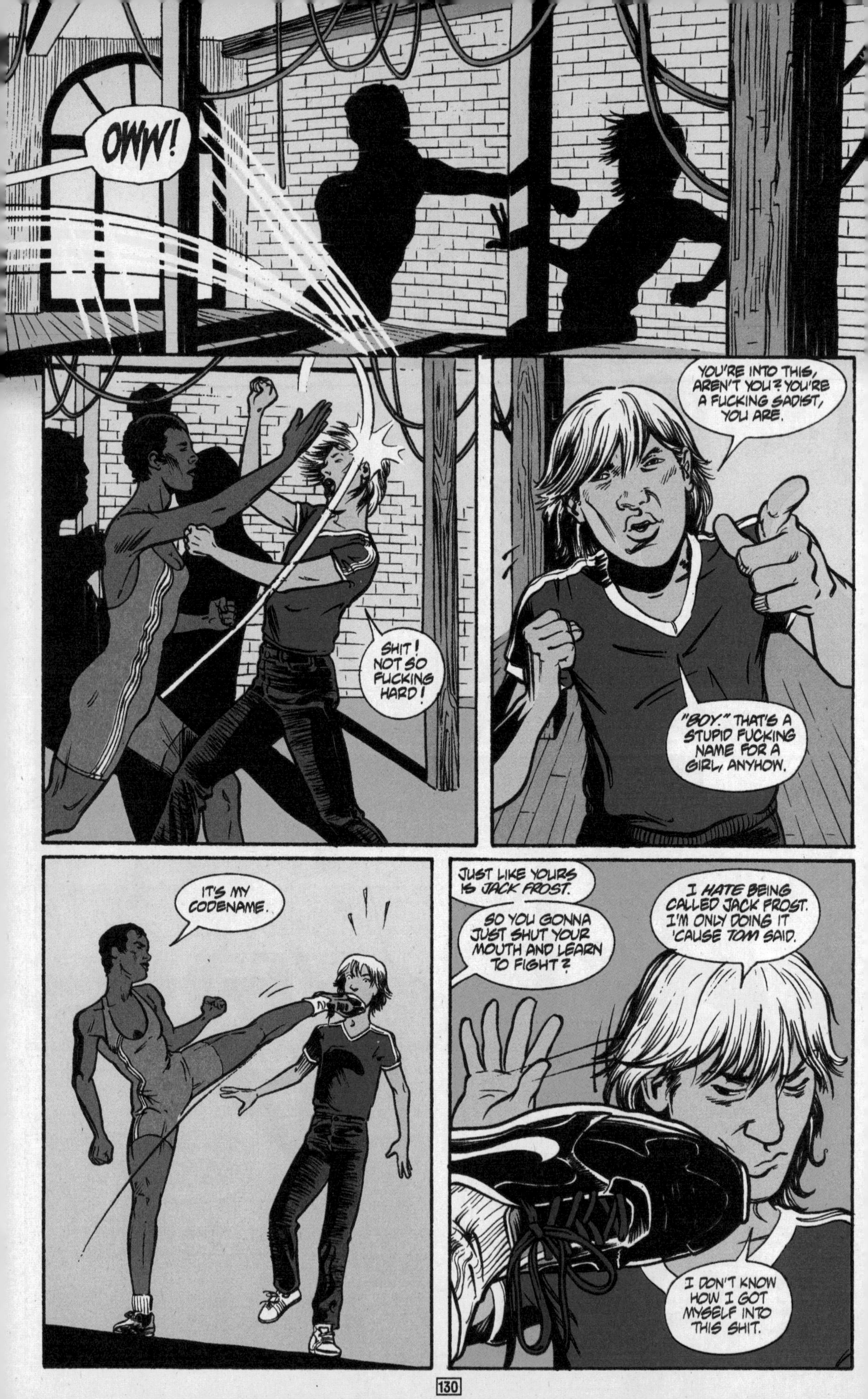
OWW!
SHIT! NOT SO FUCKING HARD!
YOU'RE INTO THIS, AREN'T YOU? YOU'RE A FUCKING SADIST, YOU ARE.
"BOY." THAT'S A STUPID FUCKING NAME FOR A GIRL, ANYHOW.
IT'S MY CODENAME.
JUST LIKE YOURS IS JACK FROST.
SO YOU GONNA JUST SHUT YOUR MOUTH AND LEARN TO FIGHT?
I HATE BEING CALLED JACK FROST. I'M ONLY DOING IT 'CAUSE TOM SAID.
I DON'T KNOW HOW I GOT MYSELF INTO THIS SHIT.

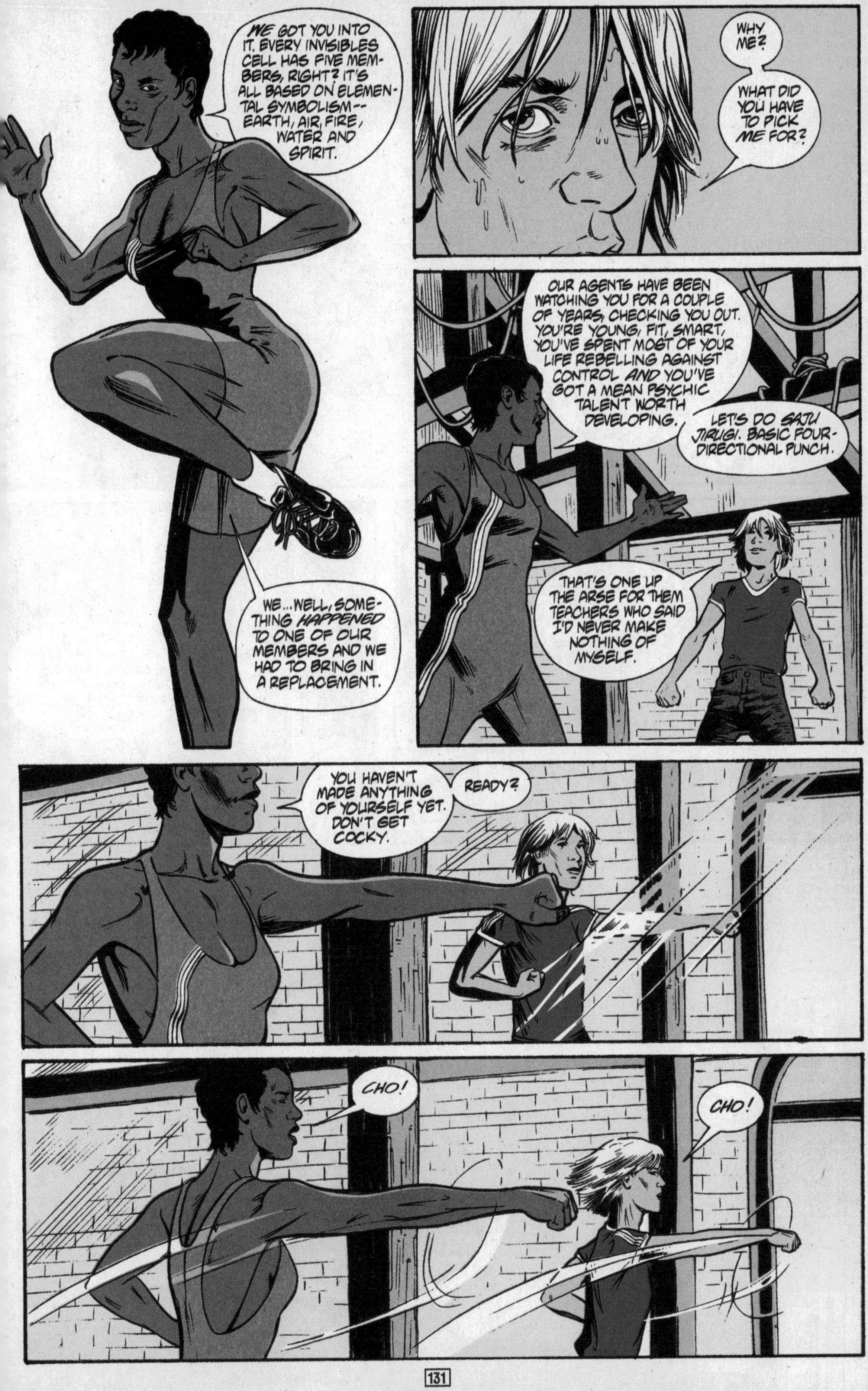

WE GOT YOU INTO IT. EVERY INVISIBLES CELL HAS FIVE MEMBERS, RIGHT? IT'S ALL BASED ON ELEMENTAL SYMBOLISM-- EARTH, AIR, FIRE, WATER AND SPIRIT.
WE...WELL, SOMETHING HAPPENED TO ONE OF OUR MEMBERS AND WE HAD TO BRING IN A REPLACEMENT.
WHY ME?
WHAT DID YOU HAVE TO PICK ME FOR?
OUR AGENTS HAVE BEEN WATCHING YOU FOR A COUPLE OF YEARS, CHECKING YOU OUT. YOU'RE YOUNG, FIT, SMART, YOU'VE SPENT MOST OF YOUR LIFE REBELLING AGAINST CONTROL AND YOU'VE GOT A MEAN PSYCHIC TALENT WORTH DEVELOPING.
LET'S DO SAJU JIRUGI. BASIC FOUR-DIRECTIONAL PUNCH.
THAT'S ONE UP THE ARSE FOR THEM TEACHERS WHO SAID I'D NEVER MAKE NOTHING OF MYSELF.
YOU HAVEN'T MADE ANYTHING OF YOURSELF YET. DON'T GET COCKY.
READY?
CHO!
CHO!

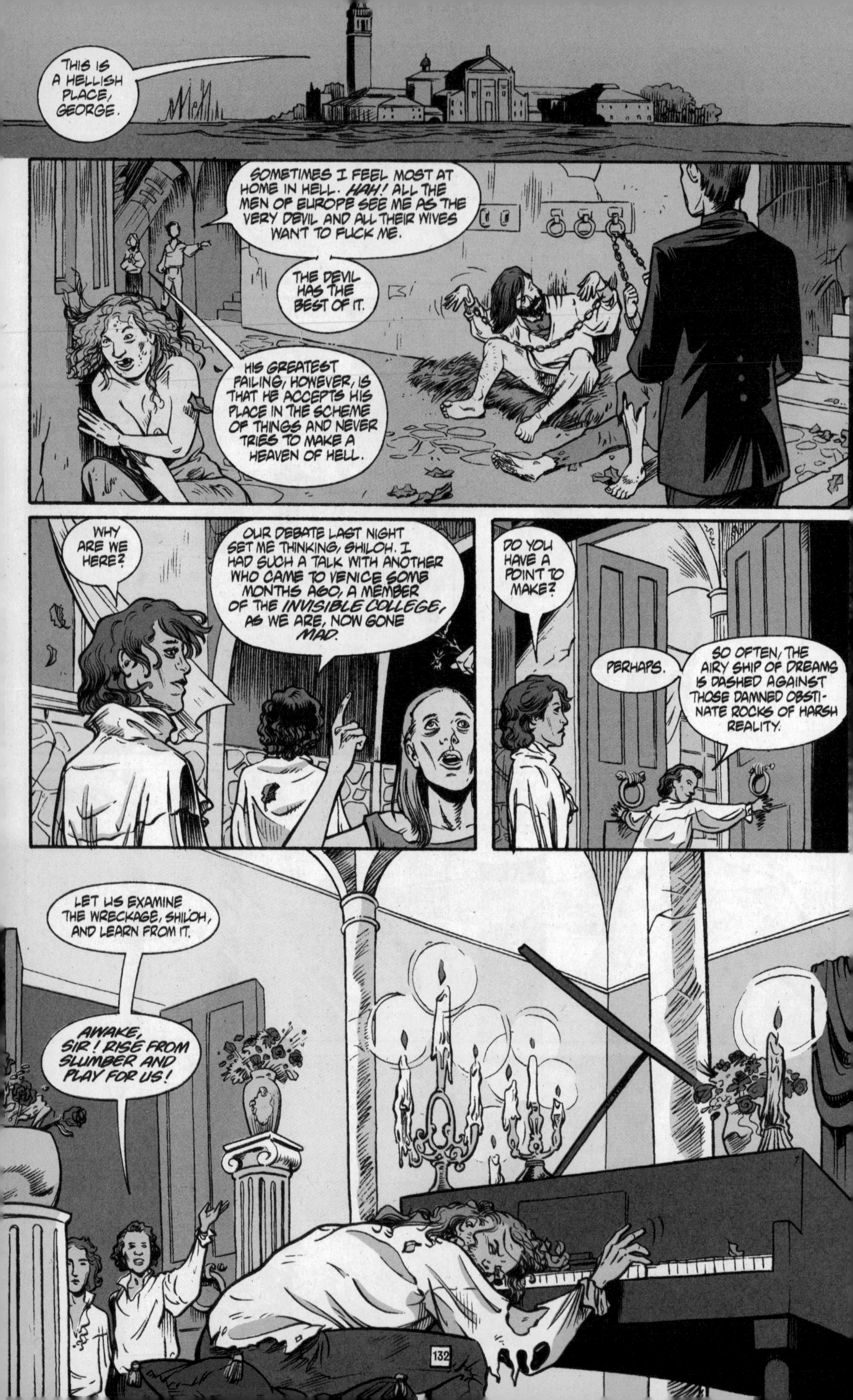

THIS IS A HELLISH PLACE, GEORGE.
SOMETIMES I FEEL MOST AT HOME IN HELL. HAH! ALL THE MEN OF EUROPE SEE ME AS THE VERY DEVIL AND ALL THEIR WIVES WANT TO FUCK ME.
THE DEVIL HAS THE BEST OF IT.
HIS GREATEST FAILING, HOWEVER, IS THAT HE ACCEPTS HIS PLACE IN THE SCHEME OF THINGS AND NEVER TRIES TO MAKE A HEAVEN OF HELL.
WHY ARE WE HERE?
OUR DEBATE LAST NIGHT SET ME THINKING, SHILOH. I HAD SUCH A TALK WITH ANOTHER WHO CAME TO VENICE SOME MONTHS AGO, A MEMBER OF THE INVISIBLE COLLEGE, AS WE ARE, NOW GONE MAD.
DO YOU HAVE A POINT TO MAKE?
PERHAPS.
SO OFTEN, THE AIRY SHIP OF DREAMS IS DASHED AGAINST THOSE DAMNED OBSTI-NATE ROCKS OF HARSH REALITY.
LET US EXAMINE THE WRECKAGE, SHILOH, AND LEARN FROM IT.
AWAKE, SIR! RISE FROM SLUMBER AND PLAY FOR US!

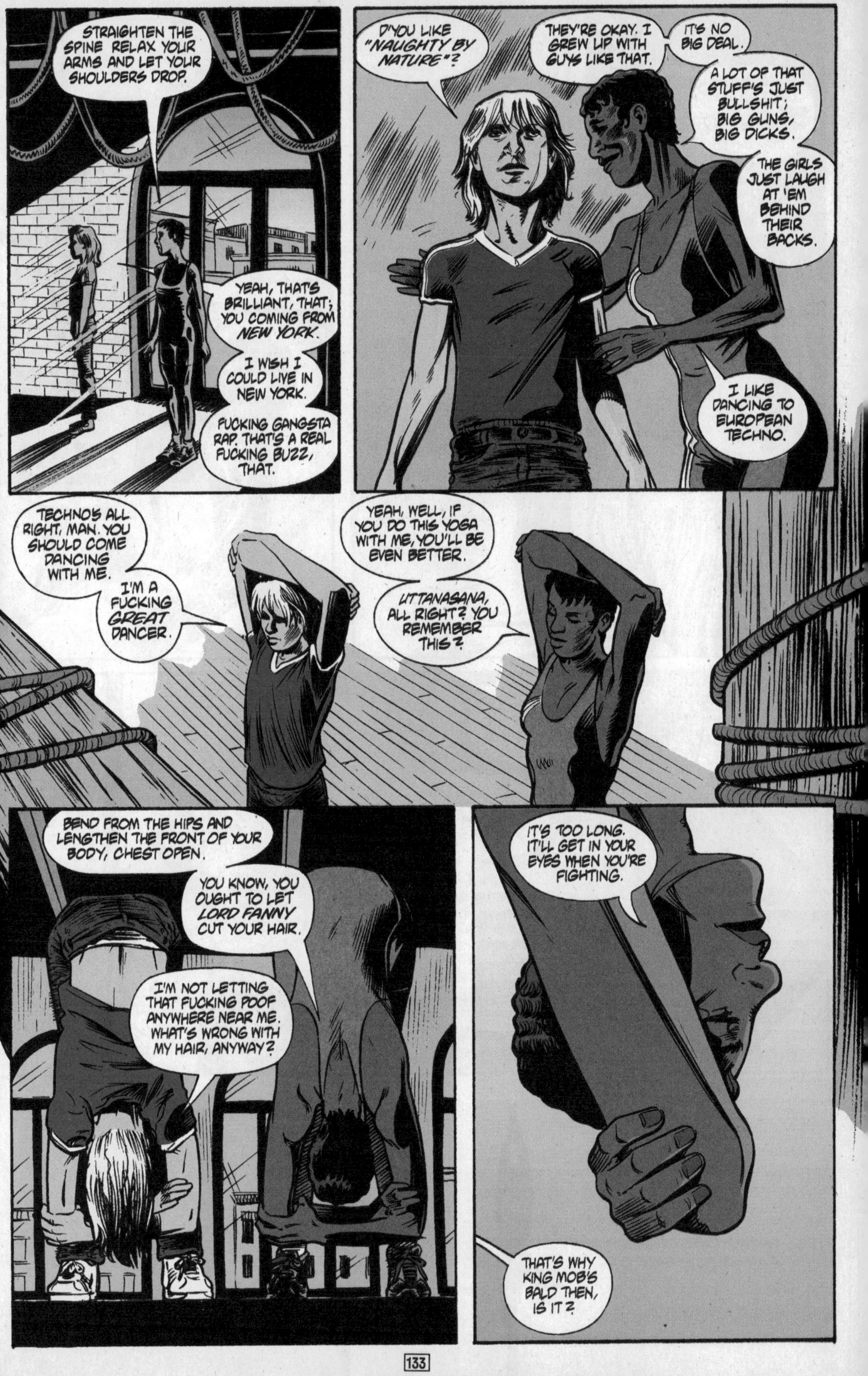
STRAIGHTEN THE SPINE RELAX YOUR ARMS AND LET YOUR SHOULDERS DROP.
YEAH, THAT'S BRILLIANT, THAT; YOU COMING FROM *NEW YORK*.
I WISH I COULD LIVE IN NEW YORK.
FUCKING GANGSTA RAP. THAT'S A REAL FUCKING BUZZ, THAT.
D'YOU LIKE *"NAUGHTY BY NATURE"*?
THEY'RE OKAY. I GREW UP WITH GUYS LIKE THAT.
IT'S NO BIG DEAL.
A LOT OF THAT STUFF'S JUST BULLSHIT; BIG GUNS, BIG DICKS.
THE GIRLS JUST LAUGH AT 'EM BEHIND THEIR BACKS.
I LIKE DANCING TO EUROPEAN TECHNO.
TECHNO'S ALL RIGHT, MAN. YOU SHOULD COME DANCING WITH ME.
I'M A FUCKING *GREAT* DANCER.
YEAH, WELL, IF YOU DO THIS YOGA WITH ME, YOU'LL BE EVEN BETTER.
UTTANASANA, ALL RIGHT? YOU REMEMBER THIS?
BEND FROM THE HIPS AND LENGTHEN THE FRONT OF YOUR BODY, CHEST OPEN.
YOU KNOW, YOU OUGHT TO LET *LORD FANNY* CUT YOUR HAIR.
I'M NOT LETTING THAT FUCKING POOF ANYWHERE NEAR ME. WHAT'S WRONG WITH MY HAIR, ANYWAY?
IT'S TOO LONG. IT'LL GET IN YOUR EYES WHEN YOU'RE FIGHTING.
THAT'S WHY KING MOB'S BALD THEN, IS IT?

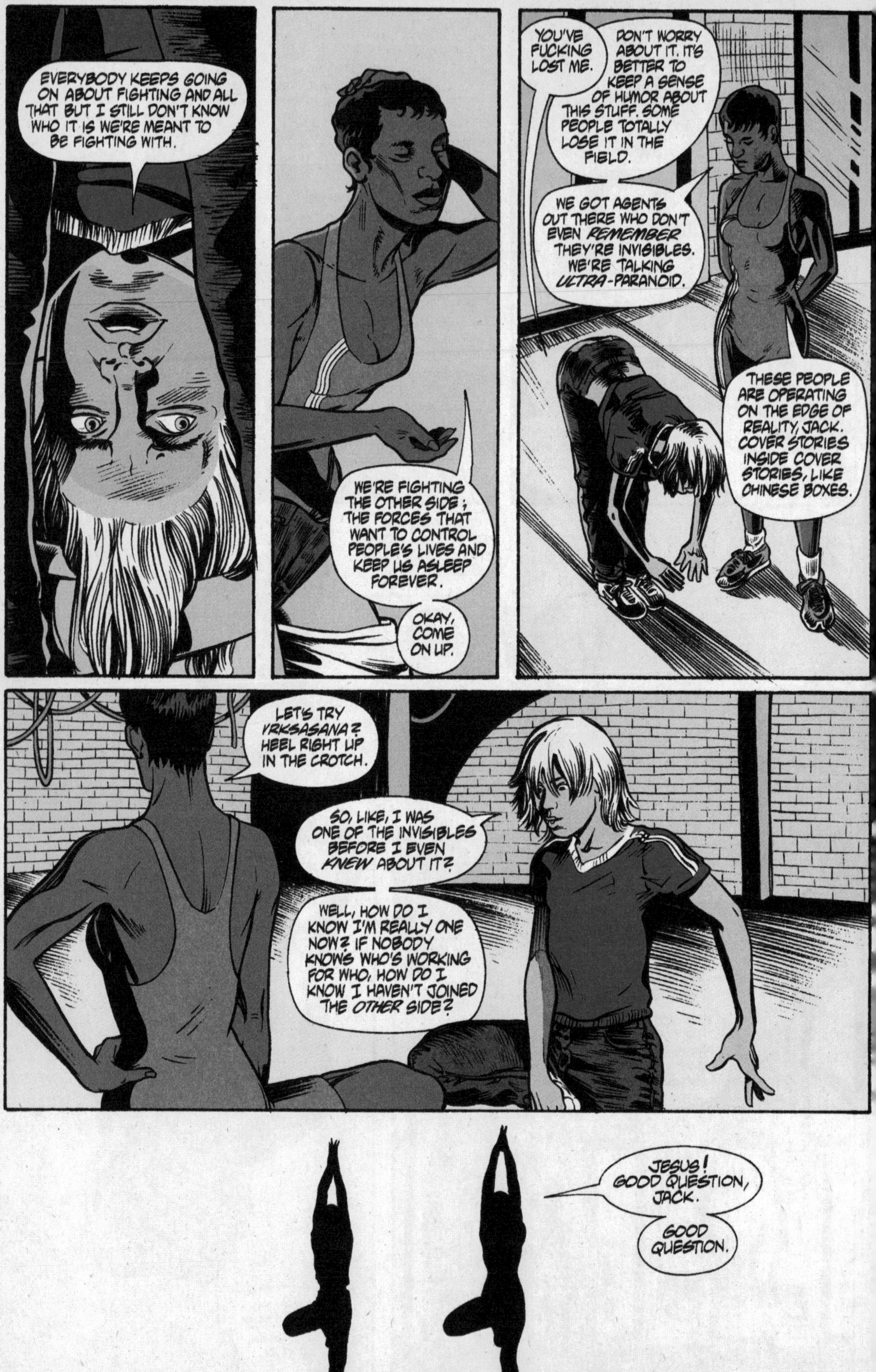

EVERYBODY KEEPS GOING ON ABOUT FIGHTING AND ALL THAT BUT I STILL DON'T KNOW WHO IT IS WE'RE MEANT TO BE FIGHTING WITH.
WE'RE FIGHTING THE OTHER SIDE; THE FORCES THAT WANT TO CONTROL PEOPLE'S LIVES AND KEEP US ASLEEP FOREVER.
OKAY, COME ON UP.
YOU'VE FUCKING LOST ME.
DON'T WORRY ABOUT IT. IT'S BETTER TO KEEP A SENSE OF HUMOR ABOUT THIS STUFF. SOME PEOPLE TOTALLY LOSE IT IN THE FIELD.
WE GOT AGENTS OUT THERE WHO DON'T EVEN *REMEMBER* THEY'RE INVISIBLES. WE'RE TALKING *ULTRA*-PARANOID.
THESE PEOPLE ARE OPERATING ON THE EDGE OF REALITY, JACK. COVER STORIES INSIDE COVER STORIES, LIKE CHINESE BOXES.
LET'S TRY *VRKSASANA*? HEEL RIGHT UP IN THE CROTCH.
SO, LIKE, I WAS ONE OF THE INVISIBLES BEFORE I EVEN *KNEW* ABOUT IT?
WELL, HOW DO I KNOW I'M REALLY ONE NOW? IF NOBODY KNOWS WHO'S WORKING FOR WHO, HOW DO I KNOW I HAVEN'T JOINED THE *OTHER* SIDE?
JESUS! GOOD QUESTION, JACK.
GOOD QUESTION.

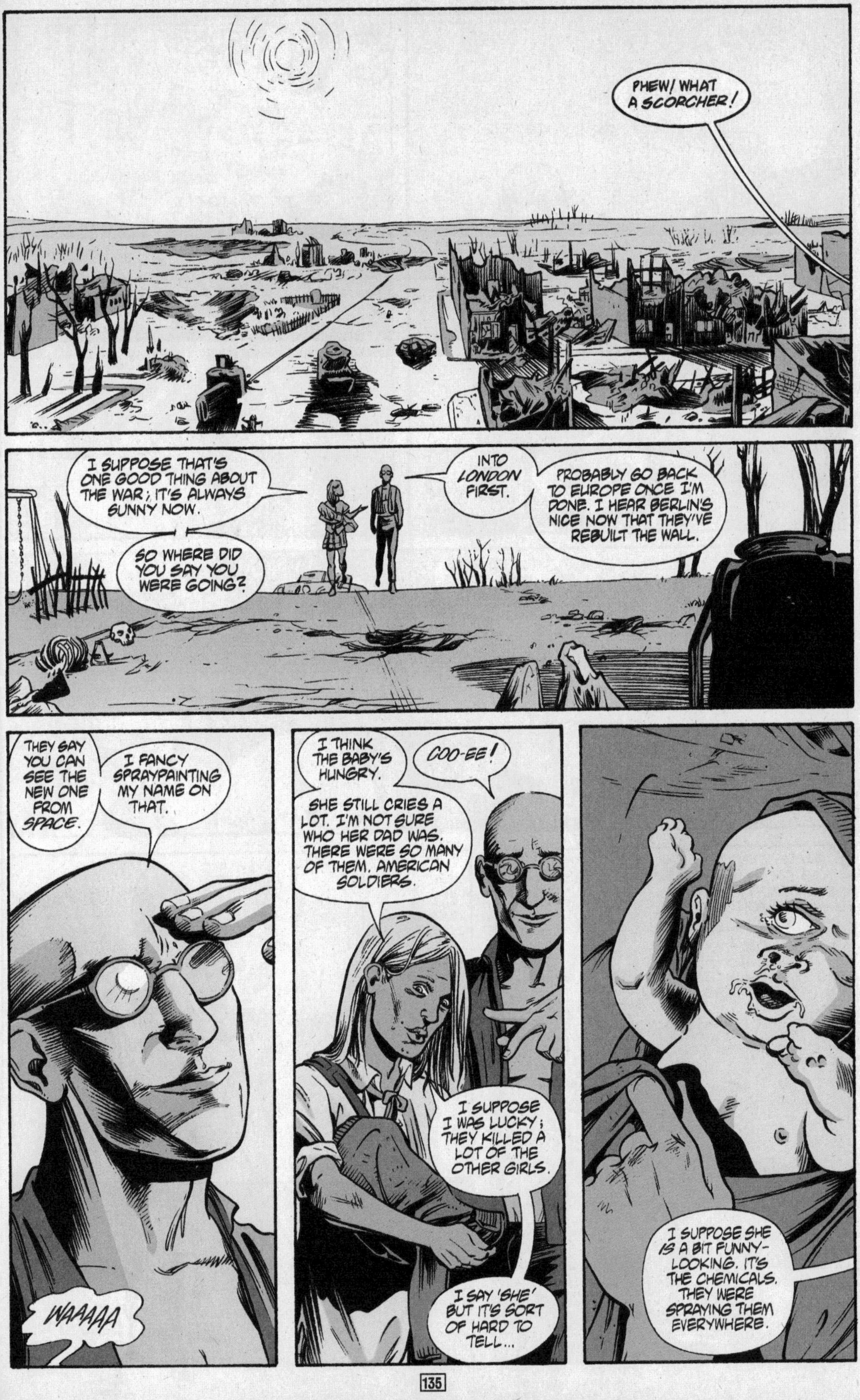
PHEW! WHAT A SCORCHER!
I SUPPOSE THAT'S ONE GOOD THING ABOUT THE WAR; IT'S ALWAYS SUNNY NOW.
SO WHERE DID YOU SAY YOU WERE GOING?
INTO LONDON FIRST.
PROBABLY GO BACK TO EUROPE ONCE I'M DONE. I HEAR BERLIN'S NICE NOW THAT THEY'VE REBUILT THE WALL.
THEY SAY YOU CAN SEE THE NEW ONE FROM SPACE.
I FANCY SPRAYPAINTING MY NAME ON THAT.
WAAAAA
I THINK THE BABY'S HUNGRY.
COO-EE!
SHE STILL CRIES A LOT. I'M NOT SURE WHO HER DAD WAS. THERE WERE SO MANY OF THEM. AMERICAN SOLDIERS.
I SUPPOSE I WAS LUCKY; THEY KILLED A LOT OF THE OTHER GIRLS.
I SAY 'SHE' BUT IT'S SORT OF HARD TO TELL...
I SUPPOSE SHE IS A BIT FUNNY-LOOKING. IT'S THE CHEMICALS. THEY WERE SPRAYING THEM EVERYWHERE.

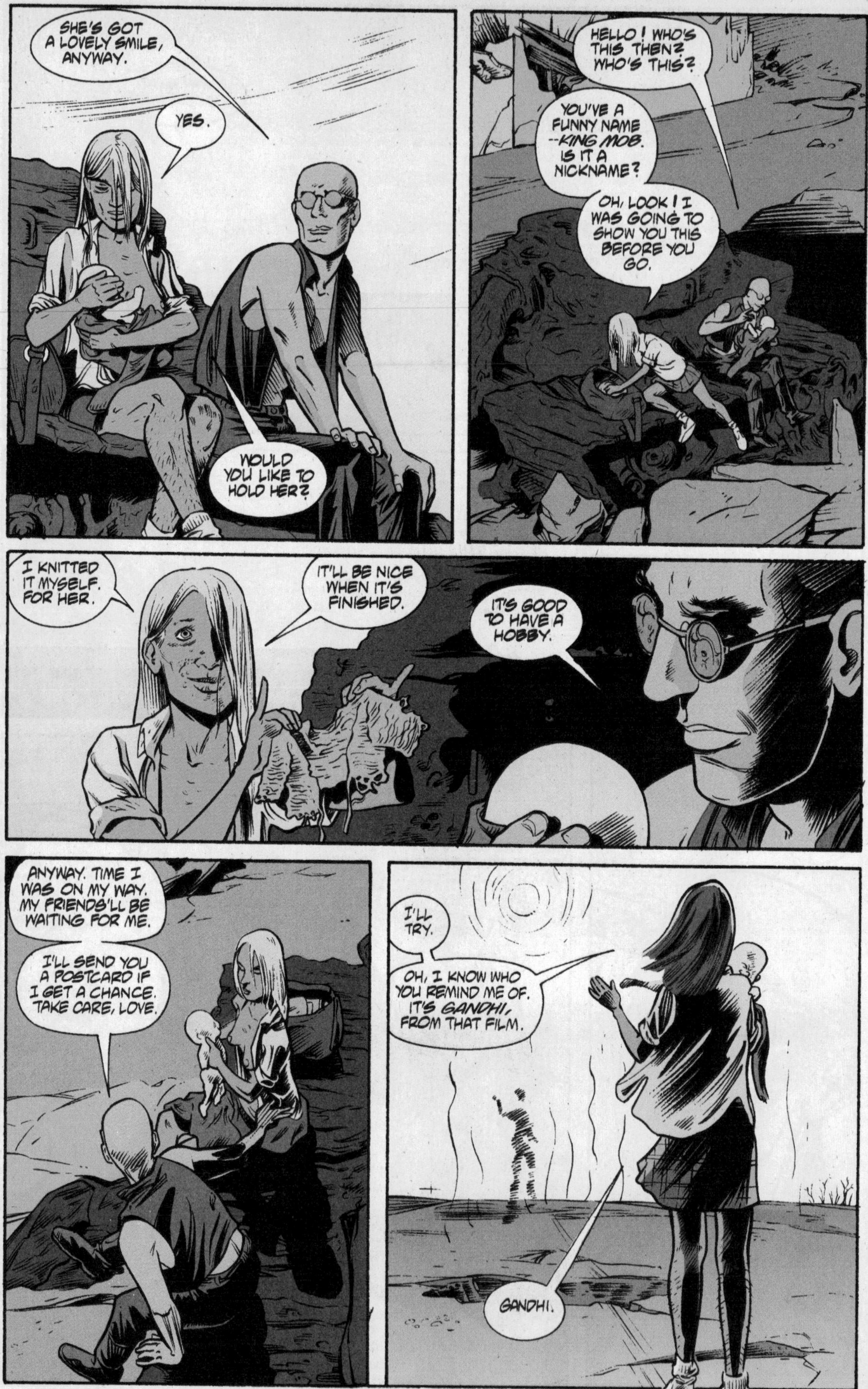
SHE'S GOT A LOVELY SMILE, ANYWAY.
YES.
WOULD YOU LIKE TO HOLD HER?
HELLO! WHO'S THIS THEN? WHO'S THIS?
YOU'VE A FUNNY NAME --KING MOB. IS IT A NICKNAME?
OH, LOOK! I WAS GOING TO SHOW YOU THIS BEFORE YOU GO.
I KNITTED IT MYSELF. FOR HER.
IT'LL BE NICE WHEN IT'S FINISHED.
IT'S GOOD TO HAVE A HOBBY.
ANYWAY. TIME I WAS ON MY WAY. MY FRIENDS'LL BE WAITING FOR ME.
I'LL SEND YOU A POSTCARD IF I GET A CHANCE. TAKE CARE, LOVE.
I'LL TRY.
OH, I KNOW WHO YOU REMIND ME OF. IT'S GANDHI, FROM THAT FILM.
GANDHI.

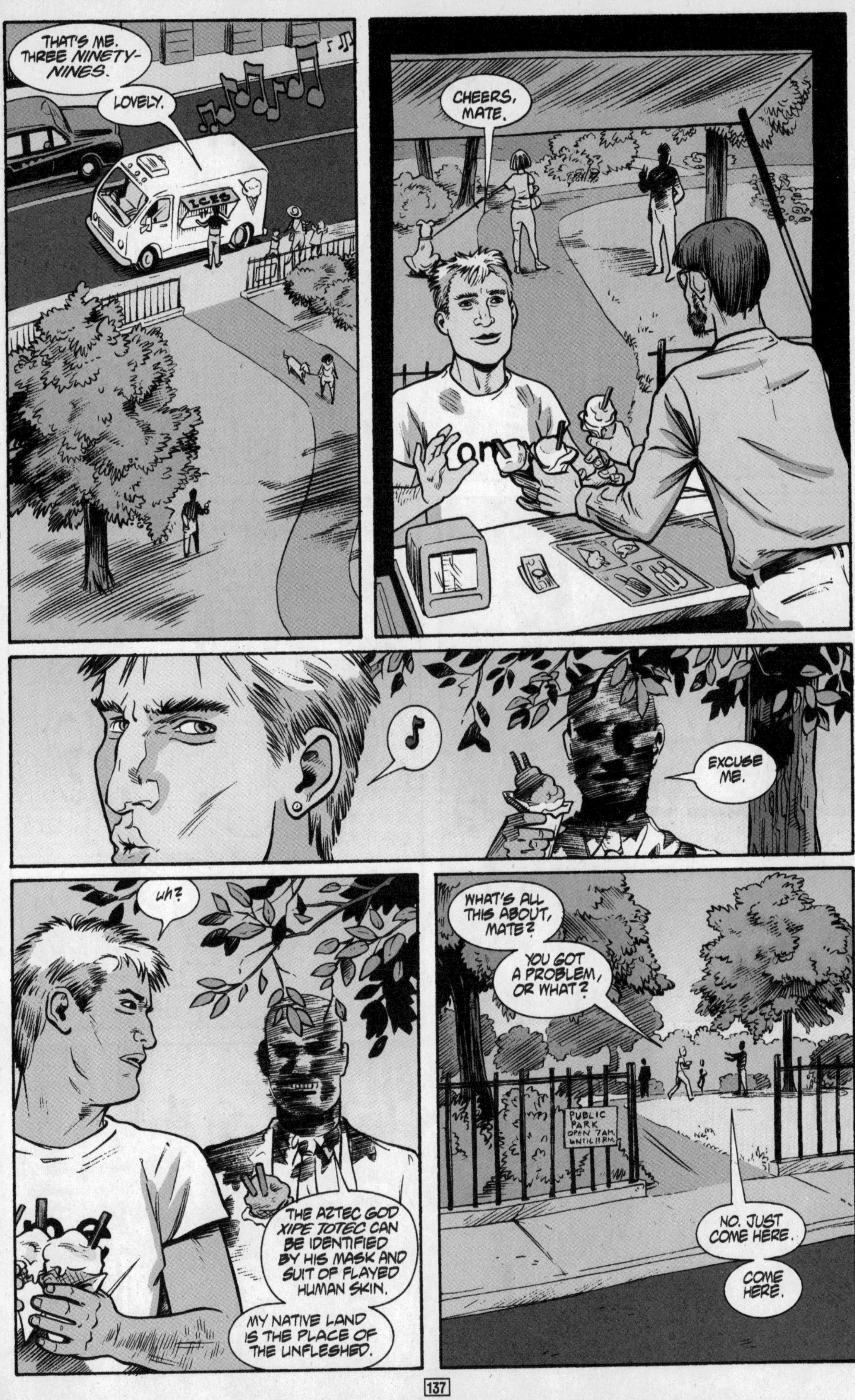

THAT'S ME. THREE NINETY-NINES.
LOVELY.
ICES
CHEERS, MATE.
EXCUSE ME.
uh?
THE AZTEC GOD XIPE TOTEC CAN BE IDENTIFIED BY HIS MASK AND SUIT OF FLAYED HUMAN SKIN.
MY NATIVE LAND IS THE PLACE OF THE UNFLESHED.
WHAT'S ALL THIS ABOUT, MATE?
YOU GOT A PROBLEM, OR WHAT?
PUBLIC PARK OPEN 7AM. UNTIL 11PM.
NO. JUST COME HERE.
COME HERE.

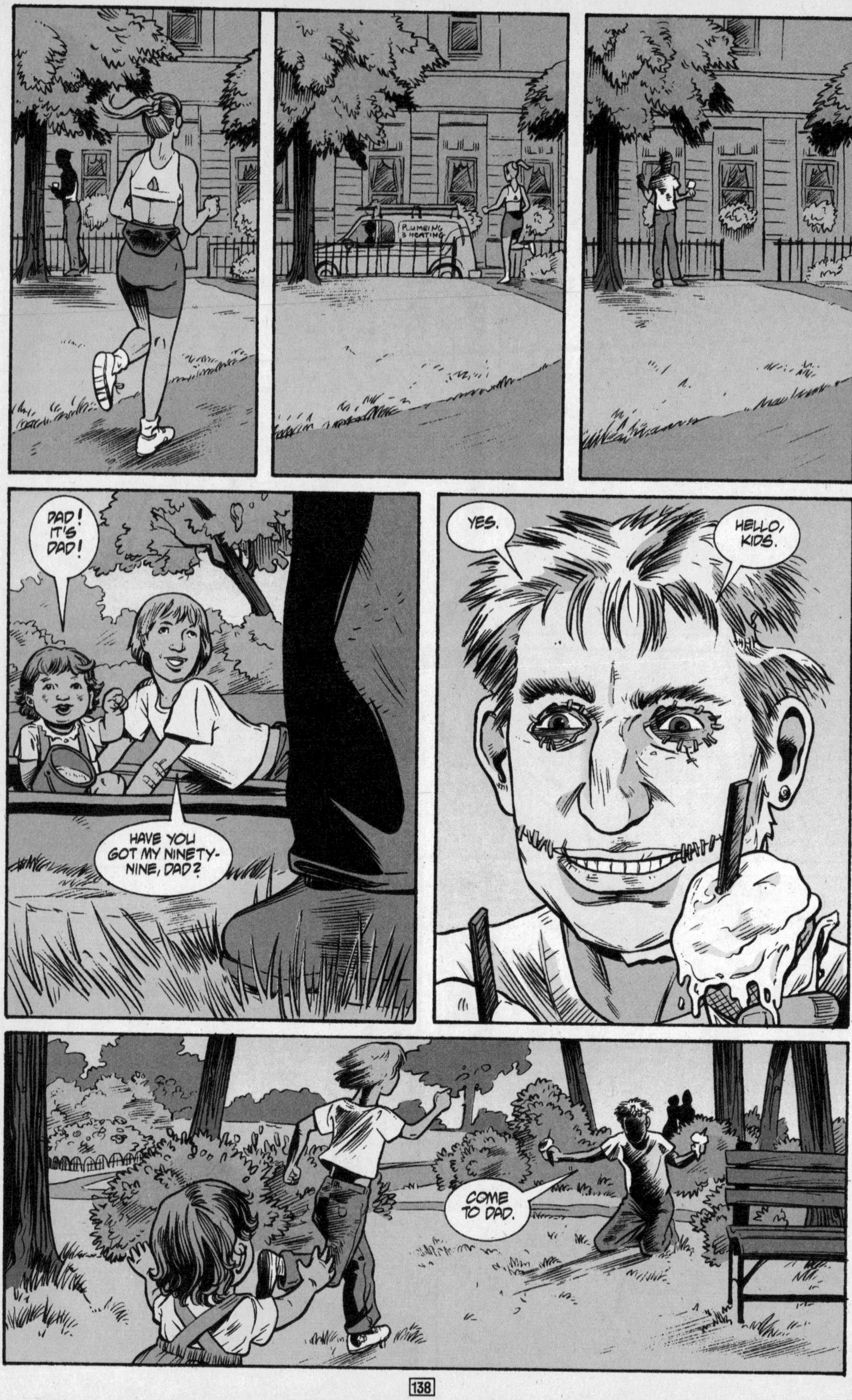
PLUMBING & HEATING
DAD! IT'S DAD!
HAVE YOU GOT MY NINETY-NINE, DAD?
YES.
HELLO, KIDS.
COME TO DAD.

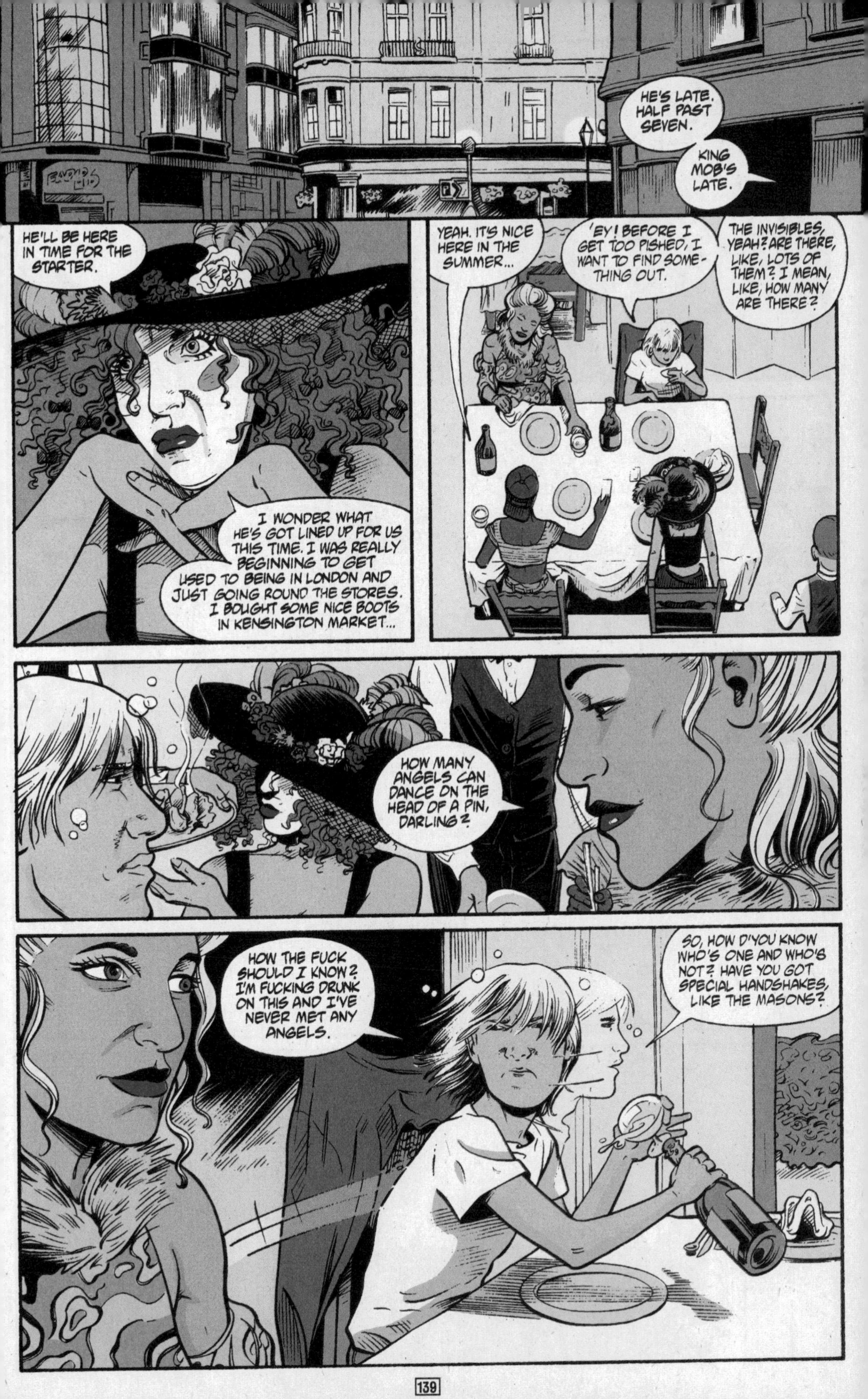
HE'S LATE. HALF PAST SEVEN.
KING MOB'S LATE.
HE'LL BE HERE IN TIME FOR THE STARTER.
I WONDER WHAT HE'S GOT LINED UP FOR US THIS TIME. I WAS REALLY BEGINNING TO GET USED TO BEING IN LONDON AND JUST GOING ROUND THE STORES. I BOUGHT SOME NICE BOOTS IN KENSINGTON MARKET...
YEAH. IT'S NICE HERE IN THE SUMMER...
'EY! BEFORE I GET TOO PISHED, I WANT TO FIND SOME-THING OUT.
THE INVISIBLES, YEAH? ARE THERE, LIKE, LOTS OF THEM? I MEAN, LIKE, HOW MANY ARE THERE?
HOW MANY ANGELS CAN DANCE ON THE HEAD OF A PIN, DARLING?
HOW THE FUCK SHOULD I KNOW? I'M FUCKING DRUNK ON THIS AND I'VE NEVER MET ANY ANGELS.
SO, HOW D'YOU KNOW WHO'S ONE AND WHO'S NOT? HAVE YOU GOT SPECIAL HANDSHAKES, LIKE THE MASONS?

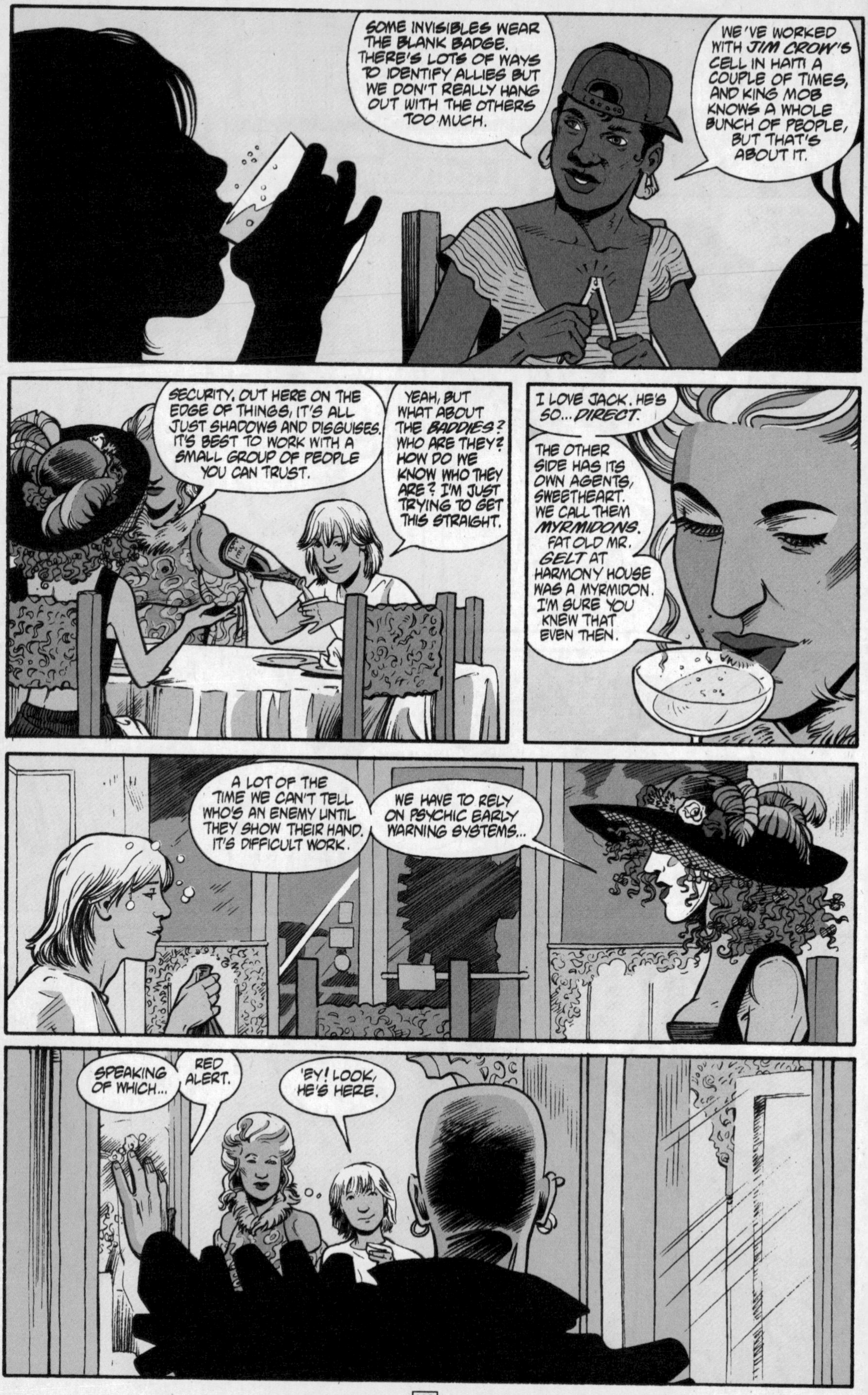
SOME INVISIBLES WEAR THE BLANK BADGE. THERE'S LOTS OF WAYS TO IDENTIFY ALLIES BUT WE DON'T REALLY HANG OUT WITH THE OTHERS TOO MUCH.
WE'VE WORKED WITH JIM CROW'S CELL IN HAITI A COUPLE OF TIMES, AND KING MOB KNOWS A WHOLE BUNCH OF PEOPLE, BUT THAT'S ABOUT IT.
SECURITY. OUT HERE ON THE EDGE OF THINGS, IT'S ALL JUST SHADOWS AND DISGUISES. IT'S BEST TO WORK WITH A SMALL GROUP OF PEOPLE YOU CAN TRUST.
YEAH, BUT WHAT ABOUT THE BADDIES? WHO ARE THEY? HOW DO WE KNOW WHO THEY ARE? I'M JUST TRYING TO GET THIS STRAIGHT.
I LOVE JACK. HE'S SO... DIRECT.
THE OTHER SIDE HAS ITS OWN AGENTS, SWEETHEART. WE CALL THEM MYRMIDONS. FAT OLD MR. GELT AT HARMONY HOUSE WAS A MYRMIDON. I'M SURE YOU KNEW THAT EVEN THEN.
A LOT OF THE TIME WE CAN'T TELL WHO'S AN ENEMY UNTIL THEY SHOW THEIR HAND. IT'S DIFFICULT WORK.
WE HAVE TO RELY ON PSYCHIC EARLY WARNING SYSTEMS...
SPEAKING OF WHICH...
RED ALERT.
'EY! LOOK, HE'S HERE.

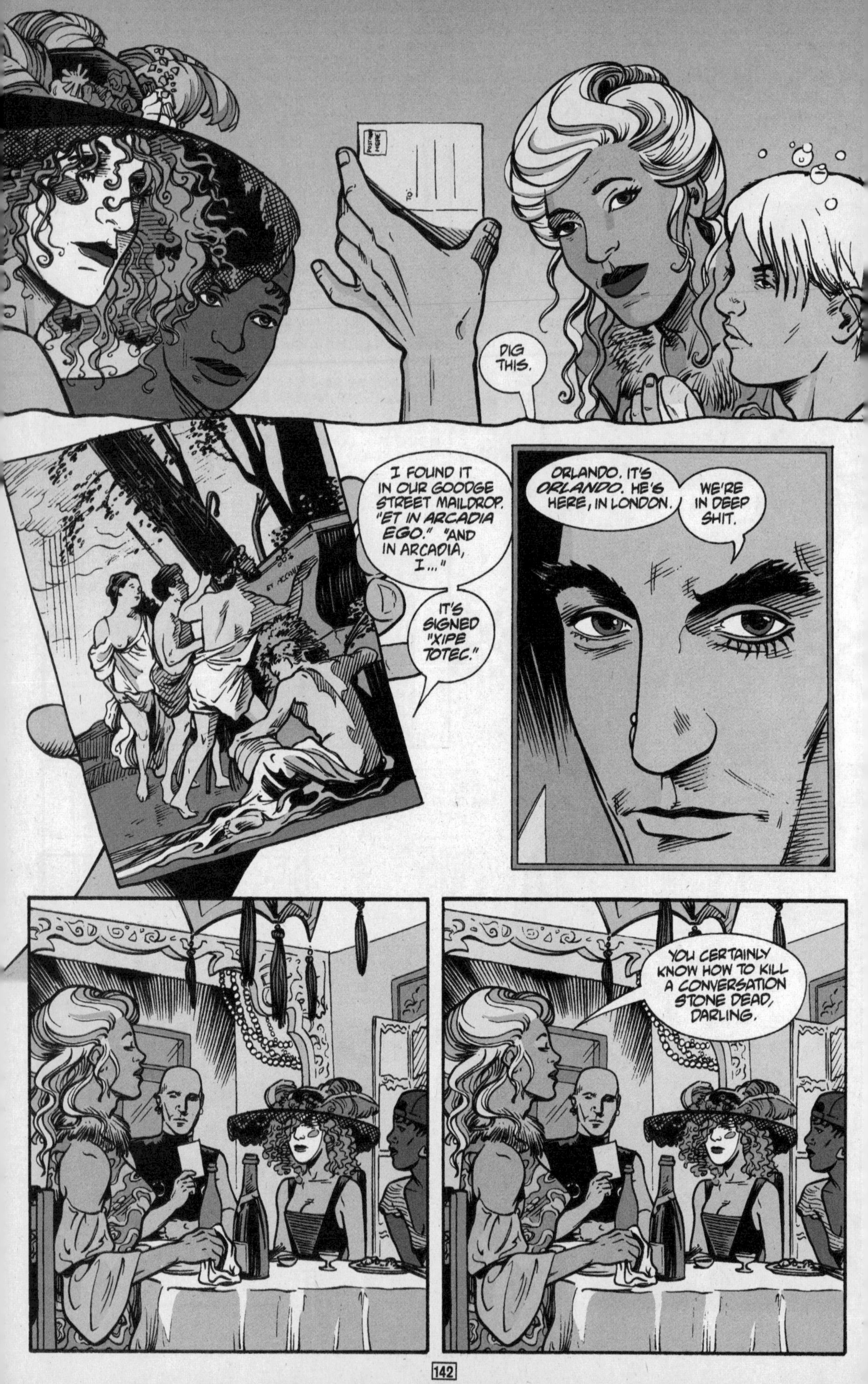
DIG THIS.
I FOUND IT IN OUR GOODGE STREET MAILDROP. "ET IN ARCADIA EGO." "AND IN ARCADIA, I..."
IT'S SIGNED "XIPE TOTEC."
ORLANDO. IT'S ORLANDO. HE'S HERE, IN LONDON.
WE'RE IN DEEP SHIT.
YOU CERTAINLY KNOW HOW TO KILL A CONVERSATION STONE DEAD, DARLING.

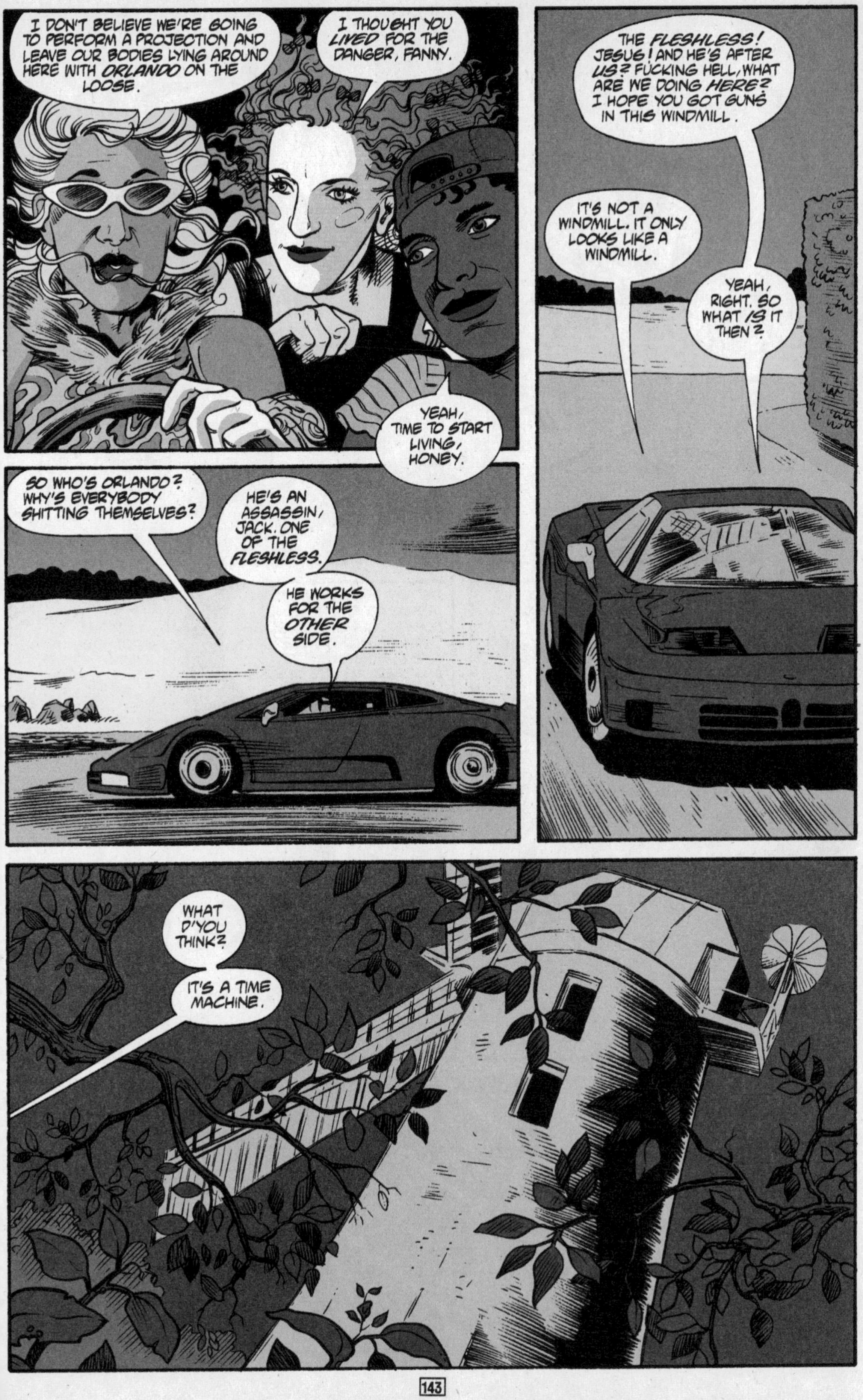
I DON'T BELIEVE WE'RE GOING TO PERFORM A PROJECTION AND LEAVE OUR BODIES LYING AROUND HERE WITH ORLANDO ON THE LOOSE.
I THOUGHT YOU LIVED FOR THE DANGER, FANNY.
YEAH, TIME TO START LIVING, HONEY.
SO WHO'S ORLANDO? WHY'S EVERYBODY SHITTING THEMSELVES?
HE'S AN ASSASSIN, JACK. ONE OF THE FLESHLESS.
HE WORKS FOR THE OTHER SIDE.
THE FLESHLESS! JESUS! AND HE'S AFTER US? FUCKING HELL, WHAT ARE WE DOING HERE? I HOPE YOU GOT GUNS IN THIS WINDMILL.
IT'S NOT A WINDMILL. IT ONLY LOOKS LIKE A WINDMILL.
YEAH, RIGHT. SO WHAT IS IT THEN?
WHAT D'YOU THINK?
IT'S A TIME MACHINE.

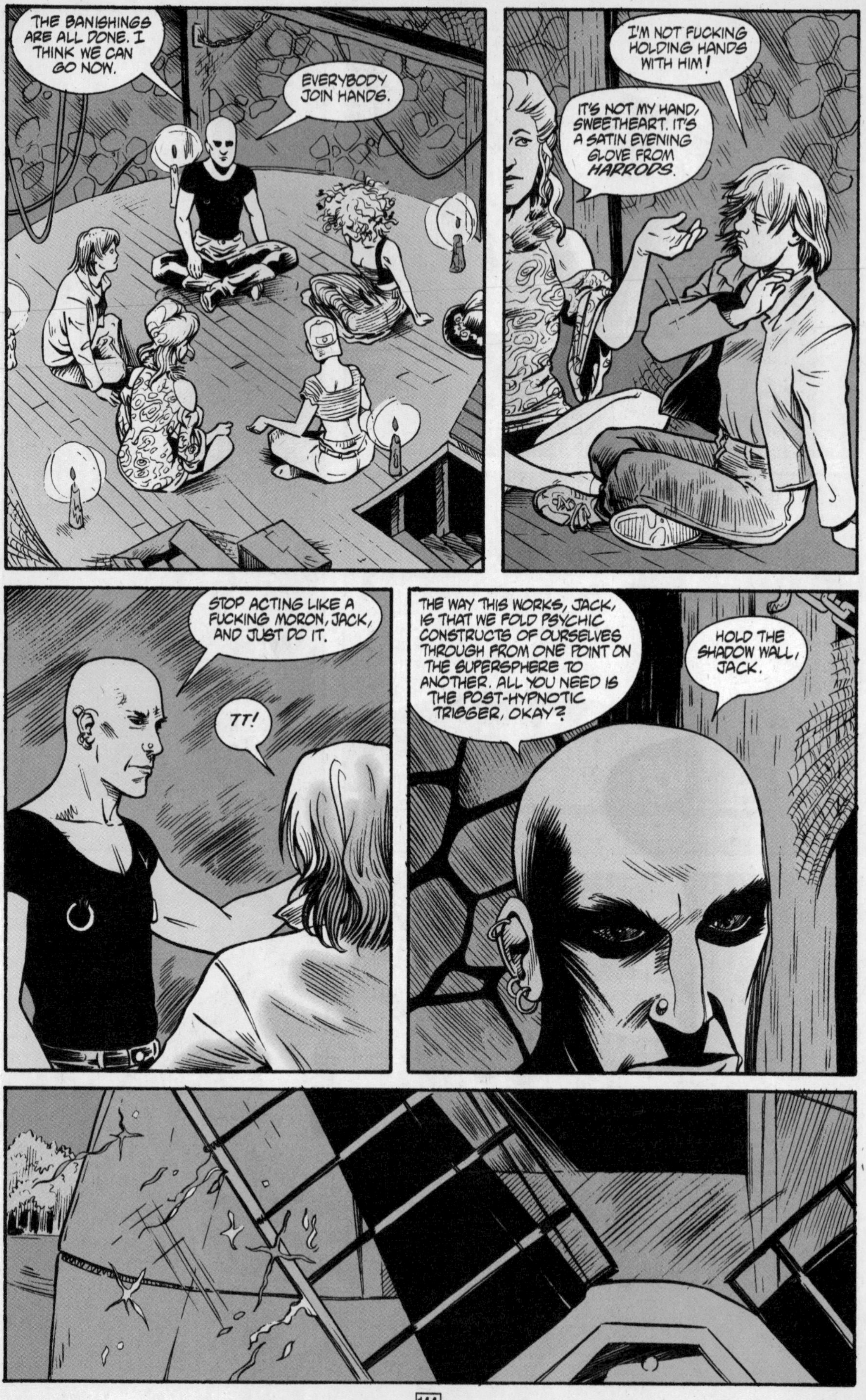
THE BANISHINGS ARE ALL DONE. I THINK WE CAN GO NOW.
EVERYBODY JOIN HANDS.
I'M NOT FUCKING HOLDING HANDS WITH HIM!
IT'S NOT MY HAND, SWEETHEART. IT'S A SATIN EVENING GLOVE FROM HARRODS.
STOP ACTING LIKE A FUCKING MORON, JACK, AND JUST DO IT.
TT!
THE WAY THIS WORKS, JACK, IS THAT WE FOLD PSYCHIC CONSTRUCTS OF OURSELVES THROUGH FROM ONE POINT ON THE SUPERSPHERE TO ANOTHER. ALL YOU NEED IS THE POST-HYPNOTIC TRIGGER, OKAY?
HOLD THE SHADOW WALL, JACK.

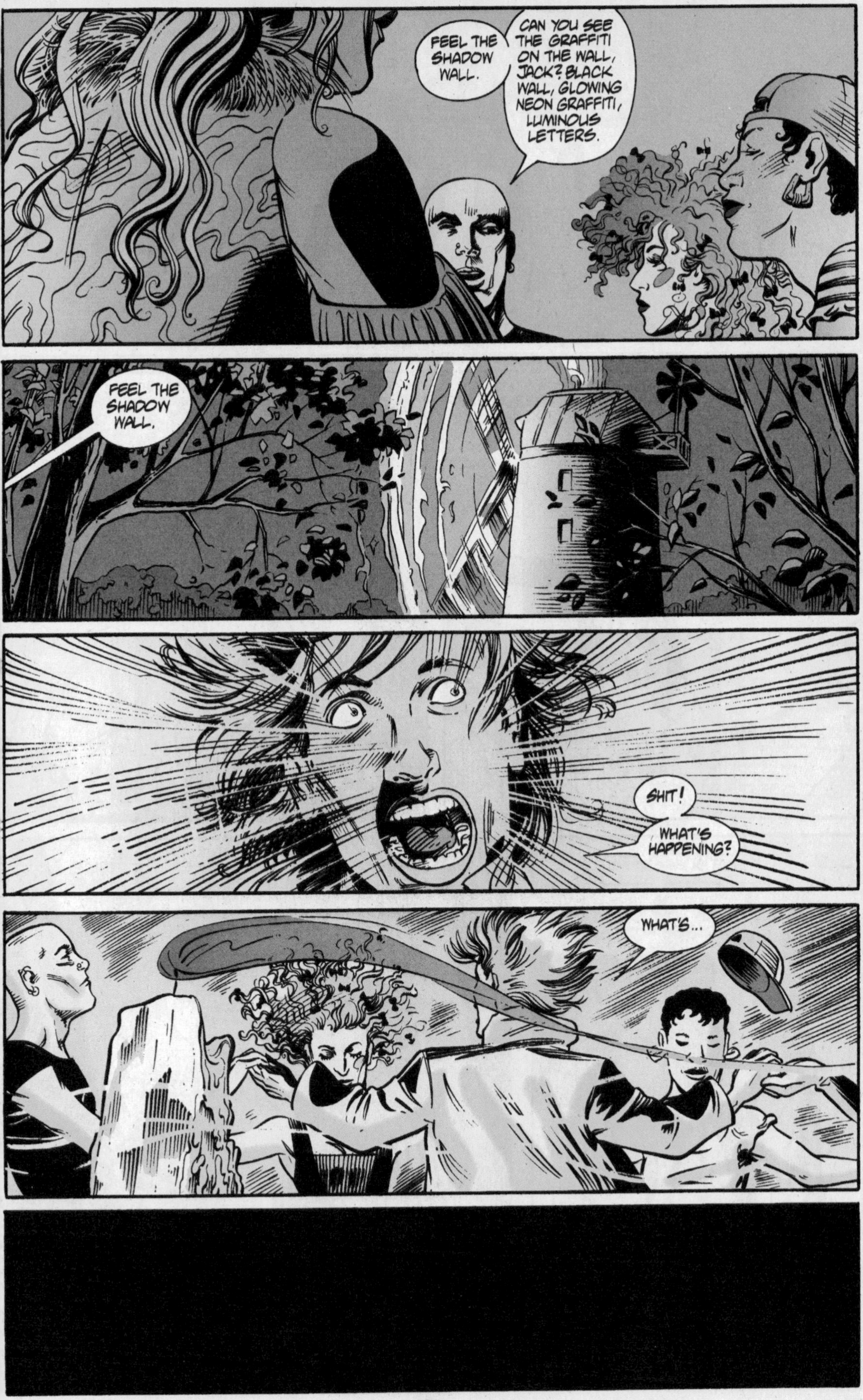
FEEL THE SHADOW WALL.
CAN YOU SEE THE GRAFFITI ON THE WALL, JACK? BLACK WALL, GLOWING NEON GRAFFITI, LUMINOUS LETTERS.
FEEL THE SHADOW WALL.
SHIT!
WHAT'S HAPPENING?
WHAT'S...

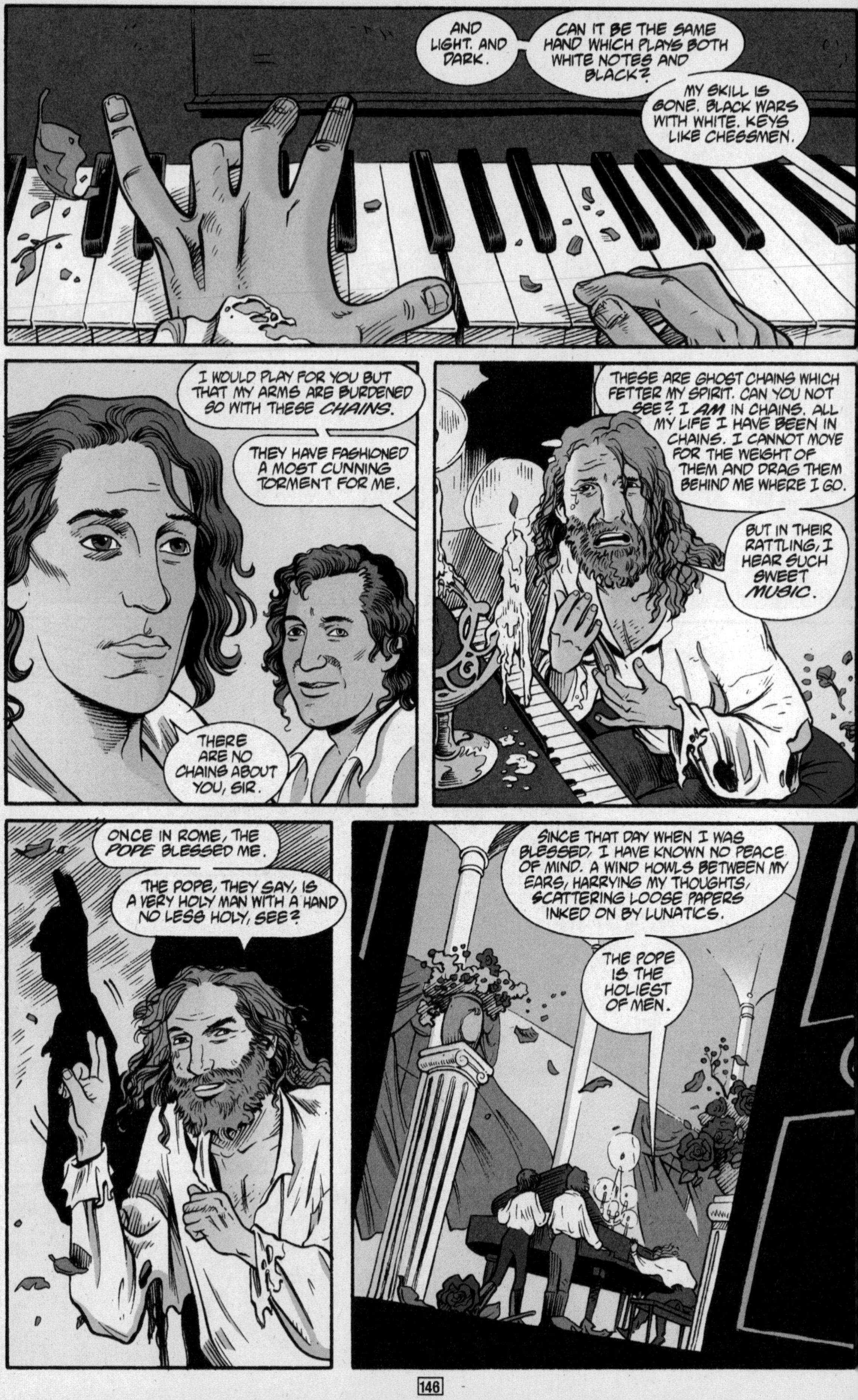

AND LIGHT. AND DARK.
CAN IT BE THE SAME HAND WHICH PLAYS BOTH WHITE NOTES AND BLACK?
MY SKILL IS GONE. BLACK WARS WITH WHITE. KEYS LIKE CHESSMEN.
I WOULD PLAY FOR YOU BUT THAT MY ARMS ARE BURDENED SO WITH THESE CHAINS.
THEY HAVE FASHIONED A MOST CUNNING TORMENT FOR ME.
THERE ARE NO CHAINS ABOUT YOU, SIR.
THESE ARE GHOST CHAINS WHICH FETTER MY SPIRIT. CAN YOU NOT SEE? I AM IN CHAINS. ALL MY LIFE I HAVE BEEN IN CHAINS. I CANNOT MOVE FOR THE WEIGHT OF THEM AND DRAG THEM BEHIND ME WHERE I GO.
BUT IN THEIR RATTLING, I HEAR SUCH SWEET MUSIC.
ONCE IN ROME, THE POPE BLESSED ME.
THE POPE, THEY SAY, IS A VERY HOLY MAN WITH A HAND NO LESS HOLY, SEE?
SINCE THAT DAY WHEN I WAS BLESSED, I HAVE KNOWN NO PEACE OF MIND. A WIND HOWLS BETWEEN MY EARS, HARRYING MY THOUGHTS, SCATTERING LOOSE PAPERS INKED ON BY LUNATICS.
THE POPE IS THE HOLIEST OF MEN.

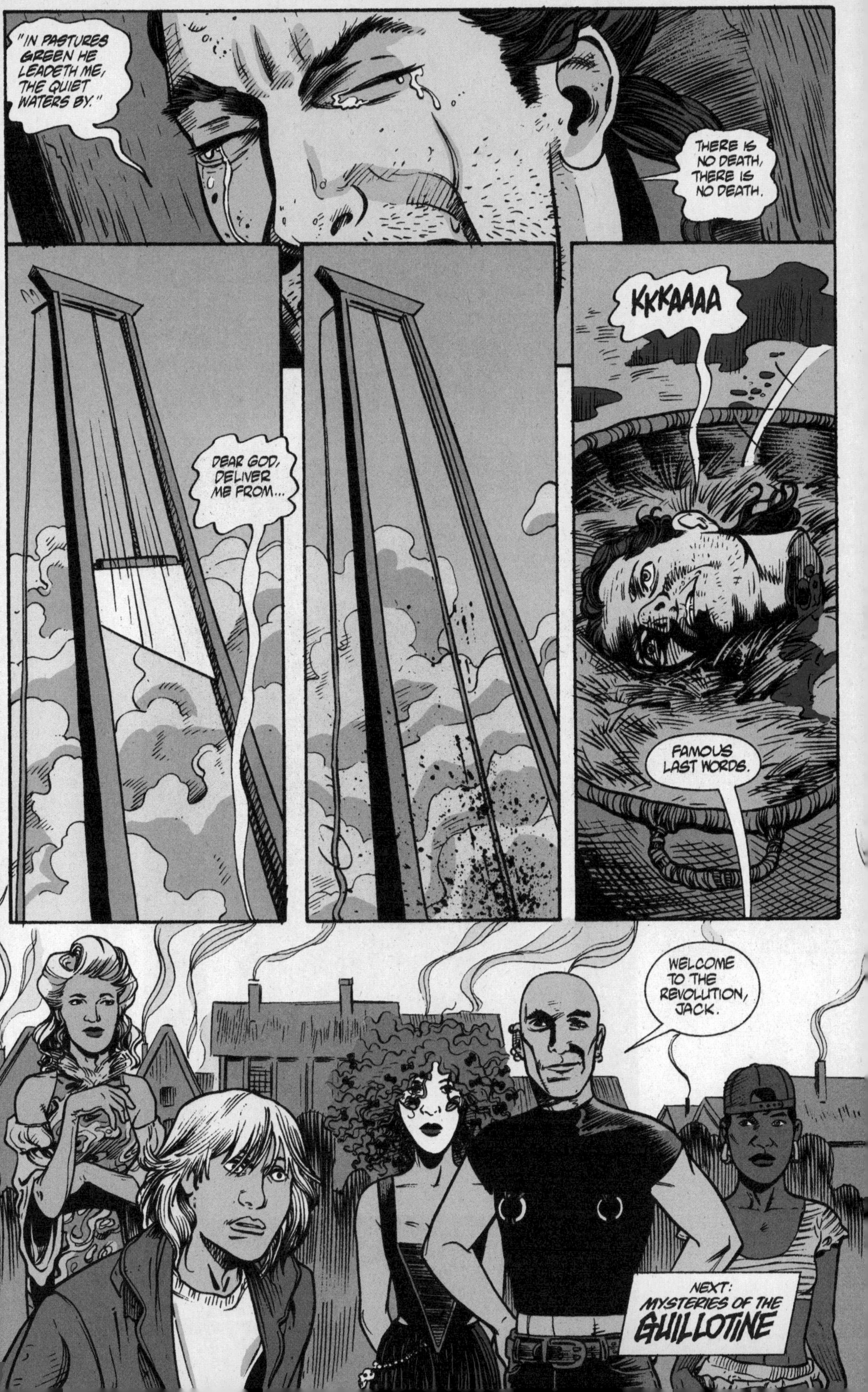
"IN PASTURES GREEN HE LEADETH ME, THE QUIET WATERS BY."
THERE IS NO DEATH, THERE IS NO DEATH.
DEAR GOD, DELIVER ME FROM...
KKKAAAA
FAMOUS LAST WORDS.
WELCOME TO THE REVOLUTION, JACK.
NEXT: MYSTERIES OF THE GUILLOTINE

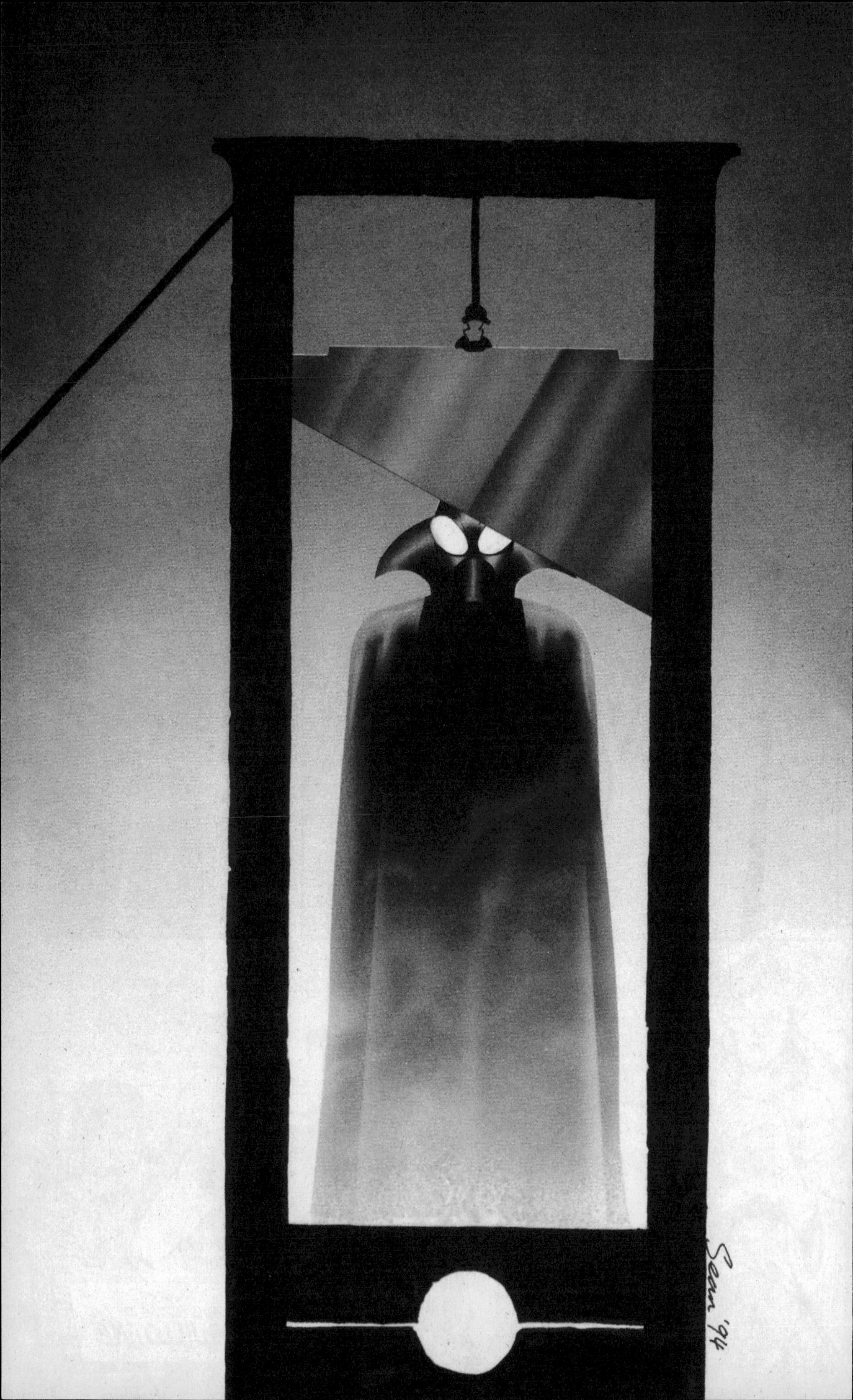
Sean '94

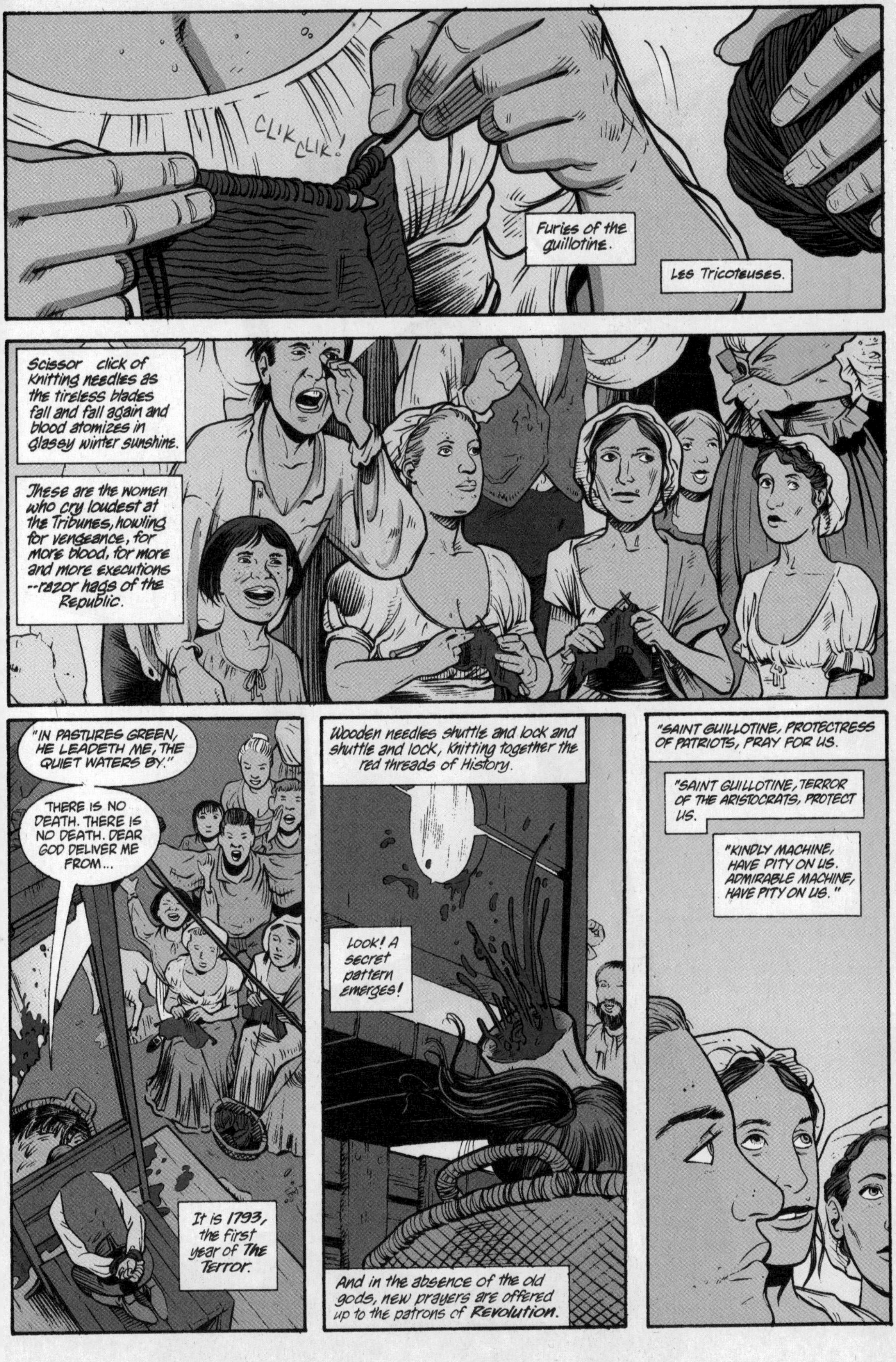
CLIK CLIK!
Furies of the guillotine.
Les Tricoteuses.
Scissor click of knitting needles as the tireless blades fall and fall again and blood atomizes in glassy winter sunshine.
These are the women who cry loudest at the Tribunes, howling for vengeance, for more blood, for more and more executions --razor hags of the Republic.
"IN PASTURES GREEN, HE LEADETH ME, THE QUIET WATERS BY."
THERE IS NO DEATH. THERE IS NO DEATH. DEAR GOD DELIVER ME FROM...
It is 1793, the first year of The Terror.
Wooden needles shuttle and lock and shuttle and lock, knitting together the red threads of History.
Look! A secret pattern emerges!
And in the absence of the old gods, new prayers are offered up to the patrons of Revolution.
"SAINT GUILLOTINE, PROTECTRESS OF PATRIOTS, PRAY FOR US.
"SAINT GUILLOTINE, TERROR OF THE ARISTOCRATS, PROTECT US.
"KINDLY MACHINE, HAVE PITY ON US. ADMIRABLE MACHINE, HAVE PITY ON US."

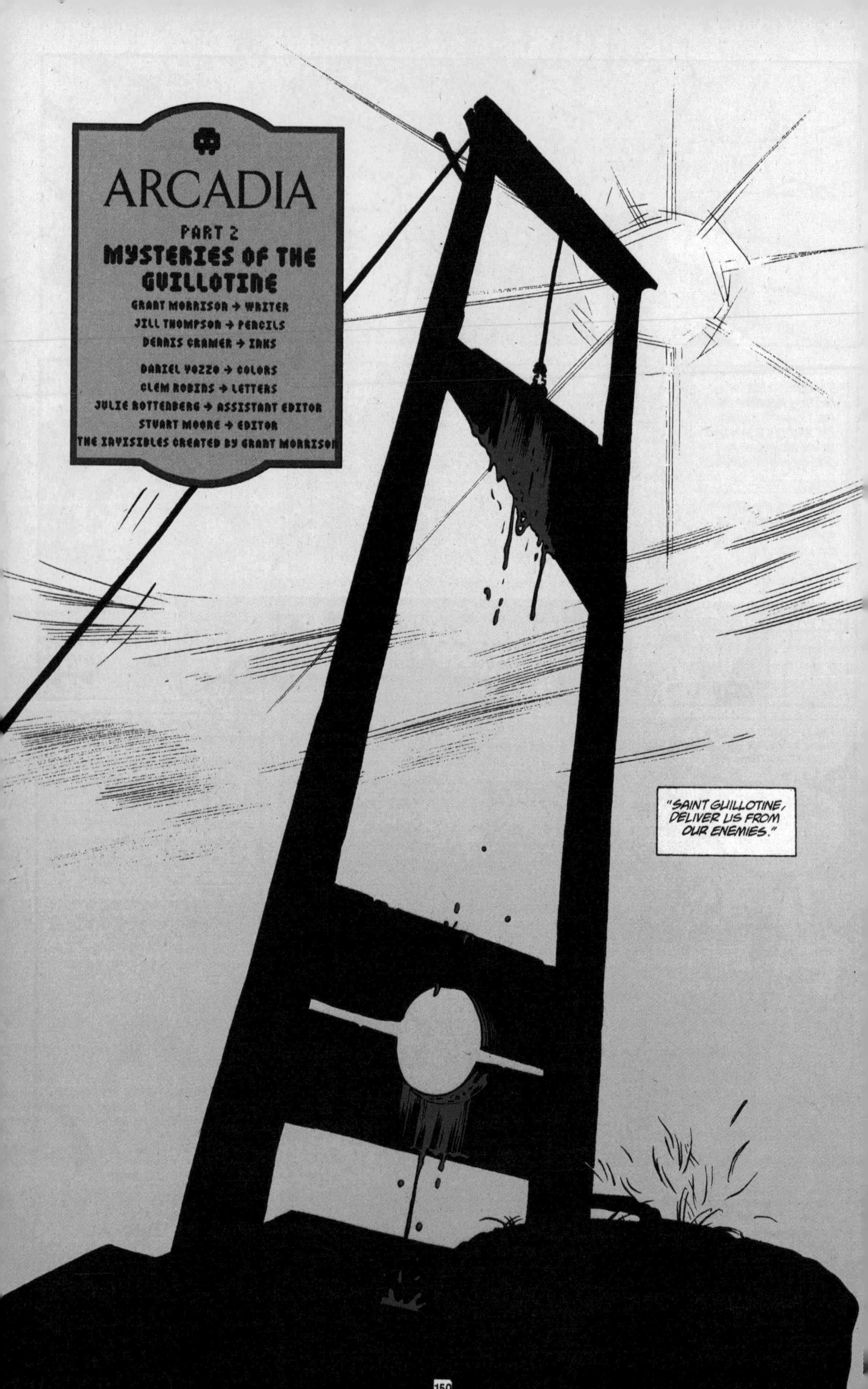
ARCADIA
PART 2
MYSTERIES OF THE GUILLOTINE
GRANT MORRISON → WRITER
JILL THOMPSON → PENCILS
DENNIS CRAMER → INKS
DANIEL VOZZO → COLORS
CLEM ROBINS → LETTERS
JULIE ROTTENBERG → ASSISTANT EDITOR
STUART MOORE → EDITOR
THE INVISIBLES CREATED BY GRANT MORRISON
"SAINT GUILLOTINE, DELIVER US FROM OUR ENEMIES."

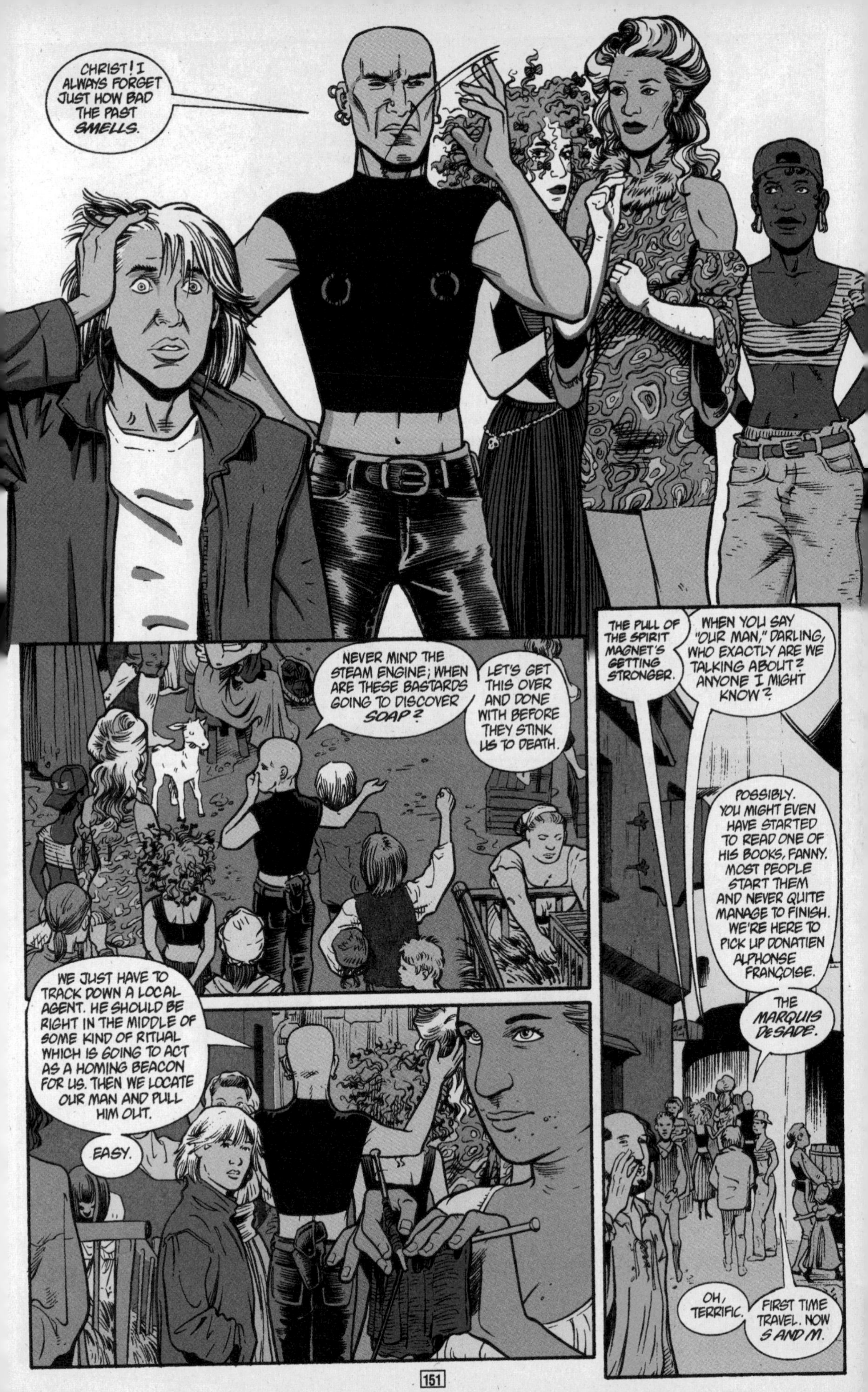

CHRIST! I ALWAYS FORGET JUST HOW BAD THE PAST SMELLS.
NEVER MIND THE STEAM ENGINE; WHEN ARE THESE BASTARDS GOING TO DISCOVER SOAP?
LET'S GET THIS OVER AND DONE WITH BEFORE THEY STINK US TO DEATH.
WE JUST HAVE TO TRACK DOWN A LOCAL AGENT. HE SHOULD BE RIGHT IN THE MIDDLE OF SOME KIND OF RITUAL WHICH IS GOING TO ACT AS A HOMING BEACON FOR US. THEN WE LOCATE OUR MAN AND PULL HIM OUT.
EASY.
THE PULL OF THE SPIRIT MAGNET'S GETTING STRONGER.
WHEN YOU SAY "OUR MAN," DARLING, WHO EXACTLY ARE WE TALKING ABOUT? ANYONE I MIGHT KNOW?
POSSIBLY. YOU MIGHT EVEN HAVE STARTED TO READ ONE OF HIS BOOKS, FANNY. MOST PEOPLE START THEM AND NEVER QUITE MANAGE TO FINISH. WE'RE HERE TO PICK UP DONATIEN ALPHONSE FRANÇOISE.
THE MARQUIS DE SADE.
OH, TERRIFIC.
FIRST TIME TRAVEL. NOW S AND M.

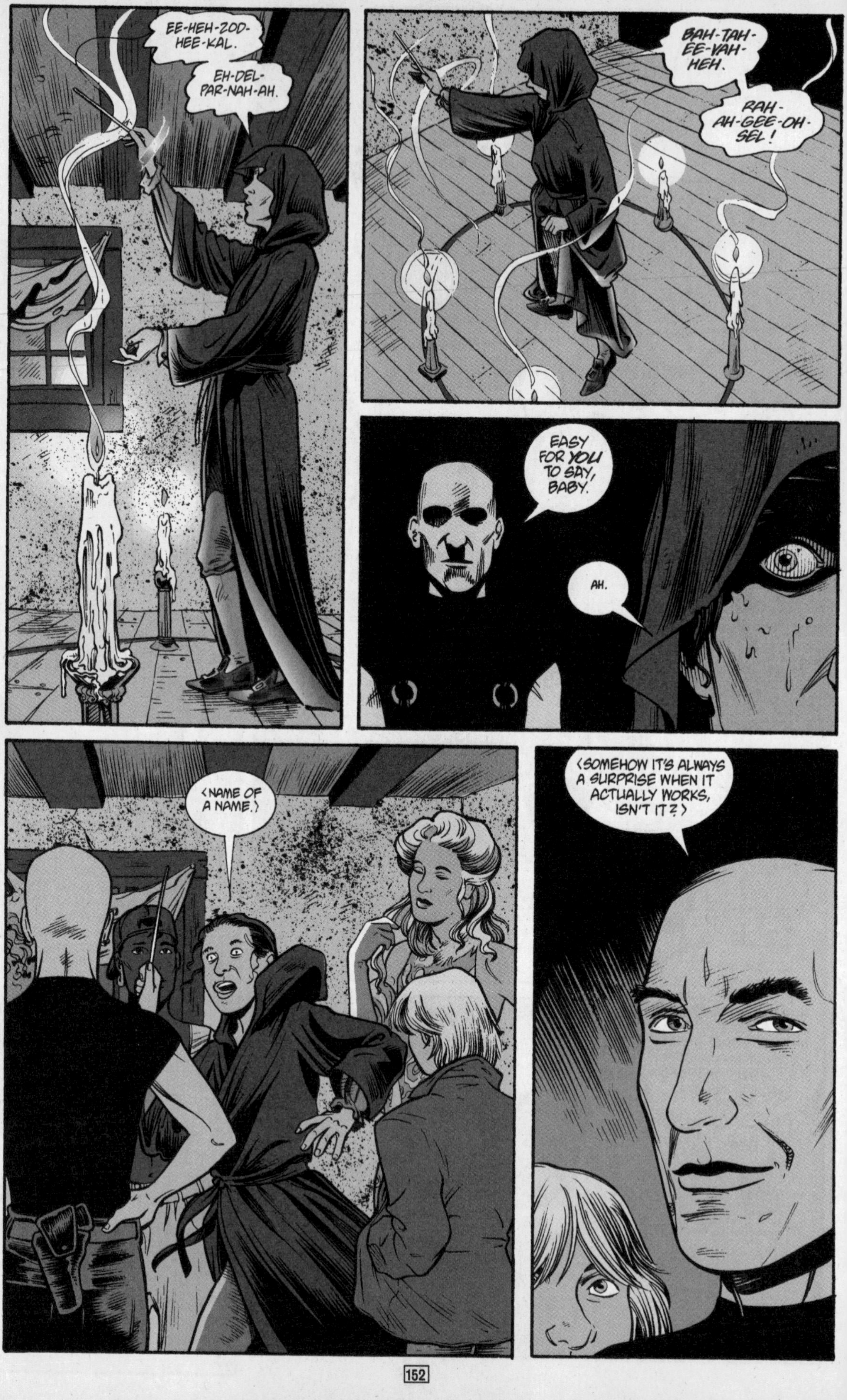
EE-HEH-ZOD-HEE-KAL.
EH-DEL-PAR-NAH-AH.
BAH-TAH-EE-VAH-HEH.
RAH-AH-GEE-OH-SEL!
EASY FOR YOU TO SAY, BABY.
AH.
‹NAME OF A NAME.›
‹SOMEHOW IT'S ALWAYS A SURPRISE WHEN IT ACTUALLY WORKS, ISN'T IT?›

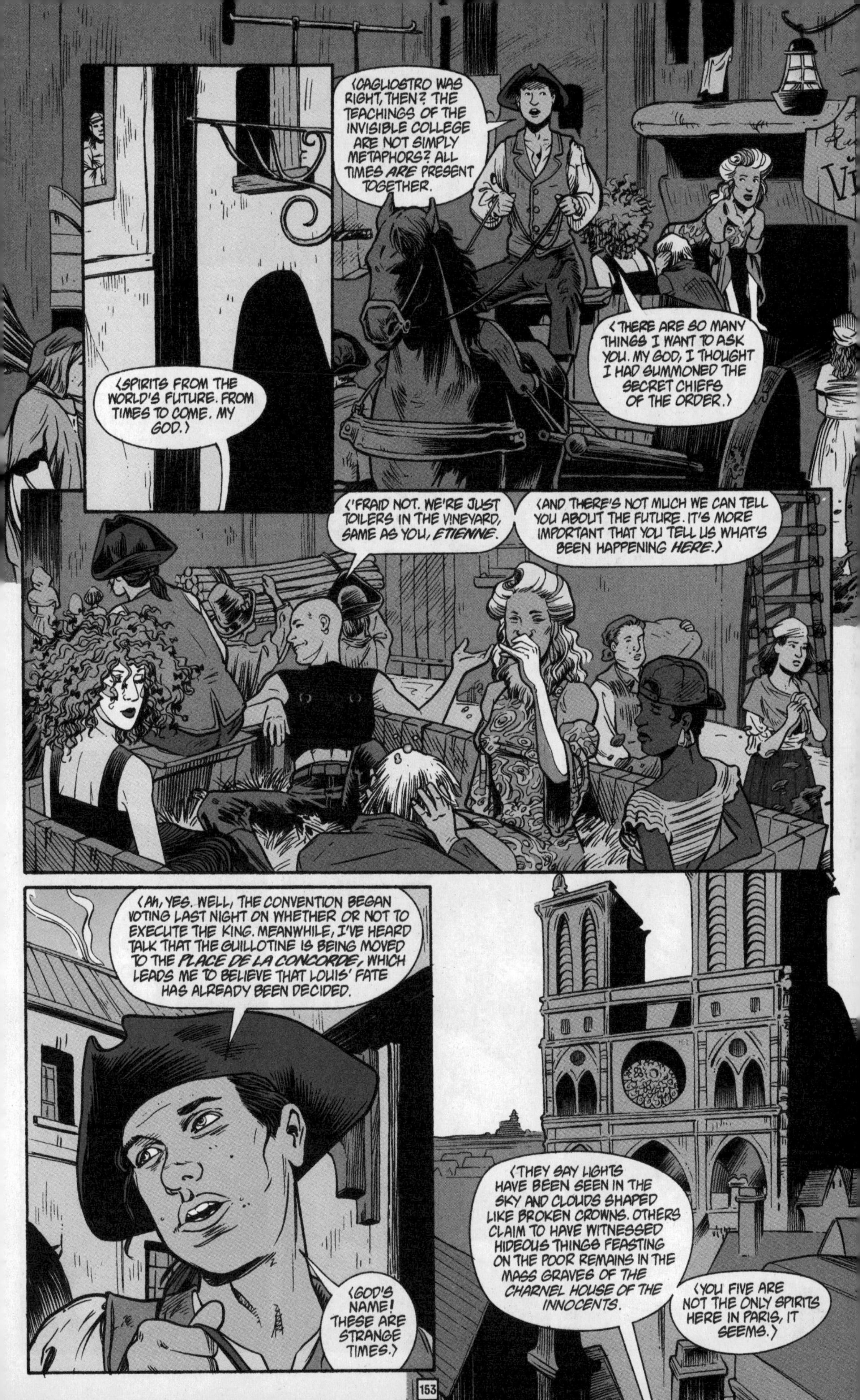

‹CAGLIOSTRO WAS RIGHT, THEN? THE TEACHINGS OF THE INVISIBLE COLLEGE ARE NOT SIMPLY METAPHORS? ALL TIMES *ARE* PRESENT TOGETHER.
‹SPIRITS FROM THE WORLD'S FUTURE. FROM TIMES TO COME. MY GOD.›
‹THERE ARE SO MANY THINGS I WANT TO ASK YOU. MY GOD, I THOUGHT I HAD SUMMONED THE SECRET CHIEFS OF THE ORDER.›
‹'FRAID NOT. WE'RE JUST TOILERS IN THE VINEYARD, SAME AS YOU, *ETIENNE*.
‹AND THERE'S NOT MUCH WE CAN TELL YOU ABOUT THE FUTURE. IT'S MORE IMPORTANT THAT YOU TELL US WHAT'S BEEN HAPPENING *HERE*.›
‹AH, YES. WELL, THE CONVENTION BEGAN VOTING LAST NIGHT ON WHETHER OR NOT TO EXECUTE THE KING. MEANWHILE, I'VE HEARD TALK THAT THE GUILLOTINE IS BEING MOVED TO THE *PLACE DE LA CONCORDE*, WHICH LEADS ME TO BELIEVE THAT LOUIS' FATE HAS ALREADY BEEN DECIDED.
‹GOD'S NAME! THESE ARE STRANGE TIMES.›
‹THEY SAY LIGHTS HAVE BEEN SEEN IN THE SKY AND CLOUDS SHAPED LIKE BROKEN CROWNS. OTHERS CLAIM TO HAVE WITNESSED HIDEOUS THINGS FEASTING ON THE POOR REMAINS IN THE MASS GRAVES OF THE *CHARNEL HOUSE OF THE INNOCENTS*.
‹YOU FIVE ARE NOT THE ONLY SPIRITS HERE IN PARIS, IT SEEMS.›

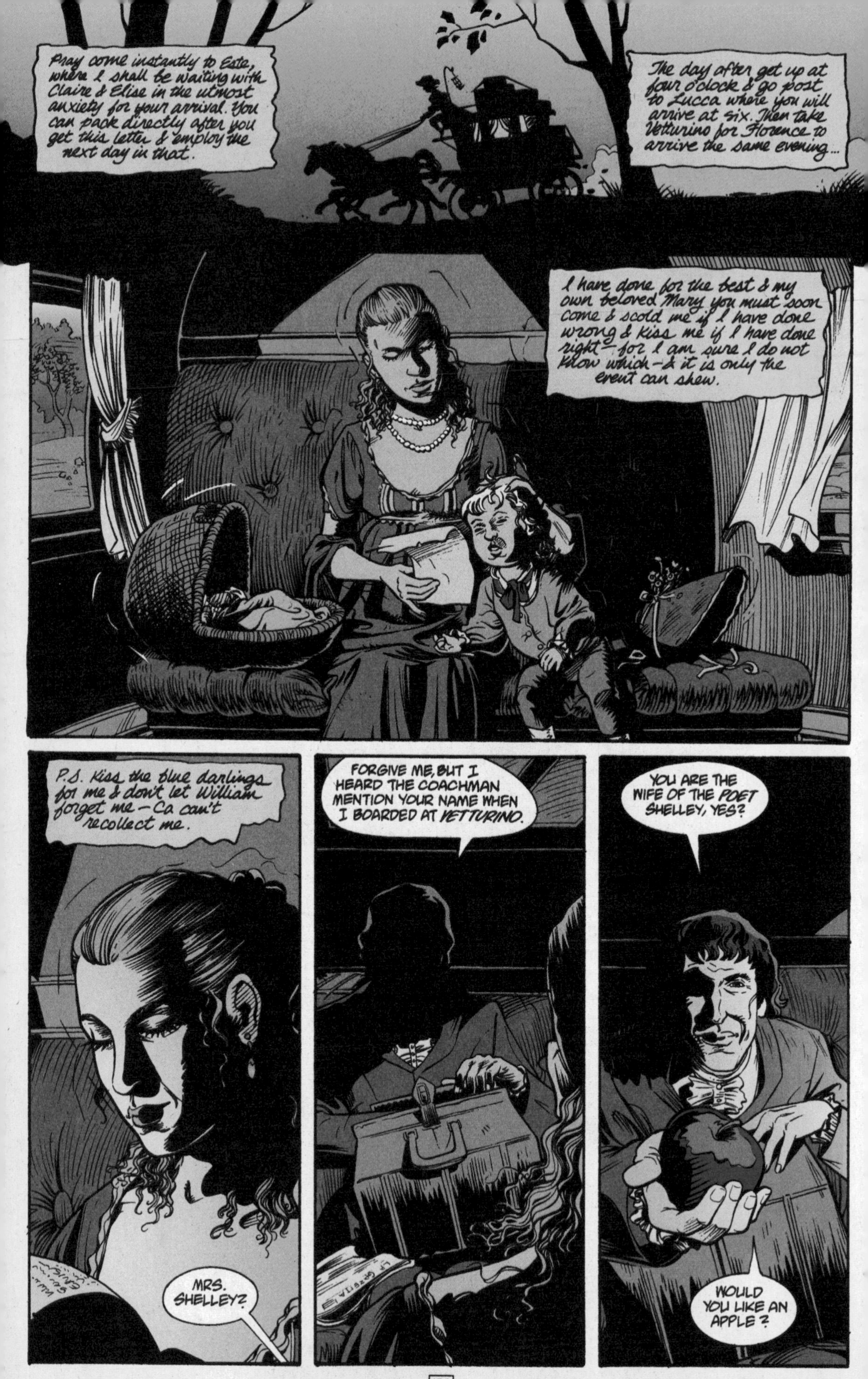
Pray come instantly to Este, where I shall be waiting with Claire & Elise in the utmost anxiety for your arrival. You can pack directly after you get this letter & employ the next day in that.
The day after get up at four o'clock & go post to Lucca where you will arrive at six. Then take Vetturino for Florence to arrive the same evening...
I have done for the best & my own beloved Mary you must soon come & scold me if I have done wrong & kiss me if I have done right — for I am sure I do not know which — & it is only the event can shew.
P.S. Kiss the blue darlings for me & don't let William forget me — Ca can't recollect me.
MRS. SHELLEY?
FORGIVE ME, BUT I HEARD THE COACHMAN MENTION YOUR NAME WHEN I BOARDED AT VETTURINO.
YOU ARE THE WIFE OF THE POET SHELLEY, YES?
WOULD YOU LIKE AN APPLE?

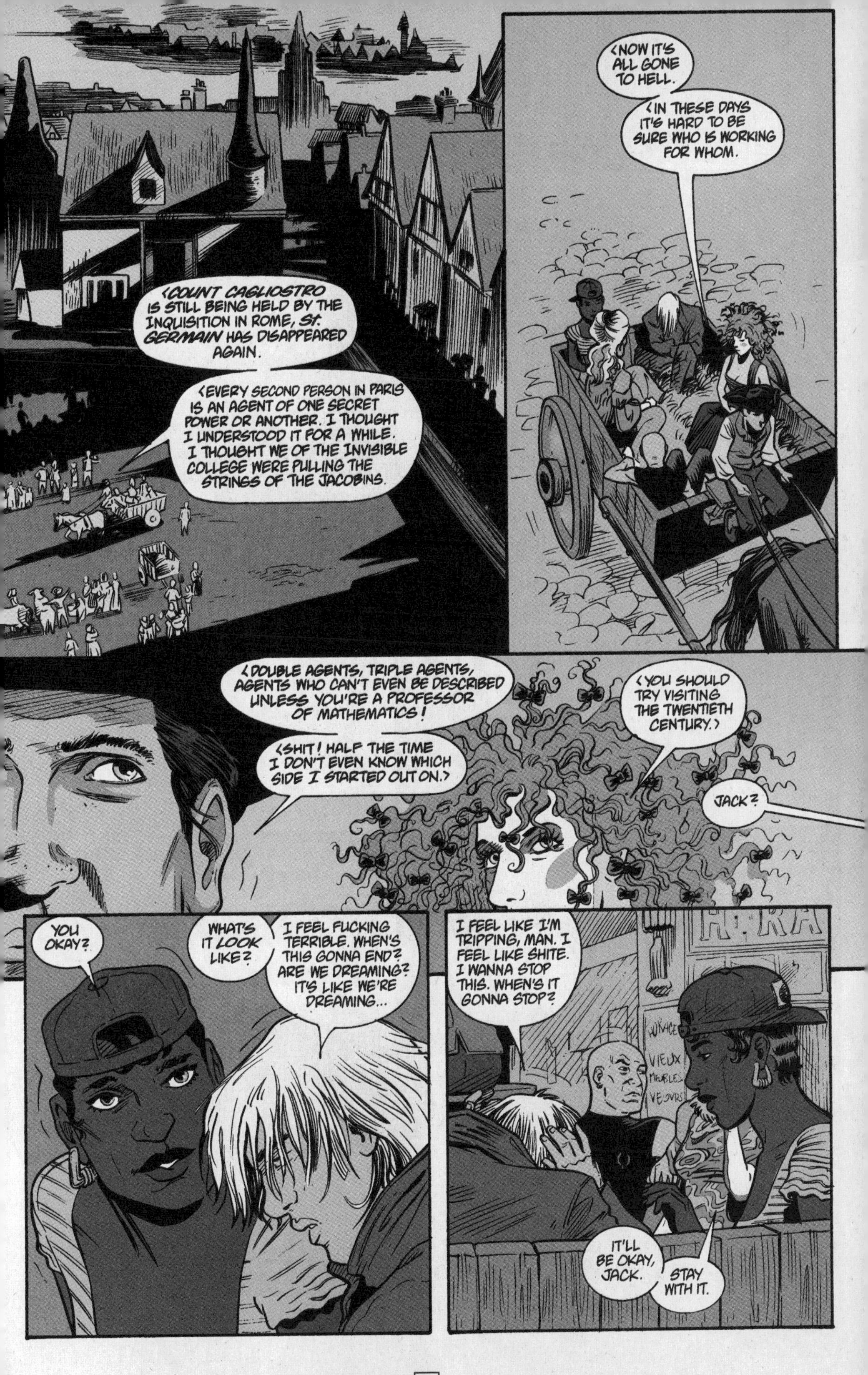

<COUNT CAGLIOSTRO IS STILL BEING HELD BY THE INQUISITION IN ROME, ST. GERMAIN HAS DISAPPEARED AGAIN.
<EVERY SECOND PERSON IN PARIS IS AN AGENT OF ONE SECRET POWER OR ANOTHER. I THOUGHT I UNDERSTOOD IT FOR A WHILE. I THOUGHT WE OF THE INVISIBLE COLLEGE WERE PULLING THE STRINGS OF THE JACOBINS.
<NOW IT'S ALL GONE TO HELL.
<IN THESE DAYS IT'S HARD TO BE SURE WHO IS WORKING FOR WHOM.
<DOUBLE AGENTS, TRIPLE AGENTS, AGENTS WHO CAN'T EVEN BE DESCRIBED UNLESS YOU'RE A PROFESSOR OF MATHEMATICS!
<SHIT! HALF THE TIME I DON'T EVEN KNOW WHICH SIDE I STARTED OUT ON.>
<YOU SHOULD TRY VISITING THE TWENTIETH CENTURY.>
JACK?
YOU OKAY?
WHAT'S IT LOOK LIKE?
I FEEL FUCKING TERRIBLE. WHEN'S THIS GONNA END? ARE WE DREAMING? IT'S LIKE WE'RE DREAMING...
I FEEL LIKE I'M TRIPPING, MAN. I FEEL LIKE SHITE. I WANNA STOP THIS. WHEN'S IT GONNA STOP?
IT'LL BE OKAY, JACK.
STAY WITH IT.

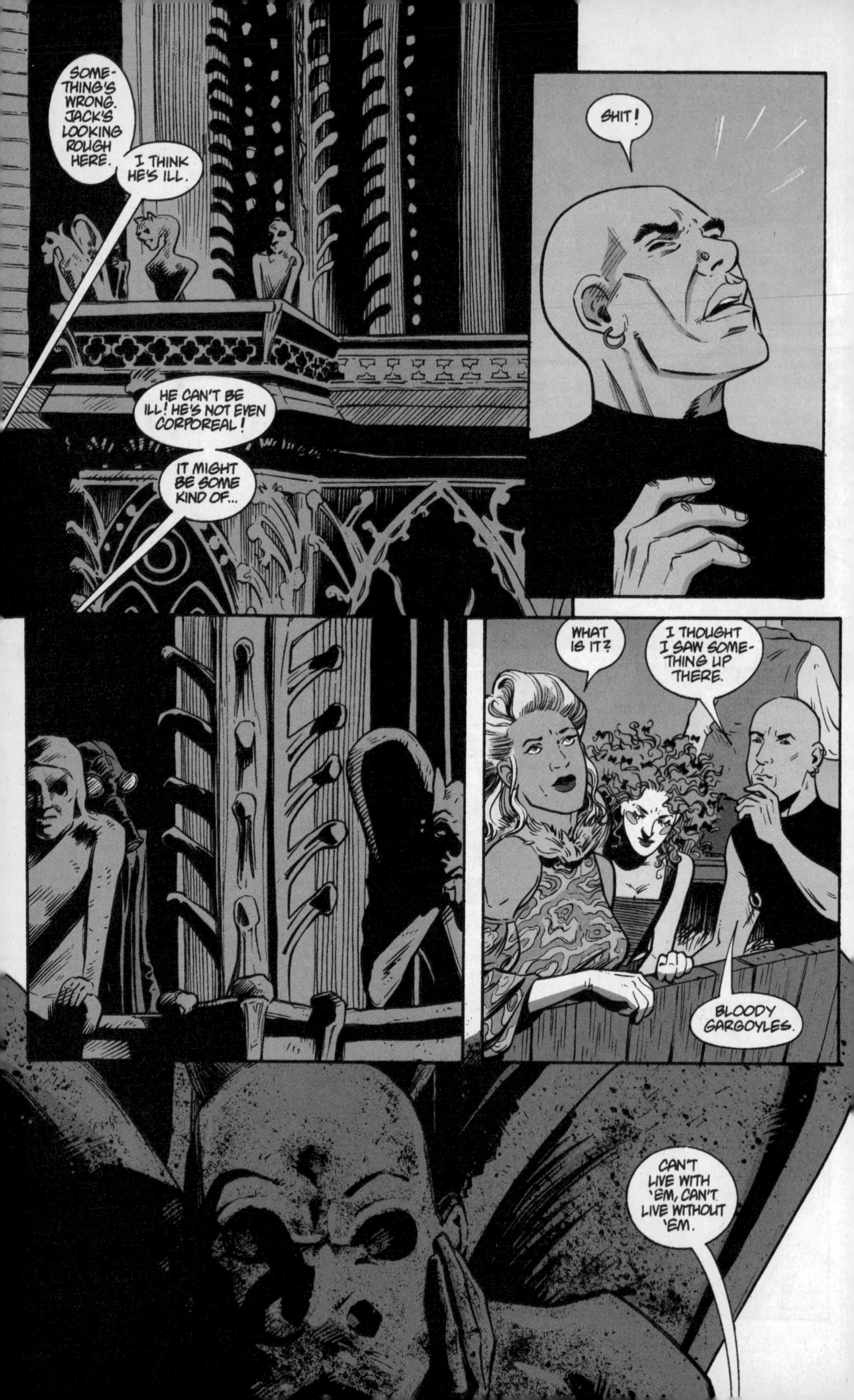
SOMETHING'S WRONG. JACK'S LOOKING ROUGH HERE.
I THINK HE'S ILL.
SHIT!
HE CAN'T BE ILL! HE'S NOT EVEN CORPOREAL!
IT MIGHT BE SOME KIND OF...
WHAT IS IT?
I THOUGHT I SAW SOMETHING UP THERE.
BLOODY GARGOYLES.
CAN'T LIVE WITH 'EM, CAN'T LIVE WITHOUT 'EM.

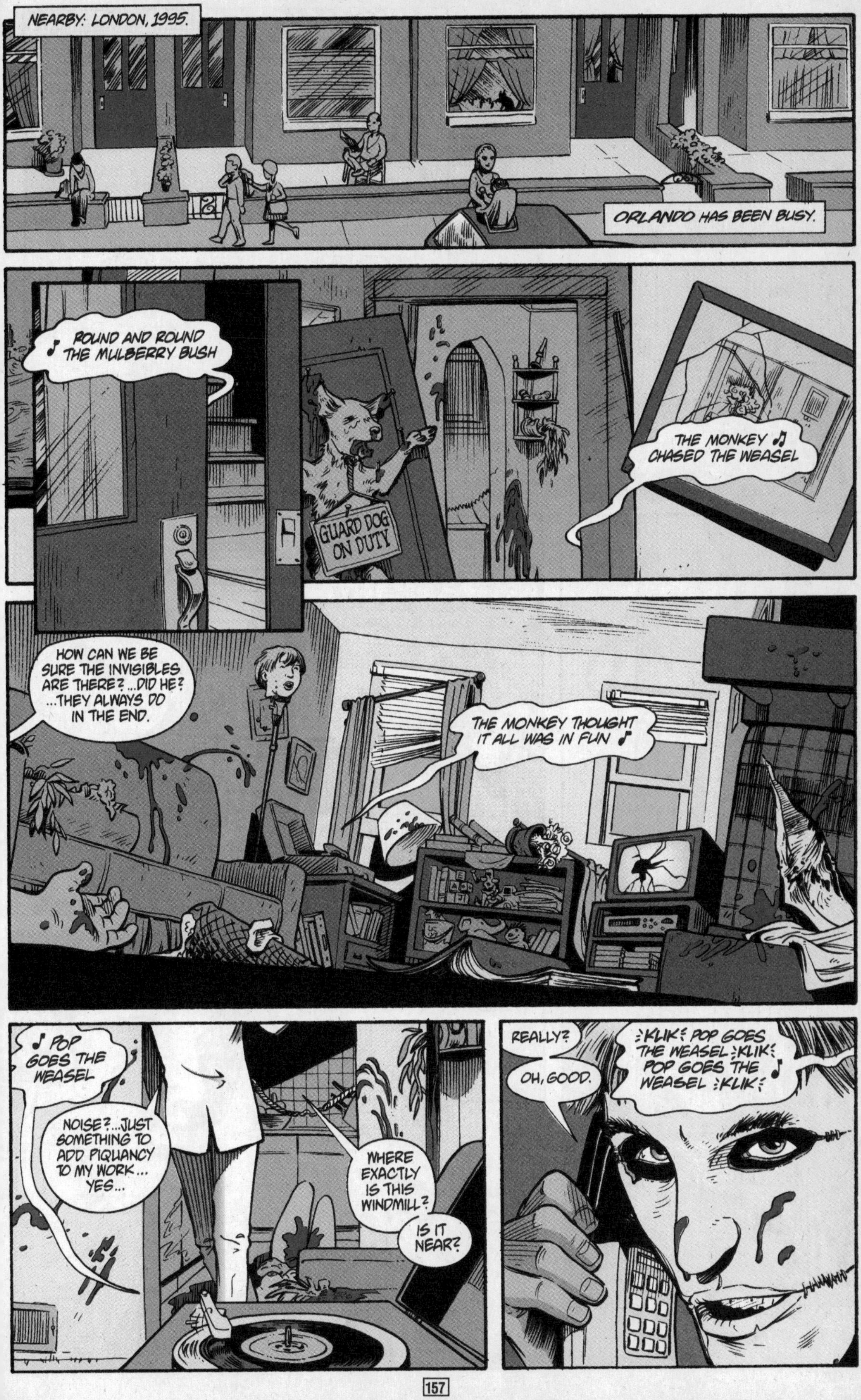
NEARBY: LONDON, 1995.
ORLANDO HAS BEEN BUSY.
♪ ROUND AND ROUND THE MULBERRY BUSH
GUARD DOG ON DUTY
THE MONKEY ♫ CHASED THE WEASEL
HOW CAN WE BE SURE THE INVISIBLES ARE THERE? ...DID HE? ...THEY ALWAYS DO IN THE END.
THE MONKEY THOUGHT IT ALL WAS IN FUN ♪
♪ POP GOES THE WEASEL
NOISE? ...JUST SOMETHING TO ADD PIQUANCY TO MY WORK... YES...
WHERE EXACTLY IS THIS WINDMILL?
IS IT NEAR?
REALLY?
OH, GOOD.
KLIK POP GOES THE WEASEL KLIK POP GOES THE WEASEL KLIK ♪

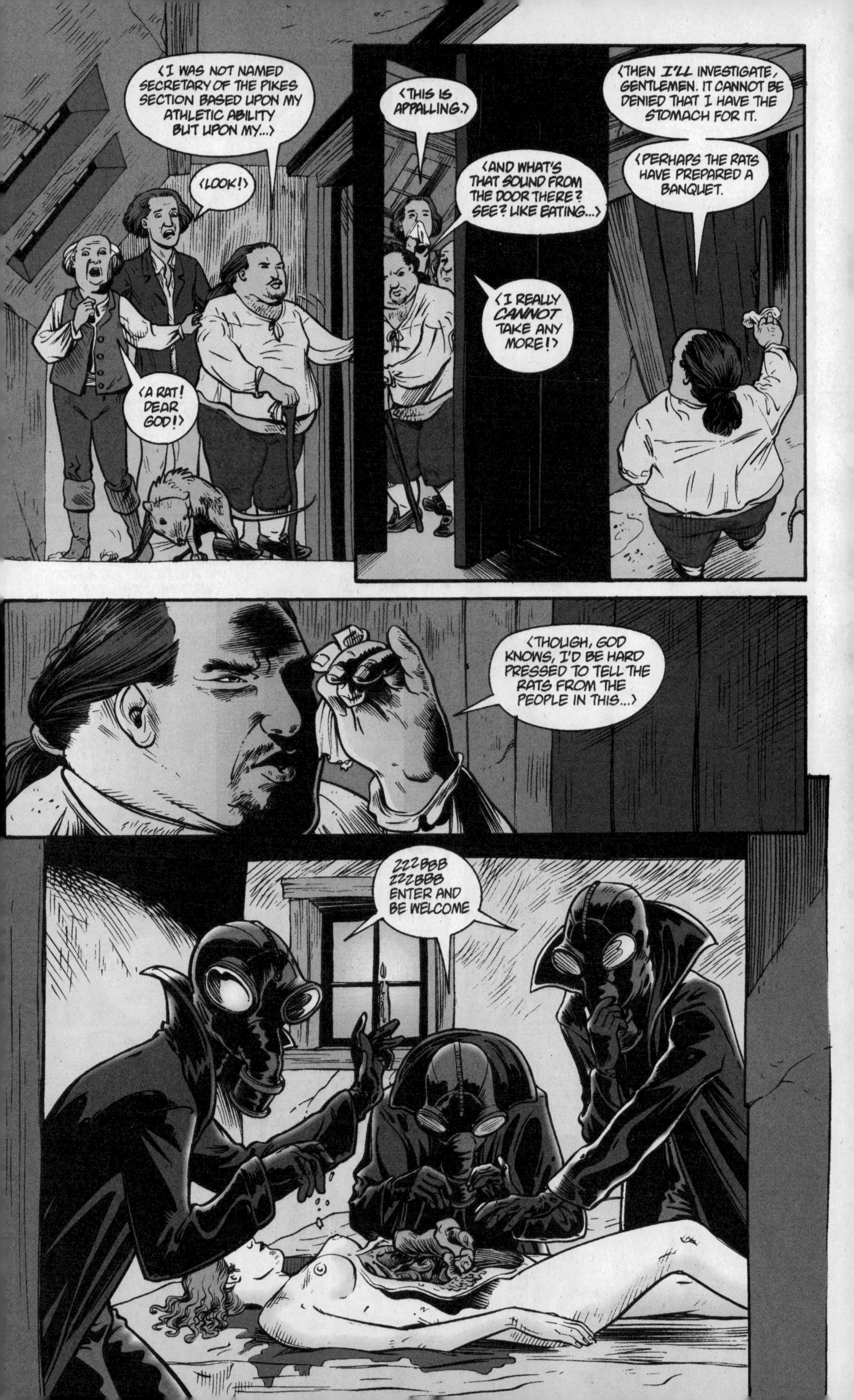

‹I WAS NOT NAMED SECRETARY OF THE PIKES SECTION BASED UPON MY ATHLETIC ABILITY BUT UPON MY...›
‹LOOK!›
‹A RAT! DEAR GOD!›
‹THIS IS APPALLING.›
‹AND WHAT'S THAT SOUND FROM THE DOOR THERE? SEE? LIKE EATING...›
‹I REALLY CANNOT TAKE ANY MORE!›
‹THEN I'LL INVESTIGATE, GENTLEMEN. IT CANNOT BE DENIED THAT I HAVE THE STOMACH FOR IT.
‹PERHAPS THE RATS HAVE PREPARED A BANQUET.
‹THOUGH, GOD KNOWS, I'D BE HARD PRESSED TO TELL THE RATS FROM THE PEOPLE IN THIS...›
ZZZBBB ZZZBBB ENTER AND BE WELCOME

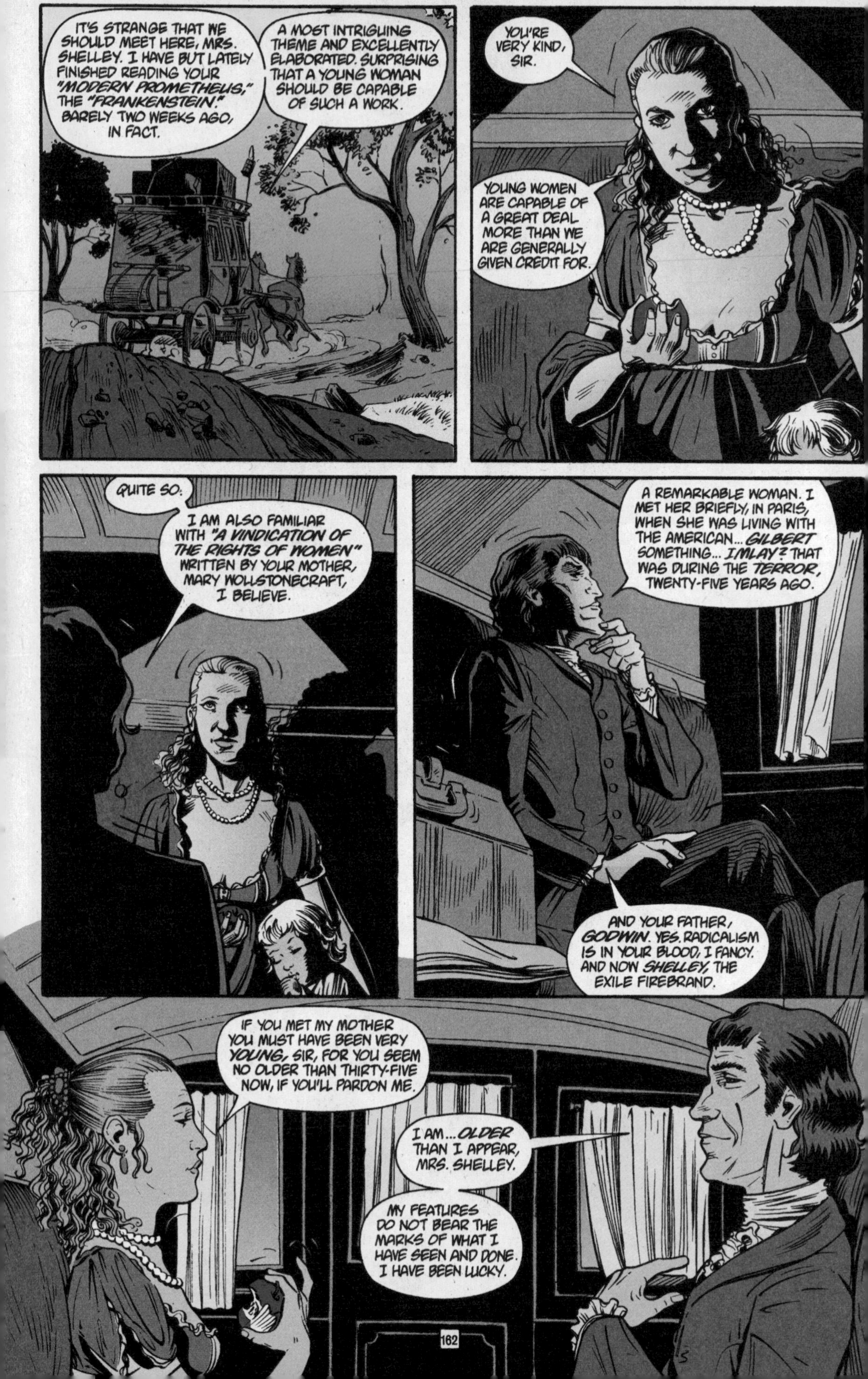
IT'S STRANGE THAT WE SHOULD MEET HERE, MRS. SHELLEY. I HAVE BUT LATELY FINISHED READING YOUR "MODERN PROMETHEUS," THE "FRANKENSTEIN." BARELY TWO WEEKS AGO, IN FACT.
A MOST INTRIGUING THEME AND EXCELLENTLY ELABORATED. SURPRISING THAT A YOUNG WOMAN SHOULD BE CAPABLE OF SUCH A WORK.
YOU'RE VERY KIND, SIR.
YOUNG WOMEN ARE CAPABLE OF A GREAT DEAL MORE THAN WE ARE GENERALLY GIVEN CREDIT FOR.
QUITE SO.
I AM ALSO FAMILIAR WITH "A VINDICATION OF THE RIGHTS OF WOMEN" WRITTEN BY YOUR MOTHER, MARY WOLLSTONECRAFT, I BELIEVE.
A REMARKABLE WOMAN. I MET HER BRIEFLY, IN PARIS, WHEN SHE WAS LIVING WITH THE AMERICAN... GILBERT SOMETHING... IMLAY? THAT WAS DURING THE TERROR, TWENTY-FIVE YEARS AGO.
AND YOUR FATHER, GODWIN. YES. RADICALISM IS IN YOUR BLOOD, I FANCY. AND NOW SHELLEY, THE EXILE FIREBRAND.
IF YOU MET MY MOTHER YOU MUST HAVE BEEN VERY YOUNG, SIR, FOR YOU SEEM NO OLDER THAN THIRTY-FIVE NOW, IF YOU'LL PARDON ME.
I AM... OLDER THAN I APPEAR, MRS. SHELLEY.
MY FEATURES DO NOT BEAR THE MARKS OF WHAT I HAVE SEEN AND DONE. I HAVE BEEN LUCKY.

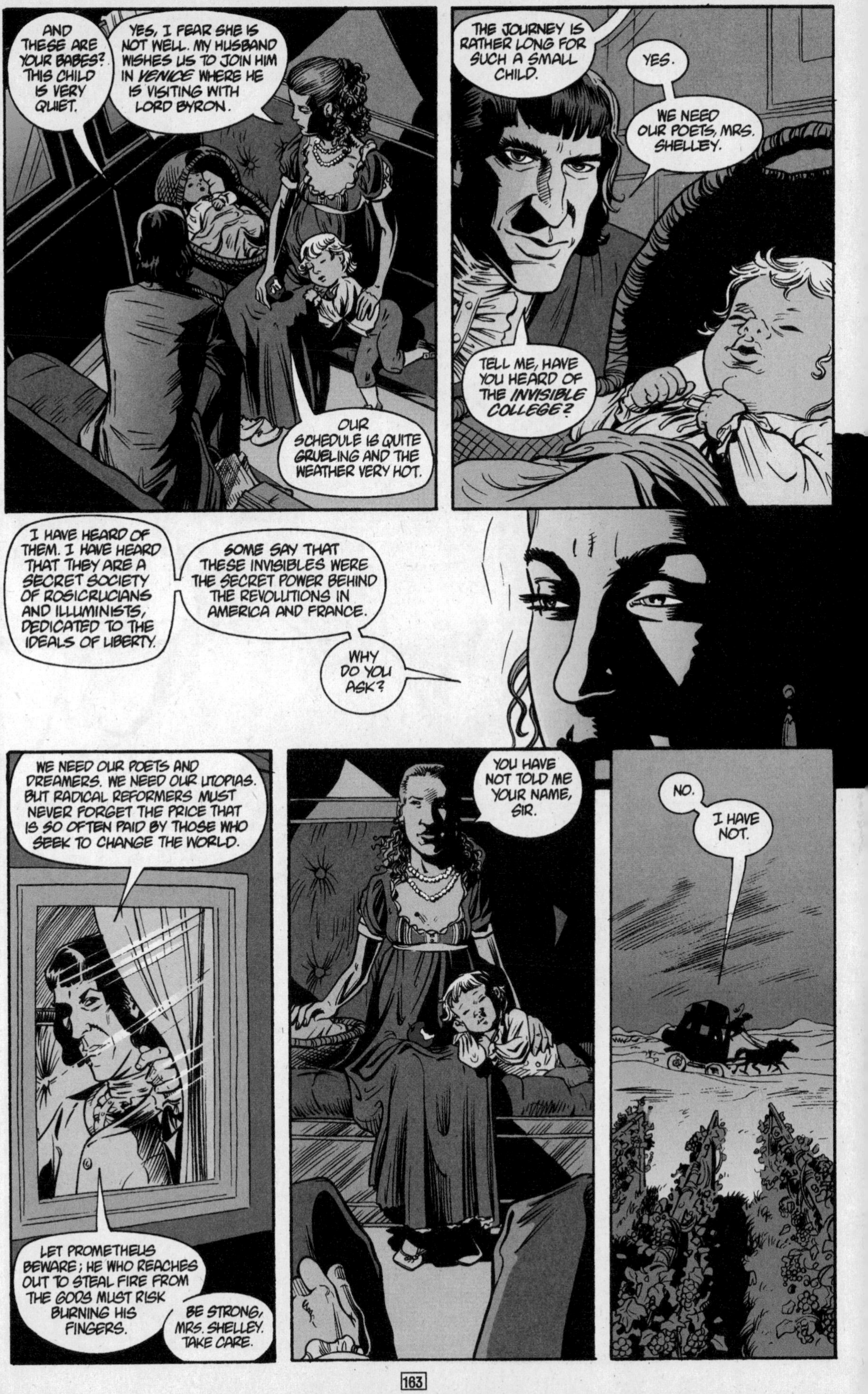
AND THESE ARE YOUR BABES? THIS CHILD IS VERY QUIET.
YES, I FEAR SHE IS NOT WELL. MY HUSBAND WISHES US TO JOIN HIM IN *VENICE* WHERE HE IS VISITING WITH LORD BYRON.
OUR SCHEDULE IS QUITE GRUELING AND THE WEATHER VERY HOT.
THE JOURNEY IS RATHER LONG FOR SUCH A SMALL CHILD.
YES.
WE NEED OUR POETS, MRS. SHELLEY.
TELL ME, HAVE YOU HEARD OF THE *INVISIBLE COLLEGE?*
I HAVE HEARD OF THEM. I HAVE HEARD THAT THEY ARE A SECRET SOCIETY OF ROSICRUCIANS AND ILLUMINISTS, DEDICATED TO THE IDEALS OF LIBERTY.
SOME SAY THAT THESE INVISIBLES WERE THE SECRET POWER BEHIND THE REVOLUTIONS IN AMERICA AND FRANCE.
WHY DO YOU ASK?
WE NEED OUR POETS AND DREAMERS. WE NEED OUR UTOPIAS. BUT RADICAL REFORMERS MUST NEVER FORGET THE PRICE THAT IS SO OFTEN PAID BY THOSE WHO SEEK TO CHANGE THE WORLD.
LET PROMETHEUS BEWARE; HE WHO REACHES OUT TO STEAL FIRE FROM THE GODS MUST RISK BURNING HIS FINGERS.
BE STRONG, MRS. SHELLEY. TAKE CARE.
YOU HAVE NOT TOLD ME YOUR NAME, SIR.
NO.
I HAVE NOT.

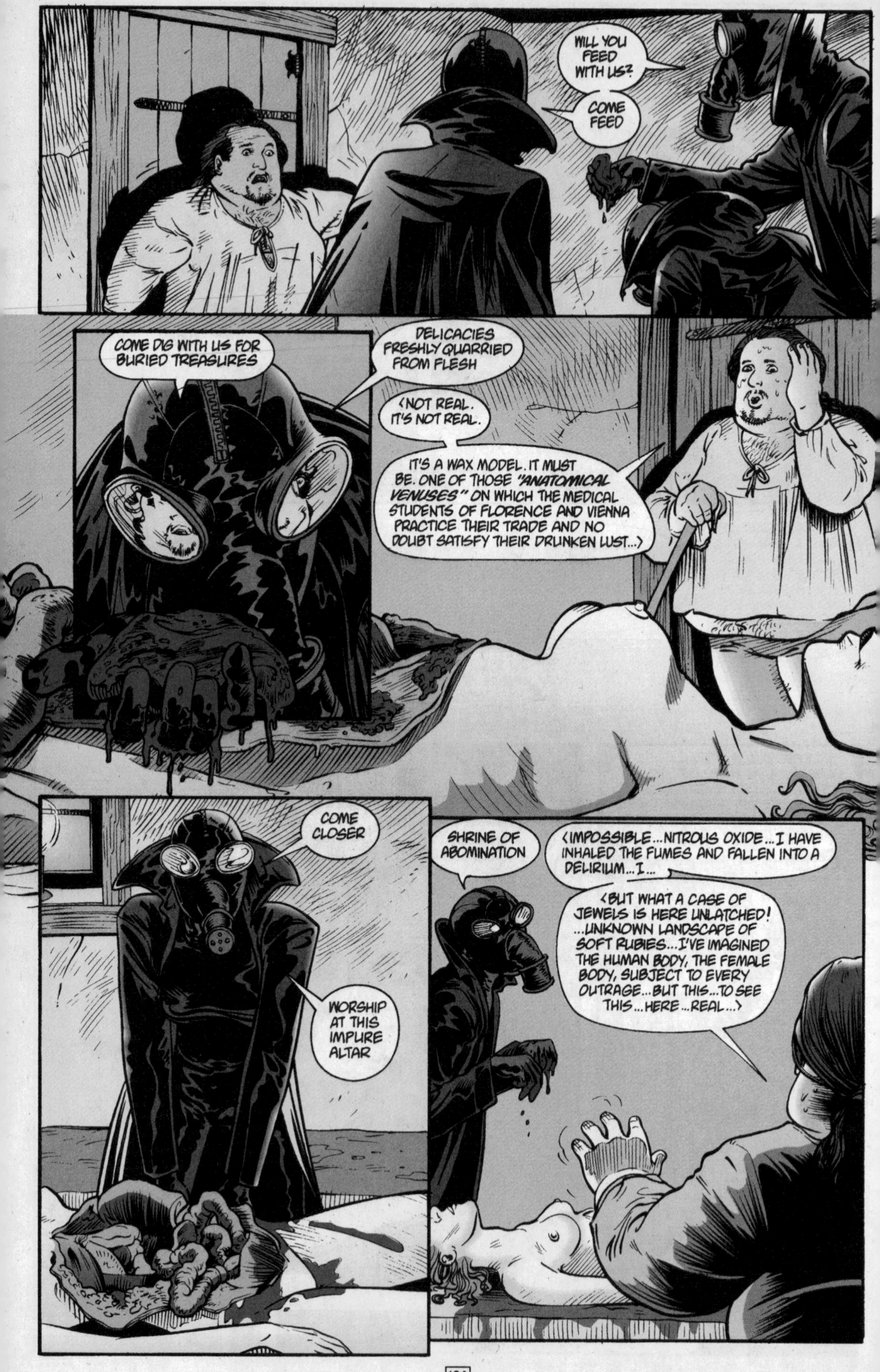
WILL YOU FEED WITH US?
COME FEED
COME DIG WITH US FOR BURIED TREASURES
DELICACIES FRESHLY QUARRIED FROM FLESH
‹NOT REAL. IT'S NOT REAL.
IT'S A WAX MODEL. IT MUST BE. ONE OF THOSE "ANATOMICAL VENUSES" ON WHICH THE MEDICAL STUDENTS OF FLORENCE AND VIENNA PRACTICE THEIR TRADE AND NO DOUBT SATISFY THEIR DRUNKEN LUST...›
COME CLOSER
WORSHIP AT THIS IMPURE ALTAR
SHRINE OF ABOMINATION
‹IMPOSSIBLE...NITROUS OXIDE...I HAVE INHALED THE FUMES AND FALLEN INTO A DELIRIUM...I...
‹BUT WHAT A CASE OF JEWELS IS HERE UNLATCHED! ...UNKNOWN LANDSCAPE OF SOFT RUBIES...I'VE IMAGINED THE HUMAN BODY, THE FEMALE BODY, SUBJECT TO EVERY OUTRAGE...BUT THIS...TO SEE THIS...HERE...REAL...›

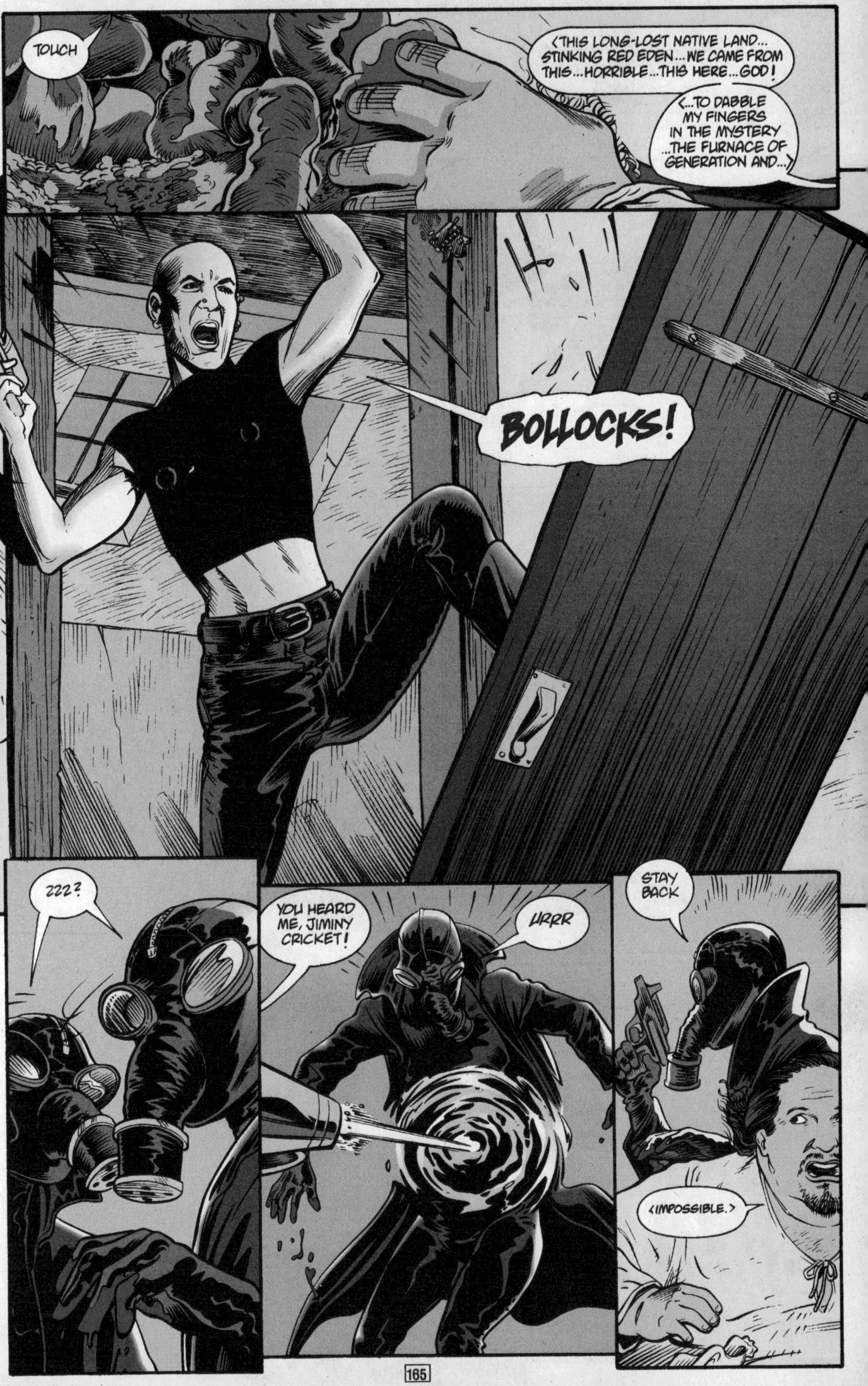
TOUCH
<THIS LONG-LOST NATIVE LAND... STINKING RED EDEN... WE CAME FROM THIS... HORRIBLE... THIS HERE... GOD!
<...TO DABBLE MY FINGERS IN THE MYSTERY ...THE FURNACE OF GENERATION AND...>
BOLLOCKS!
ZZZ?
YOU HEARD ME, JIMINY CRICKET!
URRR
STAY BACK
<IMPOSSIBLE.>

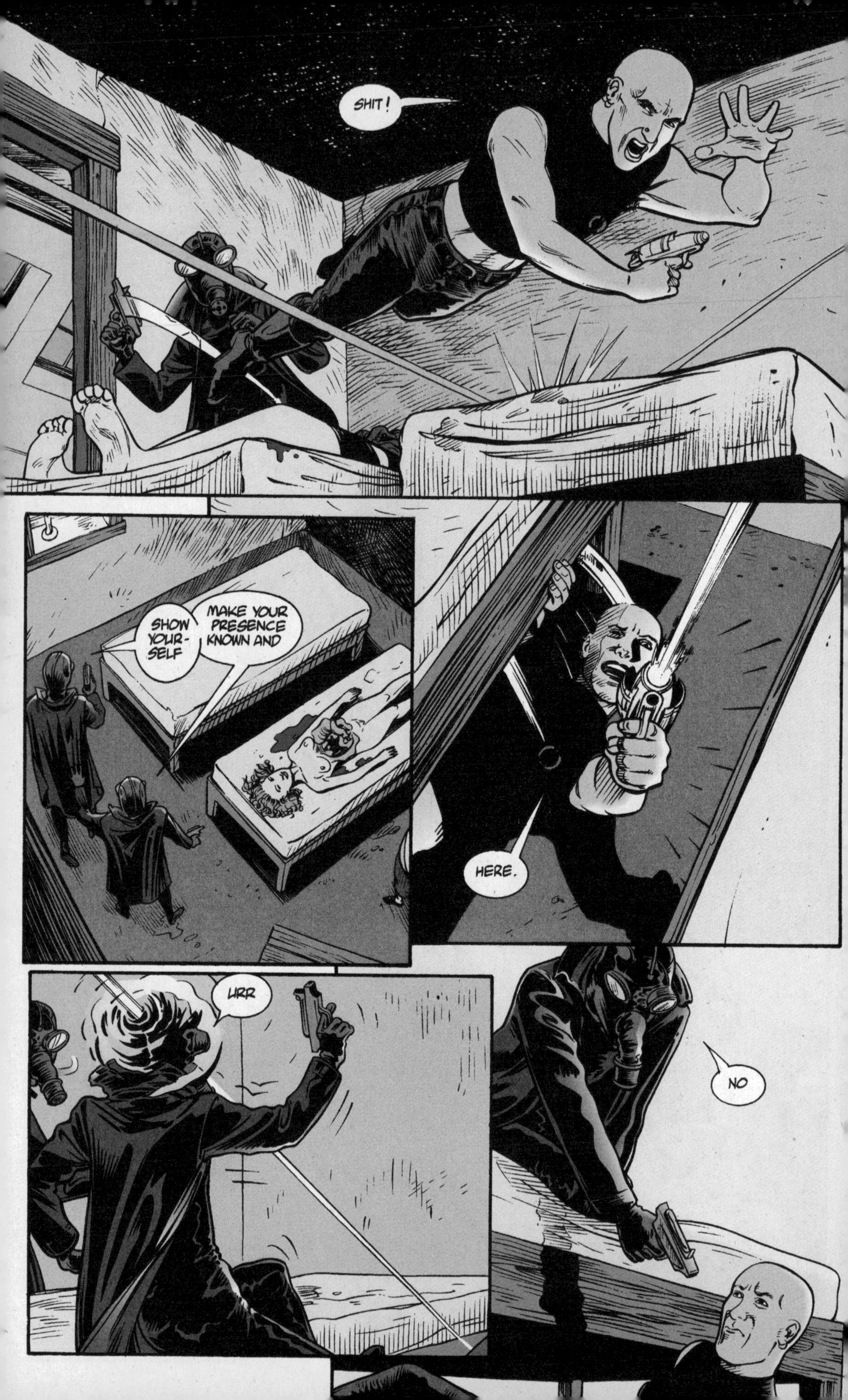
SHIT!
SHOW YOURSELF
MAKE YOUR PRESENCE KNOWN AND
HERE.
URR
NO

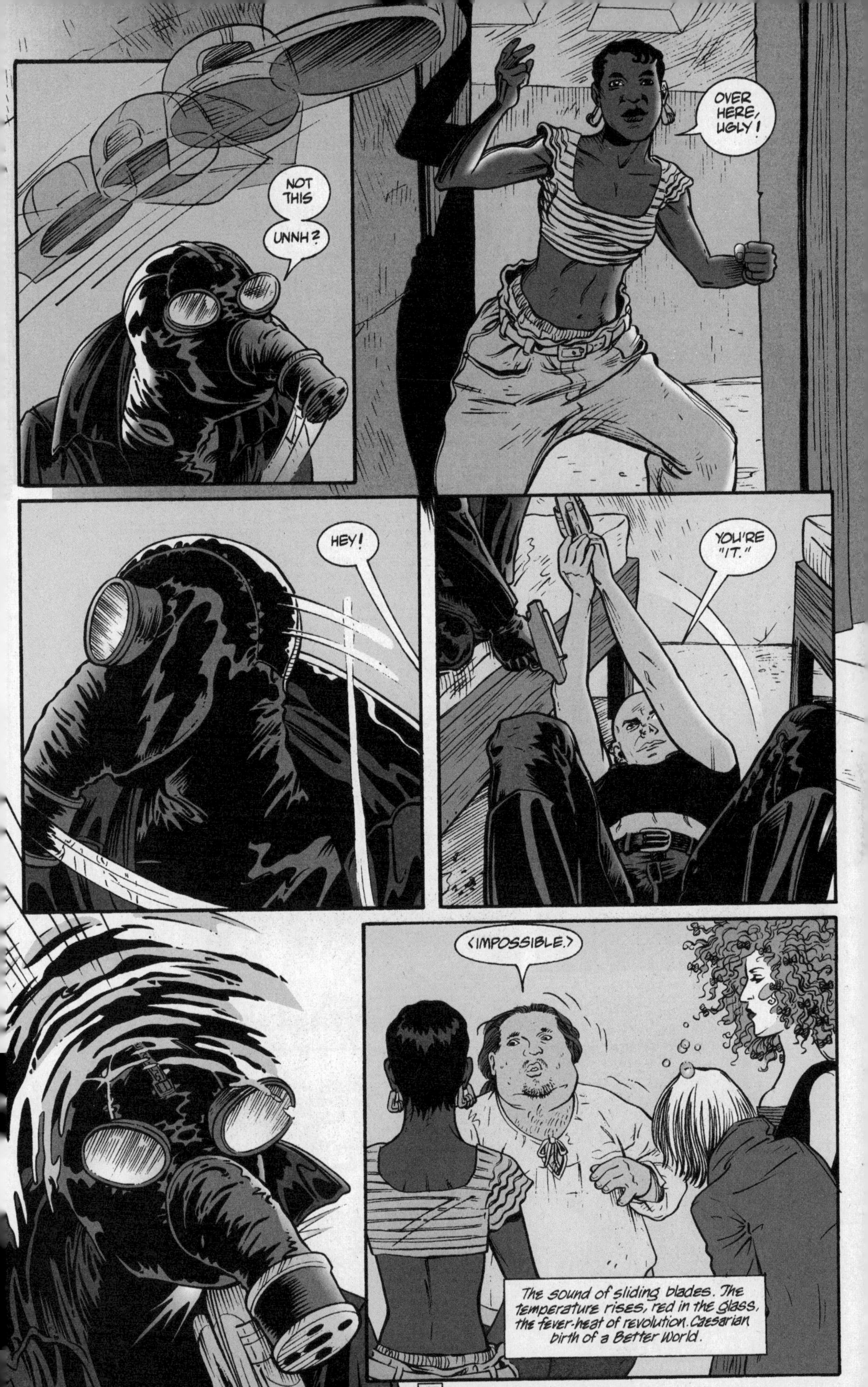
NOT THIS
UNNH?
OVER HERE, UGLY!
HEY!
YOU'RE "IT."
<IMPOSSIBLE.>
The sound of sliding blades. The temperature rises, red in the glass, the fever-heat of revolution. Caesarian birth of a Better World.

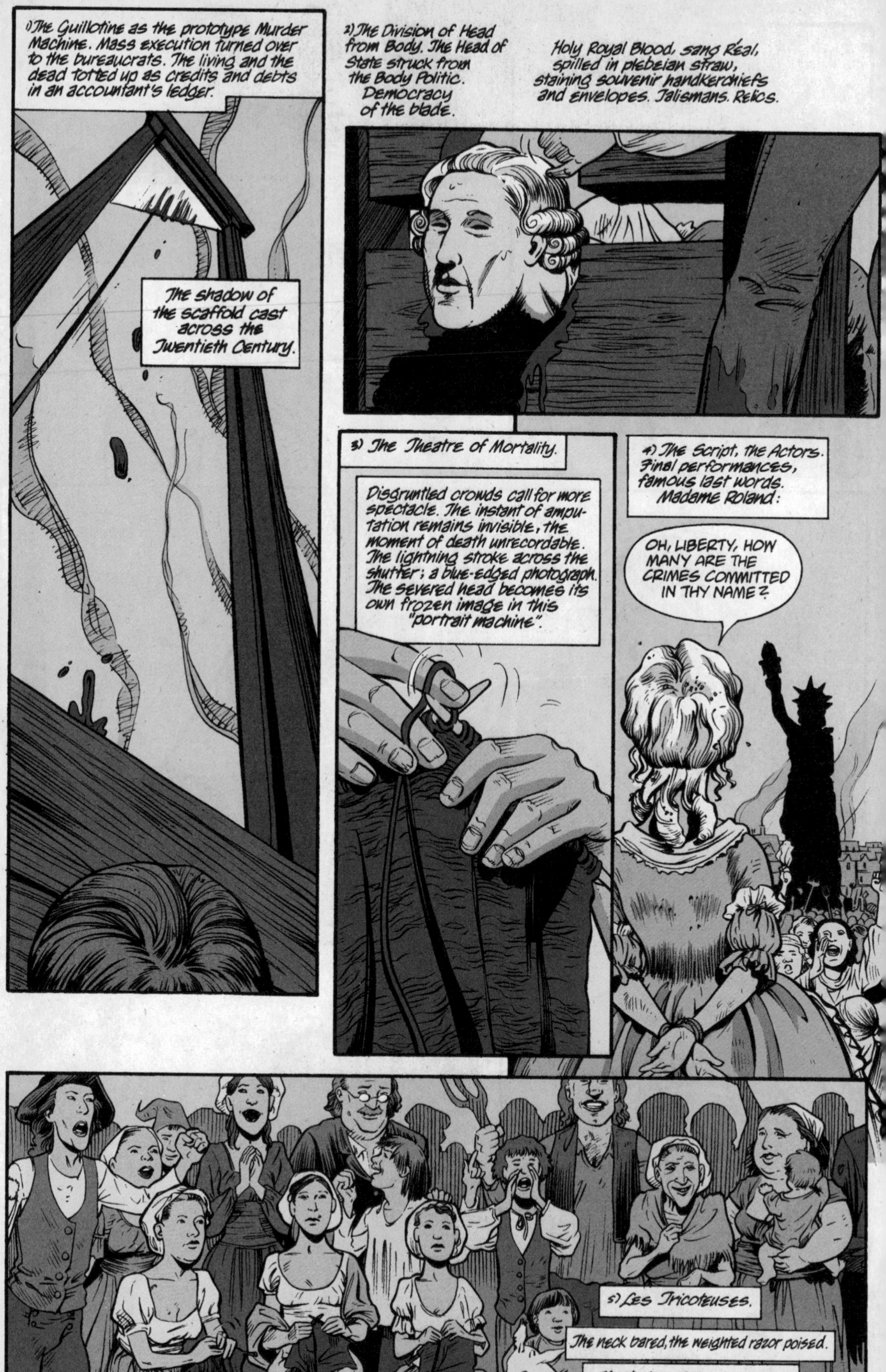
1) The Guillotine as the prototype Murder Machine. Mass execution turned over to the bureaucrats. The living and the dead totted up as credits and debts in an accountant's ledger.
The shadow of the scaffold cast across the Twentieth Century.
2) The Division of Head from Body. The Head of State struck from the Body Politic. Democracy of the blade.
Holy Royal Blood, sang Réal, spilled in plebeian straw, staining souvenir handkerchiefs and envelopes. Talismans. Relics.
3) The Theatre of Mortality.
Disgruntled crowds call for more spectacle. The instant of amputation remains invisible, the moment of death unrecordable. The lightning stroke across the shutter; a blue-edged photograph. The severed head becomes its own frozen image in this "portrait machine".
4) The Script, the Actors. Final performances, famous last words. Madame Roland:
OH, LIBERTY, HOW MANY ARE THE CRIMES COMMITTED IN THY NAME?
5) Les Tricoteuses.
The neck bared, the weighted razor poised.
Mysteries of the Guillotine.

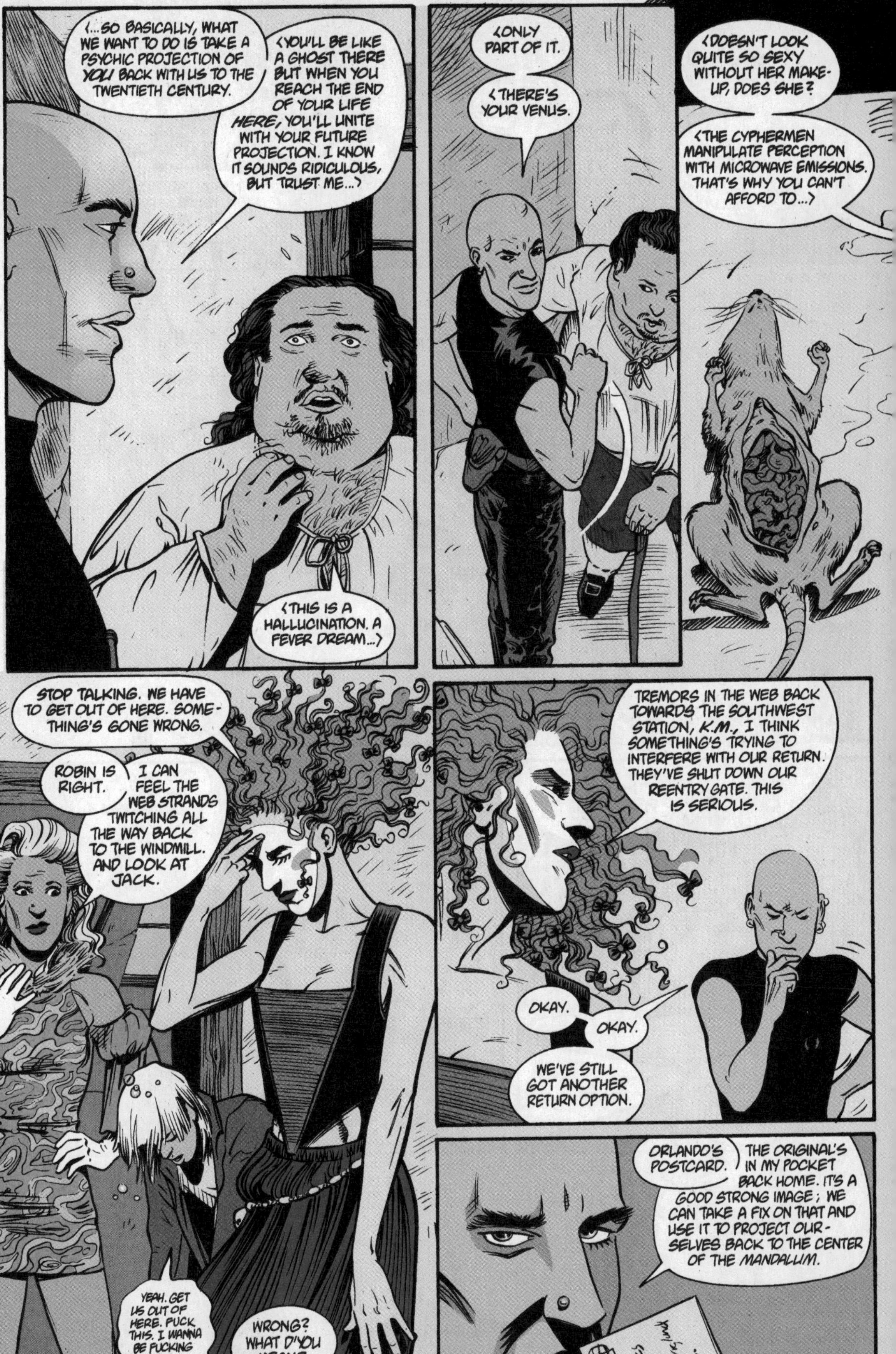
<...SO BASICALLY, WHAT WE WANT TO DO IS TAKE A PSYCHIC PROJECTION OF YOU BACK WITH US TO THE TWENTIETH CENTURY.
<YOU'LL BE LIKE A GHOST THERE BUT WHEN YOU REACH THE END OF YOUR LIFE HERE, YOU'LL UNITE WITH YOUR FUTURE PROJECTION. I KNOW IT SOUNDS RIDICULOUS, BUT TRUST ME...>
<THIS IS A HALLUCINATION. A FEVER DREAM...>
<ONLY PART OF IT.
<THERE'S YOUR VENUS.
<DOESN'T LOOK QUITE SO SEXY WITHOUT HER MAKE-UP, DOES SHE?
<THE CYPHERMEN MANIPULATE PERCEPTION WITH MICROWAVE EMISSIONS. THAT'S WHY YOU CAN'T AFFORD TO...>
STOP TALKING. WE HAVE TO GET OUT OF HERE. SOME-THING'S GONE WRONG.
ROBIN IS RIGHT.
I CAN FEEL THE WEB STRANDS TWITCHING ALL THE WAY BACK TO THE WINDMILL. AND LOOK AT JACK.
YEAH. GET US OUT OF HERE. FUCK THIS. I WANNA BE FUCKING SICK.
WRONG? WHAT D'YOU MEAN?
TREMORS IN THE WEB BACK TOWARDS THE SOUTHWEST STATION, K.M., I THINK SOMETHING'S TRYING TO INTERFERE WITH OUR RETURN. THEY'VE SHUT DOWN OUR REENTRY GATE. THIS IS SERIOUS.
OKAY.
OKAY.
WE'VE STILL GOT ANOTHER RETURN OPTION.
ORLANDO'S POSTCARD.
THE ORIGINAL'S IN MY POCKET BACK HOME. IT'S A GOOD STRONG IMAGE; WE CAN TAKE A FIX ON THAT AND USE IT TO PROJECT OUR-SELVES BACK TO THE CENTER OF THE MANDALUM.

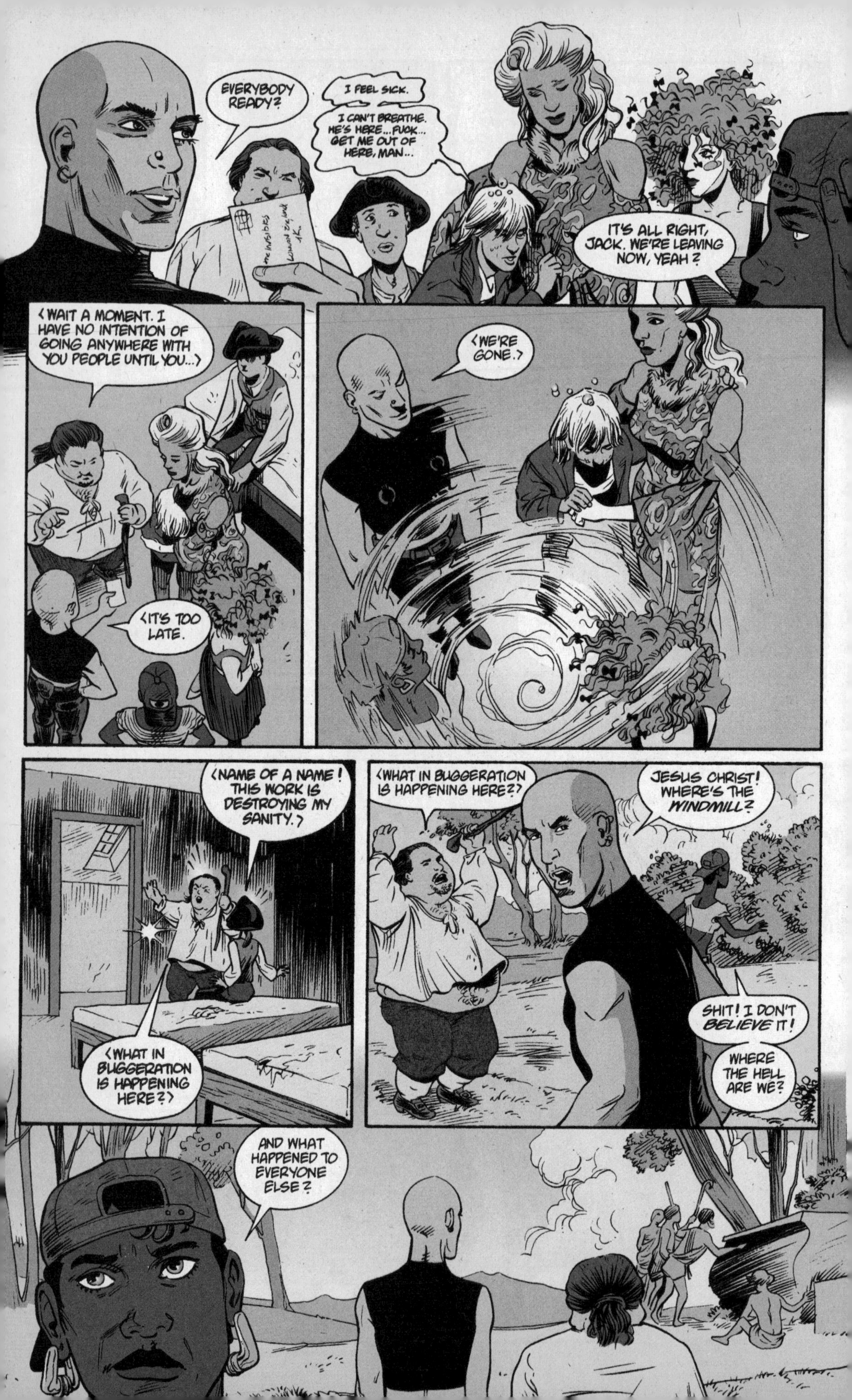
EVERYBODY READY?
I FEEL SICK.
I CAN'T BREATHE. HE'S HERE... FUCK... GET ME OUT OF HERE, MAN...
IT'S ALL RIGHT, JACK. WE'RE LEAVING NOW, YEAH?
<WAIT A MOMENT. I HAVE NO INTENTION OF GOING ANYWHERE WITH YOU PEOPLE UNTIL YOU...>
<IT'S TOO LATE.
<WE'RE GONE.>
<NAME OF A NAME! THIS WORK IS DESTROYING MY SANITY.>
<WHAT IN BUGGERATION IS HAPPENING HERE?>
<WHAT IN BUGGERATION IS HAPPENING HERE?>
JESUS CHRIST! WHERE'S THE WINDMILL?
SHIT! I DON'T BELIEVE IT!
WHERE THE HELL ARE WE?
AND WHAT HAPPENED TO EVERYONE ELSE?

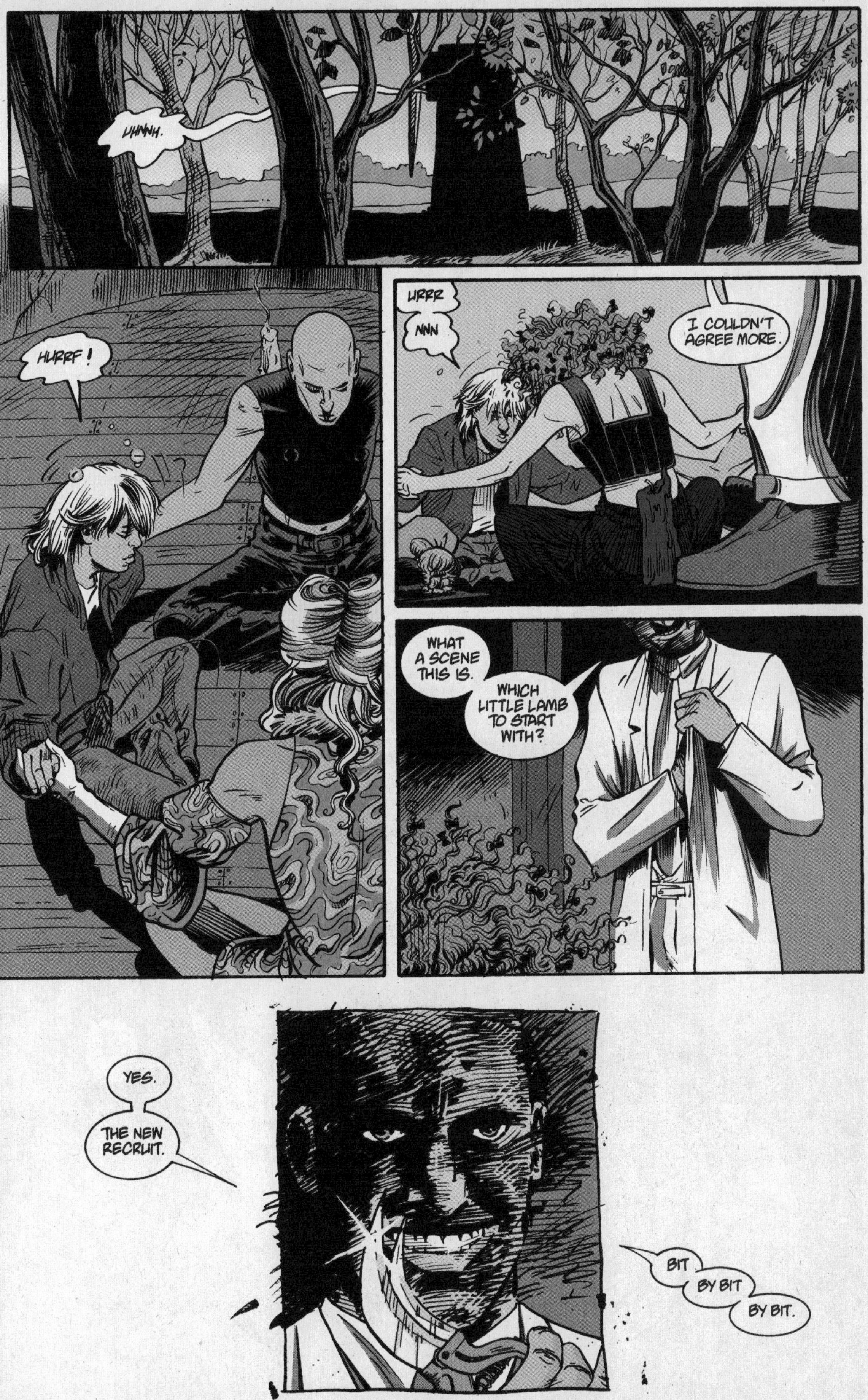
UHNNH.
HURRF!
URRR
NNN
I COULDN'T AGREE MORE.
WHAT A SCENE THIS IS.
WHICH LITTLE LAMB TO START WITH?
YES.
THE NEW RECRUIT.
BIT
BY BIT
BY BIT.

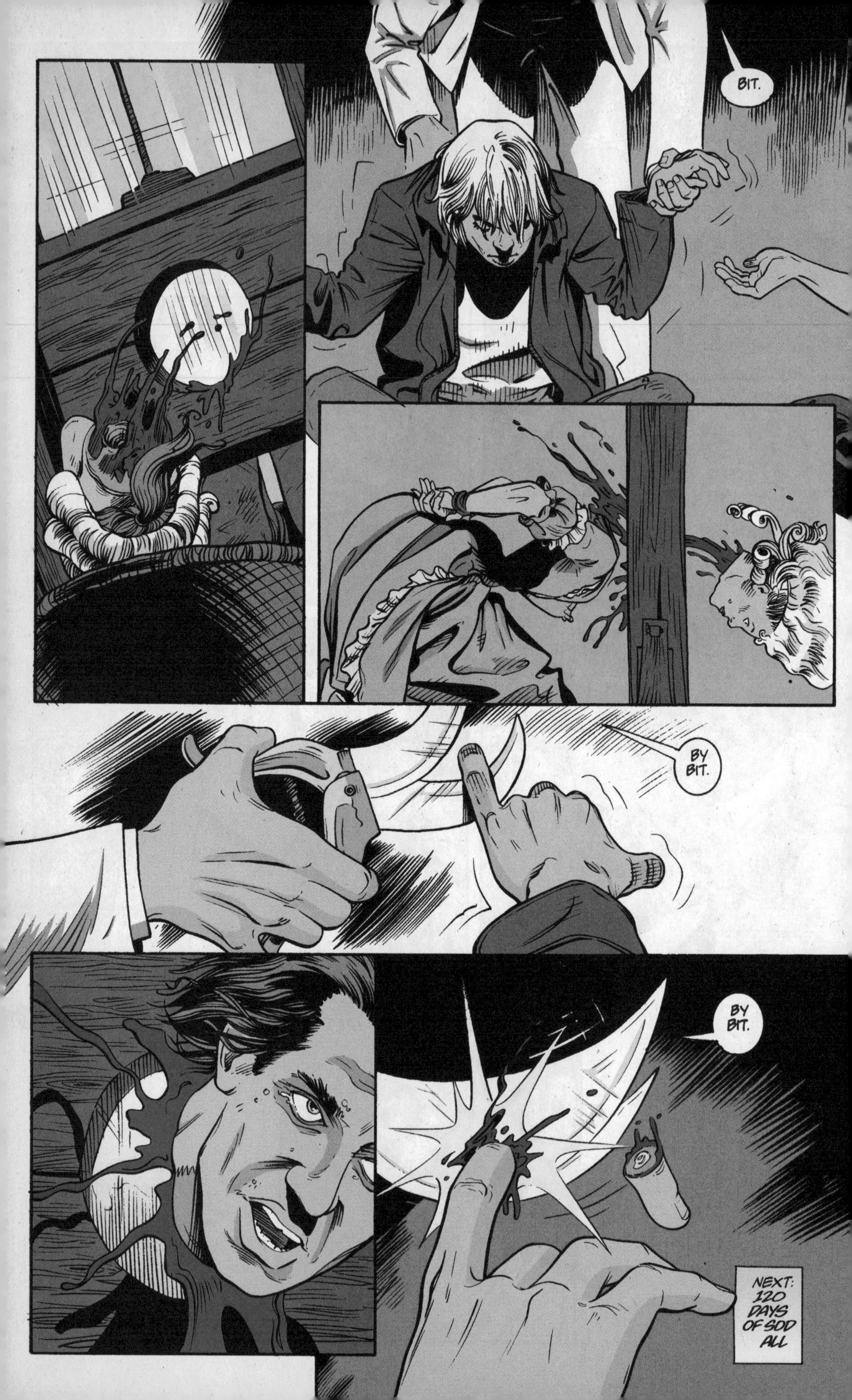
BIT.
BY BIT.
BY BIT.
NEXT: 120 DAYS OF SOD ALL

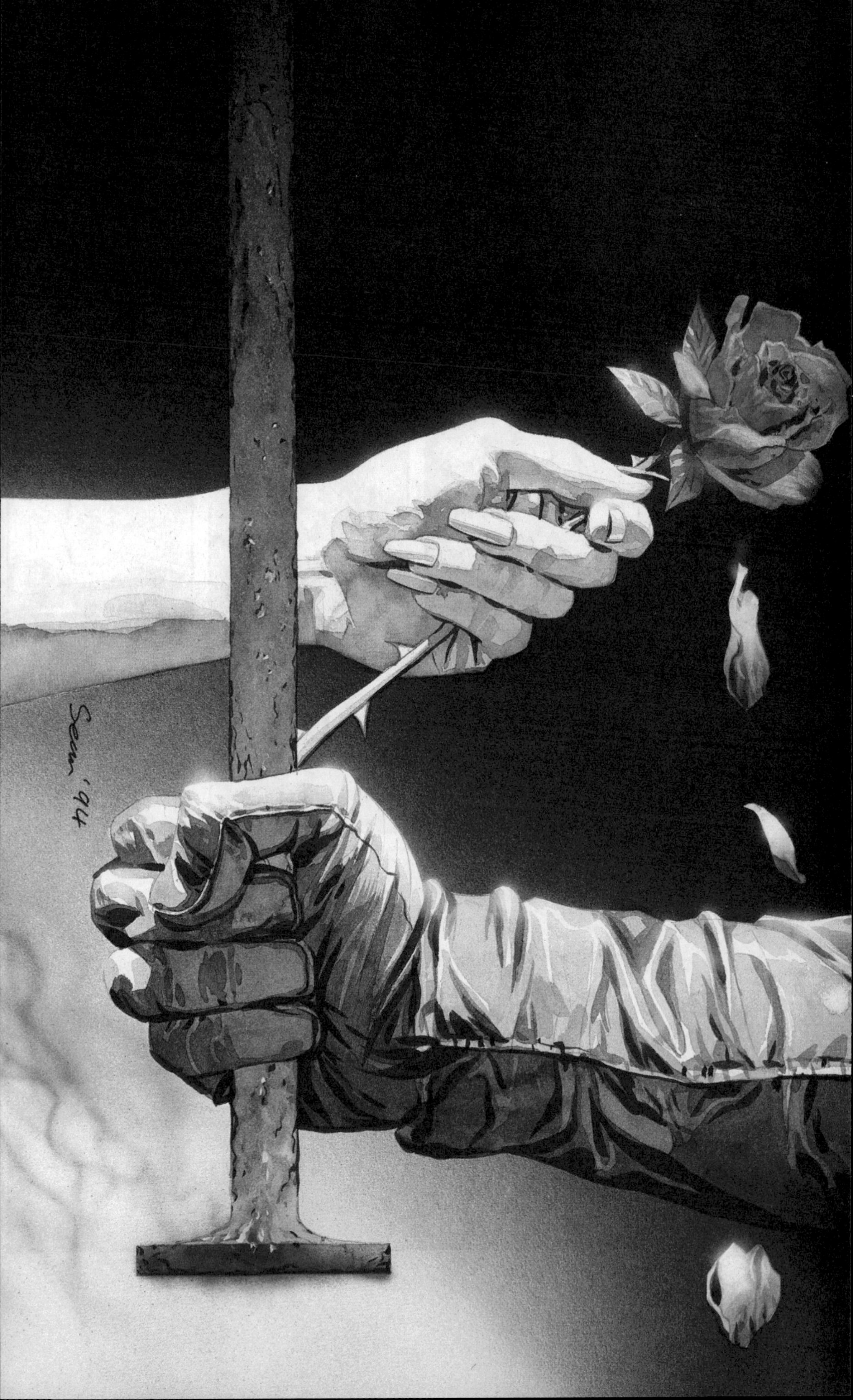

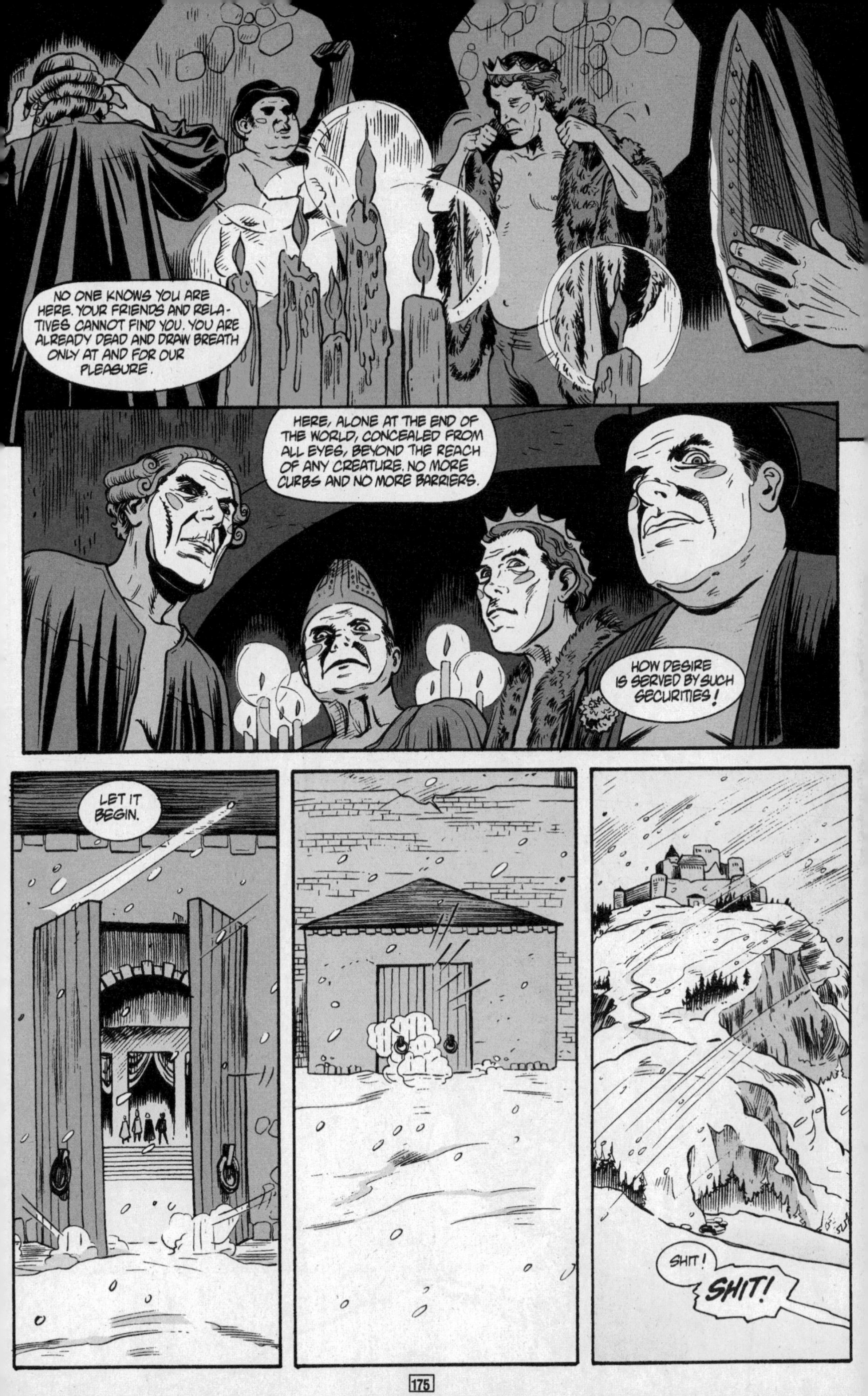
NO ONE KNOWS YOU ARE HERE. YOUR FRIENDS AND RELATIVES CANNOT FIND YOU. YOU ARE ALREADY DEAD AND DRAW BREATH ONLY AT AND FOR OUR PLEASURE.
HERE, ALONE AT THE END OF THE WORLD, CONCEALED FROM ALL EYES, BEYOND THE REACH OF ANY CREATURE. NO MORE CURBS AND NO MORE BARRIERS.
HOW DESIRE IS SERVED BY SUCH SECURITIES!
LET IT BEGIN.
SHIT!
SHIT!

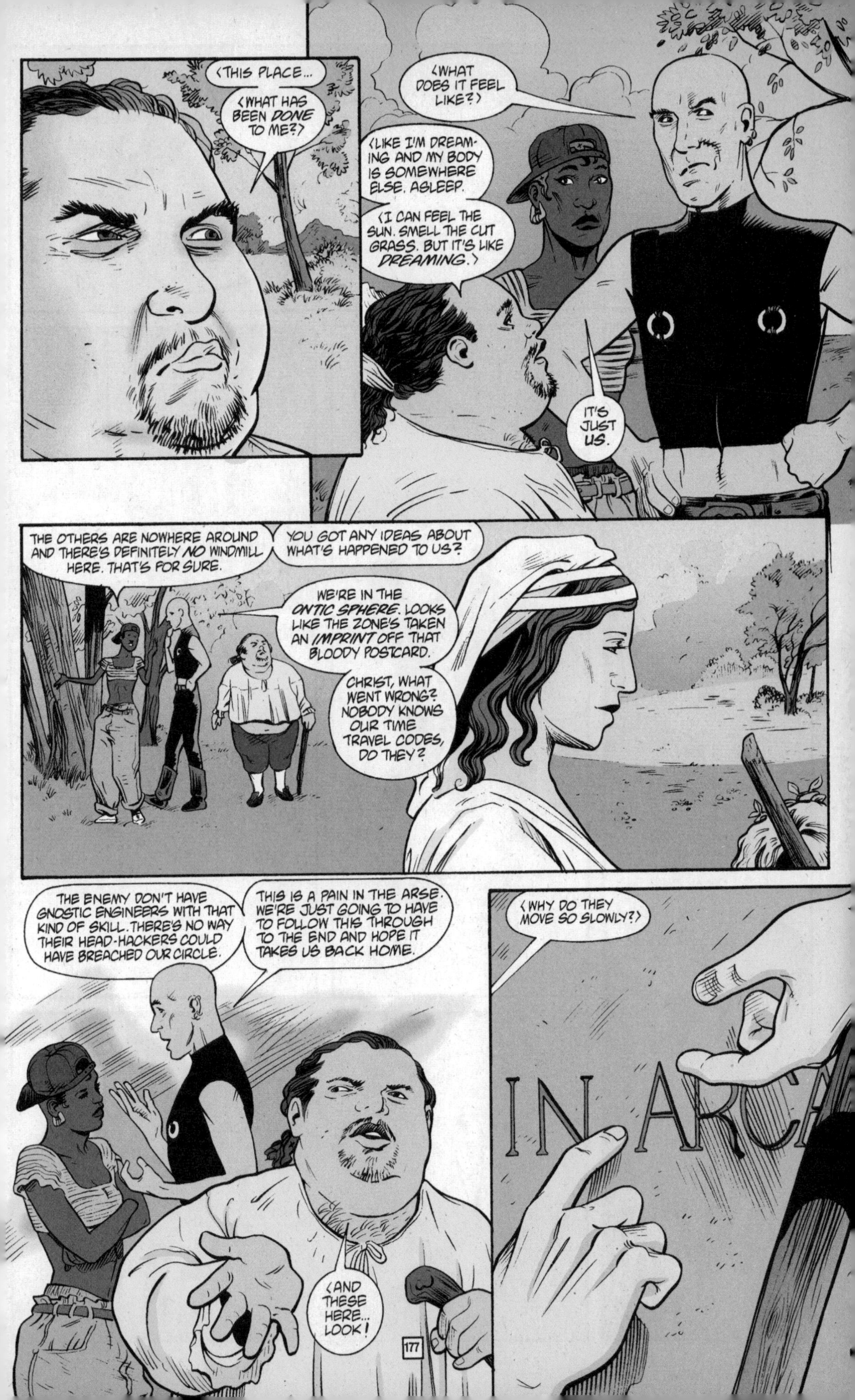

‹THIS PLACE...
‹WHAT HAS BEEN DONE TO ME?›
‹WHAT DOES IT FEEL LIKE?›
‹LIKE I'M DREAMING AND MY BODY IS SOMEWHERE ELSE. ASLEEP.
‹I CAN FEEL THE SUN. SMELL THE CUT GRASS. BUT IT'S LIKE DREAMING.›
IT'S JUST US.
THE OTHERS ARE NOWHERE AROUND AND THERE'S DEFINITELY NO WINDMILL HERE. THAT'S FOR SURE.
YOU GOT ANY IDEAS ABOUT WHAT'S HAPPENED TO US?
WE'RE IN THE ONTIC SPHERE. LOOKS LIKE THE ZONE'S TAKEN AN IMPRINT OFF THAT BLOODY POSTCARD.
CHRIST, WHAT WENT WRONG? NOBODY KNOWS OUR TIME TRAVEL CODES, DO THEY?
THE ENEMY DON'T HAVE GNOSTIC ENGINEERS WITH THAT KIND OF SKILL. THERE'S NO WAY THEIR HEAD-HACKERS COULD HAVE BREACHED OUR CIRCLE.
THIS IS A PAIN IN THE ARSE. WE'RE JUST GOING TO HAVE TO FOLLOW THIS THROUGH TO THE END AND HOPE IT TAKES US BACK HOME.
‹AND THESE HERE... LOOK!
‹WHY DO THEY MOVE SO SLOWLY?›
IN ARC

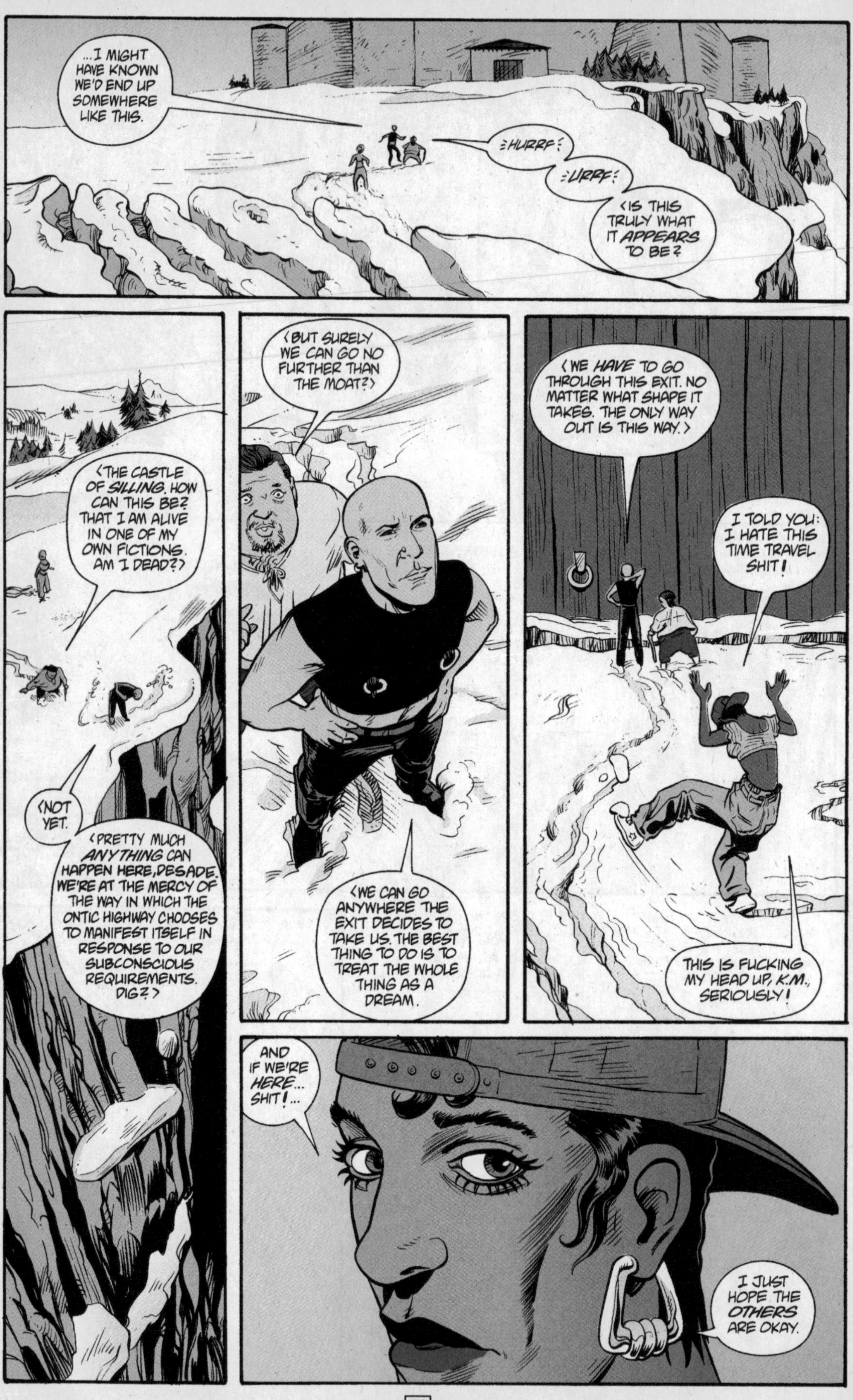
...I MIGHT HAVE KNOWN WE'D END UP SOMEWHERE LIKE THIS.
HURRF
URRF
‹IS THIS TRULY WHAT IT APPEARS TO BE?
‹THE CASTLE OF SILLING. HOW CAN THIS BE? THAT I AM ALIVE IN ONE OF MY OWN FICTIONS. AM I DEAD?›
‹NOT YET.
‹PRETTY MUCH ANYTHING CAN HAPPEN HERE, DESADE. WE'RE AT THE MERCY OF THE WAY IN WHICH THE ONTIC HIGHWAY CHOOSES TO MANIFEST ITSELF IN RESPONSE TO OUR SUBCONSCIOUS REQUIREMENTS. DIG?›
‹BUT SURELY WE CAN GO NO FURTHER THAN THE MOAT?›
‹WE CAN GO ANYWHERE THE EXIT DECIDES TO TAKE US. THE BEST THING TO DO IS TO TREAT THE WHOLE THING AS A DREAM.
‹WE HAVE TO GO THROUGH THIS EXIT. NO MATTER WHAT SHAPE IT TAKES. THE ONLY WAY OUT IS THIS WAY.›
I TOLD YOU: I HATE THIS TIME TRAVEL SHIT!
THIS IS FUCKING MY HEAD UP, K.M., SERIOUSLY!
AND IF WE'RE HERE... SHIT!...
I JUST HOPE THE OTHERS ARE OKAY.

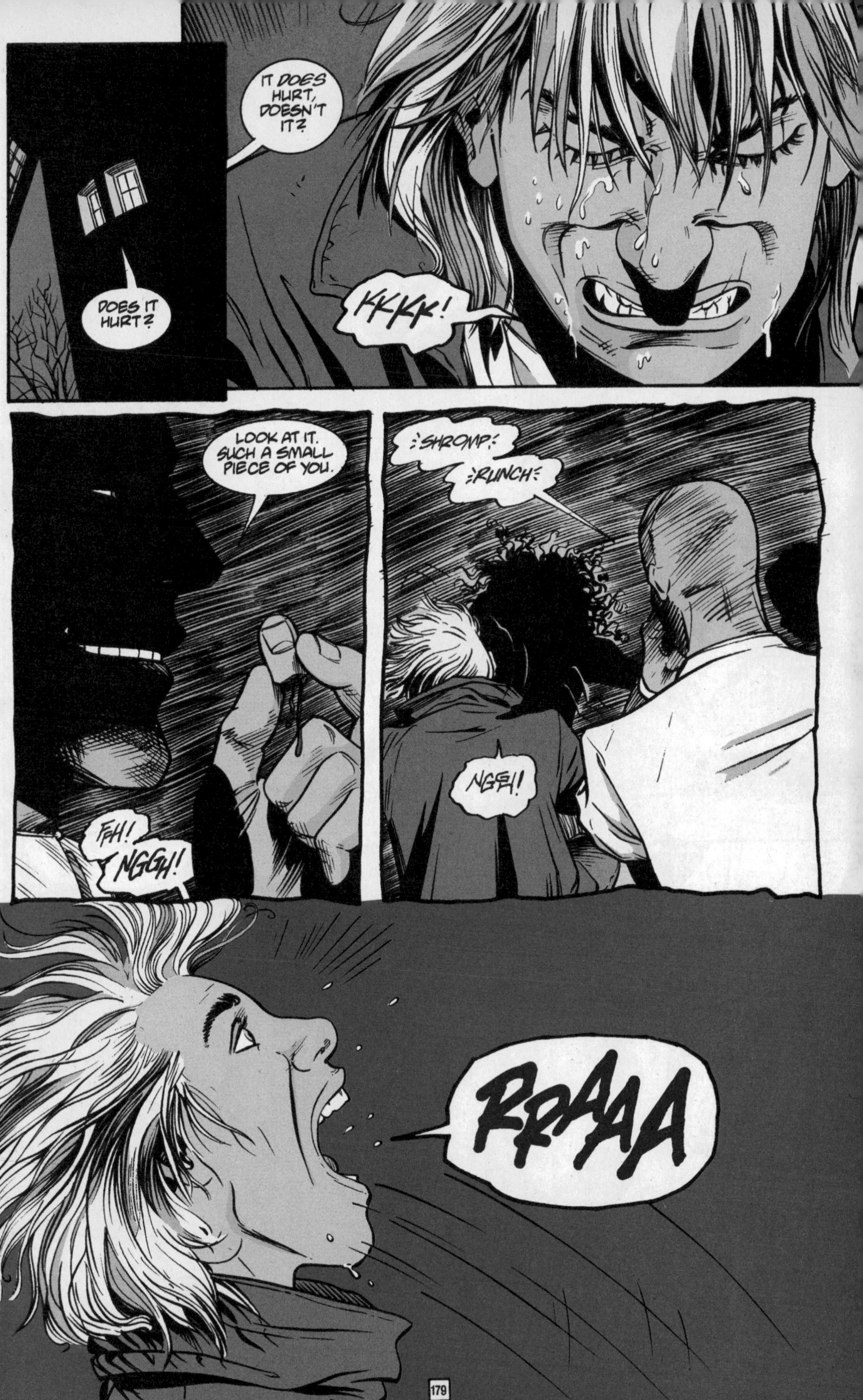
IT DOES HURT, DOESN'T IT?
DOES IT HURT?
KKKK!
LOOK AT IT. SUCH A SMALL PIECE OF YOU.
FFH!
NGGH!
SHROMP
RUNCH
NGGH!
RRAAA

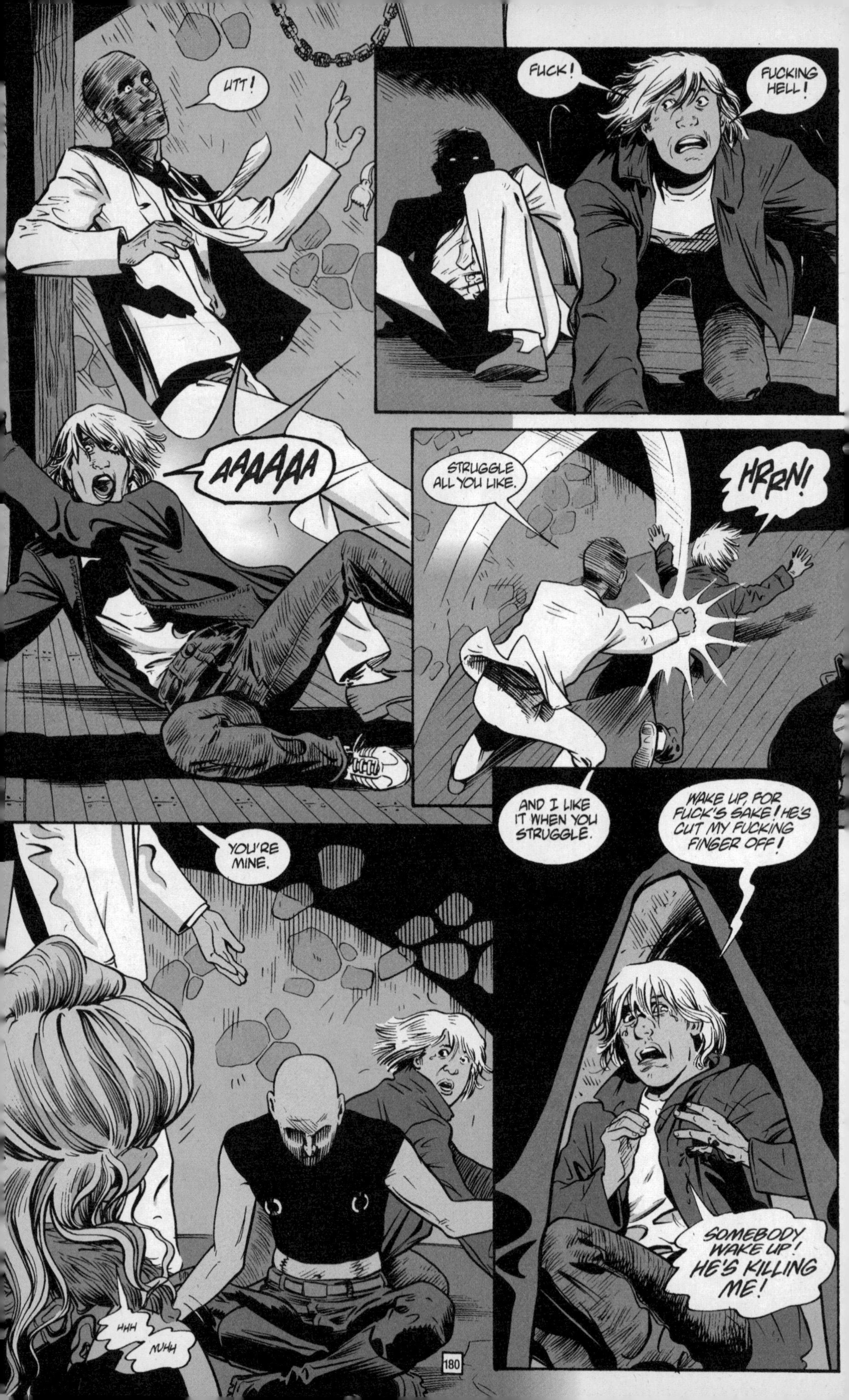
UTT!
FUCK!
FUCKING HELL!
AAAAAA
STRUGGLE ALL YOU LIKE.
HRRN!
AND I LIKE IT WHEN YOU STRUGGLE.
WAKE UP, FOR FUCK'S SAKE! HE'S CUT MY FUCKING FINGER OFF!
YOU'RE MINE.
HHH
NUHH
SOMEBODY WAKE UP! HE'S KILLING ME!

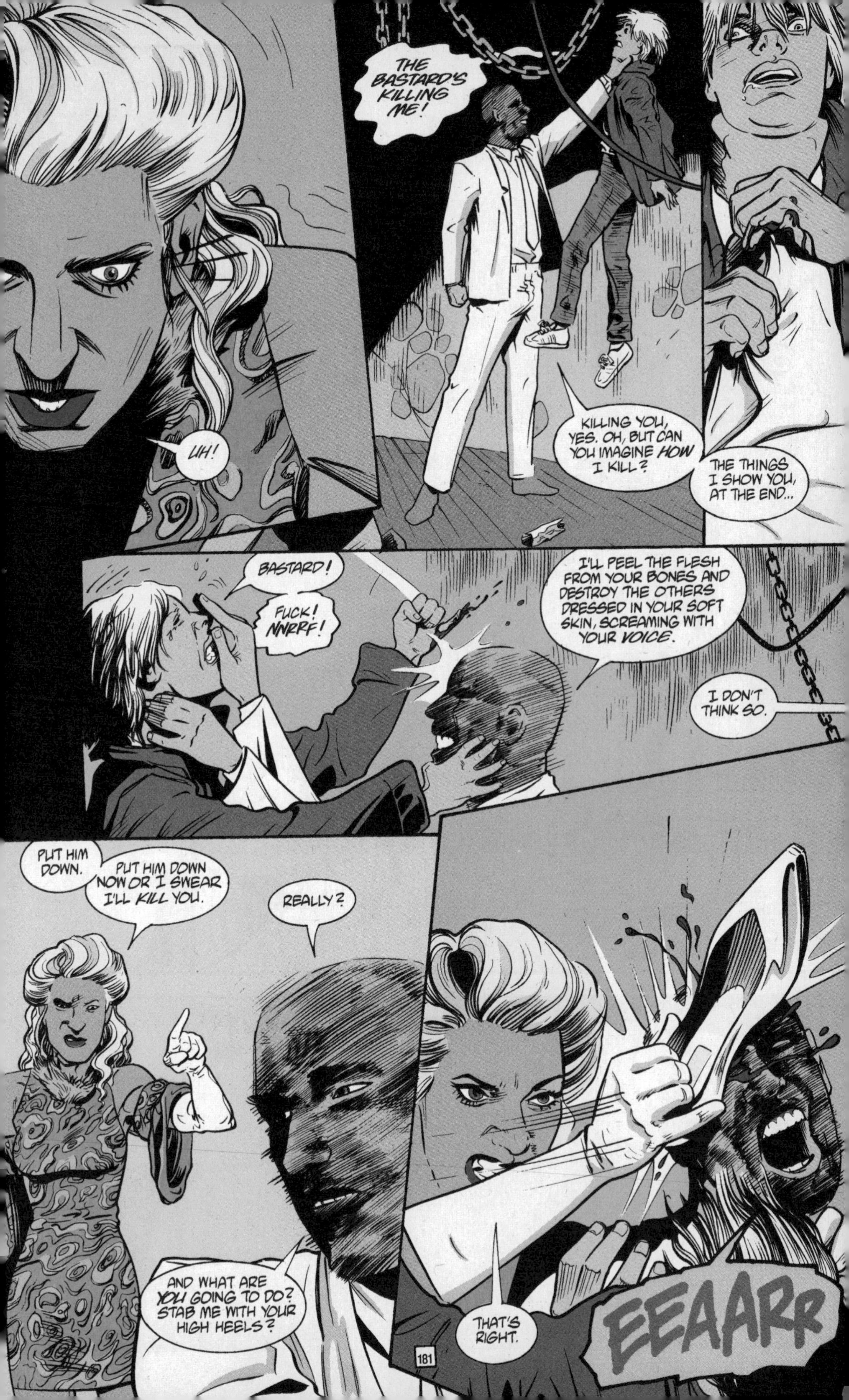
THE BASTARD'S KILLING ME!
UH!
KILLING YOU, YES. OH, BUT CAN YOU IMAGINE HOW I KILL?
THE THINGS I SHOW YOU, AT THE END...
BASTARD!
FUCK! NNRRF!
I'LL PEEL THE FLESH FROM YOUR BONES AND DESTROY THE OTHERS DRESSED IN YOUR SOFT SKIN, SCREAMING WITH YOUR VOICE.
I DON'T THINK SO.
PUT HIM DOWN.
PUT HIM DOWN NOW OR I SWEAR I'LL KILL YOU.
REALLY?
AND WHAT ARE YOU GOING TO DO? STAB ME WITH YOUR HIGH HEELS?
THAT'S RIGHT.
EEAARR

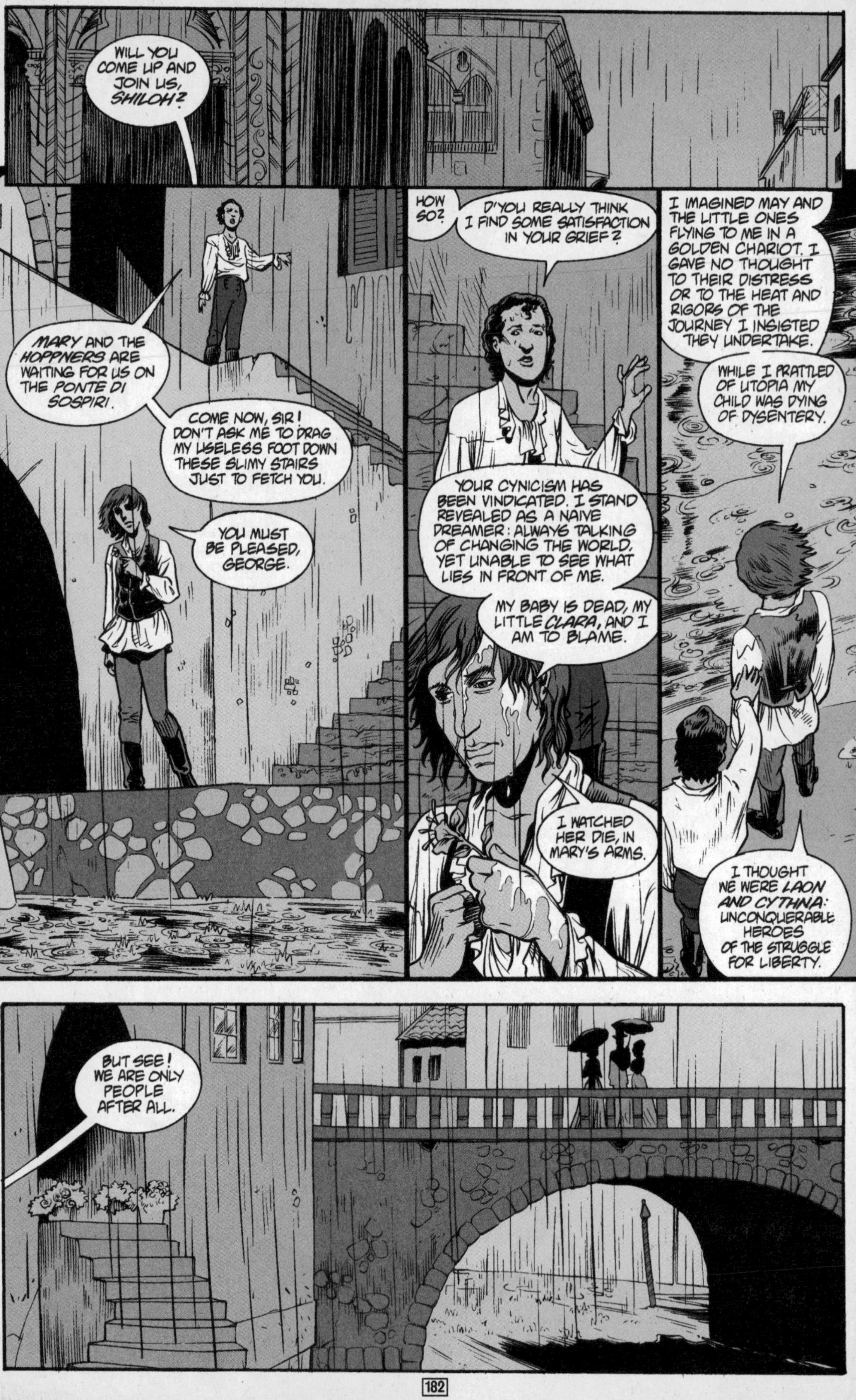
WILL YOU COME UP AND JOIN US, SHILOH?
MARY AND THE HOPPNERS ARE WAITING FOR US ON THE PONTE DI SOSPIRI.
COME NOW, SIR! DON'T ASK ME TO DRAG MY USELESS FOOT DOWN THESE SLIMY STAIRS JUST TO FETCH YOU.
YOU MUST BE PLEASED, GEORGE.
HOW SO?
D'YOU REALLY THINK I FIND SOME SATISFACTION IN YOUR GRIEF?
YOUR CYNICISM HAS BEEN VINDICATED. I STAND REVEALED AS A NAIVE DREAMER: ALWAYS TALKING OF CHANGING THE WORLD, YET UNABLE TO SEE WHAT LIES IN FRONT OF ME.
MY BABY IS DEAD, MY LITTLE CLARA, AND I AM TO BLAME.
I WATCHED HER DIE, IN MARY'S ARMS.
I IMAGINED MAY AND THE LITTLE ONES FLYING TO ME IN A GOLDEN CHARIOT. I GAVE NO THOUGHT TO THEIR DISTRESS OR TO THE HEAT AND RIGORS OF THE JOURNEY I INSISTED THEY UNDERTAKE.
WHILE I PRATTLED OF UTOPIA MY CHILD WAS DYING OF DYSENTERY.
I THOUGHT WE WERE LAON AND CYTHNA: UNCONQUERABLE HEROES OF THE STRUGGLE FOR LIBERTY.
BUT SEE! WE ARE ONLY PEOPLE AFTER ALL.

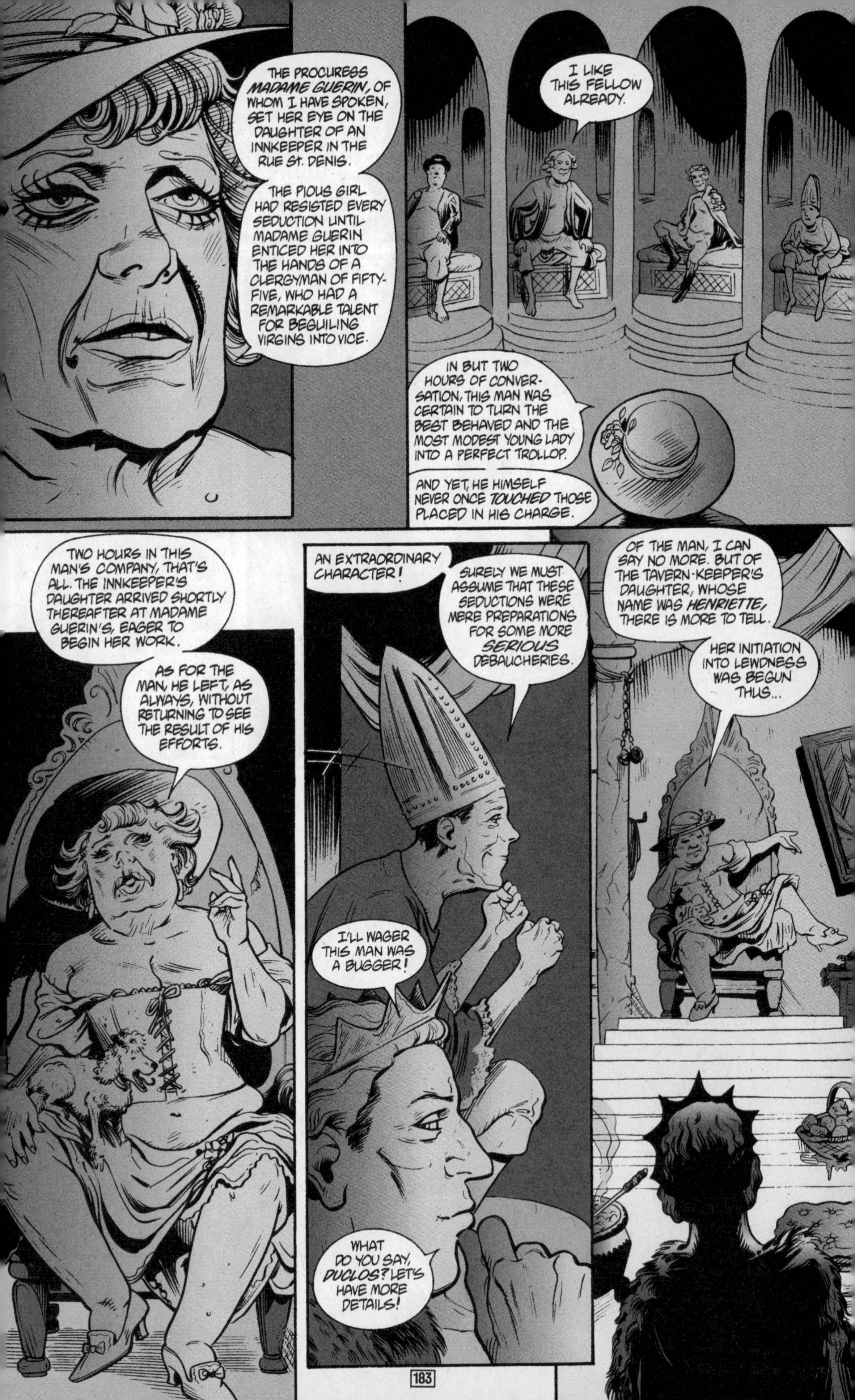
THE PROCURESS MADAME GUERIN, OF WHOM I HAVE SPOKEN, SET HER EYE ON THE DAUGHTER OF AN INNKEEPER IN THE RUE St. DENIS.
THE PIOUS GIRL HAD RESISTED EVERY SEDUCTION UNTIL MADAME GUERIN ENTICED HER INTO THE HANDS OF A CLERGYMAN OF FIFTY-FIVE, WHO HAD A REMARKABLE TALENT FOR BEGUILING VIRGINS INTO VICE.
I LIKE THIS FELLOW ALREADY.
IN BUT TWO HOURS OF CONVERSATION, THIS MAN WAS CERTAIN TO TURN THE BEST BEHAVED AND THE MOST MODEST YOUNG LADY INTO A PERFECT TROLLOP.
AND YET, HE HIMSELF NEVER ONCE TOUCHED THOSE PLACED IN HIS CHARGE.
TWO HOURS IN THIS MAN'S COMPANY, THAT'S ALL. THE INNKEEPER'S DAUGHTER ARRIVED SHORTLY THEREAFTER AT MADAME GUERIN'S, EAGER TO BEGIN HER WORK.
AS FOR THE MAN, HE LEFT, AS ALWAYS, WITHOUT RETURNING TO SEE THE RESULT OF HIS EFFORTS.
AN EXTRAORDINARY CHARACTER!
SURELY WE MUST ASSUME THAT THESE SEDUCTIONS WERE MERE PREPARATIONS FOR SOME MORE SERIOUS DEBAUCHERIES.
I'LL WAGER THIS MAN WAS A BUGGER!
WHAT DO YOU SAY, DUCLOS? LET'S HAVE MORE DETAILS!
OF THE MAN, I CAN SAY NO MORE. BUT OF THE TAVERN-KEEPER'S DAUGHTER, WHOSE NAME WAS HENRIETTE, THERE IS MORE TO TELL.
HER INITIATION INTO LEWDNESS WAS BEGUN THUS...

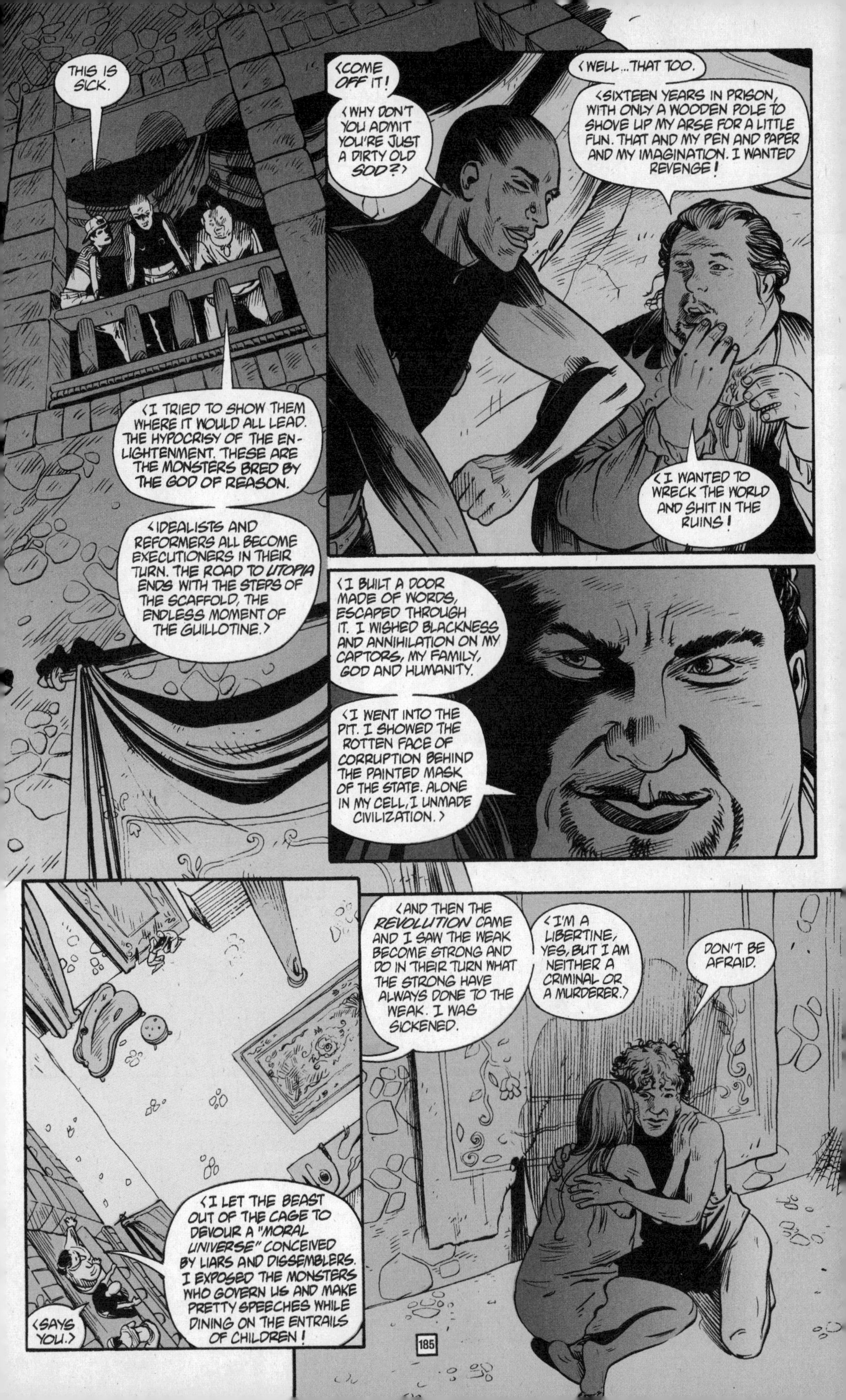
THIS IS SICK.
<I TRIED TO SHOW THEM WHERE IT WOULD ALL LEAD. THE HYPOCRISY OF THE EN-LIGHTENMENT. THESE ARE THE MONSTERS BRED BY THE GOD OF REASON.
<IDEALISTS AND REFORMERS ALL BECOME EXECUTIONERS IN THEIR TURN. THE ROAD TO UTOPIA ENDS WITH THE STEPS OF THE SCAFFOLD, THE ENDLESS MOMENT OF THE GUILLOTINE.>
<COME OFF IT!
<WHY DON'T YOU ADMIT YOU'RE JUST A DIRTY OLD SOD?>
<WELL...THAT TOO.
<SIXTEEN YEARS IN PRISON, WITH ONLY A WOODEN POLE TO SHOVE UP MY ARSE FOR A LITTLE FUN. THAT AND MY PEN AND PAPER AND MY IMAGINATION. I WANTED REVENGE!
<I WANTED TO WRECK THE WORLD AND SHIT IN THE RUINS!
<I BUILT A DOOR MADE OF WORDS, ESCAPED THROUGH IT. I WISHED BLACKNESS AND ANNIHILATION ON MY CAPTORS, MY FAMILY, GOD AND HUMANITY.
<I WENT INTO THE PIT. I SHOWED THE ROTTEN FACE OF CORRUPTION BEHIND THE PAINTED MASK OF THE STATE. ALONE IN MY CELL, I UNMADE CIVILIZATION.>
<I LET THE BEAST OUT OF THE CAGE TO DEVOUR A "MORAL UNIVERSE" CONCEIVED BY LIARS AND DISSEMBLERS. I EXPOSED THE MONSTERS WHO GOVERN US AND MAKE PRETTY SPEECHES WHILE DINING ON THE ENTRAILS OF CHILDREN!
<SAYS YOU.>
<AND THEN THE REVOLUTION CAME AND I SAW THE WEAK BECOME STRONG AND DO IN THEIR TURN WHAT THE STRONG HAVE ALWAYS DONE TO THE WEAK. I WAS SICKENED.
<I'M A LIBERTINE, YES, BUT I AM NEITHER A CRIMINAL OR A MURDERER.>
DON'T BE AFRAID.

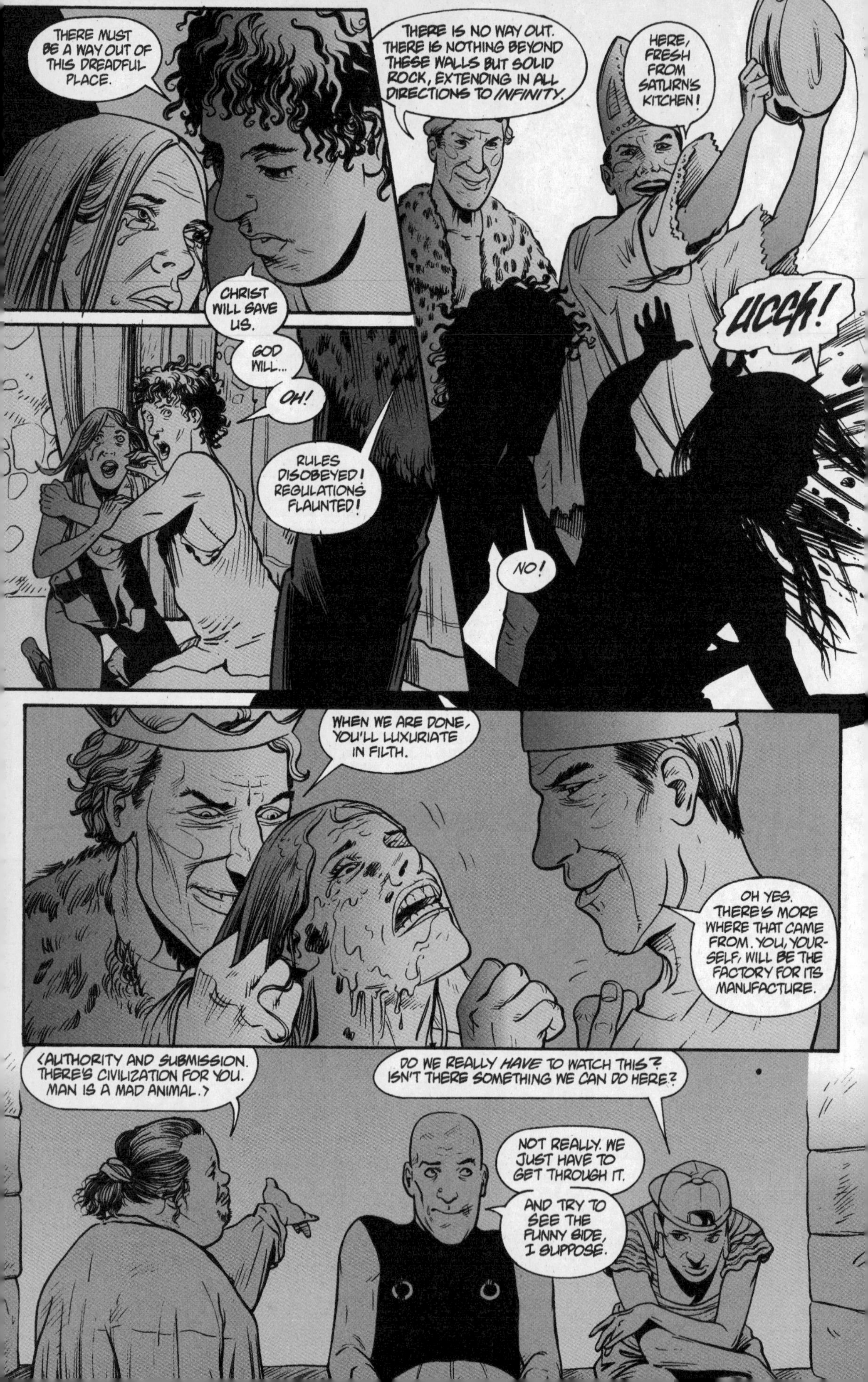
THERE MUST BE A WAY OUT OF THIS DREADFUL PLACE.
CHRIST WILL SAVE US.
THERE IS NO WAY OUT. THERE IS NOTHING BEYOND THESE WALLS BUT SOLID ROCK, EXTENDING IN ALL DIRECTIONS TO INFINITY.
HERE, FRESH FROM SATURN'S KITCHEN!
GOD WILL...
OH!
RULES DISOBEYED! REGULATIONS FLAUNTED!
UCCH!
NO!
WHEN WE ARE DONE, YOU'LL LUXURIATE IN FILTH.
OH YES. THERE'S MORE WHERE THAT CAME FROM. YOU, YOURSELF, WILL BE THE FACTORY FOR ITS MANUFACTURE.
<AUTHORITY AND SUBMISSION. THERE'S CIVILIZATION FOR YOU. MAN IS A MAD ANIMAL.>
DO WE REALLY HAVE TO WATCH THIS? ISN'T THERE SOMETHING WE CAN DO HERE?
NOT REALLY. WE JUST HAVE TO GET THROUGH IT.
AND TRY TO SEE THE FUNNY SIDE, I SUPPOSE.

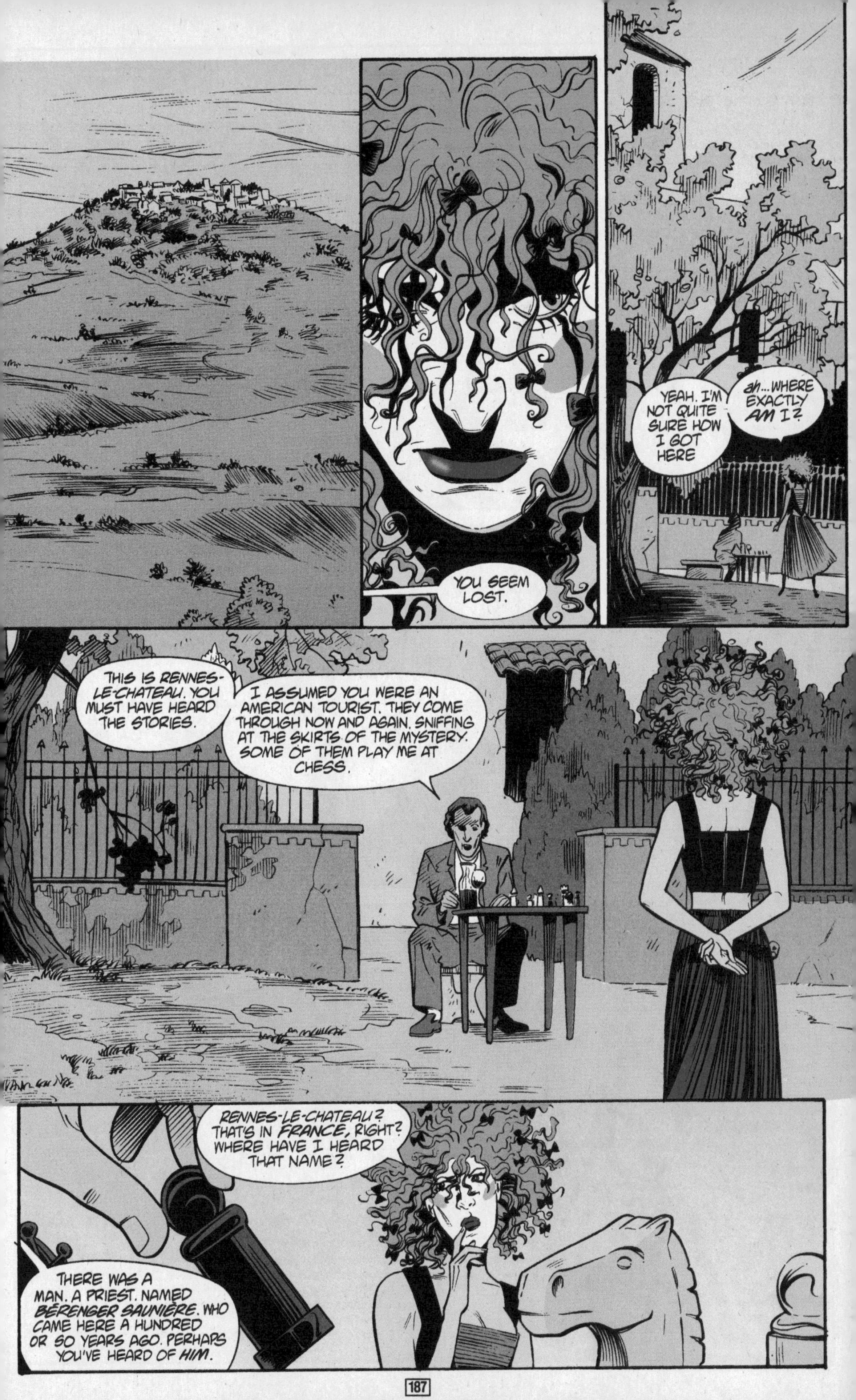
YOU SEEM LOST.
YEAH. I'M NOT QUITE SURE HOW I GOT HERE
ah... WHERE EXACTLY AM I?
THIS IS RENNES-LE-CHATEAU. YOU MUST HAVE HEARD THE STORIES.
I ASSUMED YOU WERE AN AMERICAN TOURIST. THEY COME THROUGH NOW AND AGAIN, SNIFFING AT THE SKIRTS OF THE MYSTERY. SOME OF THEM PLAY ME AT CHESS.
RENNES-LE-CHATEAU? THAT'S IN FRANCE, RIGHT? WHERE HAVE I HEARD THAT NAME?
THERE WAS A MAN. A PRIEST. NAMED BÉRENGER SAUNIÈRE. WHO CAME HERE A HUNDRED OR SO YEARS AGO. PERHAPS YOU'VE HEARD OF HIM.

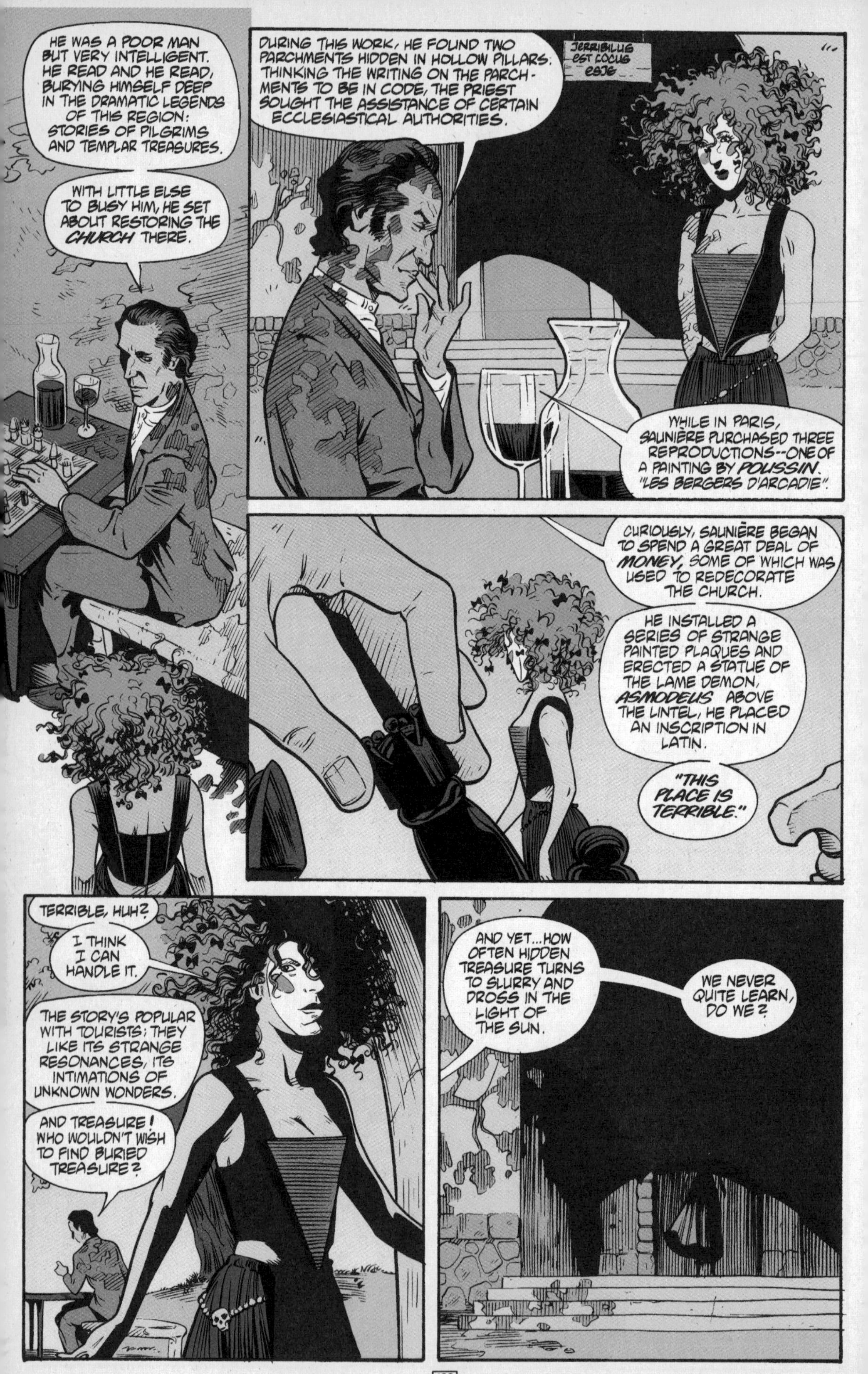
HE WAS A POOR MAN BUT VERY INTELLIGENT. HE READ AND HE READ, BURYING HIMSELF DEEP IN THE DRAMATIC LEGENDS OF THIS REGION: STORIES OF PILGRIMS AND TEMPLAR TREASURES.
WITH LITTLE ELSE TO BUSY HIM, HE SET ABOUT RESTORING THE CHURCH THERE.
DURING THIS WORK, HE FOUND TWO PARCHMENTS HIDDEN IN HOLLOW PILLARS: THINKING THE WRITING ON THE PARCHMENTS TO BE IN CODE, THE PRIEST SOUGHT THE ASSISTANCE OF CERTAIN ECCLESIASTICAL AUTHORITIES.
WHILE IN PARIS, SAUNIÈRE PURCHASED THREE REPRODUCTIONS--ONE OF A PAINTING BY POUSSIN. "LES BERGERS D'ARCADIE".
CURIOUSLY, SAUNIÈRE BEGAN TO SPEND A GREAT DEAL OF MONEY, SOME OF WHICH WAS USED TO REDECORATE THE CHURCH.
HE INSTALLED A SERIES OF STRANGE PAINTED PLAQUES AND ERECTED A STATUE OF THE LAME DEMON, ASMODEUS ABOVE THE LINTEL, HE PLACED AN INSCRIPTION IN LATIN.
"THIS PLACE IS TERRIBLE."
TERRIBLE, HUH?
I THINK I CAN HANDLE IT.
THE STORY'S POPULAR WITH TOURISTS; THEY LIKE ITS STRANGE RESONANCES, ITS INTIMATIONS OF UNKNOWN WONDERS.
AND TREASURE! WHO WOULDN'T WISH TO FIND BURIED TREASURE?
AND YET...HOW OFTEN HIDDEN TREASURE TURNS TO SLURRY AND DROSS IN THE LIGHT OF THE SUN.
WE NEVER QUITE LEARN, DO WE?

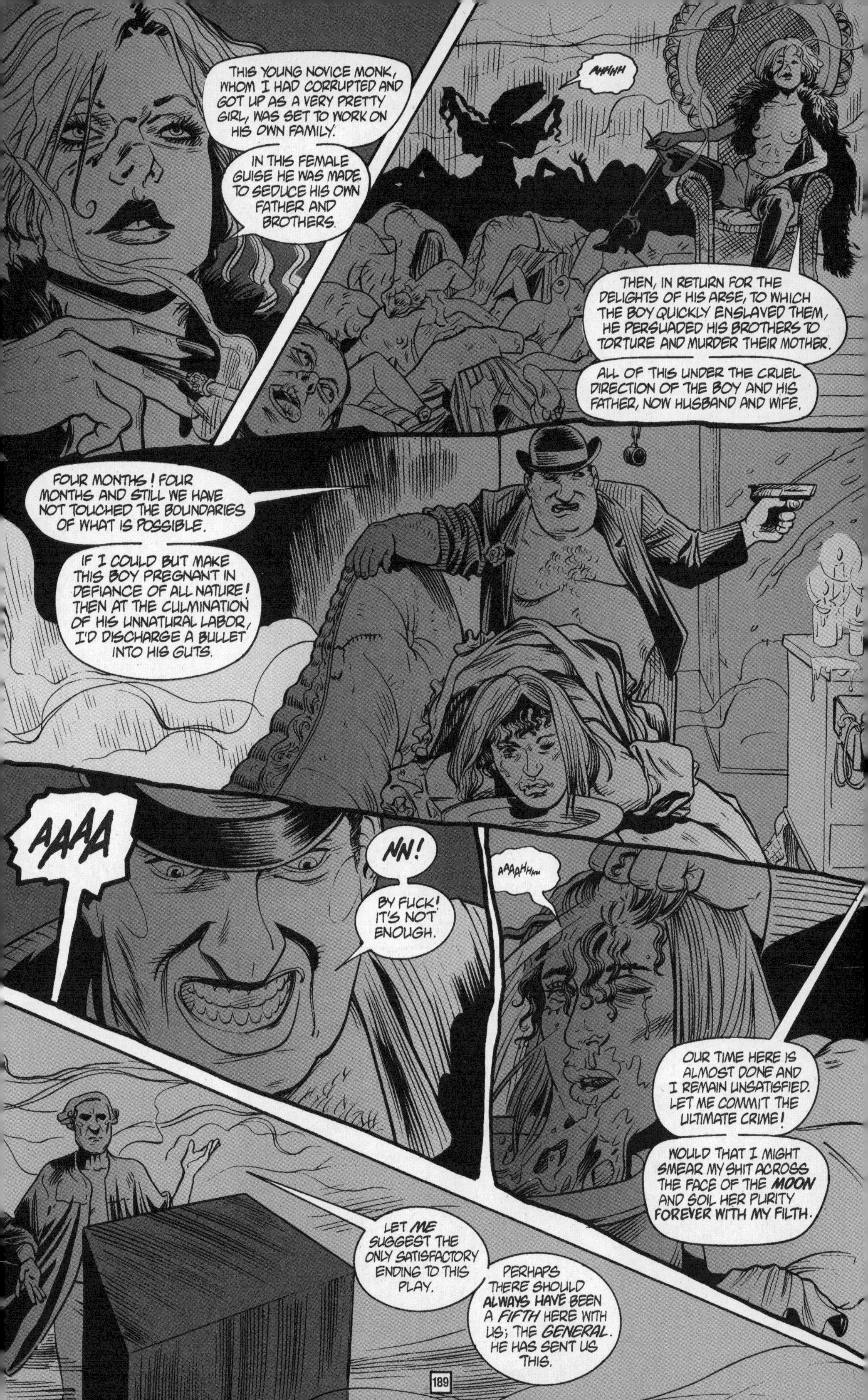

THIS YOUNG NOVICE MONK, WHOM I HAD CORRUPTED AND GOT UP AS A VERY PRETTY GIRL, WAS SET TO WORK ON HIS OWN FAMILY.
IN THIS FEMALE GUISE HE WAS MADE TO SEDUCE HIS OWN FATHER AND BROTHERS.
AHHHH
THEN, IN RETURN FOR THE DELIGHTS OF HIS ARSE, TO WHICH THE BOY QUICKLY ENSLAVED THEM, HE PERSUADED HIS BROTHERS TO TORTURE AND MURDER THEIR MOTHER.
ALL OF THIS UNDER THE CRUEL DIRECTION OF THE BOY AND HIS FATHER, NOW HUSBAND AND WIFE.
FOUR MONTHS! FOUR MONTHS AND STILL WE HAVE NOT TOUCHED THE BOUNDARIES OF WHAT IS POSSIBLE.
IF I COULD BUT MAKE THIS BOY PREGNANT IN DEFIANCE OF ALL NATURE! THEN AT THE CULMINATION OF HIS UNNATURAL LABOR, I'D DISCHARGE A BULLET INTO HIS GUTS.
AAAA
NN!
BY FUCK! IT'S NOT ENOUGH.
AAAAHHhhh
OUR TIME HERE IS ALMOST DONE AND I REMAIN UNSATISFIED. LET ME COMMIT THE ULTIMATE CRIME!
WOULD THAT I MIGHT SMEAR MY SHIT ACROSS THE FACE OF THE MOON AND SOIL HER PURITY FOREVER WITH MY FILTH.
LET ME SUGGEST THE ONLY SATISFACTORY ENDING TO THIS PLAY.
PERHAPS THERE SHOULD ALWAYS HAVE BEEN A FIFTH HERE WITH US; THE GENERAL. HE HAS SENT US THIS.

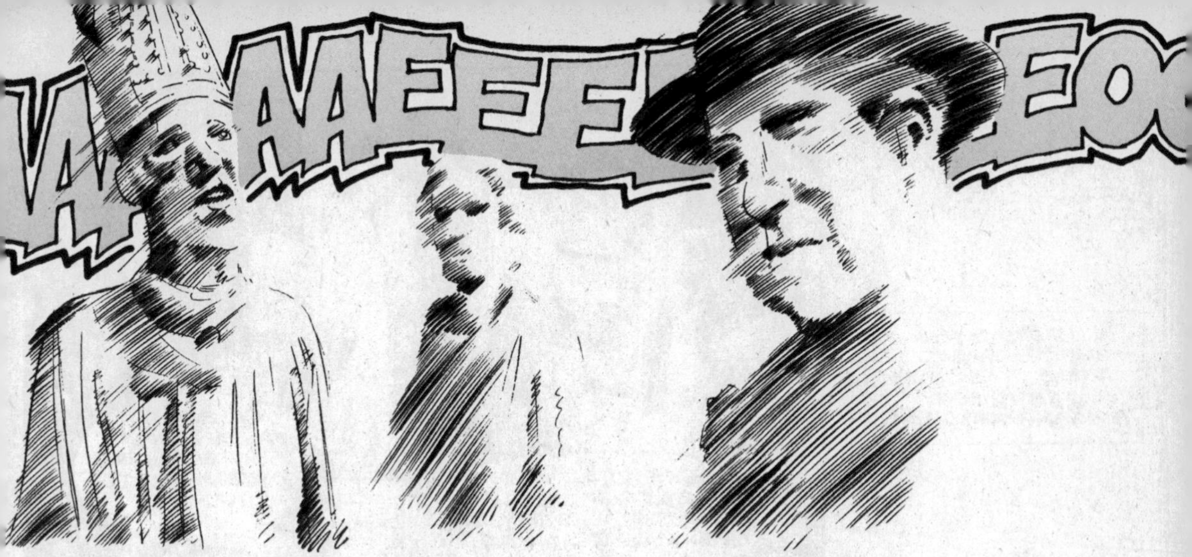

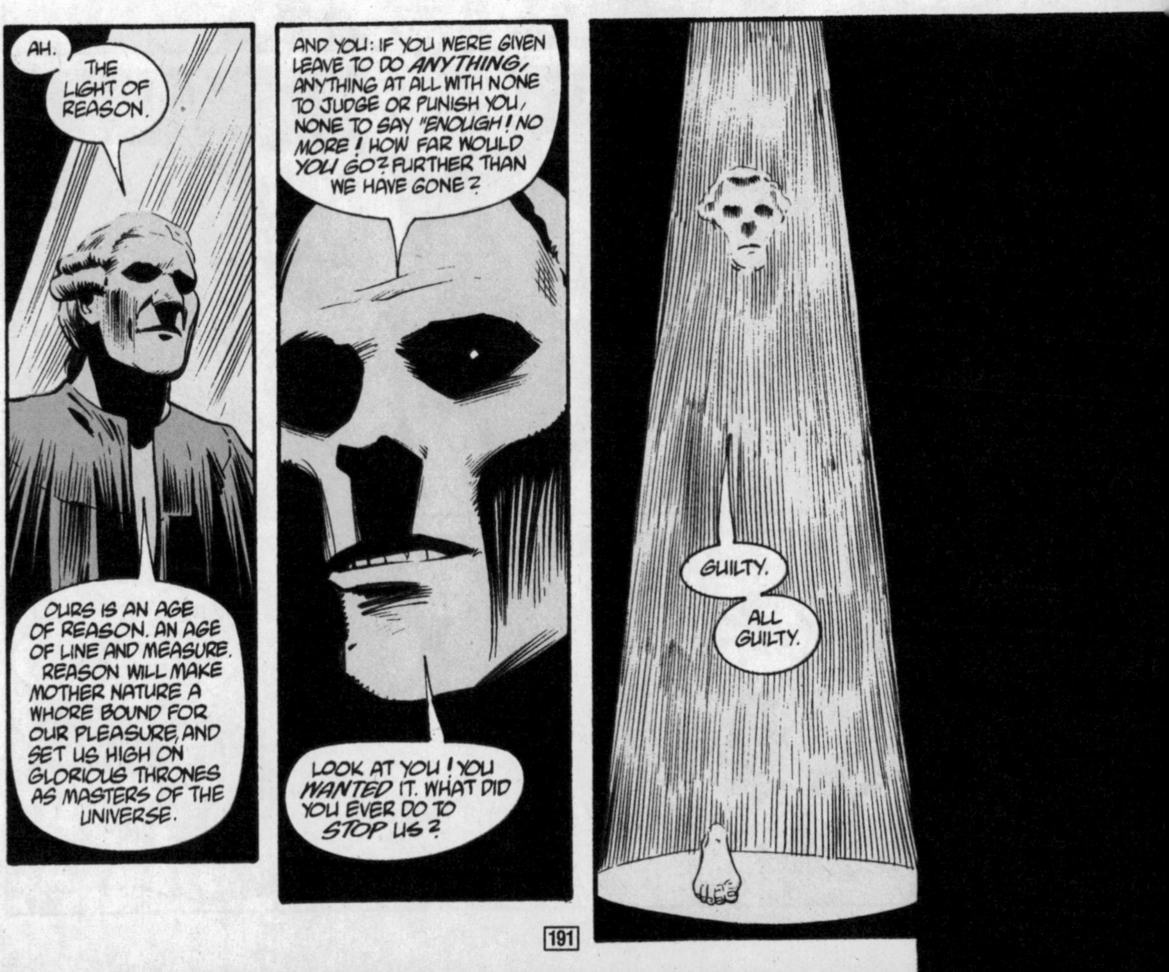
AH.
THE LIGHT OF REASON.
OURS IS AN AGE OF REASON. AN AGE OF LINE AND MEASURE. REASON WILL MAKE MOTHER NATURE A WHORE BOUND FOR OUR PLEASURE, AND SET US HIGH ON GLORIOUS THRONES AS MASTERS OF THE UNIVERSE.
AND YOU: IF YOU WERE GIVEN LEAVE TO DO *ANYTHING*, ANYTHING AT ALL WITH NONE TO JUDGE OR PUNISH YOU, NONE TO SAY "ENOUGH! NO MORE! HOW FAR WOULD *YOU GO*? FURTHER THAN WE HAVE GONE?
LOOK AT YOU! YOU *WANTED* IT. WHAT DID YOU EVER DO TO *STOP* US?
GUILTY.
ALL GUILTY.

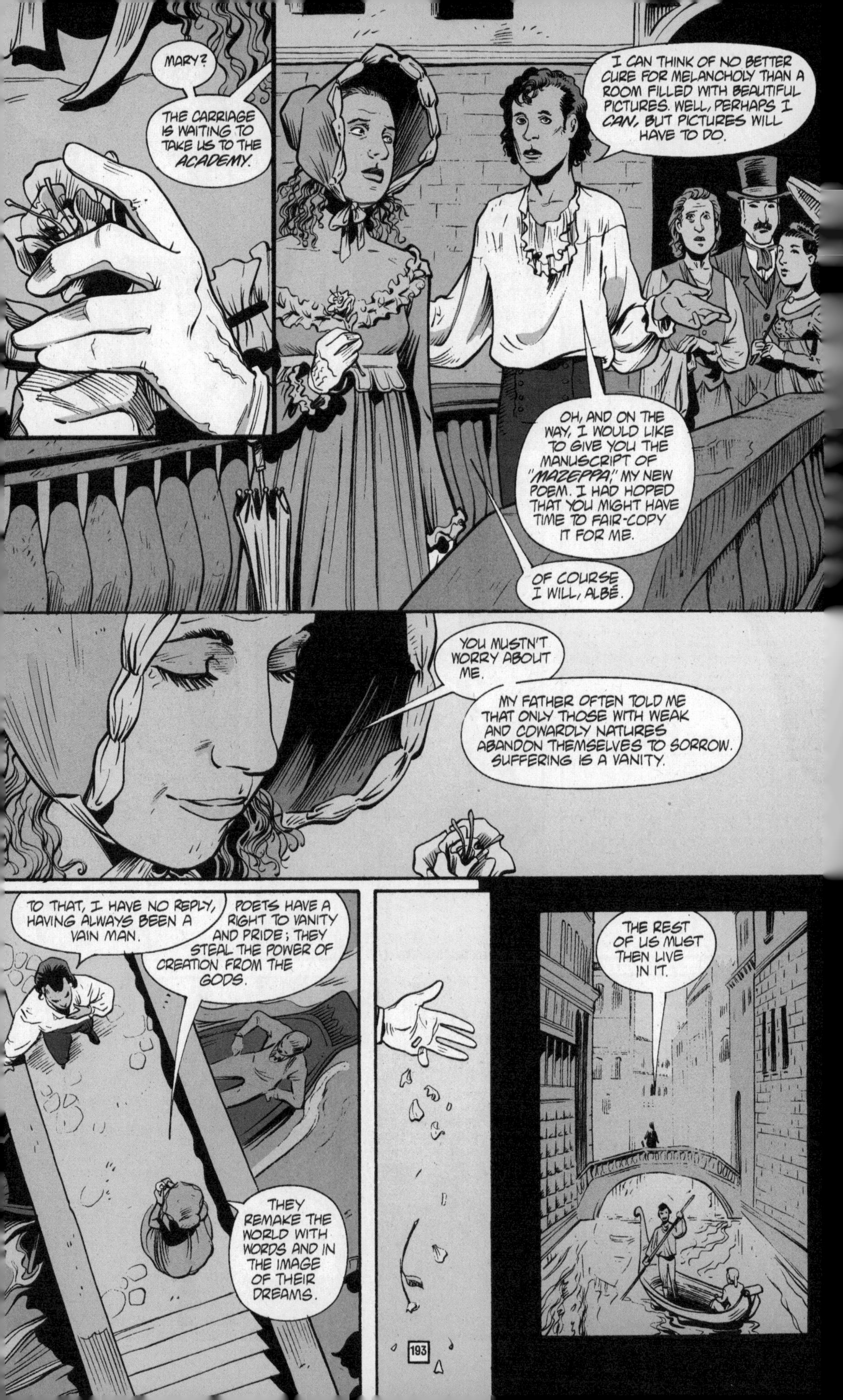
MARY?
THE CARRIAGE IS WAITING TO TAKE US TO THE *ACADEMY*.
I CAN THINK OF NO BETTER CURE FOR MELANCHOLY THAN A ROOM FILLED WITH BEAUTIFUL PICTURES. WELL, PERHAPS I *CAN*, BUT PICTURES WILL HAVE TO DO.
OH, AND ON THE WAY, I WOULD LIKE TO GIVE YOU THE MANUSCRIPT OF "*MAZEPPA*," MY NEW POEM. I HAD HOPED THAT YOU MIGHT HAVE TIME TO FAIR-COPY IT FOR ME.
OF COURSE I WILL, ALBÉ.
YOU MUSTN'T WORRY ABOUT ME.
MY FATHER OFTEN TOLD ME THAT ONLY THOSE WITH WEAK AND COWARDLY NATURES ABANDON THEMSELVES TO SORROW. SUFFERING IS A VANITY.
TO THAT, I HAVE NO REPLY, HAVING ALWAYS BEEN A VAIN MAN.
POETS HAVE A RIGHT TO VANITY AND PRIDE; THEY STEAL THE POWER OF CREATION FROM THE GODS.
THEY REMAKE THE WORLD WITH WORDS AND IN THE IMAGE OF THEIR DREAMS.
THE REST OF US MUST THEN LIVE IN IT.

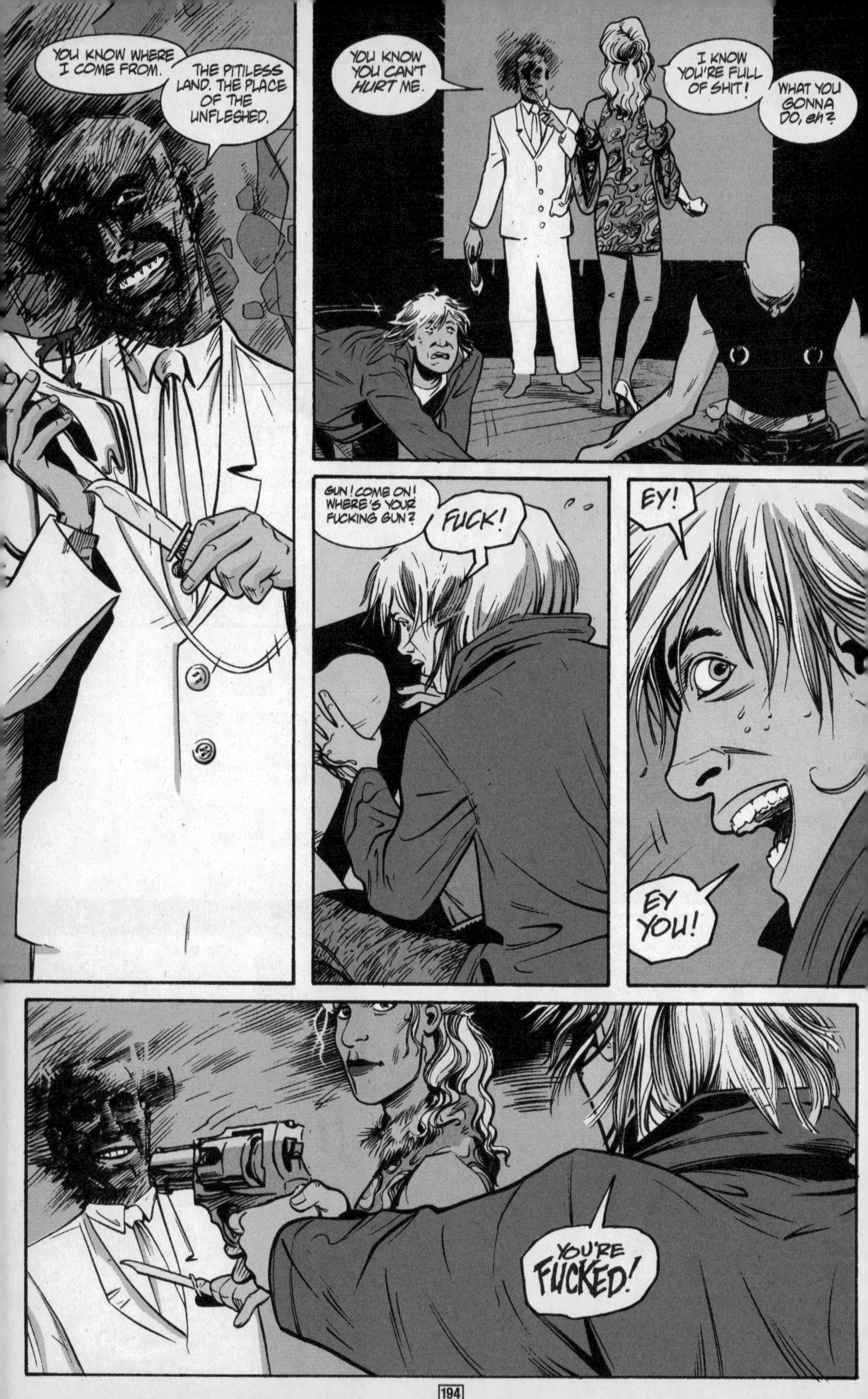
YOU KNOW WHERE I COME FROM.
THE PITILESS LAND. THE PLACE OF THE UNFLESHED.
YOU KNOW YOU CAN'T HURT ME.
I KNOW YOU'RE FULL OF SHIT!
WHAT YOU GONNA DO, eh?
GUN! COME ON! WHERE'S YOUR FUCKING GUN?
FUCK!
EY!
EY YOU!
YOU'RE FUCKED!

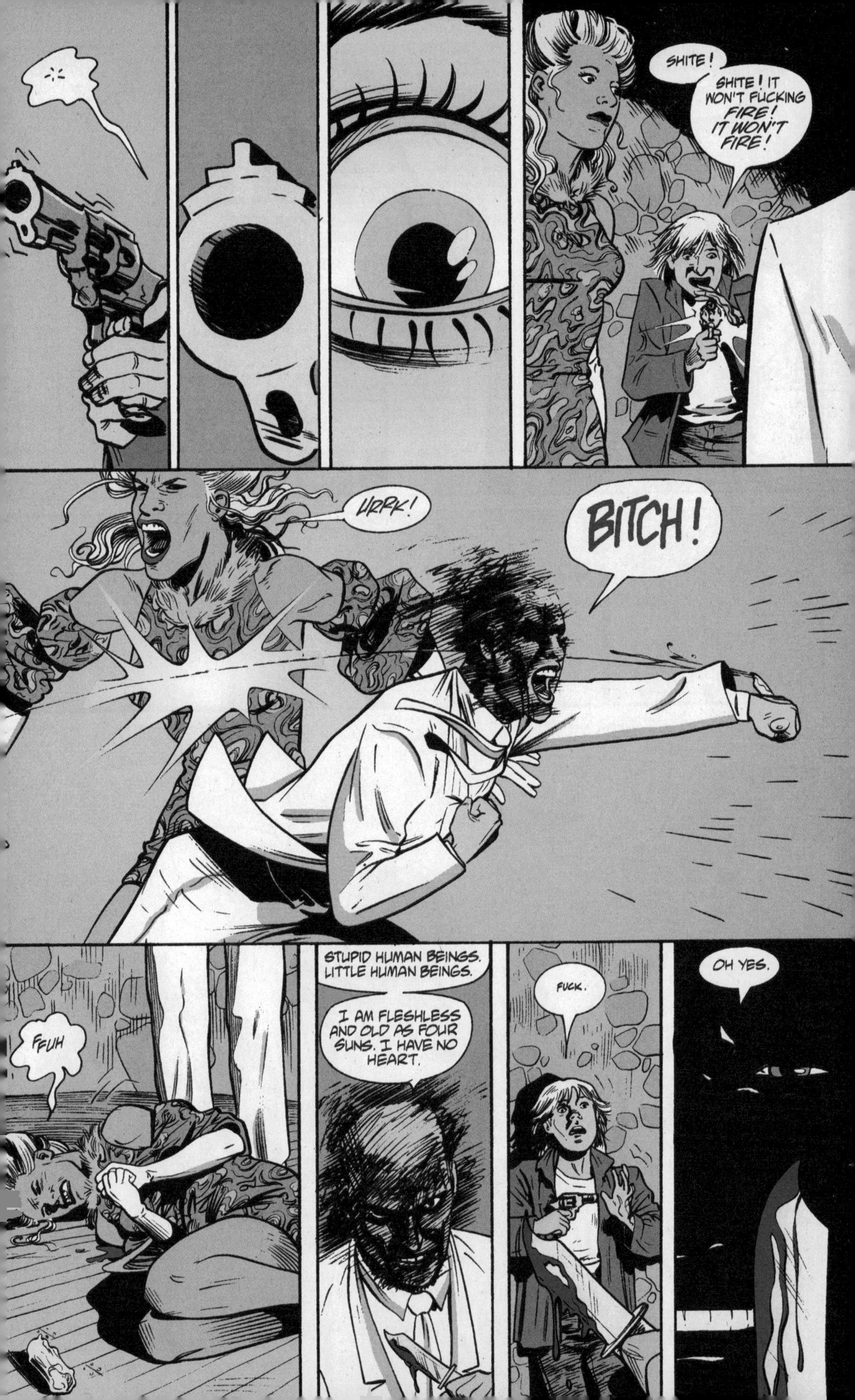
SHITE!
SHITE! IT WON'T FUCKING FIRE! IT WON'T FIRE!
URRK!
BITCH!
FFUH
STUPID HUMAN BEINGS. LITTLE HUMAN BEINGS.
I AM FLESHLESS AND OLD AS FOUR SUNS. I HAVE NO HEART.
FUCK.
OH YES.

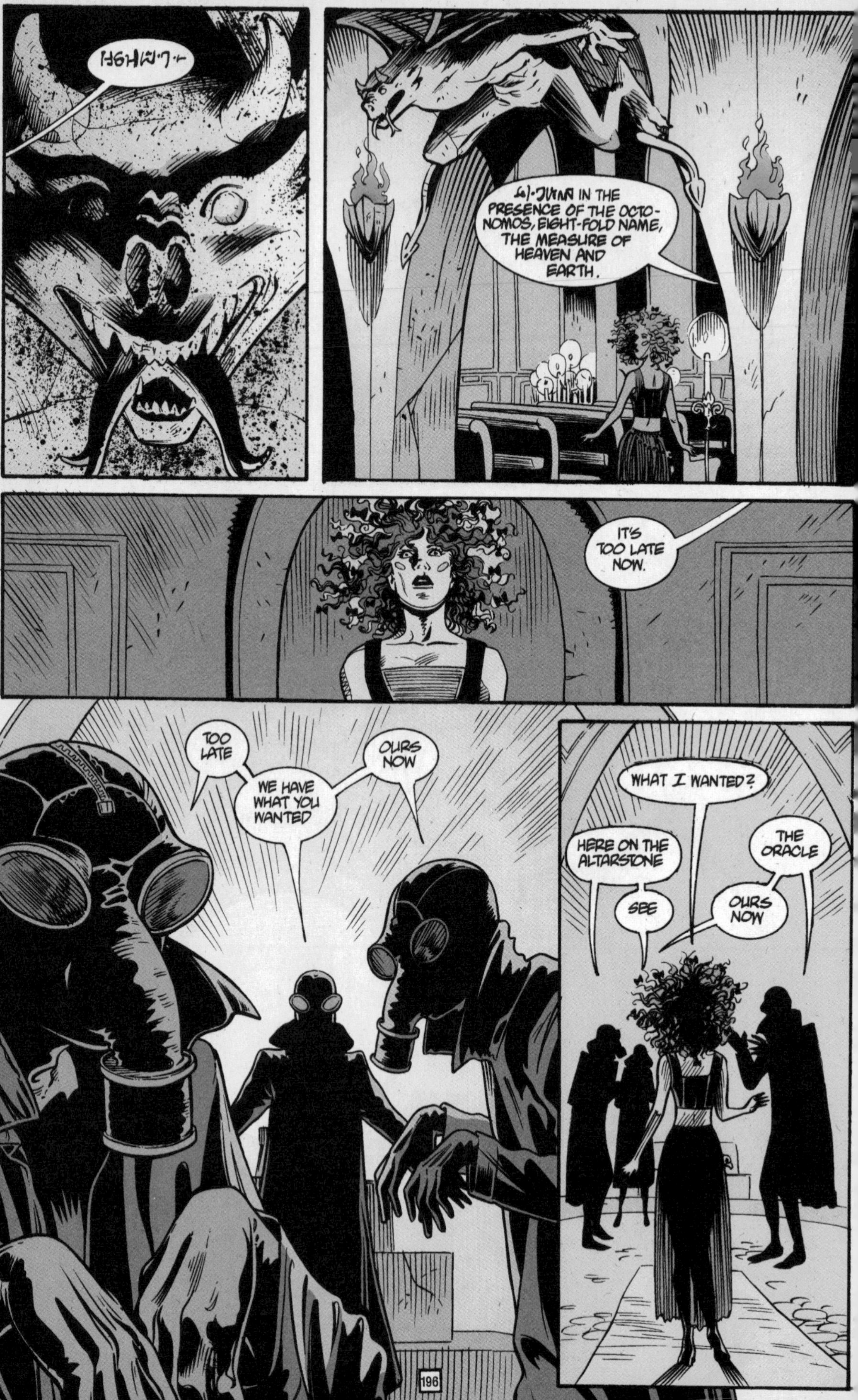

IN THE PRESENCE OF THE OCTO-NOMOS, EIGHT-FOLD NAME, THE MEASURE OF HEAVEN AND EARTH.
IT'S TOO LATE NOW.
TOO LATE
WE HAVE WHAT YOU WANTED
OURS NOW
WHAT I WANTED?
HERE ON THE ALTARSTONE
SEE
THE ORACLE
OURS NOW

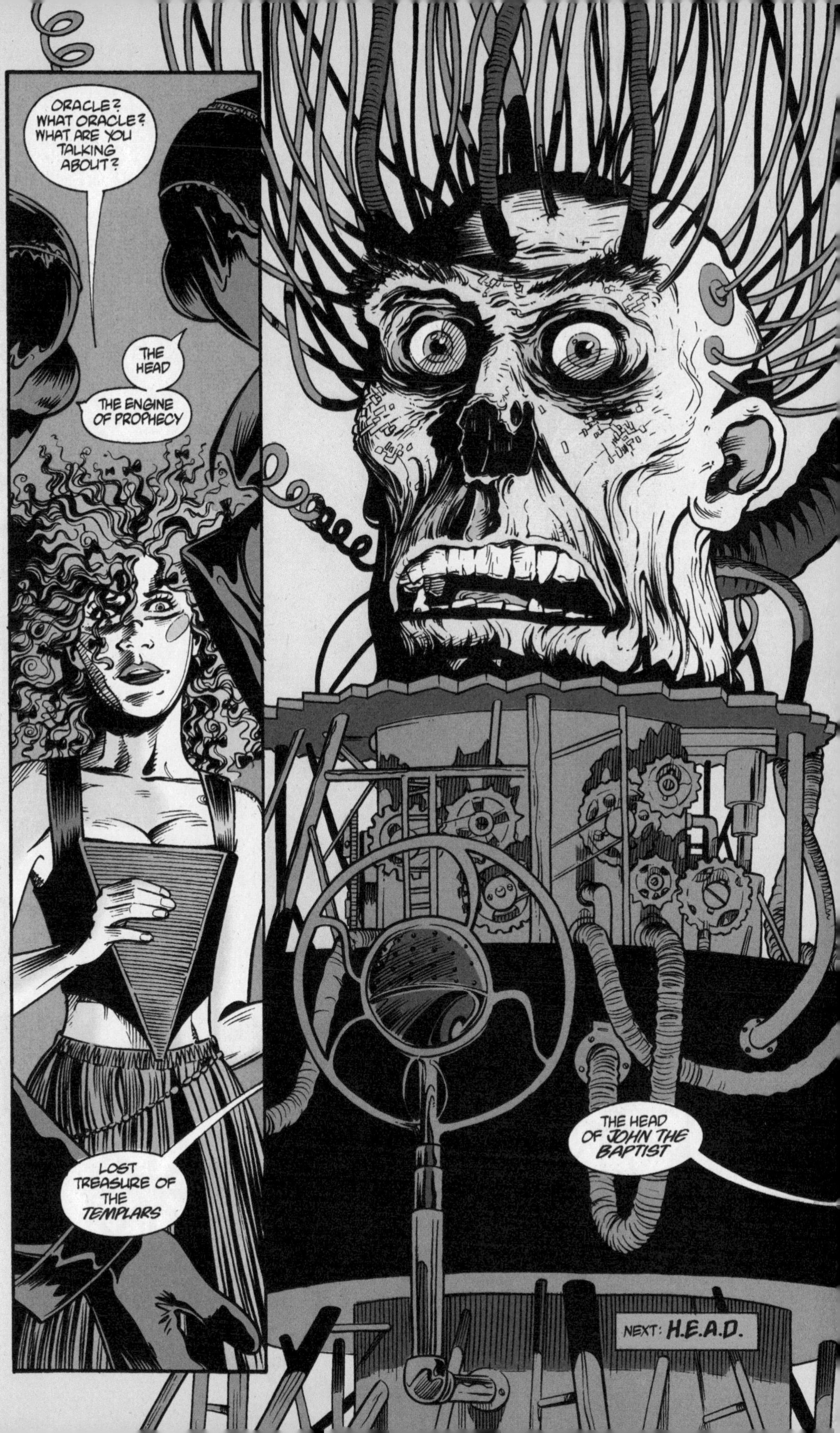

ORACLE? WHAT ORACLE? WHAT ARE YOU TALKING ABOUT?
THE HEAD
THE ENGINE OF PROPHECY
LOST TREASURE OF THE *TEMPLARS*
THE HEAD OF *JOHN THE BAPTIST*
NEXT: H.E.A.D.

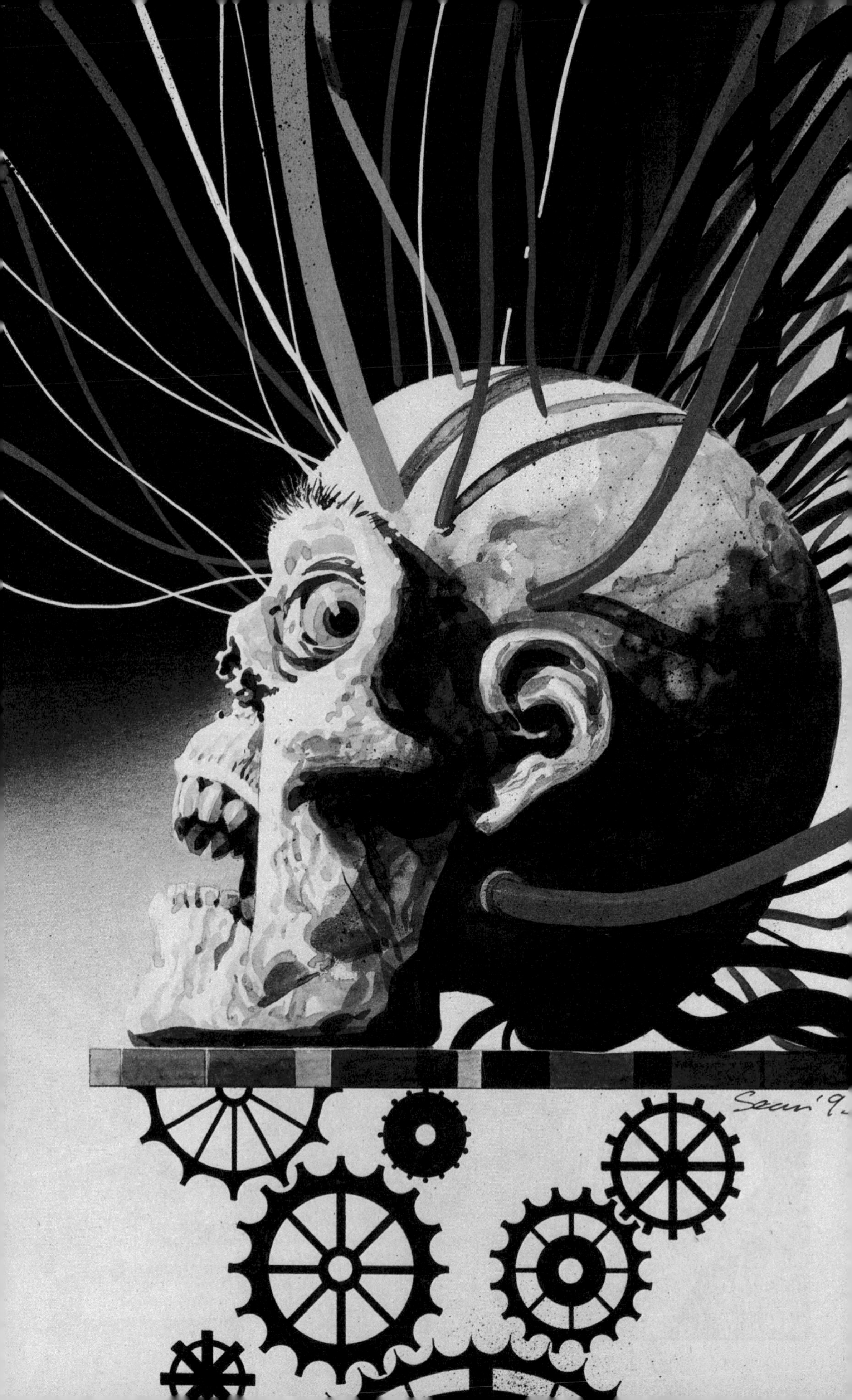

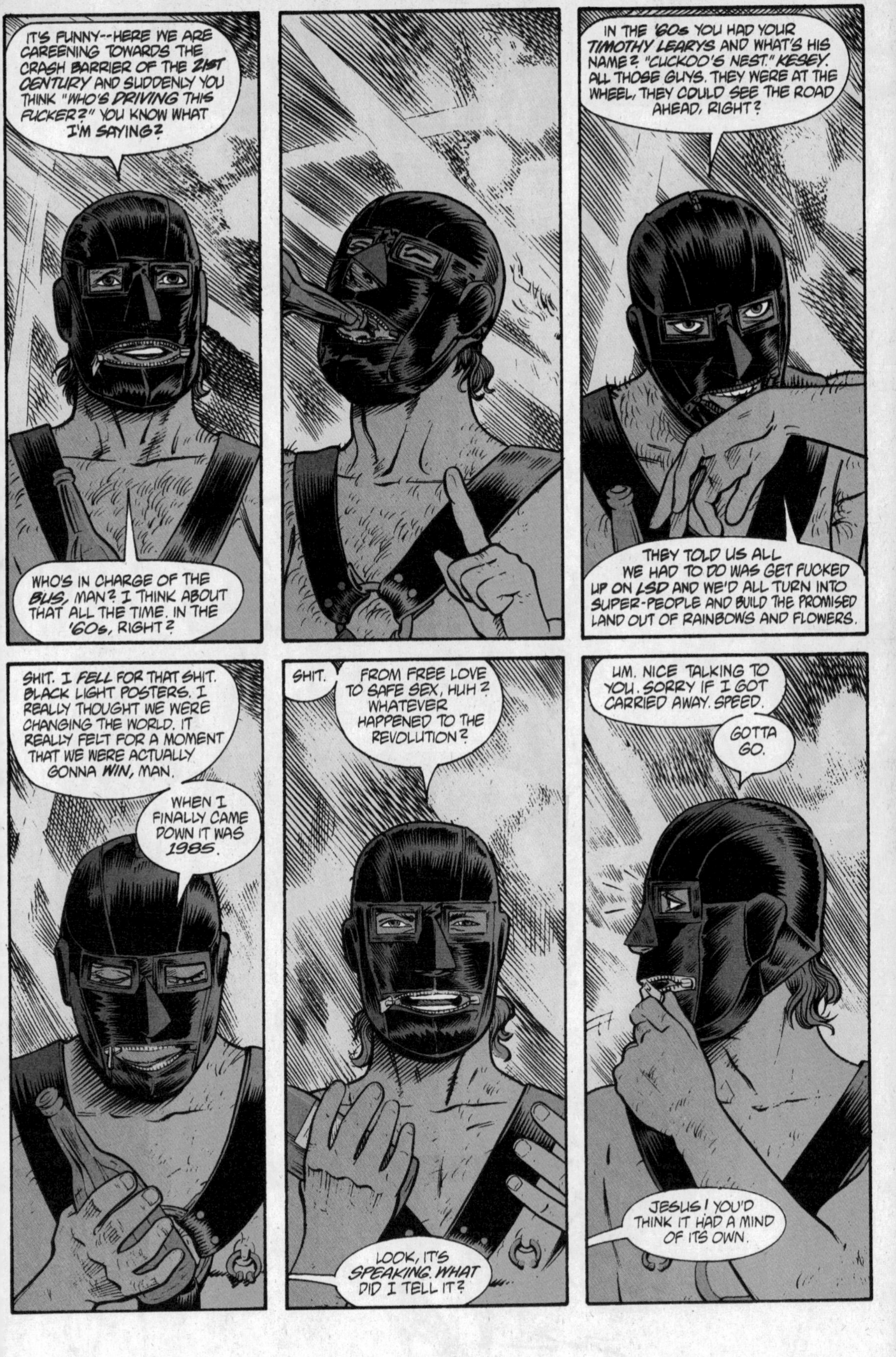
IT'S FUNNY--HERE WE ARE CAREENING TOWARDS THE CRASH BARRIER OF THE 21ST CENTURY AND SUDDENLY YOU THINK "WHO'S DRIVING THIS FUCKER?" YOU KNOW WHAT I'M SAYING?
WHO'S IN CHARGE OF THE BUS, MAN? I THINK ABOUT THAT ALL THE TIME. IN THE '60s, RIGHT?
IN THE '60s YOU HAD YOUR TIMOTHY LEARYS AND WHAT'S HIS NAME? "CUCKOO'S NEST." KESEY. ALL THOSE GUYS. THEY WERE AT THE WHEEL, THEY COULD SEE THE ROAD AHEAD, RIGHT?
THEY TOLD US ALL WE HAD TO DO WAS GET FUCKED UP ON LSD AND WE'D ALL TURN INTO SUPER-PEOPLE AND BUILD THE PROMISED LAND OUT OF RAINBOWS AND FLOWERS.
SHIT. I FELL FOR THAT SHIT. BLACK LIGHT POSTERS. I REALLY THOUGHT WE WERE CHANGING THE WORLD. IT REALLY FELT FOR A MOMENT THAT WE WERE ACTUALLY GONNA WIN, MAN.
WHEN I FINALLY CAME DOWN IT WAS 1985.
SHIT.
FROM FREE LOVE TO SAFE SEX, HUH? WHATEVER HAPPENED TO THE REVOLUTION?
LOOK, IT'S SPEAKING. WHAT DID I TELL IT?
UM. NICE TALKING TO YOU. SORRY IF I GOT CARRIED AWAY. SPEED.
GOTTA GO.
JESUS! YOU'D THINK IT HAD A MIND OF ITS OWN.

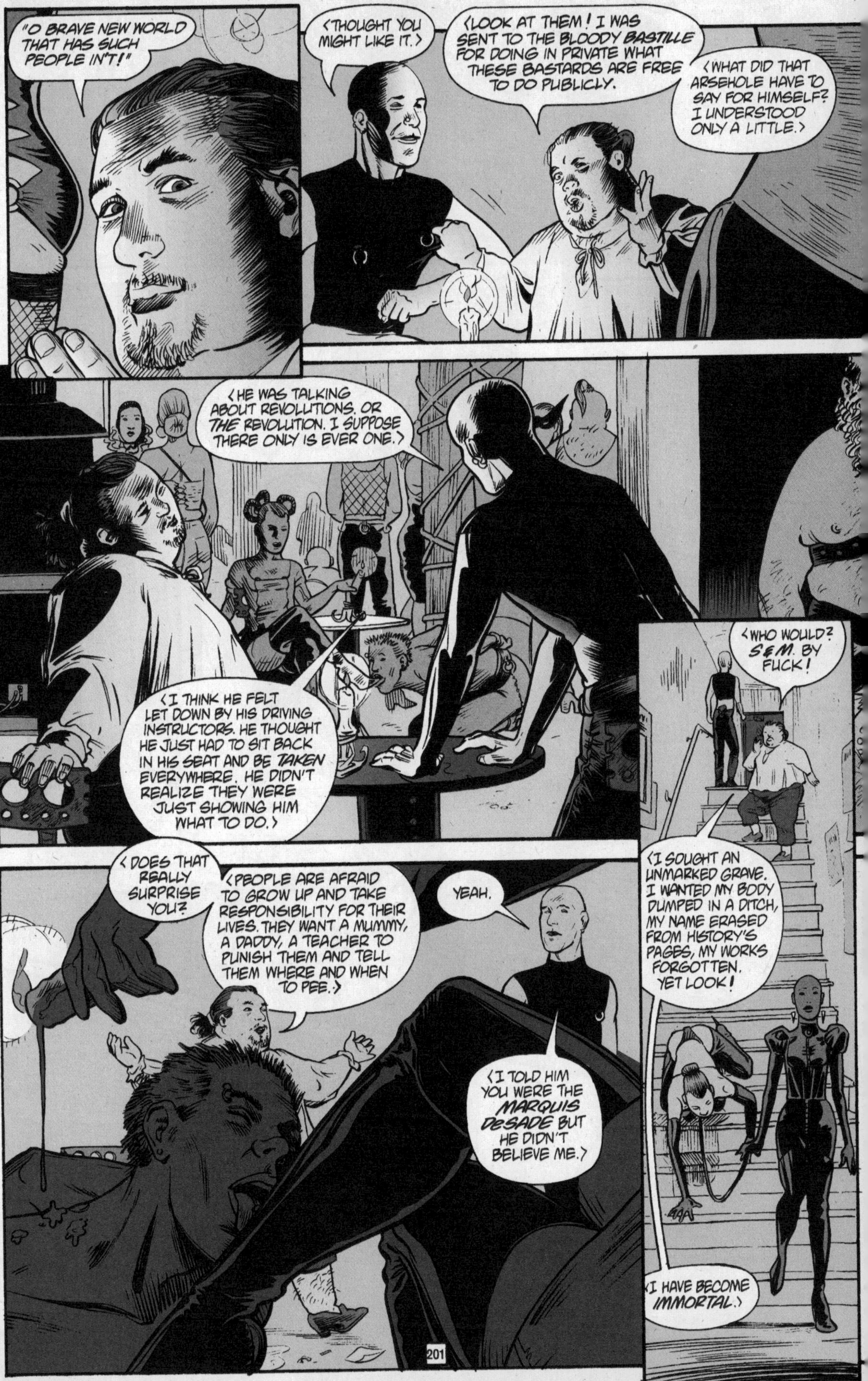
"O BRAVE NEW WORLD THAT HAS SUCH PEOPLE IN'T!"
<THOUGHT YOU MIGHT LIKE IT.>
<LOOK AT THEM! I WAS SENT TO THE BLOODY BASTILLE FOR DOING IN PRIVATE WHAT THESE BASTARDS ARE FREE TO DO PUBLICLY.
<WHAT DID THAT ARSEHOLE HAVE TO SAY FOR HIMSELF? I UNDERSTOOD ONLY A LITTLE.>
<HE WAS TALKING ABOUT REVOLUTIONS, OR THE REVOLUTION. I SUPPOSE THERE ONLY IS EVER ONE.>
<I THINK HE FELT LET DOWN BY HIS DRIVING INSTRUCTORS. HE THOUGHT HE JUST HAD TO SIT BACK IN HIS SEAT AND BE TAKEN EVERYWHERE. HE DIDN'T REALIZE THEY WERE JUST SHOWING HIM WHAT TO DO.>
<DOES THAT REALLY SURPRISE YOU?
<PEOPLE ARE AFRAID TO GROW UP AND TAKE RESPONSIBILITY FOR THEIR LIVES. THEY WANT A MUMMY, A DADDY, A TEACHER TO PUNISH THEM AND TELL THEM WHERE AND WHEN TO PEE.>
YEAH.
<I TOLD HIM YOU WERE THE MARQUIS DeSADE BUT HE DIDN'T BELIEVE ME.>
<WHO WOULD? S&M. BY FUCK!
<I SOUGHT AN UNMARKED GRAVE. I WANTED MY BODY DUMPED IN A DITCH, MY NAME ERASED FROM HISTORY'S PAGES, MY WORKS FORGOTTEN. YET LOOK!
<I HAVE BECOME IMMORTAL.>

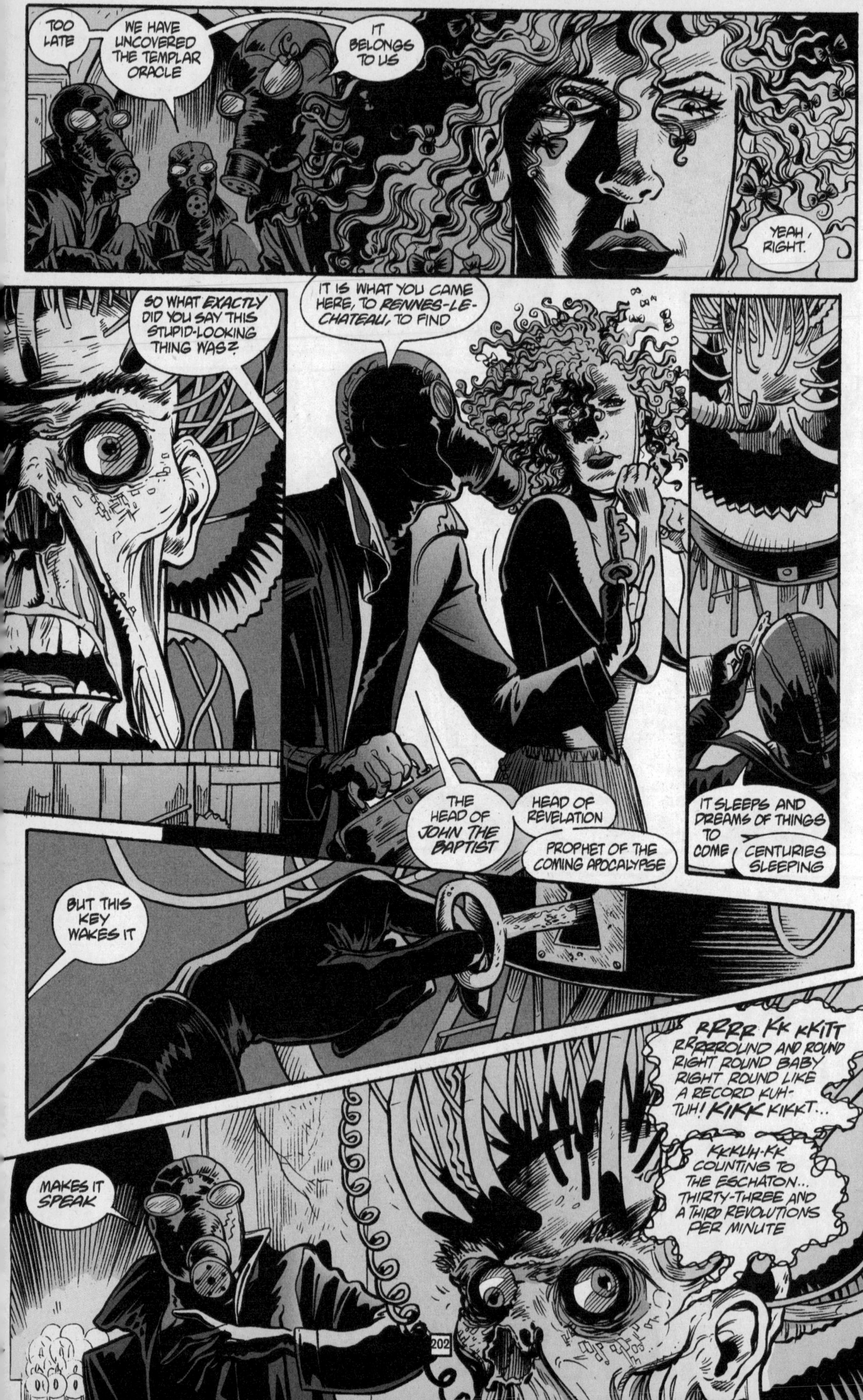

TOO LATE
WE HAVE UNCOVERED THE TEMPLAR ORACLE
IT BELONGS TO US
YEAH, RIGHT.
SO WHAT EXACTLY DID YOU SAY THIS STUPID-LOOKING THING WAS?
IT IS WHAT YOU CAME HERE, TO RENNES-LE-CHATEAU, TO FIND
THE HEAD OF JOHN THE BAPTIST
HEAD OF REVELATION
PROPHET OF THE COMING APOCALYPSE
IT SLEEPS AND DREAMS OF THINGS TO COME
CENTURIES SLEEPING
BUT THIS KEY WAKES IT
RRRR KK KKITT RRRRROUND AND ROUND RIGHT ROUND BABY RIGHT ROUND LIKE A RECORD KUH-TUH! KIKK KIKKT...
KKKUH-KK COUNTING TO THE ESCHATON... THIRTY-THREE AND A THIRD REVOLUTIONS PER MINUTE
MAKES IT SPEAK

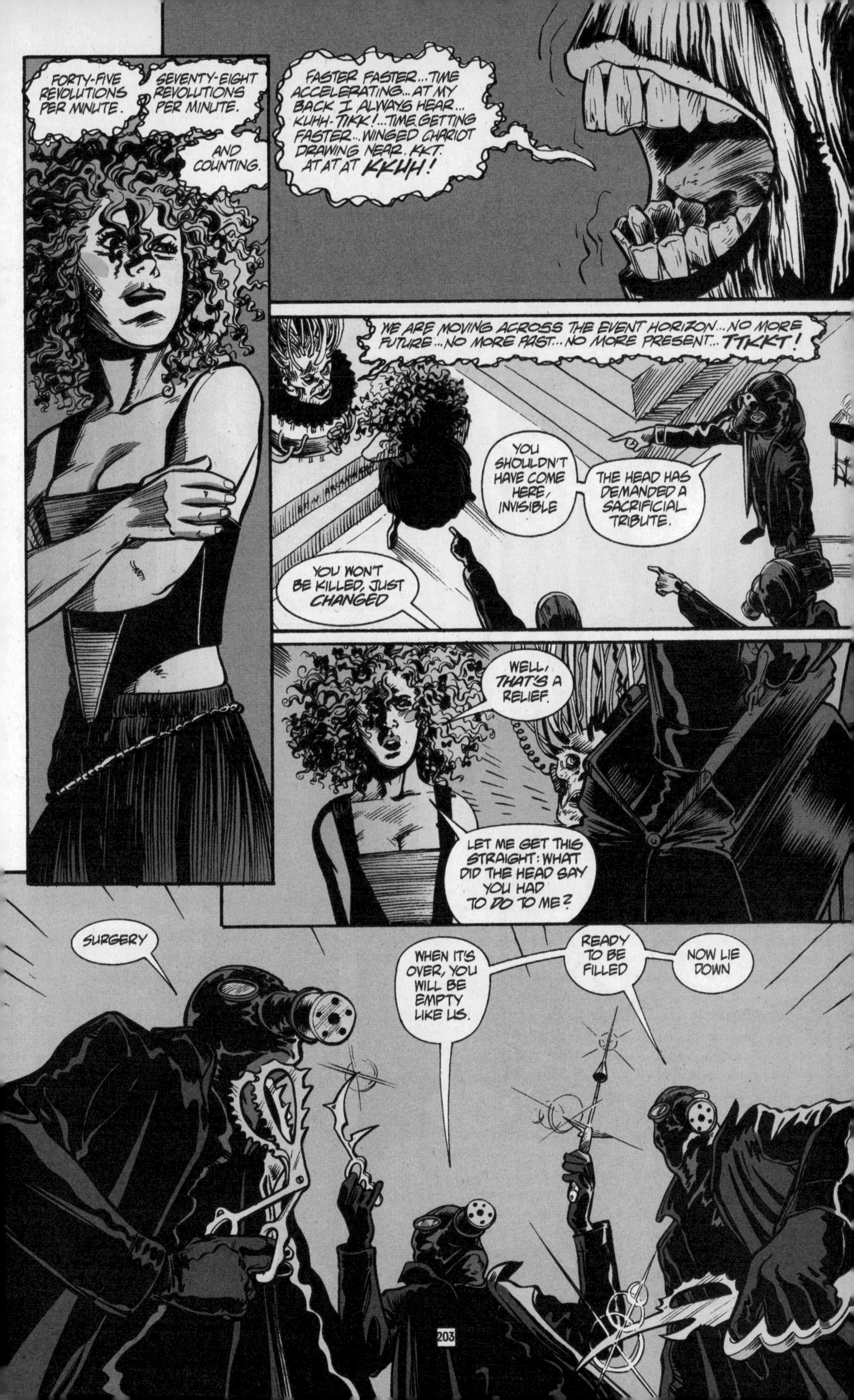

FORTY-FIVE REVOLUTIONS PER MINUTE.
SEVENTY-EIGHT REVOLUTIONS PER MINUTE.
AND COUNTING.
FASTER FASTER... TIME ACCELERATING... AT MY BACK I ALWAYS HEAR... KUHH-TIKK!... TIME GETTING FASTER... WINGED CHARIOT DRAWING NEAR.. KKT. AT AT AT KKUH!
WE ARE MOVING ACROSS THE EVENT HORIZON... NO MORE FUTURE... NO MORE PAST... NO MORE PRESENT... TTKKT!
YOU SHOULDN'T HAVE COME HERE, INVISIBLE
THE HEAD HAS DEMANDED A SACRIFICIAL TRIBUTE.
YOU WON'T BE KILLED, JUST CHANGED
WELL, THAT'S A RELIEF.
LET ME GET THIS STRAIGHT: WHAT DID THE HEAD SAY YOU HAD TO DO TO ME?
SURGERY
WHEN IT'S OVER, YOU WILL BE EMPTY LIKE US.
READY TO BE FILLED
NOW LIE DOWN

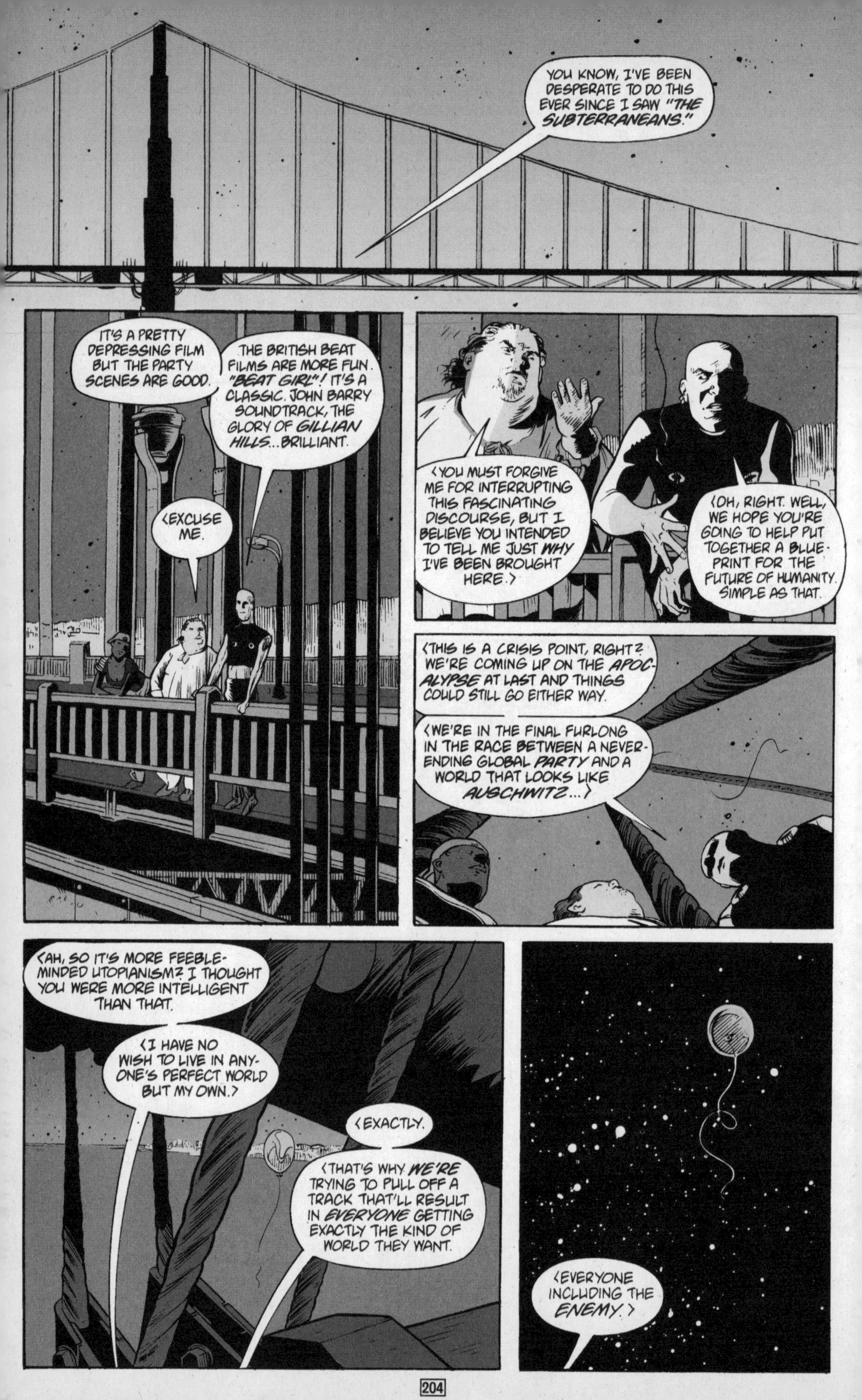
YOU KNOW, I'VE BEEN DESPERATE TO DO THIS EVER SINCE I SAW "THE SUBTERRANEANS."
IT'S A PRETTY DEPRESSING FILM BUT THE PARTY SCENES ARE GOOD.
THE BRITISH BEAT FILMS ARE MORE FUN. "BEAT GIRL"! IT'S A CLASSIC. JOHN BARRY SOUNDTRACK, THE GLORY OF GILLIAN HILLS...BRILLIANT.
<EXCUSE ME.
<YOU MUST FORGIVE ME FOR INTERRUPTING THIS FASCINATING DISCOURSE, BUT I BELIEVE YOU INTENDED TO TELL ME JUST WHY I'VE BEEN BROUGHT HERE.>
<OH, RIGHT. WELL, WE HOPE YOU'RE GOING TO HELP PUT TOGETHER A BLUEPRINT FOR THE FUTURE OF HUMANITY. SIMPLE AS THAT.
<THIS IS A CRISIS POINT, RIGHT? WE'RE COMING UP ON THE APOCALYPSE AT LAST AND THINGS COULD STILL GO EITHER WAY.
<WE'RE IN THE FINAL FURLONG IN THE RACE BETWEEN A NEVER-ENDING GLOBAL PARTY AND A WORLD THAT LOOKS LIKE AUSCHWITZ...>
<AH, SO IT'S MORE FEEBLE-MINDED UTOPIANISM? I THOUGHT YOU WERE MORE INTELLIGENT THAN THAT.
<I HAVE NO WISH TO LIVE IN ANYONE'S PERFECT WORLD BUT MY OWN.>
<EXACTLY.
<THAT'S WHY WE'RE TRYING TO PULL OFF A TRACK THAT'LL RESULT IN EVERYONE GETTING EXACTLY THE KIND OF WORLD THEY WANT.
<EVERYONE INCLUDING THE ENEMY.>

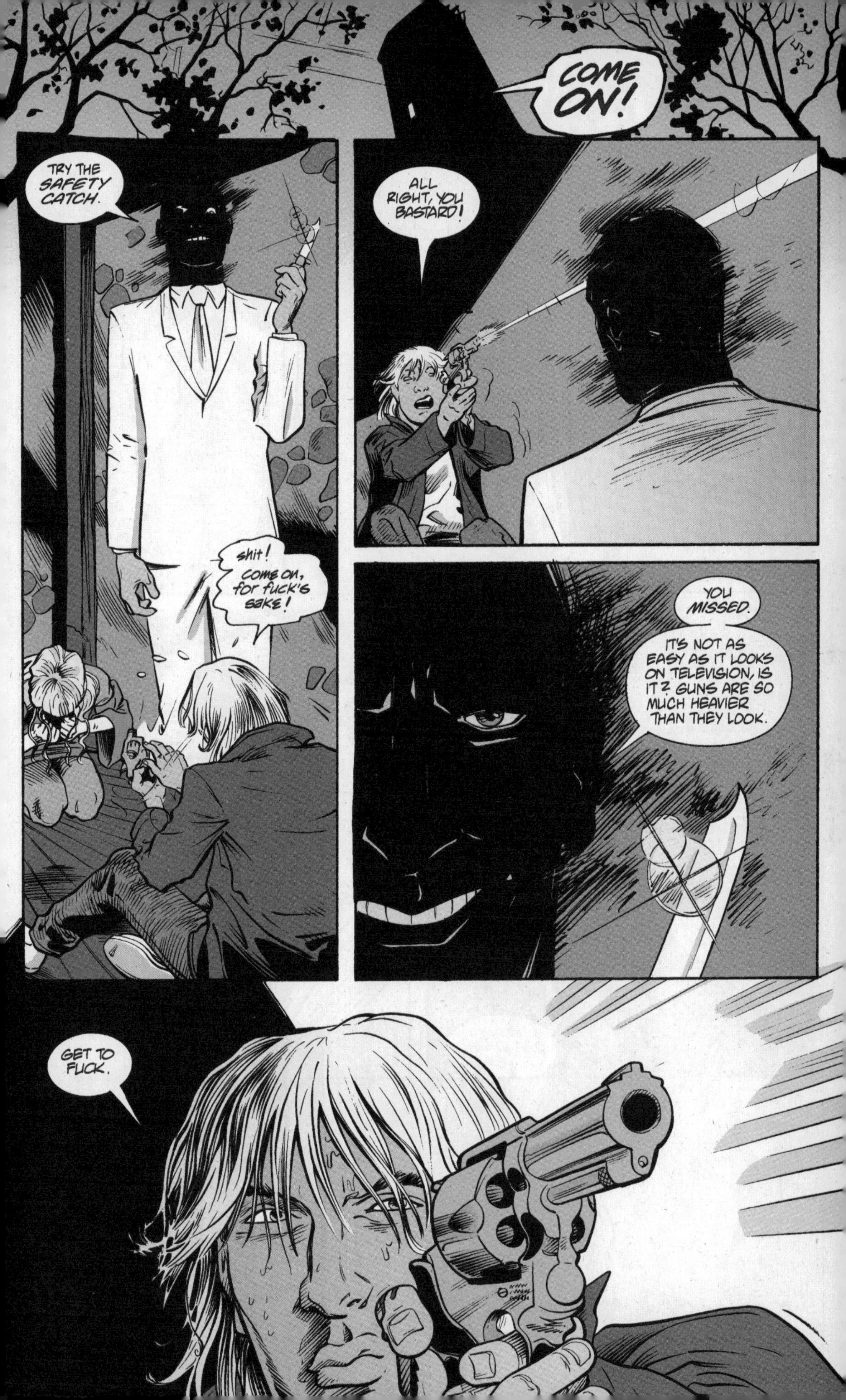
COME ON!
TRY THE SAFETY CATCH.
shit! come on, for fuck's sake!
ALL RIGHT, YOU BASTARD!
YOU MISSED.
IT'S NOT AS EASY AS IT LOOKS ON TELEVISION, IS IT? GUNS ARE SO MUCH HEAVIER THAN THEY LOOK.
GET TO FUCK.

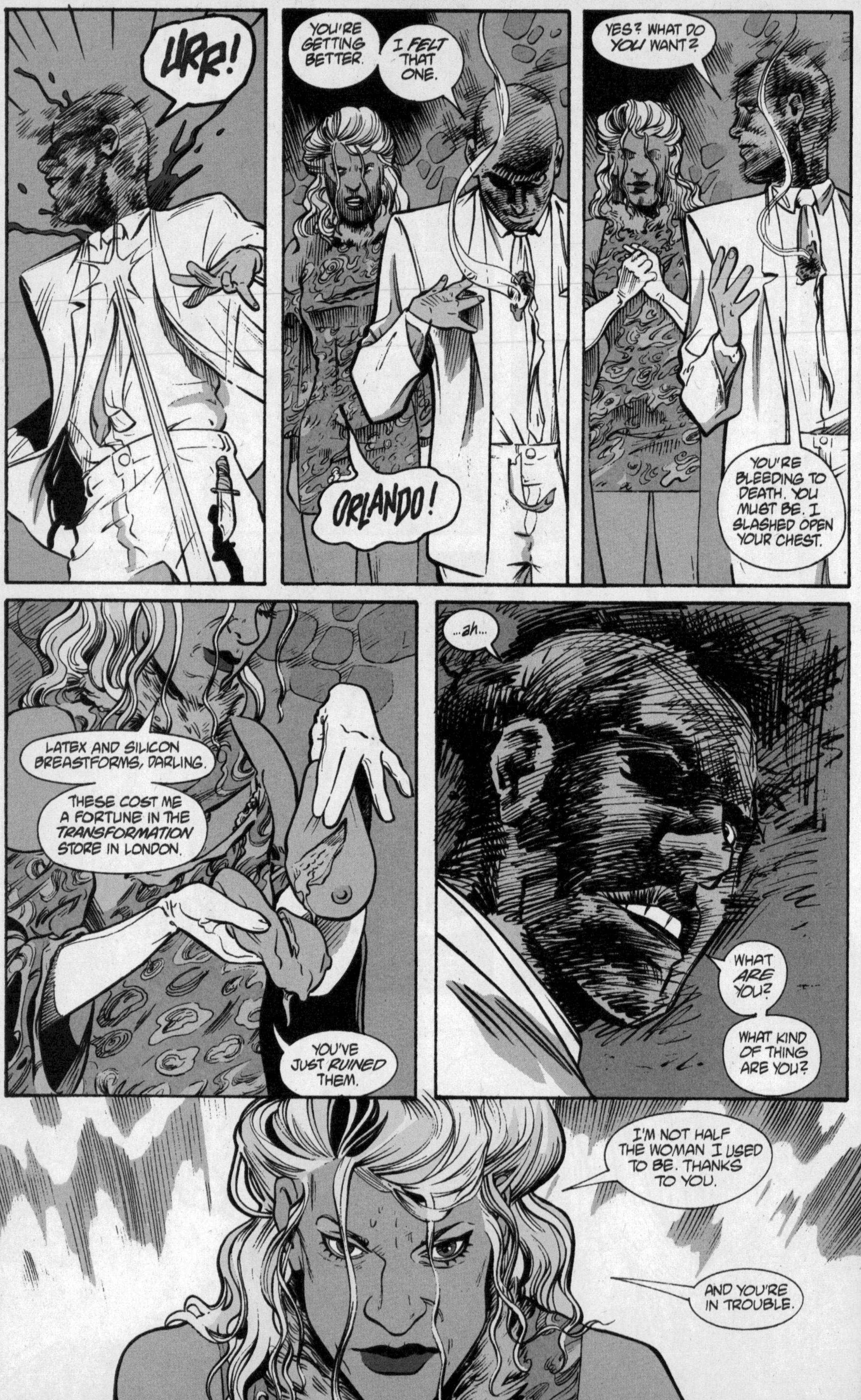
URR!
YOU'RE GETTING BETTER.
I FELT THAT ONE.
ORLANDO!
YES? WHAT DO YOU WANT?
YOU'RE BLEEDING TO DEATH. YOU MUST BE. I SLASHED OPEN YOUR CHEST.
LATEX AND SILICON BREASTFORMS, DARLING.
THESE COST ME A FORTUNE IN THE TRANSFORMATION STORE IN LONDON.
YOU'VE JUST RUINED THEM.
...ah...
WHAT ARE YOU?
WHAT KIND OF THING ARE YOU?
I'M NOT HALF THE WOMAN I USED TO BE. THANKS TO YOU.
AND YOU'RE IN TROUBLE.

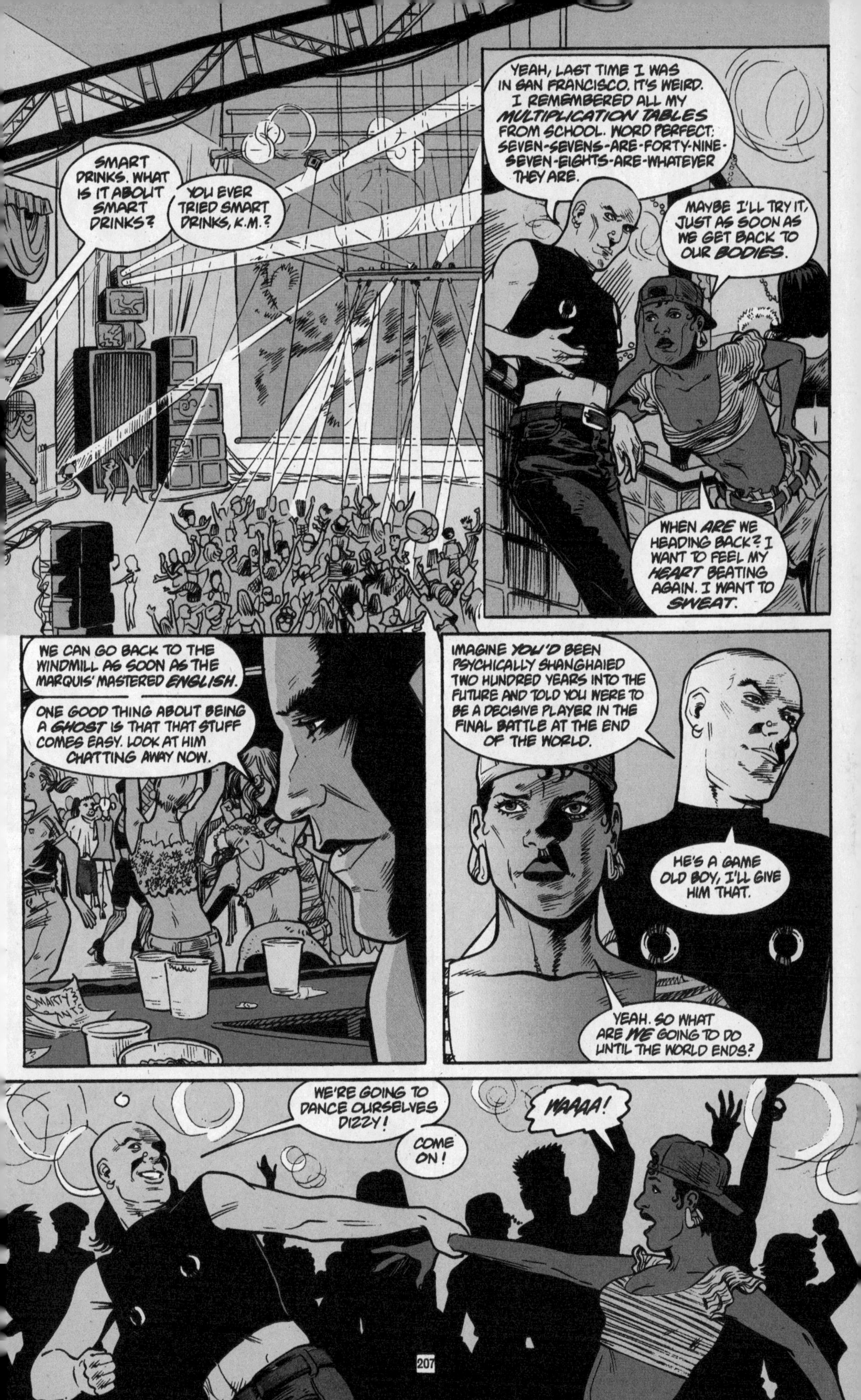
SMART DRINKS. WHAT IS IT ABOUT SMART DRINKS?
YOU EVER TRIED SMART DRINKS, K.M.?
YEAH, LAST TIME I WAS IN SAN FRANCISCO. IT'S WEIRD. I REMEMBERED ALL MY MULTIPLICATION TABLES FROM SCHOOL. WORD PERFECT: SEVEN-SEVENS-ARE-FORTY-NINE-SEVEN-EIGHTS-ARE-WHATEVER THEY ARE.
MAYBE I'LL TRY IT, JUST AS SOON AS WE GET BACK TO OUR BODIES.
WHEN ARE WE HEADING BACK? I WANT TO FEEL MY HEART BEATING AGAIN. I WANT TO SWEAT.
WE CAN GO BACK TO THE WINDMILL AS SOON AS THE MARQUIS' MASTERED ENGLISH.
ONE GOOD THING ABOUT BEING A GHOST IS THAT THAT STUFF COMES EASY. LOOK AT HIM CHATTING AWAY NOW.
IMAGINE YOU'D BEEN PSYCHICALLY SHANGHAIED TWO HUNDRED YEARS INTO THE FUTURE AND TOLD YOU WERE TO BE A DECISIVE PLAYER IN THE FINAL BATTLE AT THE END OF THE WORLD.
HE'S A GAME OLD BOY, I'LL GIVE HIM THAT.
YEAH. SO WHAT ARE WE GOING TO DO UNTIL THE WORLD ENDS?
WE'RE GOING TO DANCE OURSELVES DIZZY!
COME ON!
WAAAA!

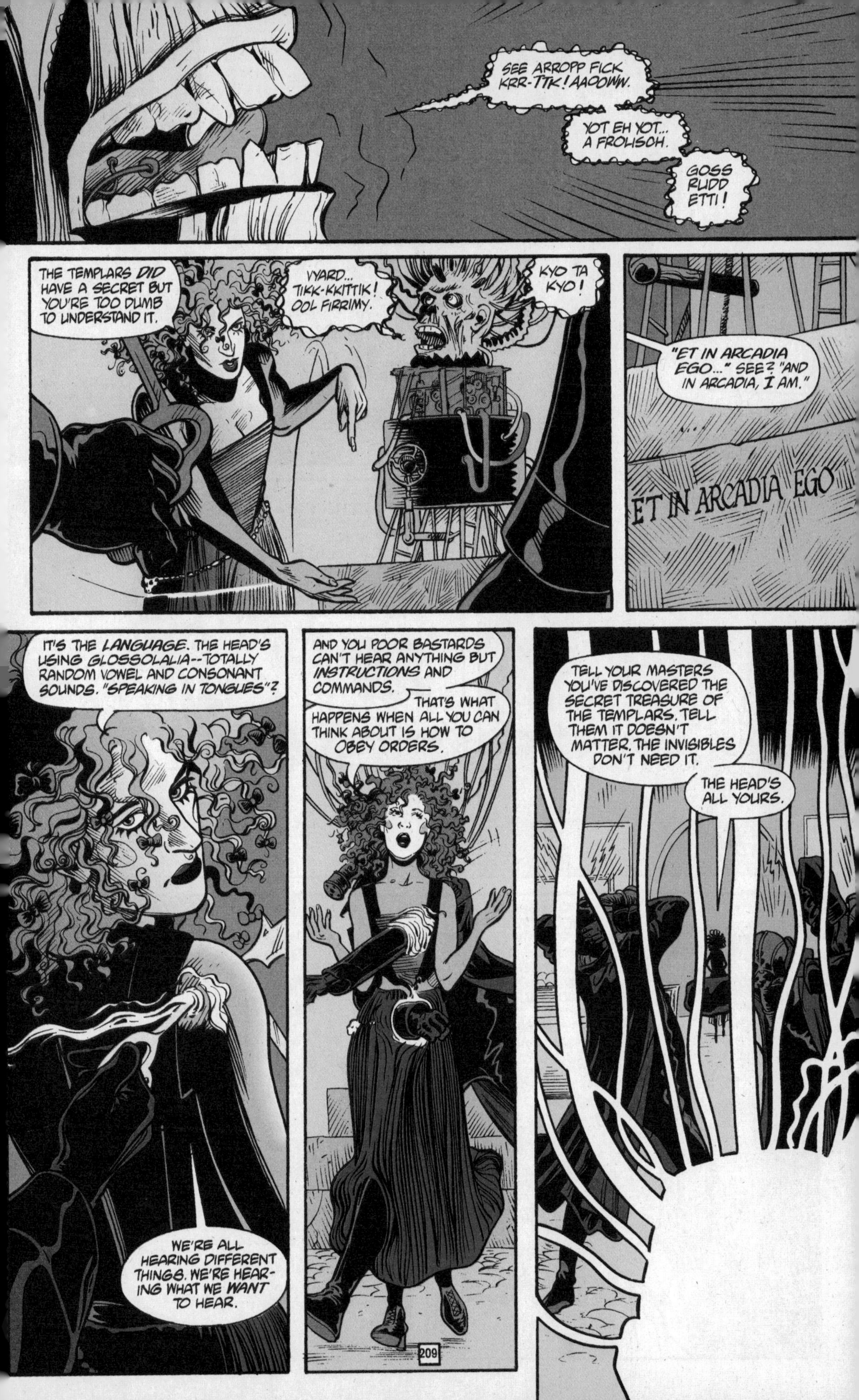

SEE ARROPP FICK KRR-TTK! AAOOWW.
YOT EH YOT... A FROUSOH.
GOSS RUDD ETTI!
THE TEMPLARS DID HAVE A SECRET BUT YOU'RE TOO DUMB TO UNDERSTAND IT.
VYARD... TIKK-KKITTIK! OOL FIRRIMY.
KYO TA KYO!
"ET IN ARCADIA EGO..." SEE? "AND IN ARCADIA, I AM."
ET IN ARCADIA EGO
IT'S THE LANGUAGE. THE HEAD'S USING GLOSSOLALIA--TOTALLY RANDOM VOWEL AND CONSONANT SOUNDS. "SPEAKING IN TONGUES"?
WE'RE ALL HEARING DIFFERENT THINGS. WE'RE HEARING WHAT WE WANT TO HEAR.
AND YOU POOR BASTARDS CAN'T HEAR ANYTHING BUT INSTRUCTIONS AND COMMANDS.
THAT'S WHAT HAPPENS WHEN ALL YOU CAN THINK ABOUT IS HOW TO OBEY ORDERS.
TELL YOUR MASTERS YOU'VE DISCOVERED THE SECRET TREASURE OF THE TEMPLARS. TELL THEM IT DOESN'T MATTER. THE INVISIBLES DON'T NEED IT.
THE HEAD'S ALL YOURS.

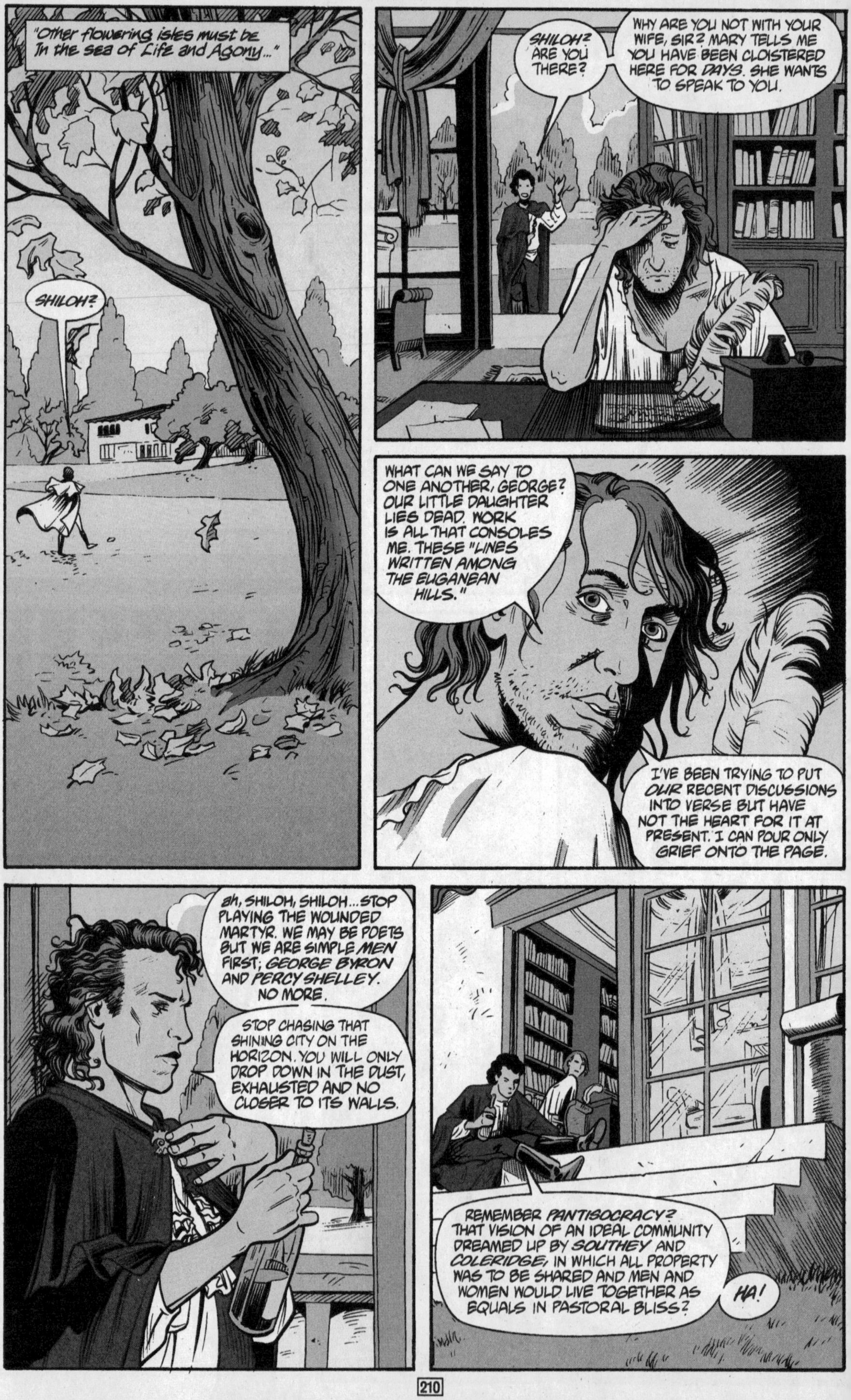
"Other flowering isles must be In the sea of Life and Agony..."
SHILOH?
SHILOH? ARE YOU THERE?
WHY ARE YOU NOT WITH YOUR WIFE, SIR? MARY TELLS ME YOU HAVE BEEN CLOISTERED HERE FOR DAYS. SHE WANTS TO SPEAK TO YOU.
WHAT CAN WE SAY TO ONE ANOTHER, GEORGE? OUR LITTLE DAUGHTER LIES DEAD. WORK IS ALL THAT CONSOLES ME. THESE "LINES WRITTEN AMONG THE EUGANEAN HILLS."
I'VE BEEN TRYING TO PUT OUR RECENT DISCUSSIONS INTO VERSE BUT HAVE NOT THE HEART FOR IT AT PRESENT. I CAN POUR ONLY GRIEF ONTO THE PAGE.
ah, SHILOH, SHILOH... STOP PLAYING THE WOUNDED MARTYR. WE MAY BE POETS BUT WE ARE SIMPLE MEN FIRST; GEORGE BYRON AND PERCY SHELLEY. NO MORE.
STOP CHASING THAT SHINING CITY ON THE HORIZON. YOU WILL ONLY DROP DOWN IN THE DUST, EXHAUSTED AND NO CLOSER TO ITS WALLS.
REMEMBER PANTISOCRACY? THAT VISION OF AN IDEAL COMMUNITY DREAMED UP BY SOUTHEY AND COLERIDGE, IN WHICH ALL PROPERTY WAS TO BE SHARED AND MEN AND WOMEN WOULD LIVE TOGETHER AS EQUALS IN PASTORAL BLISS?
HA!

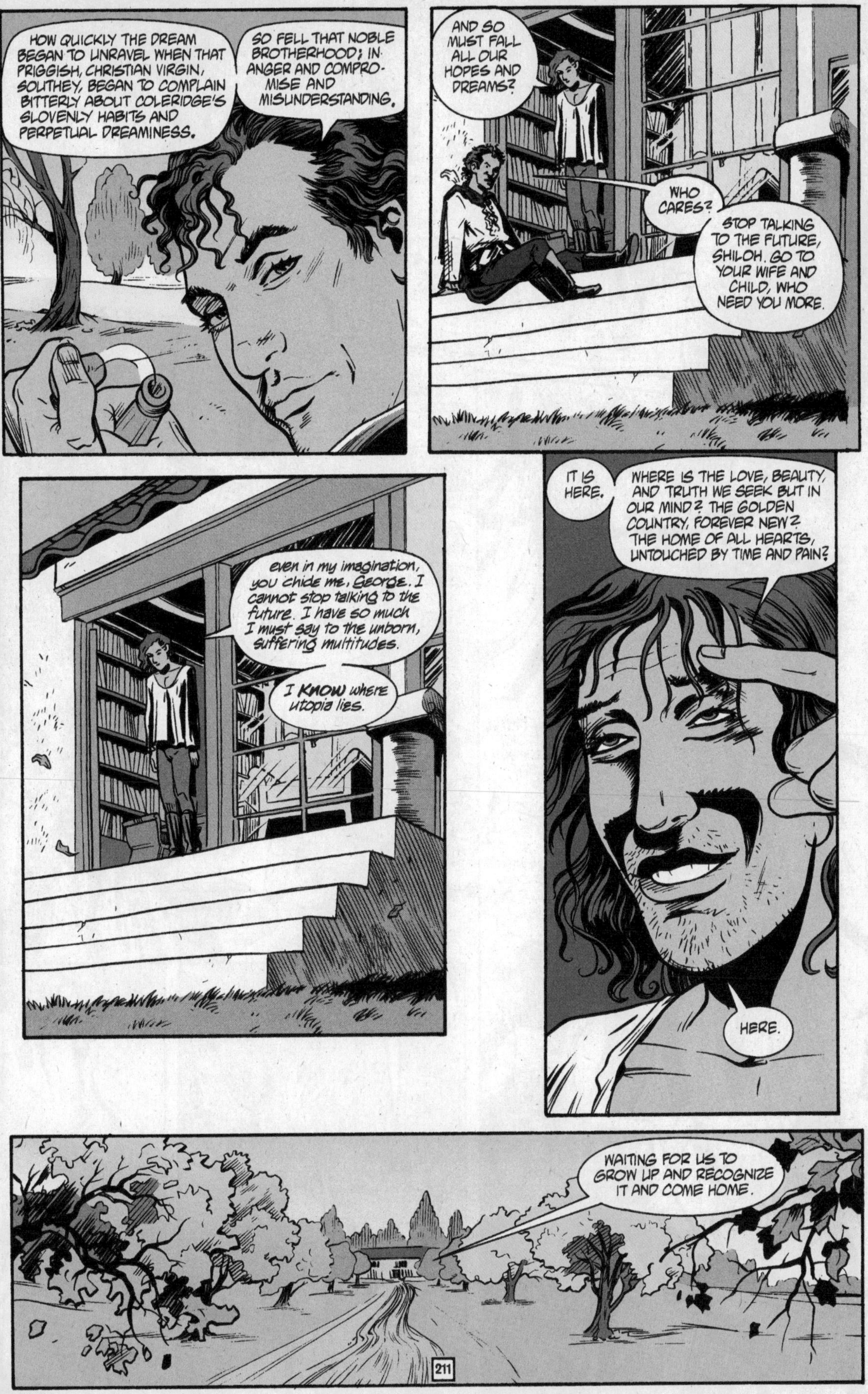
HOW QUICKLY THE DREAM BEGAN TO UNRAVEL WHEN THAT PRIGGISH, CHRISTIAN VIRGIN, SOUTHEY, BEGAN TO COMPLAIN BITTERLY ABOUT COLERIDGE'S SLOVENLY HABITS AND PERPETUAL DREAMINESS.
SO FELL THAT NOBLE BROTHERHOOD; IN ANGER AND COMPROMISE AND MISUNDERSTANDING.
AND SO MUST FALL ALL OUR HOPES AND DREAMS?
WHO CARES?
STOP TALKING TO THE FUTURE, SHILOH. GO TO YOUR WIFE AND CHILD, WHO NEED YOU MORE.
even in my imagination, you chide me, George. I cannot stop talking to the future. I have so much I must say to the unborn, suffering multitudes.
I KNOW where utopia lies.
IT IS HERE.
WHERE IS THE LOVE, BEAUTY, AND TRUTH WE SEEK BUT IN OUR MIND? THE GOLDEN COUNTRY, FOREVER NEW? THE HOME OF ALL HEARTS, UNTOUCHED BY TIME AND PAIN?
HERE.
WAITING FOR US TO GROW UP AND RECOGNIZE IT AND COME HOME.

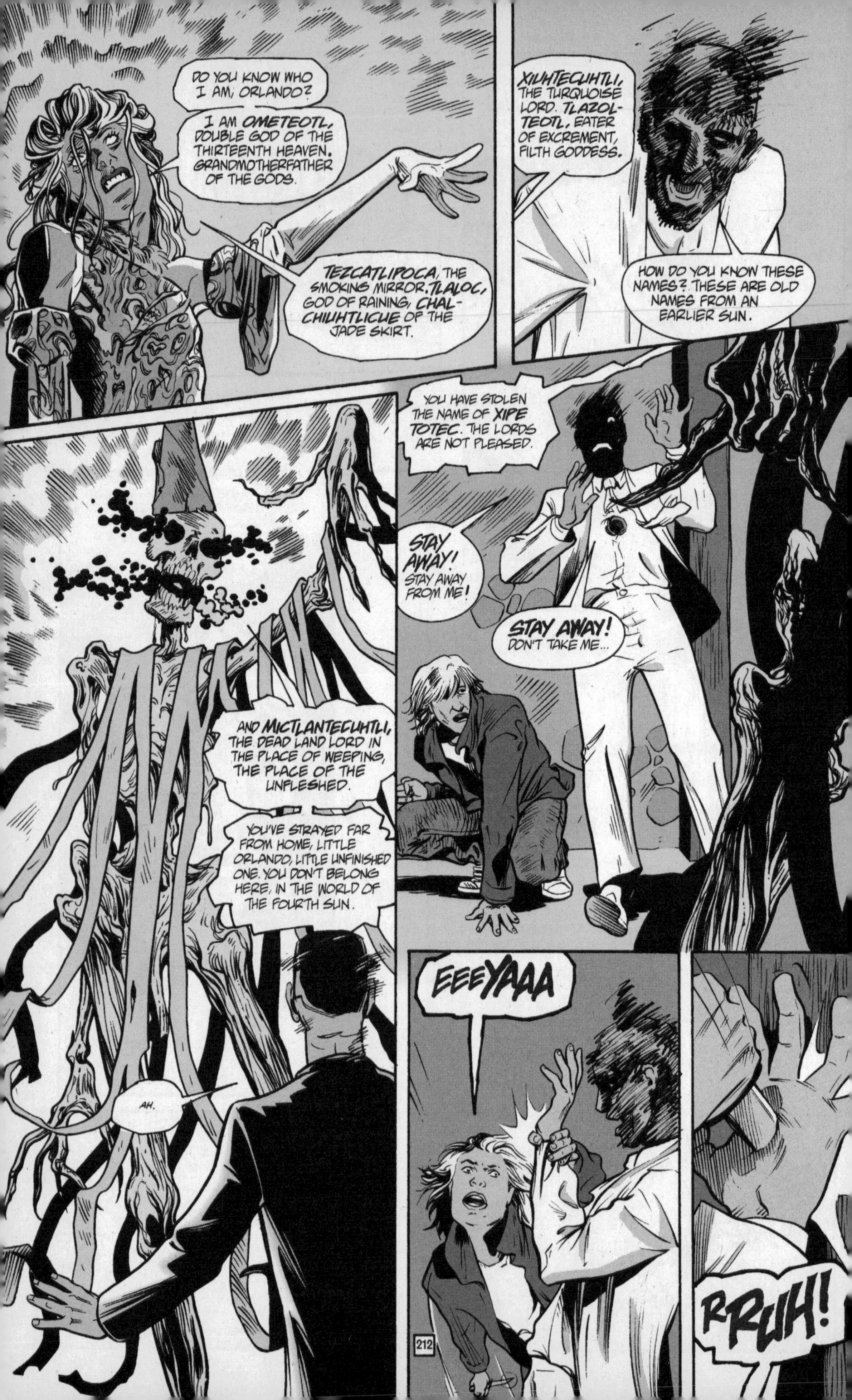
DO YOU KNOW WHO I AM, ORLANDO?
I AM OMETEOTL, DOUBLE GOD OF THE THIRTEENTH HEAVEN. GRANDMOTHERFATHER OF THE GODS.
TEZCATLIPOCA, THE SMOKING MIRROR. TLALOC, GOD OF RAINING, CHALCHIUHTLICUE OF THE JADE SKIRT.
XIUHTECUHTLI, THE TURQUOISE LORD. TLAZOLTEOTL, EATER OF EXCREMENT, FILTH GODDESS.
HOW DO YOU KNOW THESE NAMES? THESE ARE OLD NAMES FROM AN EARLIER SUN.
AND MICTLANTECUHTLI, THE DEAD LAND LORD IN THE PLACE OF WEEPING, THE PLACE OF THE UNFLESHED.
YOU'VE STRAYED FAR FROM HOME, LITTLE ORLANDO, LITTLE UNFINISHED ONE. YOU DON'T BELONG HERE, IN THE WORLD OF THE FOURTH SUN.
AH.
YOU HAVE STOLEN THE NAME OF XIPE TOTEC. THE LORDS ARE NOT PLEASED.
STAY AWAY! STAY AWAY FROM ME!
STAY AWAY! DON'T TAKE ME...
EEEYAAA
RRUH!

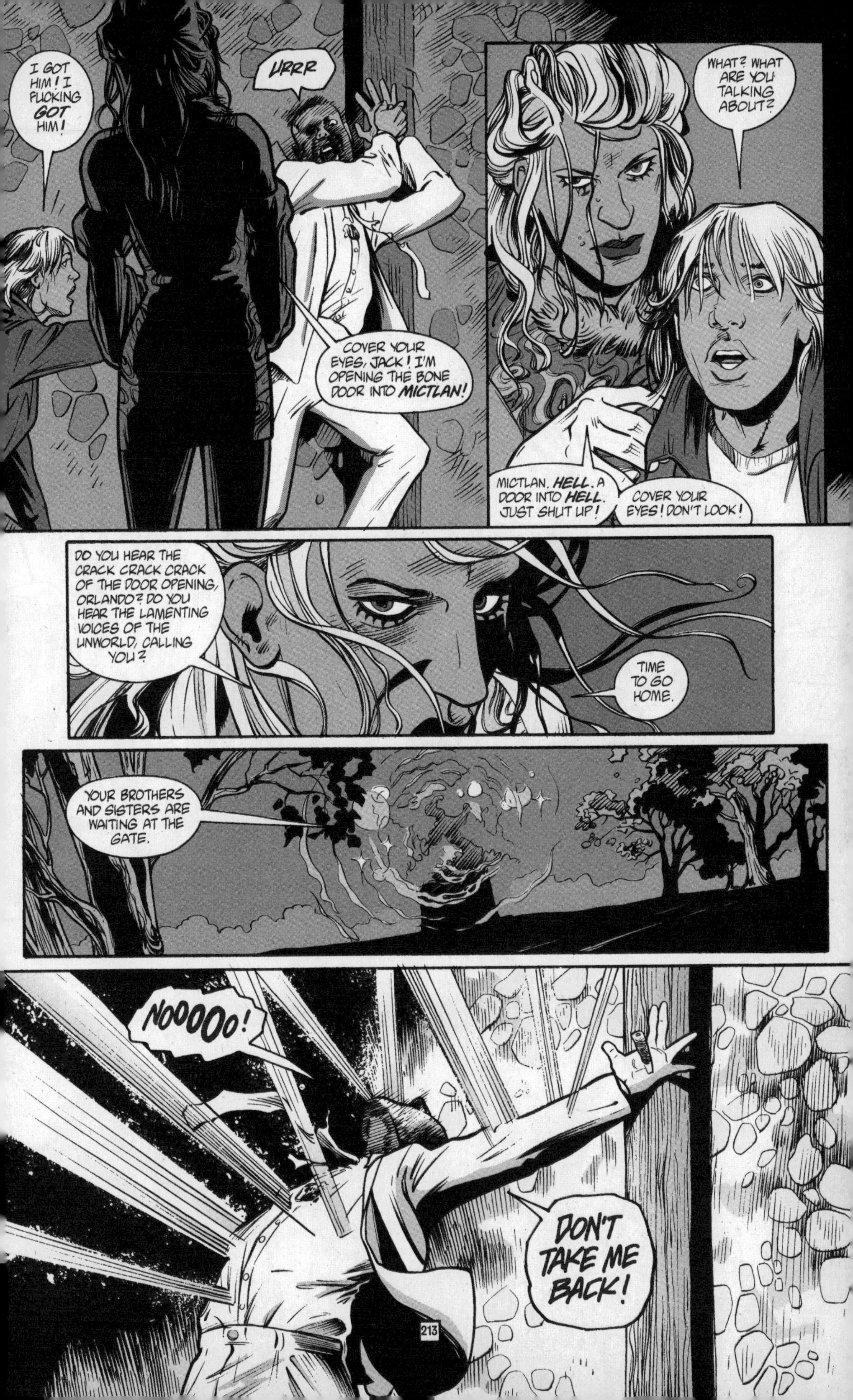
I GOT HIM! I FUCKING GOT HIM!
URRR
COVER YOUR EYES, JACK! I'M OPENING THE BONE DOOR INTO MICTLAN!
WHAT? WHAT ARE YOU TALKING ABOUT?
MICTLAN. HELL. A DOOR INTO HELL. JUST SHUT UP!
COVER YOUR EYES! DON'T LOOK!
DO YOU HEAR THE CRACK CRACK CRACK OF THE DOOR OPENING, ORLANDO? DO YOU HEAR THE LAMENTING VOICES OF THE UNWORLD, CALLING YOU?
TIME TO GO HOME.
YOUR BROTHERS AND SISTERS ARE WAITING AT THE GATE.
NOOOOo!
DON'T TAKE ME BACK!

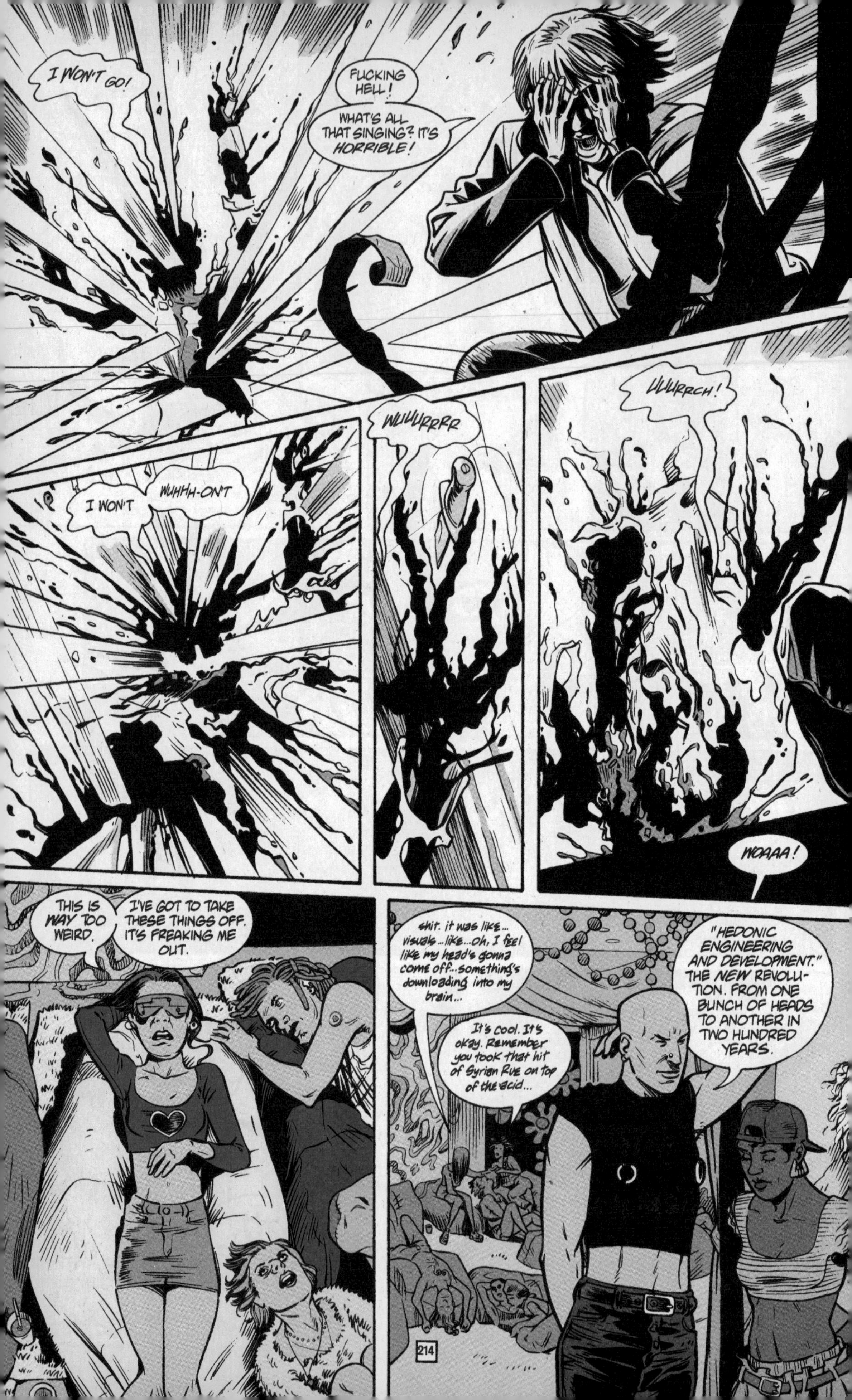
I WON'T GO!
FUCKING HELL!
WHAT'S ALL THAT SINGING? IT'S HORRIBLE!
I WON'T
WUHHH-ON'T
WUUURRRR
UUURRCH!
WOAAA!
THIS IS WAY TOO WEIRD.
I'VE GOT TO TAKE THESE THINGS OFF. IT'S FREAKING ME OUT.
shit. it was like... visuals...like...oh, I feel like my head's gonna come off...something's downloading into my brain...
It's cool. It's okay. Remember you took that hit of Syrian Rue on top of the acid...
"HEDONIC ENGINEERING AND DEVELOPMENT." THE NEW REVOLUTION. FROM ONE BUNCH OF HEADS TO ANOTHER IN TWO HUNDRED YEARS.

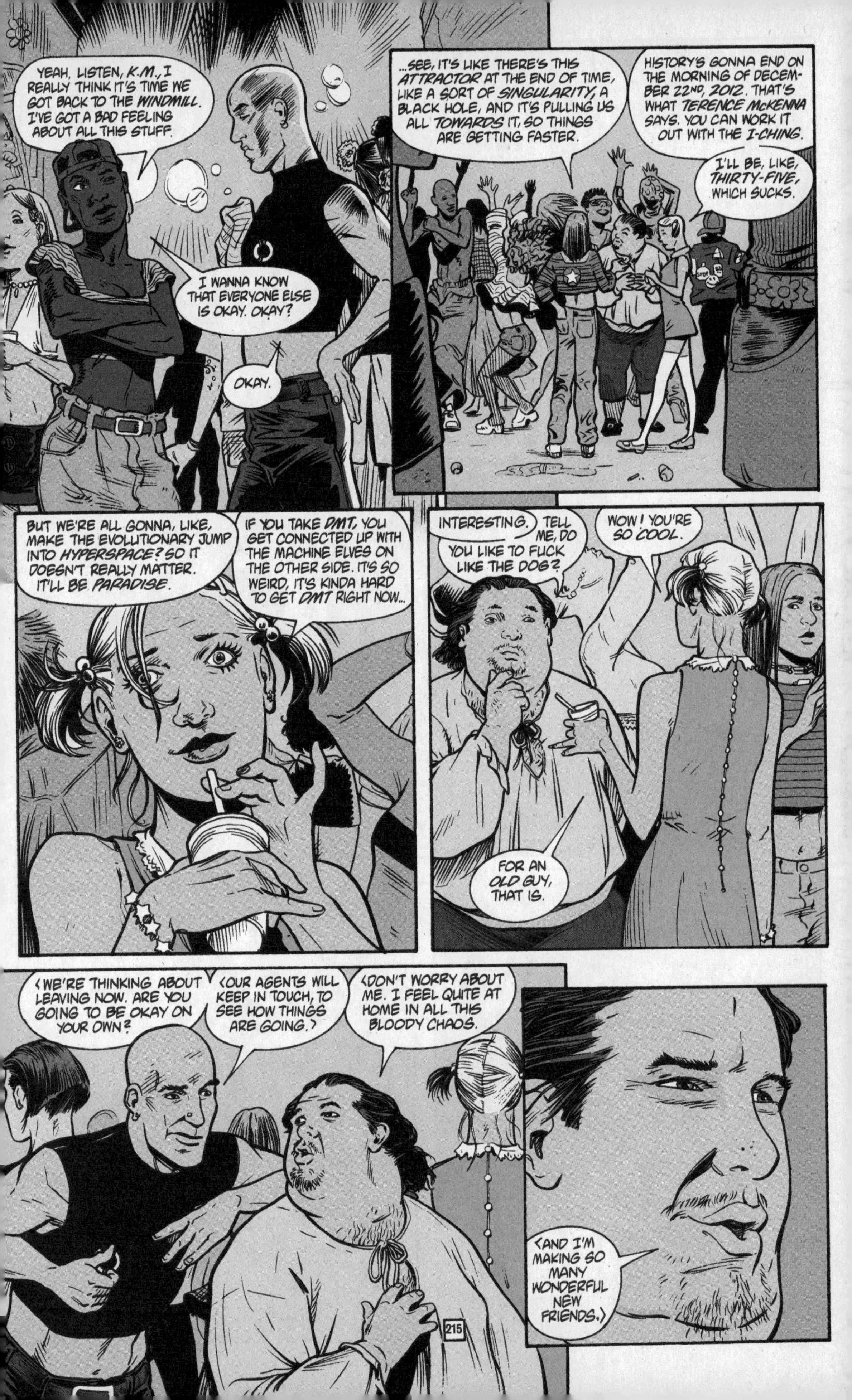
YEAH, LISTEN, K.M., I REALLY THINK IT'S TIME WE GOT BACK TO THE WINDMILL. I'VE GOT A BAD FEELING ABOUT ALL THIS STUFF.
I WANNA KNOW THAT EVERYONE ELSE IS OKAY. OKAY?
OKAY.
...SEE, IT'S LIKE THERE'S THIS ATTRACTOR AT THE END OF TIME, LIKE A SORT OF SINGULARITY, A BLACK HOLE, AND IT'S PULLING US ALL TOWARDS IT, SO THINGS ARE GETTING FASTER.
HISTORY'S GONNA END ON THE MORNING OF DECEMBER 22ND, 2012. THAT'S WHAT TERENCE McKENNA SAYS. YOU CAN WORK IT OUT WITH THE I-CHING.
I'LL BE, LIKE, THIRTY-FIVE, WHICH SUCKS.
BUT WE'RE ALL GONNA, LIKE, MAKE THE EVOLUTIONARY JUMP INTO HYPERSPACE? SO IT DOESN'T REALLY MATTER. IT'LL BE PARADISE.
IF YOU TAKE DMT, YOU GET CONNECTED UP WITH THE MACHINE ELVES ON THE OTHER SIDE. IT'S SO WEIRD, IT'S KINDA HARD TO GET DMT RIGHT NOW...
INTERESTING.
TELL ME, DO YOU LIKE TO FUCK LIKE THE DOG?
WOW! YOU'RE SO COOL.
FOR AN OLD GUY, THAT IS.
<WE'RE THINKING ABOUT LEAVING NOW. ARE YOU GOING TO BE OKAY ON YOUR OWN?
<OUR AGENTS WILL KEEP IN TOUCH, TO SEE HOW THINGS ARE GOING.>
<DON'T WORRY ABOUT ME. I FEEL QUITE AT HOME IN ALL THIS BLOODY CHAOS.
<AND I'M MAKING SO MANY WONDERFUL NEW FRIENDS.>

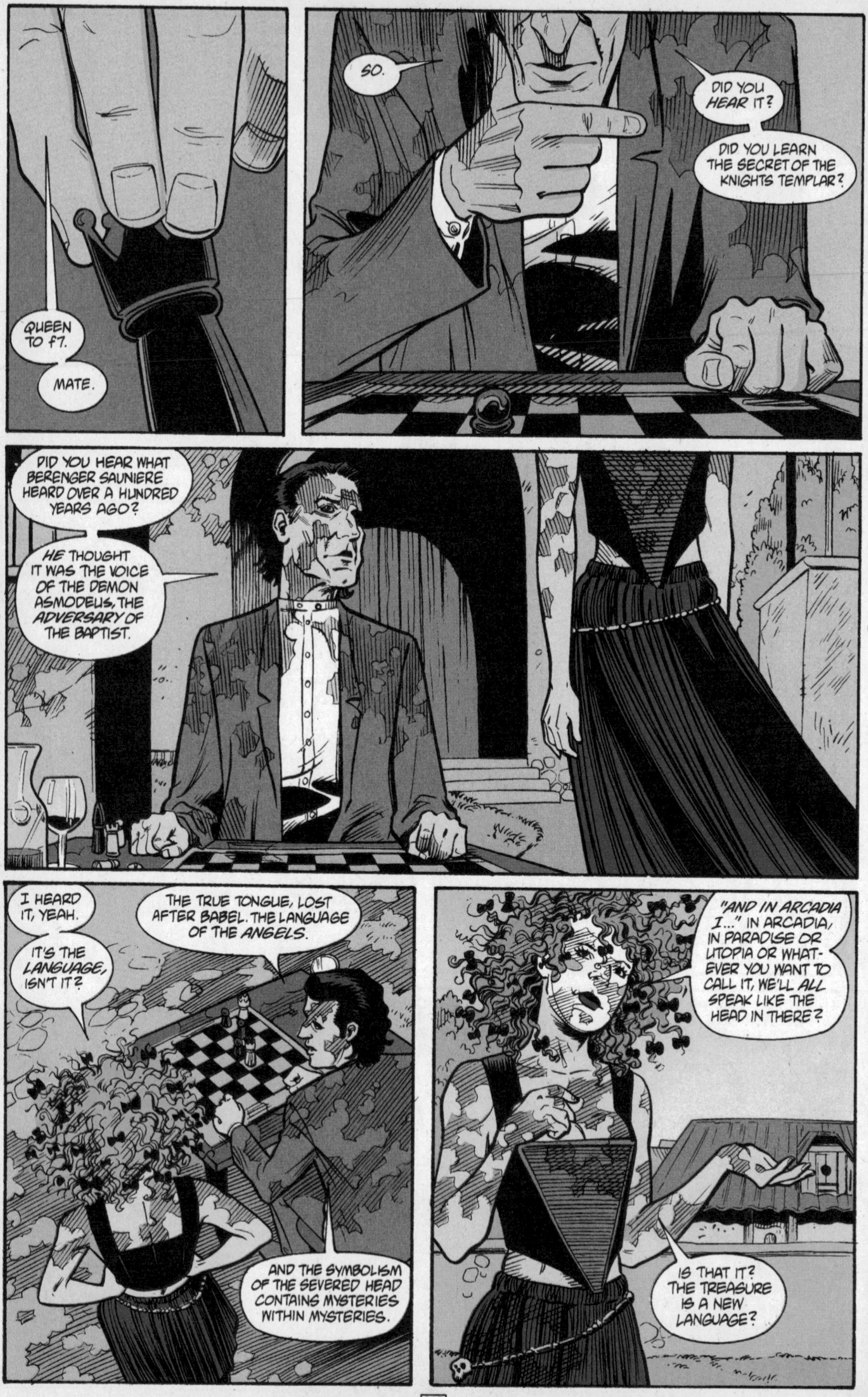
QUEEN TO f7.
MATE.
SO.
DID YOU HEAR IT?
DID YOU LEARN THE SECRET OF THE KNIGHTS TEMPLAR?
DID YOU HEAR WHAT BERENGER SAUNIERE HEARD OVER A HUNDRED YEARS AGO?
HE THOUGHT IT WAS THE VOICE OF THE DEMON ASMODEUS, THE ADVERSARY OF THE BAPTIST.
I HEARD IT, YEAH.
IT'S THE LANGUAGE, ISN'T IT?
THE TRUE TONGUE, LOST AFTER BABEL. THE LANGUAGE OF THE ANGELS.
AND THE SYMBOLISM OF THE SEVERED HEAD CONTAINS MYSTERIES WITHIN MYSTERIES.
"AND IN ARCADIA I..." IN ARCADIA, IN PARADISE OR UTOPIA OR WHATEVER YOU WANT TO CALL IT, WE'LL ALL SPEAK LIKE THE HEAD IN THERE?
IS THAT IT? THE TREASURE IS A NEW LANGUAGE?

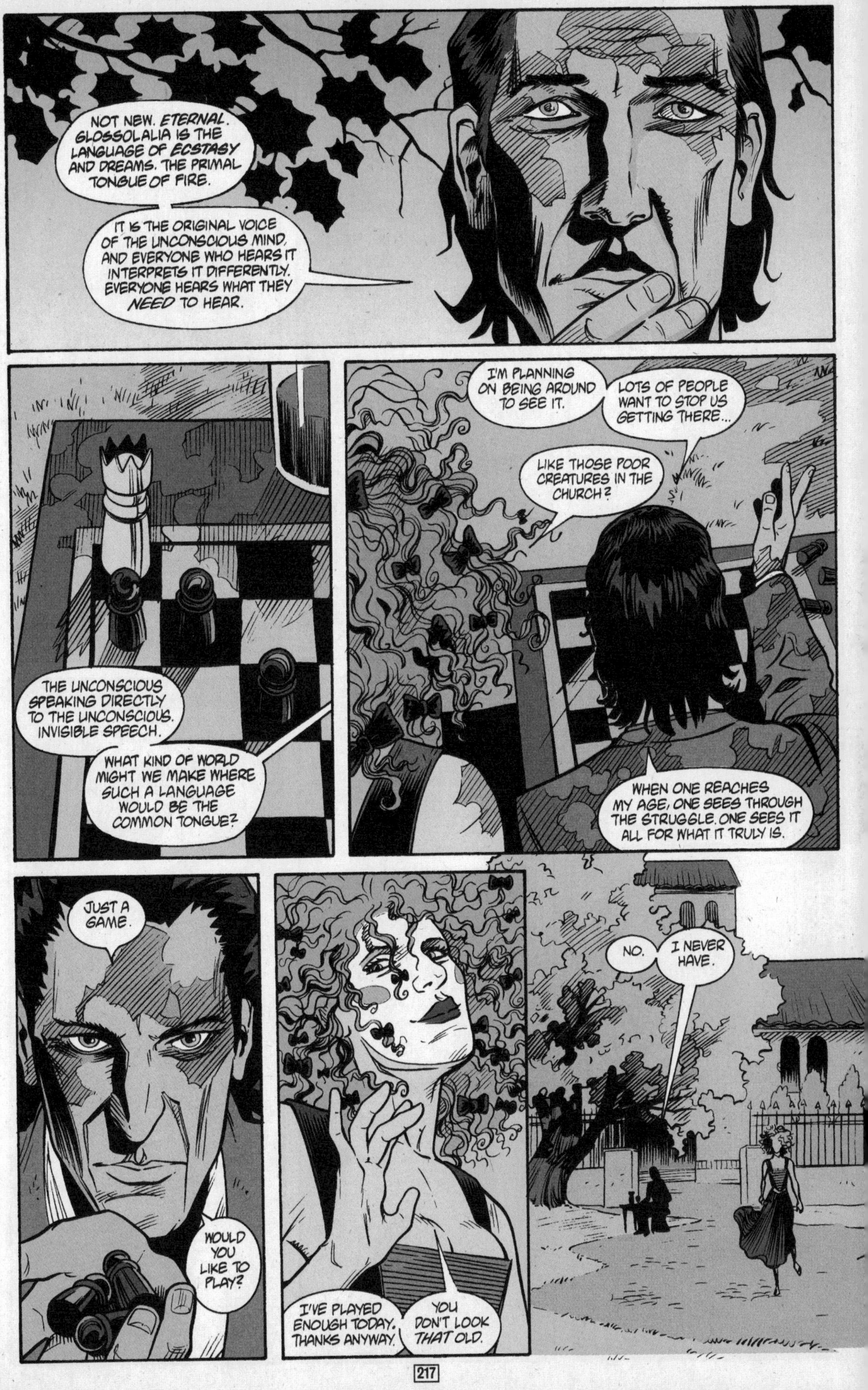

NOT NEW. ETERNAL. GLOSSOLALIA IS THE LANGUAGE OF ECSTASY AND DREAMS. THE PRIMAL TONGUE OF FIRE.
IT IS THE ORIGINAL VOICE OF THE UNCONSCIOUS MIND, AND EVERYONE WHO HEARS IT INTERPRETS IT DIFFERENTLY. EVERYONE HEARS WHAT THEY NEED TO HEAR.
THE UNCONSCIOUS SPEAKING DIRECTLY TO THE UNCONSCIOUS. INVISIBLE SPEECH.
WHAT KIND OF WORLD MIGHT WE MAKE WHERE SUCH A LANGUAGE WOULD BE THE COMMON TONGUE?
I'M PLANNING ON BEING AROUND TO SEE IT.
LOTS OF PEOPLE WANT TO STOP US GETTING THERE...
LIKE THOSE POOR CREATURES IN THE CHURCH?
WHEN ONE REACHES MY AGE, ONE SEES THROUGH THE STRUGGLE. ONE SEES IT ALL FOR WHAT IT TRULY IS.
JUST A GAME.
WOULD YOU LIKE TO PLAY?
I'VE PLAYED ENOUGH TODAY. THANKS ANYWAY.
YOU DON'T LOOK THAT OLD.
NO.
I NEVER HAVE.

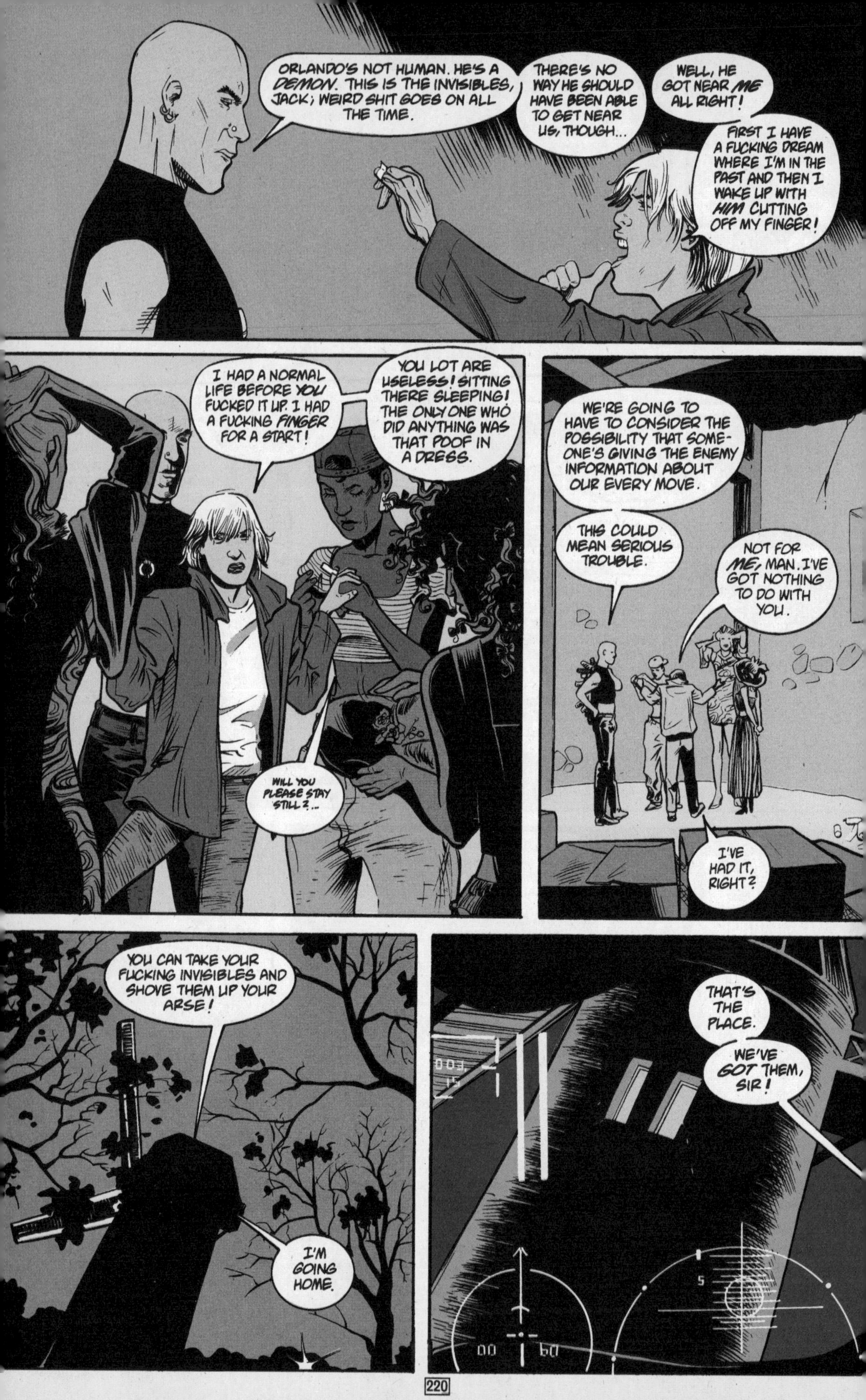
ORLANDO'S NOT HUMAN. HE'S A DEMON. THIS IS THE INVISIBLES, JACK; WEIRD SHIT GOES ON ALL THE TIME.
THERE'S NO WAY HE SHOULD HAVE BEEN ABLE TO GET NEAR US, THOUGH...
WELL, HE GOT NEAR ME ALL RIGHT!
FIRST I HAVE A FUCKING DREAM WHERE I'M IN THE PAST AND THEN I WAKE UP WITH HIM CUTTING OFF MY FINGER!
I HAD A NORMAL LIFE BEFORE YOU FUCKED IT UP. I HAD A FUCKING FINGER FOR A START!
YOU LOT ARE USELESS! SITTING THERE SLEEPING! THE ONLY ONE WHO DID ANYTHING WAS THAT POOF IN A DRESS.
WILL YOU PLEASE STAY STILL?...
WE'RE GOING TO HAVE TO CONSIDER THE POSSIBILITY THAT SOME-ONE'S GIVING THE ENEMY INFORMATION ABOUT OUR EVERY MOVE.
THIS COULD MEAN SERIOUS TROUBLE.
NOT FOR ME, MAN. I'VE GOT NOTHING TO DO WITH YOU.
I'VE HAD IT, RIGHT?
YOU CAN TAKE YOUR FUCKING INVISIBLES AND SHOVE THEM UP YOUR ARSE!
I'M GOING HOME.
THAT'S THE PLACE.
WE'VE GOT THEM, SIR!

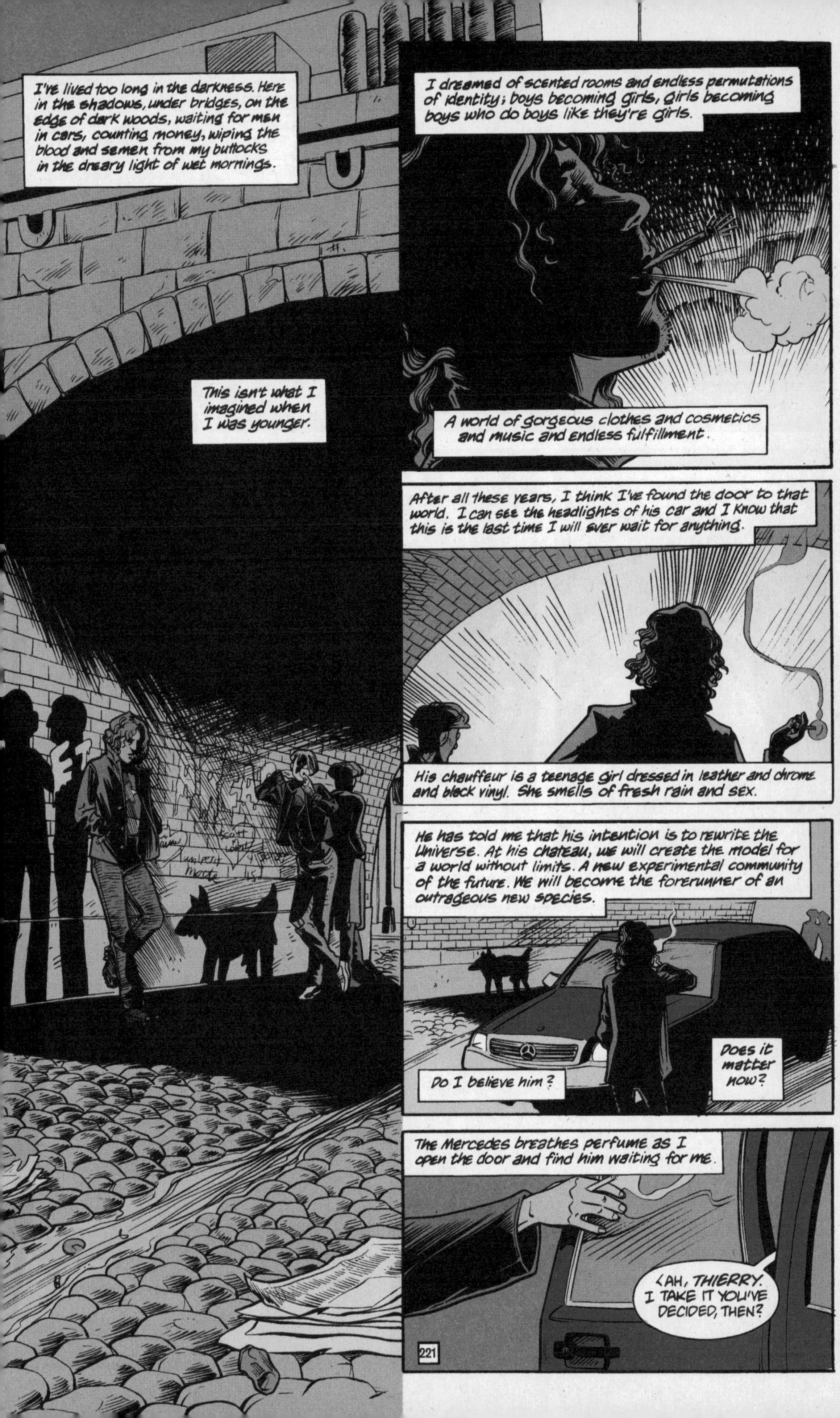
I've lived too long in the darkness. Here in the shadows, under bridges, on the edge of dark woods, waiting for men in cars, counting money, wiping the blood and semen from my buttocks in the dreary light of wet mornings.
This isn't what I imagined when I was younger.
I dreamed of scented rooms and endless permutations of identity; boys becoming girls, girls becoming boys who do boys like they're girls.
A world of gorgeous clothes and cosmetics and music and endless fulfillment.
After all these years, I think I've found the door to that world. I can see the headlights of his car and I know that this is the last time I will ever wait for anything.
His chauffeur is a teenage girl dressed in leather and chrome and black vinyl. She smells of fresh rain and sex.
He has told me that his intention is to rewrite the Universe. At his chateau, we will create the model for a world without limits. A new experimental community of the future. We will become the forerunner of an outrageous new species.
Do I believe him?
Does it matter now?
The Mercedes breathes perfume as I open the door and find him waiting for me.
<AH, THIERRY. I TAKE IT YOU'VE DECIDED, THEN?

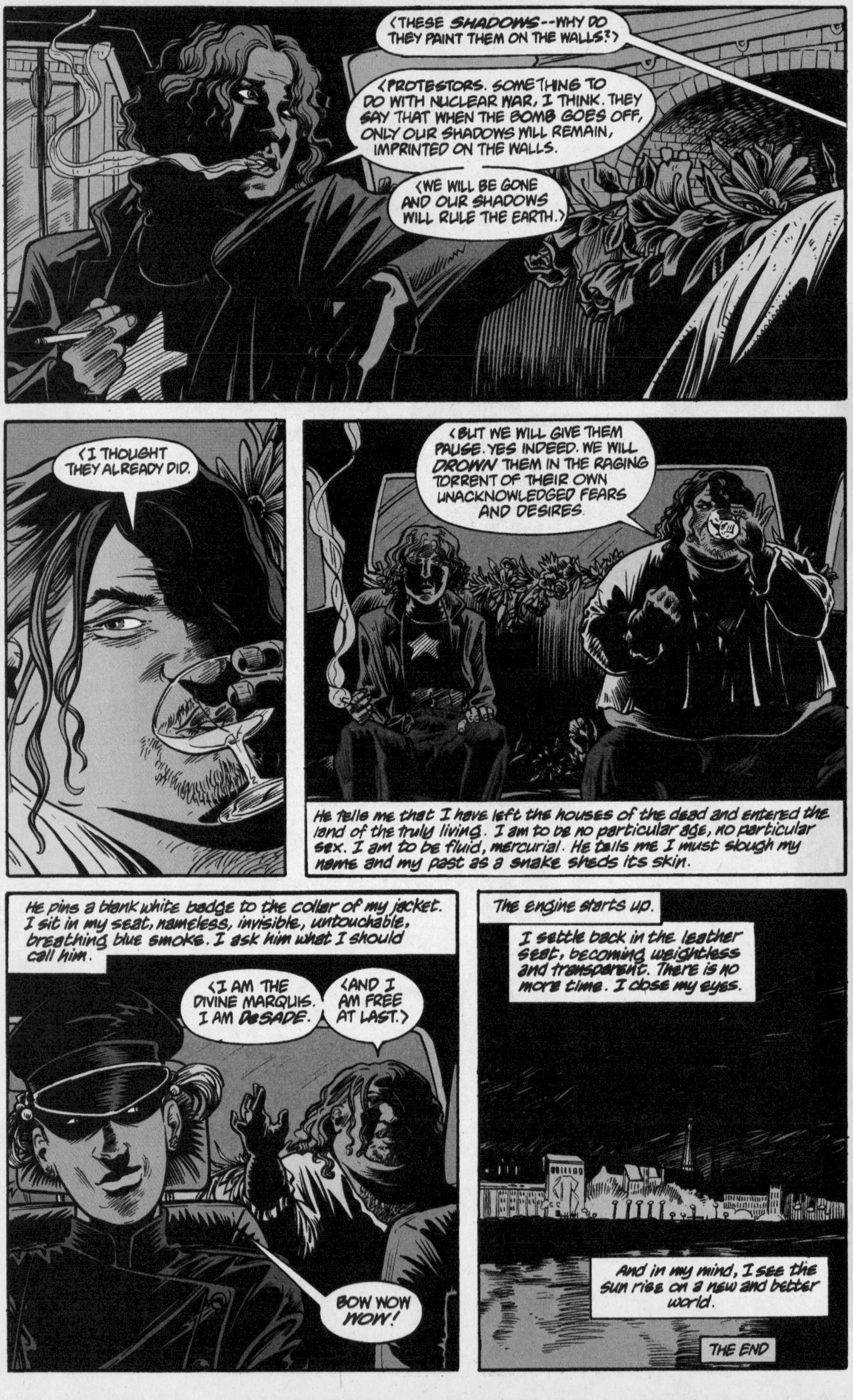
<THESE SHADOWS--WHY DO THEY PAINT THEM ON THE WALLS?>
<PROTESTORS. SOMETHING TO DO WITH NUCLEAR WAR, I THINK. THEY SAY THAT WHEN THE BOMB GOES OFF, ONLY OUR SHADOWS WILL REMAIN, IMPRINTED ON THE WALLS.
<WE WILL BE GONE AND OUR SHADOWS WILL RULE THE EARTH.>
<I THOUGHT THEY ALREADY DID.
<BUT WE WILL GIVE THEM PAUSE. YES INDEED. WE WILL DROWN THEM IN THE RAGING TORRENT OF THEIR OWN UNACKNOWLEDGED FEARS AND DESIRES.
He tells me that I have left the houses of the dead and entered the land of the truly living. I am to be no particular age, no particular sex. I am to be fluid, mercurial. He tells me I must slough my name and my past as a snake sheds its skin.
He pins a blank white badge to the collar of my jacket. I sit in my seat, nameless, invisible, untouchable, breathing blue smoke. I ask him what I should call him.
<I AM THE DIVINE MARQUIS. I AM DESADE.
<AND I AM FREE AT LAST.>
BOW WOW WOW!
The engine starts up.
I settle back in the leather seat, becoming weightless and transparent. There is no more time. I close my eyes.
And in my mind, I see the sun rise on a new and better world.
THE END

THE GRANT MORRISON LIBRARY

From VERTIGO. Suggested for mature readers.

THE INVISIBLES

The saga of a terrifying conspiracy and the resistance movement combatting it — a secret underground of ultra-cool guerrilla cells trained in ontological and physical anarchy.

Volume 1: SAY YOU WANT A REVOLUTION
With Steve Yeowell and Jill Thompson

Volume 2: APOCALIPSTICK
With Jill Thompson, Chris Weston and various

Volume 3: ENTROPY IN THE U.K.
With Phil Jimenez, John Stokes and various

Volume 4: BLOODY HELL IN AMERICA
With Phil Jimenez and John Stokes

Volume 5: COUNTING TO NONE
With Phil Jimenez and John Stokes

Volume 6: KISSING MR. QUIMPER
With Chris Weston and various

Volume 7: THE INVISIBLE KINGDOM
With Philip Bond, Sean Phillips and various

THE INVISIBLES
Apocalipstick

VERTIGO
INVISIBLES
ENTROPY IN THE U.K.

VERTIGO
THE INVISIBLES
BLOODY HELL IN AMERICA

INVISIBLES
COUNTING TO NONE

INVISIBLES
KISSING MISTER QUIMPER

THE INVISIBLES

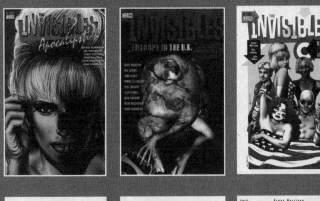

From DC COMICS

BATMAN: ARKHAM ASYLUM
With Dave McKean
suggested for mature readers.

BATMAN: GOTHIC
With Klaus Janson

JLA: EARTH 2
With Frank Quitely

JLA: NEW WORLD ORDER
With Howard Porter and John Dell

JLA: AMERICAN DREAMS
With Howard Porter, John Dell and various

JLA: ROCK OF AGES
With Howard Porter, John Dell and various

JLA: ONE MILLION
With Val Semeiks, Prentis Rollins and various

ARKHAM ASYLUM
GRANT MORRISON DAVE McKEAN

Batman
Gothic
Grant Morrison Klaus Janson

JLA
earth 2

JLA
NEW WORLD ORDER
GRANT MORRISON
HOWARD PORTER
JOHN DELL

JLA
AMERICAN DREAMS

JLA
ROCK OF AGES

JLA
ONE MILLION
GRANT MORRISON

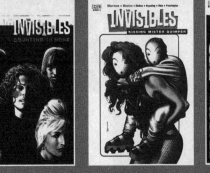

DOOM PATROL

The World's Strangest Heroes are reimagined even stranger and more otherworldly in this groundbreaking series exploring the mysteries of identity and madness.

Volume 1:
CRAWLING FROM THE WRECKAGE
With Richard Case, Doug Braithwaite, Scott Hanna, Carlos Garzon and John Nyberg

Volume 2:
THE PAINTING THAT ATE PARIS
With Richard Case and John Nyberg

SEAGUY
With Cameron Stewart

ANIMAL MAN

A minor super-hero's consciousness is raised higher and higher until he becomes aware of his own fictitious nature in this revolutionary and existential series.

Volume 1: ANIMAL MAN
With Chas Truog, Doug Hazlewood and Tom Grummett

Volume 2: ORIGIN OF THE SPECIES
With Chas Truog, Doug Hazlewood and Tom Grummett

Volume 3: DEUS EX MACHINA
With Chas Truog, Doug Hazlewood and various

THE FILTH
With Chris Weston and Gary Erskine

THE MYSTERY PLAY
With Jon J Muth

SEBASTIAN O
With Steve Yeowell

From VERTIGO. Suggested for mature readers.